Shaping Truth:
Culture, Expression, and Creativity

Lynchburg College Symposium Readings

Third Edition

2005

Volume III

Shaping Truth:
Culture, Expression, and Creativity

Edited by

Barbara Rothermel, M.L.S.

To order additional copies of this book, contact:
Xlibris Corporation
1-888-795-4274
www.Xlibris.com
Orders@Xlibris.com
23023

CONTENTS

Volume III

ACKNOWLEDGEMENTS

The editors acknowledge with appreciation the permissions granted by these holders of the respective copyrights.

"Archaic Torso of Apollo" by Rilke, Used by permission of Howard A. Landman, translator.

"Beethoven's Heiligenstadt Testament," ©1967. In *Letters of Composers Through Six Centuries,* Piero Weiss, (ed.), Philadelphia: Chilton Books. Permission granted by Piero Weiss.

Confessions by St. Augustine. Reprinted from Great Books of the Western World, © 1952, 1990 Encyclopedia Britannica, Inc.

Description of Greece. Reprinted by permission of the publishers and the Trustees of the Loeb Classical Library from PAUSANIAS VOLUME IX, Loeb Classical Library Volume 297, translated by W. H. S. Jones, Cambridge, Mass.: Harvard University Press, copyright 1935 by the President and Fellows of Harvard College. The Loeb Classical Library ® is a registered trademark of the President and Fellows of Harvard College.

"God is Red" by Vine Deloria. Used by permission from GOD IS RED by Vine Deloria, Jr. © 1994. Fulcrum Publishing, Inc., Golden, Colorado. All rights reserved.

"In this mere living stone . . ." by Michelangelo. Used by permission of New York University Press.

LYNCHBURG COLLEGE SYMPOSIUM READINGS, SENIOR SYMPOSIUM, AND THE LCSR PROGRAM

The ten-volume series, Lynchburg College Symposium Readings, has been developed by Lynchburg College faculty for use in the Senior Symposium and the Lynchburg College Symposium Readings Program (SS/LCSR). Each volume presents primary source material organized around interdisciplinary, liberal arts themes.

In 1976, the College developed the Senior Symposium as a two-hour, interdisciplinary course, required of all graduating seniors. On Mondays students in all sections of the course come together for public lectures, given by invited guest speakers. On Wednesdays, Symposium students meet in their sections for student-led discussions and presentations on associated readings from the LCSR series. The course requires students, who have spent their later college years in narrowing the scope of their studies, to expand their fields of vision within a discussion group composed of and led by their peers. Students can apply analytical and problem-solving capabilities learned in their major fields of study to issues raised by guest speakers and classical readings.

This approach works against convention in higher education, which typically emphasizes the gradual exclusion of subject areas outside of a student's major field. But Senior Symposium leads students, poised for graduation, into their post-College intellectual responsibilities. They gain experience in taking their liberal education into real world problems, using it to address contemporary problems thoughtfully and critically. In order to do this successfully, students must abandon their habitual posture as docile receptors of authoritative information for a much more skeptical attitude toward opinion, proof, reasoning, and authoritative experience. The effort to think constructively through a variety of conflicting opinions—on a weekly basis—prepares them well for the mature, independent, well-reasoned points of view expected of educated adults.

The LCSR Program's primary goals are to foster an appreciation of the connection between basic skills and interdisciplinary knowledge, and to promote greater cross-disciplinary communication among faculty and students. General education core courses or courses that serve other program requirements may be classified as "LCSR," as long as they fulfill certain speaking and writing activities connected to LCSR readings. The effect of the program has been to help create the atmosphere of a residential academic community; shared learning creates a climate in which teaching and learning take root more forcefully.

Since its inception, the SS/LCSR Program has helped create opportunities for faculty interaction across the disciplines in "pre-service" and "in-service" workshops. Each May, the LCSR Program sponsors a four-day pre-service workshop to which all new full-time and part-time faculty members are invited. Participants receive individual sets of the Lynchburg College Symposium Readings, which they make their own by using them during the workshop in exercises designed to promote familiarity with a wide variety of the readings. The goals of the workshop are several: for those unfamiliar with the program, to begin planning an LCSR course; for new faculty, to become acquainted with those they have not met and get to know their acquaintances better; for other faculty of various experiential levels, to share their pedagogical successes; for new teachers, to ask questions about teaching, about the College, and about the students in an informal setting; for experienced teachers to re-visit some of their assumptions, pedagogies, and strategies; to inspire strong scholarship, creative teaching, risk-taking, and confidence among all participants.

Another opportunity comes with the "in-service" workshops, which occur each month during the school year. The LCSR Program sponsors luncheons and dinners at which faculty teaching in the program give informal presentations on their use of specific teaching strategies or reading selections. Attendance is voluntary, but many try to be present for every session. For those involved in the LCSR program, teaching has become what Lee Schulman, President of the Carnegie Foundation, calls "community property."

On the Lynchburg College campus, there is evidence of a systematic change in teaching effectiveness as well as sustained faculty commitment to the program. By the 2002-2003 academic year, nearly two-thirds of all full-time faculty members and more than half of all part-time faculty members had completed the workshop at some time during their time at Lynchburg College. In any given semester, roughly ten to fifteen percent of the total class enrollments are in LCSR courses, not counting the required Senior Symposium. An important feature of this program is that participation is voluntary on the part of the faculty and, except for the required Senior Symposium, on the part of students. The program's influence quietly pervades the campus community, improving teaching and scholarship. Many see the LCSR Program as the College's premier academic program.

The Senior Symposium/LCSR program publishes *The Agora*, an in-house journal that features the best of student writings responding to LCSR texts. The journal selections by students must integrate classical ideas and issues with contemporary ones. Faculty may also submit writings that address innovative teaching strategies. The journal takes its title from the marketplace at the heart of classical Athens, where much of Athenian public life was carried on: mercantile exchange, performance, political debate, athletic contests, and the public worship of deities—all took place within the hustle and bustle of the Athenian agora. Similarly, the journal seeks to be a marketplace for compelling ideas and issues. Faculty members and students serve together on the editorial committee.

Since 1976, the Senior Symposium and the LCSR Program have affected the academic community both on and beyond the Lynchburg College campus. In 1991, Professor Richard Marius from Harvard University's writing center in reviewing the program favorably said, "I have seldom in my life been so impressed by an innovation in college education. I suppose the highest compliment that I could pay to the program was that I wished I could teach in it." Also in 1991, Professor Donald Boileau of George Mason University's communication studies department wrote, "what I discovered was a sound program that not only enriches the education of students at Lynchburg College, but what I hope can be a model for many other colleges and universities throughout our country." In spring 2003, in an article titled, "Whither the Great Books," Dr. William Casement described the LCSR program as the "most fully organized version" of the recent growth of great-books programs that employ an "across-the-disciplines structure." According to him, this approach perhaps encourages the use of the great books across the curriculum, which can be less isolating than even interdisciplinary programs. The Senior Symposium and LCSR Programs have received national acclaim in such publications as Loren Popes's *Colleges That Change Lives* and Charles Sykes and Brad Miner's *The National Review of College Guide, America's 50 Top Liberal Arts Schools.*

Shaping Truth: Culture, Expression, and Creativity is the third volume of the third edition of the Lynchburg College Symposium Readings series. The first edition, published in the early 1980s, included several selections also printed in the third edition. We gratefully acknowledge the work of Dr. James Campbell, Professor of English, Virginia Berger, Associate Professor of Music, Emerita, Dr. Clifton Potter Jr., Turner Distinguished Professor in the Humanities, Professor of History, and Dr. Dorothy Bundy Potter, Assistant Professor of History for their contributions to previous editions of this volume. The Senior Symposium was the creation of Dr. James Huston, Dean of the College, Emeritus (1972-1984);

he and Dr. Michael Santos, Professor of History, co-founded the LCSR program. Dean Huston served as the first series editor, and with Dr. Julius Sigler, Professor of Physics, as co-editor of the second series. All four remain committed to the program today, and for this we are grateful.

Peggy Pittas, Ph.D.
Katherine Gray, Ph. D
Series Co-Editors

ON TRUTHS AND ON SHAPES

> Truth for me is what I cannot help believing. To make clear what I understand by this will perhaps take a little explaining. I say that this proposition appears to me almost in the nature of a truism so far as it goes. Certainly that which I do *not* believe I cannot in any intelligible sense call true; this would be to empty terms of all accepted meaning. And indeed everything that I really *do* believe must for the moment come under the head of what I call the true. But the words "*cannot help* believing" are intended to limit the field somewhat; for we are engaged on a philosophical inquiry, and what we are after in the end is not anything that may *seem* true, but what approves itself as true to the persistent inquirer. If we simply believed things, the problem of truth would not yet have arisen. (Rogers 1923)

Truth. What is it? How is it determined? How is it recognized? People search for the truth in many ways: some are convinced they possess the truth; some believe they are living the truth; some are unconcerned with the very idea of truth; some deny there is any truth; others seek truth knowing they will never find the whole truth.

Does truth exist in the process of seeking? Or is truth shaped by societal forces? Truth has been defined as conformity to knowledge, fact, actuality, or logic. Is truth, then, relative to the human community? Can truth exist without cultural relativism? "Considering the variety of human nature as a result of evolution why should it not require an indefinite number of systems to express human nature in the various stages of its development and in its various moods? And why are they not all true, in so far they are really genuine and really express human nature then and there?" (Boodin 1911).

More questions must follow. If truth is relative, is truth shaped— developed or given definitive form? What are these shapes? What are the circumstances that determine these shapes? The seminal writings that comprise the LCSR volume, *Shaping Truth: Culture, Expression, and Creativity*, address these concerns. Although there are no definitive answers to the questions, this collection is a reflection of the world's on-going conversation about the concept and nature of truth.

Every culture develops a traditional repertoire of forms in which the concept of truth is given shape—narrative, drama, verse, music, and art. These forms are given shape through the creative processes in which the creator—the storyteller, the playwright, the poet, the musician, the artist—gives oral, tangible, or visual shape to ideas, philosophies, or feelings that seek to find universal truth. These shapes are responsive to the ways in which diverse societies, through collective history, customs, and beliefs, find answers. Yet these shapes are also determined by the imagination and creativity of the individual maker, the one who envisions a picture or composes a song. Through expression, the creator seeks to fulfill the innate human urge to understand ourselves and our universe and thus becomes the articulator of shared beliefs and values that give shape to the concept of truth. The creator thus becomes the vessel through which humanity seeks truth.

The meanings and content that are given shape are inseparable from their formal stylistic and characteristic compositional qualities that are both conditioned by culture and determined by the maker's creativity and intentions. But the makers are conversant with the Muses who give creative inspiration to poetry, song, and other arts. And the temple of the Muses is first of all a school. Each creator modifies shapes through imagination and interpretation of the original concept or belief. Truth, therefore, becomes subject to interpretation and is constructed to fit expectations, convey a message, or support a particular agenda. These shapes then become part of a continuum, an unbroken thread of influence and impact, a progression of shape and idea transcending time and culture.

The process is made dramatically clear in John Gardner's *Grendel* as the monster/narrator recounts the arrival of the poet at the meadhall of his enemy, Hrothgar*:

> One night, inevitably, a blind man turned up at Hrothgar's temporary meadhall. He was carrying a harp . . . . As if all by itself, then, the harp made a curious run of sounds, almost words, and then a moment later, arresting as a voice from a hollow tree, the harper began to chant . . . . So he sang— or intoned, with the harp behind him—twisting together like sailors' ropes the bits and pieces of the best old songs. The people were hushed. Even the surrounding hills were hushed, as if brought low by language. He knew his art. He was king of the Shapers, harpstring scratchers . . . . [W]hat had brought him over wilderness, down blindman's alleys of time and space, to Hrothgar's famous hall . . . What was he? The man had changed the world, had torn up the past by its thick, gnarled roots and had transmuted it, and they, who knew the truth, remembered it his way—and so did I.

Barbara Rothermel, M.L.S.
Director, Daura Gallery

---

*   *This 1989 novel retells the 8th-century story of the Anglo-Saxon hero Beowulf (excerpted in the "Verse" section of this volume) from the perspective of the story's monster, the hero's enemy, Grendel. The monster is portrayed as an angst-ridden adolescent who struggles for intergrity and understanding in a world he sees as controlled by malcontents, liars, illusionists, and cowards. Over the course of the conflict, we see the storyteller in the mead hall (the "Shaper" or the "scop") inventing*

Sources

Boodin, John Elof. 1911. *Truth and Reality: An Introduction to the Theory of Knowledge.* New York: Macmillan. 3.

Gardner, John. 1989. *Grendel.* New York: Vintage. 40-43.

Rogers, Arthur Kenyon. 1923. "What Is Truth? An Essay in the Theory of Knowledge." New Haven: Yale University Press. 1.

---

the tale for future generations, shaping events from the point of view of the warriors. Enraged at humankind's enchantment with the artistic rendering of its own bravery and glory, Grendel launches the attacks that propel him and the "Shaper" into cultural history.

PART I

TRUTHS: PHILOSOPHICAL, THEORETICAL, CULTURAL

Philosophy, Theory, Cultural Heritage

The writings in this section are all artifacts from the past. Archeologists piece together pottery chards in order to understand better the people who lived at a site. Equally, these writings, these statements of ideas, values, and beliefs, can be analyzed to understand better the experiences of the people who wrote them, as well as our own lives, our own experiences.

From a social science perspective, by the late 19th century, culture was argued to include all of the immaterial elements of human experience—information, beliefs, art, moral codes, laws, customs, all and any of the capabilities or habits we learn directly or indirectly from others within the context of a specific, ongoing, self-identified set of people, within the context of a society. More simply, culture is the totality of the ideas, beliefs, and values shared more-or-less by an ongoing set of people and which provide a blueprint, a guide, for survival and continuation of the group across time. The readings here, the ideas, beliefs, and values discussed here, are elements from past cultures which have been brought forward into our present culture. By definition and default these readings then are part of our cultural heritage which we can use to understand our own experiences better.

The cultural heritage of any people, at any point in time, consists of (1) static segments of the past which are within our present culture, elements which are frozen and unchanging, e.g., ancient Greek or Roman statuary pieces; and (2) those elements of the past which are dynamically important within our daily lives, those elements which we are taught to value and to use, e.g., ideas of democracy, of justice. Importantly, the cultural heritage of any people, at any time, always consists of those elements of the past which have been purposively selected in some manner that reflects the people and the culture who make that selection, to be saved and to be represented to each new generation of citizens, of students. Our cultural heritage consists of the elements of past cultures which have been identified and brought forward as valued examples and exemplars for thinking and behaving.

All of the readings here are examples of how other people from both the immediate and the distant past—from Plato to Deloria— have perceived and interpreted the world which they experienced and how they worked to understand that world. Some of the readings can also be seen as exemplars of how to think about, to interpret, or to describe a specific phenomenon. Some of these authors discuss broad sets of ideas and beliefs, e.g., Plato on government, Aristotle on poetry, or Marx and Engels on the political state and private property. Others present and discuss specific information about the world in which they lived, e.g. Pausanias writing about Delphi or Barthes discussing toys, as a means of better understanding the experiences of those who lived in both ancient Greece and contemporary America. Equally, others—Boas and Deloria—provide examples of examining the culture of one people in order to understand better the abstract, larger, human experiences as well as their own experiences.

Together these readings move us across a wide spread of time and a broad array of human experiences. Together these authors provide guides for a better understanding and appreciation of both our own experiences and of the world in which we live.

Charles L. Shull, Professor of Sociology

PLATO

428-347 B.C.E.

THE REPUBLIC

360 B.C.E.

Although Plato had political ambitions, he became disillusioned by the political leadership in Athens and instead became a student of Socrates, accepting his basic philosophy and dialectical style of debate: the pursuit of truth through questions, answers, and additional questions. After witnessing the death of Socrates at the hands of the Athenian democracy in 399 B.C. E., Plato left Athens to travel to Italy, Sicily, and Egypt. In 387 B.C.E., Plato founded the Academy in Athens, the institution often described as the first European university. The Academy provided a comprehensive curriculum, including such subjects as astronomy, biology, mathematics, political theory, and philosophy. Aristotle was the Academy's most prominent student. Plato's Academy continued after his death until it was closed in 529 C.E. by the Byzantine emperor Justinian I, who objected to its pagan teachings.

The Republic, Plato's major political work, is concerned with the question of justice. The ideal state, according to Plato, is composed of three classes: the economic structure of the state is met by the merchant class with its virtue of restraint; security needs are maintained by the military class with its virtue of courage; and political leadership is sustained by the philosopher-kings, with their virtue of wisdom. A person's class was determined by an educational process, with those who complete the entire process and whose minds have been so developed that they are able to grasp the Forms, becoming philosopher-kings. Justice, the fourth virtue, characterizes society as a whole. Plato, likewise, divided the human soul into three parts: the rational part, the will, and the appetites. The just person is the one in whom the rational, supported by the will, controls the appetites.

In Book X of *The Republic*, Plato questions the nature and reality of poetry and art. His theory is that art is a copy or imitation of the universal Forms; the physical object is one step removed from reality, that is, the Forms. An image is then two steps removed from reality. This also meant that the artist was two steps removed from knowledge. Plato's frequent criticism of artists is that they lack knowledge of what they are doing, thus making artistic creation an irrational act.

Platonic thought had a crucial role in the development of Christian theology and also in medieval Islamic thought: the theologian Saint Augustine was an early Christian exponent of its perspective; in the 15th century, the primary focus of Platonic influence was the Florentine Academy. Plato's influence continues to be pervasive in Western philosophy.

SOURCE

Plato. 360 B.C.E. *The Republic*. Book X. In *The Republic of Plato*. B. Jowett, Ed. and Trans. New York: P.F. Collier & Son. 1901. 378-396.

THE REPUBLIC

BOOK X

SOCRATES—GLAUCON

Of the many excellences which I perceive in the order of our State, there is none which upon reflection pleases me better than the rule about poetry.

To what do you refer?
To the rejection of imitative poetry, which certainly ought not to be received; as I see far more clearly now that the parts of the soul have been distinguished.

What do you mean?
Speaking in confidence, for I should not like to have my words repeated to the tragedians and the rest of the imitative tribe—but I do not mind saying to you, that all poetical imitations are ruinous to the understanding of the hearers, and that the knowledge of their true nature is the only antidote to them.

Explain the purport of your remark.
Well, I will tell you, although I have always from my earliest youth had an awe and love of Homer, which even now makes the words falter on my lips, for he is the great captain and teacher of the whole of that charming tragic company; but a man is not to be reverenced more than the truth, and therefore I will speak out.

Very good, he said.
Listen to me then, or rather, answer me.
Put your question.
Can you tell me what imitation is? for I really do not know.
A likely thing, then, that I should know.
Why not? for the duller eye may often see a thing sooner than the keener.

Very true, he said; but in your presence, even if I had any faint notion, I could not muster courage to utter it. Will you enquire yourself?

Well then, shall we begin the enquiry in our usual manner: Whenever a number of individuals have a common name, we assume them to have also a corresponding idea or form. Do you understand me?

I do.

Let us take any common instance; there are beds and tables in the world—plenty of them, are there not?

Yes.

But there are only two ideas or forms of them—one the idea of a bed, the other of a table.

True.

And the maker of either of them makes a bed or he makes a table for our use, in accordance with the idea—that is our way of speaking in this and similar instances—but no artificer makes the ideas themselves: how could he?

Impossible.

And there is another artist,—I should like to know what you would say of him.

Who is he?

One who is the maker of all the works of all other workmen.

What an extraordinary man!

Wait a little, and there will be more reason for your saying so. For this is he who is able to make not only vessels of every kind, but plants and animals, himself and all other things—the earth and heaven, and the things which are in heaven or under the earth; he makes the gods also.

He must be a wizard and no mistake.

Oh! you are incredulous, are you? Do you mean that there is no such maker or creator, or that in one sense there might be a maker of all these things but in another not? Do you see that there is a way in which you could make them all yourself?

What way?

An easy way enough; or rather, there are many ways in which the

feat might be quickly and easily accomplished, none quicker than that of turning a mirror round and round—you would soon enough make the sun and the heavens, and the earth and yourself, and other animals and plants, and all the other things of which we were just now speaking, in the mirror.

Yes, he said; but they would be appearances only.
Very good, I said, you are coming to the point now. And the painter too is, as I conceive, just such another—a creator of appearances, is he not?

Of course.
But then I suppose you will say that what he creates is untrue. And yet there is a sense in which the painter also creates a bed?

Yes, he said, but not a real bed.
And what of the maker of the bed? Were you not saying that he too makes, not the idea which, according to our view, is the essence of the bed, but only a particular bed?

Yes, I did.
Then if he does not make that which exists he cannot make true existence, but only some semblance of existence; and if any one were to say that the work of the maker of the bed, or of any other workman, has real existence, he could hardly be supposed to be speaking the truth.

At any rate, he replied, philosophers would say that he was not speaking the truth.

No wonder, then, that his work too is an indistinct expression of truth.

No wonder.
Suppose now that by the light of the examples just offered we enquire who this imitator is?

If you please.

Well then, here are three beds: one existing in nature, which is made by God, as I think that we may say—for no one else can be the maker?

No.

There is another which is the work of the carpenter?

Yes.

And the work of the painter is a third?

Yes.

Beds, then, are of three kinds, and there are three artists who superintend them: God, the maker of the bed, and the painter?

Yes, there are three of them.

God, whether from choice or from necessity, made one bed in nature and one only; two or more such ideal beds neither ever have been nor ever will be made by God.

Why is that?

Because even if He had made but two, a third would still appear behind them which both of them would have for their idea, and that would be the ideal bed and the two others.

Very true, he said.

God knew this, and He desired to be the real maker of a real bed, not a particular maker of a particular bed, and therefore He created a bed which is essentially and by nature one only.

So we believe.

Shall we, then, speak of Him as the natural author or maker of the bed?

Yes, he replied; inasmuch as by the natural process of creation He is the author of this and of all other things.

And what shall we say of the carpenter—is not he also the maker of the bed?

[handwritten note: bed = Carpenter = Painter]

Yes. .

But would you call the painter a creator and maker?

Certainly not.

Yet if he is not the maker, what is he in relation to the bed?

I think, he said, that we may fairly designate him as the imitator of that which the others make.

Good, I said; then you call him who is third in the descent from nature an imitator?

Certainly, he said.

And the tragic poet is an imitator, and therefore, like all other imitators, he is thrice removed from the king and from the truth?

That appears to be so.

Then about the imitator we are agreed. And what about the painter?—I would like to know whether he may be thought to imitate that which originally exists in nature, or only the creations of artists?

The latter.

As they are or as they appear? You have still to determine this.

What do you mean?

I mean, that you may look at a bed from different points of view, obliquely or directly or from any other point of view, and the bed will appear different, but there is no difference in reality. And the same of all things.

[handwritten note: Point of view does not change performance]

Yes, he said, the difference is only apparent.

Now let me ask you another question: Which is the art of painting designed to be—an imitation of things as they are, or as they appear—of appearance or of reality?

Of appearance.

Then the imitator, I said, is a long way off the truth, and can do all things because he lightly touches on a small part of them, and that part an image. For example: A painter will paint a cobbler, carpenter, or any other artist, though he knows nothing of their arts; and, if he is a good artist, he may deceive children or simple persons, when he shows them his picture of a carpenter from a distance, and they will fancy that they are looking at a real carpenter.

Certainly.

And whenever any one informs us that he has found a man knows all the arts, and all things else that anybody knows, and every single thing with a higher degree of accuracy than any other man— whoever tells us this, I think that we can only imagine to be a simple creature who is likely to have been deceived by some wizard or actor whom he met, and whom he thought all-knowing, because he himself was unable to analyse the nature of knowledge and ignorance and imitation.

Most true.

And so, when we hear persons saying that the tragedians, and Homer, who is at their head, know all the arts and all things human, virtue as well as vice, and divine things too, for that the good poet cannot compose well unless he knows his subject, and that he who has not this knowledge can never be a poet, we ought to consider whether here also there may not be a similar illusion. Perhaps they may have come across imitators and been deceived by them; they may not have remembered when they saw their works that these were but imitations thrice removed from the truth, and could easily be made without any knowledge of the truth, because they are appearances only and not realities? Or, after all, they may be in the right, and poets do really know the things about which they seem to the many to speak so well?

The question, he said, should by all means be considered.

Now do you suppose that if a person were able to make the original as well as the image, he would seriously devote himself to the image-making branch? Would he allow imitation to be the ruling principle of his life, as if he had nothing higher in him?

I should say not.

The real artist, who knew what he was imitating, would be interested in realities and not in imitations; and would desire to leave as memorials of himself works many and fair; and, instead of being the author of encomiums, he would prefer to be the theme of them.

Yes, he said, that would be to him a source of much greater honour and profit.

Then, I said, we must put a question to Homer; not about medicine, or any of the arts to which his poems only incidentally refer: we are not going to ask him, or any other poet, whether he has cured patients like Asclepius, or left behind him a school of medicine such as the Asclepiads were, or whether he only talks about medicine and other arts at second hand; but we have a right to know respecting military tactics, politics, education, which are the chiefest and noblest subjects of his poems, and we may fairly ask him about them. 'Friend Homer,' then we say to him, 'if you are only in the second remove from truth in what you say of virtue, and not in the third—not an image maker or imitator—and if you are able to discern what pursuits make men better or worse in private or public life, tell us what State was ever better governed by your help? The good order of Lacedaemon is due to Lycurgus, and many other cities great and small have been similarly benefited by others; but who says that you have been a good legislator to them and have done them any good? Italy and Sicily boast of

Charondas, and there is Solon who is renowned among us; but what city has anything to say about you?' Is there any city which he might name?

I think not, said Glaucon; not even the Homerids themselves pretend that he was a legislator.

Well, but is there any war on record which was carried on successfully by him, or aided by his counsels, when he was alive?

There is not.
Or is there any invention of his, applicable to the arts or to human life, such as Thales the Milesian or Anacharsis the Scythian, and other ingenious men have conceived, which is attributed to him?

There is absolutely nothing of the kind.
But, if Homer never did any public service, was he privately a guide or teacher of any? Had he in his lifetime friends who loved to associate with him, and who handed down to posterity an Homeric way of life, such as was established by Pythagoras who was so greatly beloved for his wisdom, and whose followers are to this day quite celebrated for the order which was named after him?

Nothing of the kind is recorded of him. For surely, Socrates, Creophylus, the companion of Homer, that child of flesh, whose name always makes us laugh, might be more justly ridiculed for his stupidity, if, as is said, Homer was greatly neglected by him and others in his own day when he was alive?

Yes, I replied, that is the tradition. But can you imagine, Glaucon, that if Homer had really been able to educate and improve mankind—if he had possessed knowledge and not been a mere imitator—can you imagine, I say, that he would not have had many followers, and been honoured and loved by them? Protagoras of Abdera, and Prodicus of Ceos, and a host of others, have only to whisper to their contemporaries: 'You will never be able to manage

either your own house or your own State until you appoint us to
be your ministers of education'—and this ingenious device of theirs
has such an effect in making them love them that their companions
all but carry them about on their shoulders. And is it conceivable
that the contemporaries of Homer, or again of Hesiod, would have
allowed either of them to go about as rhapsodists, if they had
really been able to make mankind virtuous? Would they not have
been as unwilling to part with them as with gold, and have
compelled them to stay at home with them? Or, if the master
would not stay, then the disciples would have followed him about
everywhere, until they had got education enough?

Yes, Socrates, that, I think, is quite true.

Then must we not infer that all these poetical individuals,
beginning with Homer, are only imitators; they copy images of
virtue and the like, but the truth they never reach? The poet is like
a painter who, as we have already observed, will make a likeness of
a cobbler though he understands nothing of cobbling; and his
picture is good enough for those who know no more than he does,
and judge only by colours and figures.

Quite so.

In like manner the poet with his words and phrases may be said to
lay on the colours of the several arts, himself understanding their
nature only enough to imitate them; and other people, who are as
ignorant as he is, and judge only from his words, imagine that if
he speaks of cobbling, or of military tactics, or of anything else, in
metre and harmony and rhythm, he speaks very well—such is the
sweet influence which melody and rhythm by nature have. And I
think that you must have observed again and again what a poor
appearance the tales of poets make when stripped of the colours
which music puts upon them, and recited in simple prose.

Yes, he said.

They are like faces which were never really beautiful, but only blooming;
and now the bloom of youth has passed away from them?

Exactly.

Here is another point: The imitator or maker of the image knows nothing of true existence; he knows appearances only. Am I not right?

Yes.

Then let us have a clear understanding, and not be satisfied with half an explanation.

Proceed.

Of the painter we say that he will paint reins, and he will paint a bit?

Yes.

And the worker in leather and brass will make them?

Certainly.

But does the painter know the right form of the bit and reins? Nay, hardly even the workers in brass and leather who make them; only the horseman who knows how to use them—he knows their right form.

Most true.

And may we not say the same of all things?

What?

That there are three arts which are concerned with all things: one which uses, another which makes, a third which imitates them?

Yes.

And the excellence or beauty or truth of every structure, animate or inanimate, and of every action of man, is relative to the use for which nature or the artist has intended them.

True.

Then the user of them must have the greatest experience of them, and he must indicate to the maker the good or bad qualities which develop themselves in use; for example, the flute-player will tell the flute-maker which of his flutes is satisfactory to the performer;

he will tell him how he ought to make them, and the other will attend to his instructions?

Of course.

The one knows and therefore speaks with authority about the goodness and badness of flutes, while the other, confiding in him, will do what he is told by him?

True.

The instrument is the same, but about the excellence or badness of it the maker will only attain to a correct belief; and this he will gain from him who knows, by talking to him and being compelled to hear what he has to say, whereas the user will have knowledge?

True.

But will the imitator have either? Will he know from use whether or no his drawing is correct or beautiful? Or will he have right opinion from being compelled to associate with another who knows and gives him instructions about what he should draw?

Neither.

Then he will no more have true opinion than he will have knowledge about the goodness or badness of his imitations?

I suppose not.

The imitative artist will be in a brilliant state of intelligence about his own creations?

Nay, very much the reverse.

And still he will go on imitating without knowing what makes a thing good or bad, and may be expected therefore to imitate only that which appears to be good to the ignorant multitude?

Just so.

Thus far then we are pretty well agreed that the imitator has no knowledge worth mentioning of what he imitates. Imitation is only a kind of play or sport, and the tragic poets, whether they write in iambic or in Heroic verse, are imitators in the highest degree?

Very true.

And now tell me, I conjure you, has not imitation been shown by us to be concerned with that which is thrice removed from the truth?

Certainly.   Sight

And what is the faculty in man to which imitation is addressed?

What do you mean?

I will explain: The body which is large when seen near, appears small when seen at a distance?

True.

And the same object appears straight when looked at out of the water, and crooked when in the water; and the concave becomes convex, owing to the illusion about colours to which the sight is liable. Thus every sort of confusion is revealed within us; and this is that weakness of the human mind on which the art of conjuring and of deceiving by light and shadow and other ingenious devices imposes, having an effect upon us like magic.

True.

And the arts of measuring and numbering and weighing come to the rescue of the human understanding—there is the beauty of them—and the apparent greater or less, or more or heavier, no longer have the mastery over us, but give way before calculation and measure and weight?

Most true.

And this, surely, must be the work of the calculating and rational principle in the soul

To be sure.

And when this principle measures and certifies that some things are equal, or that some are greater or less than others, there occurs an apparent contradiction?

True.

But were we not saying that such a contradiction is the same faculty cannot have contrary opinions at the same time about the same thing?

Very true.

Then that part of the soul which has an opinion contrary to measure is not the same with that which has an opinion in accordance with measure?

True.

And the better part of the soul is likely to be that which trusts to measure and calculation?

— interesting Conclusion

Certainly.

And that which is opposed to them is one of the inferior principles of the soul?

No doubt.

This was the conclusion at which I was seeking to arrive when I said that painting or drawing, and imitation in general, when doing their own proper work, are far removed from truth, and the companions and friends and associates of a principle within us which is equally removed from reason, and that they have no true or healthy aim.

Exactly.

The imitative art is an inferior who marries an inferior, and has inferior offspring.

Very true.

And is this confined to the sight only, or does it extend to the hearing also, relating in fact to what we term poetry?

Probably the same would be true of poetry.

Do not rely, I said, on a probability derived from the analogy of painting; but let us examine further and see whether the faculty with which poetical imitation is concerned is good or bad.

By all means.

We may state the question thus:—Imitation imitates the actions of men, whether voluntary or involuntary, on which, as they imagine, a good or bad result has ensued, and they rejoice or sorrow accordingly. Is there anything more?

No, there is nothing else.

But in all this variety of circumstances is the man at unity with himself—or rather, as in the instance of sight there was confusion and opposition in his opinions about the same things, so here also is there not strife and inconsistency in his life? Though I need hardly raise the question again, for I remember that all this has been already admitted; and the soul has been acknowledged by us to be full of these and ten thousand similar oppositions occurring at the same moment?

And we were right, he said.

Yes, I said, thus far we were right; but there was an omission which must now be supplied.

What was the omission?

Were we not saying that a good man, who has the misfortune to lose his son or anything else which is most dear to him, will bear the loss with more equanimity than another?

Yes.

But will he have no sorrow, or shall we say that although he cannot
help sorrowing, he will moderate his sorrow?

The latter, he said, is the truer statement.

Tell me: will he be more likely to struggle and hold out against his
sorrow when he is seen by his equals, or when he is alone?

It will make a great difference whether he is seen or not.

When he is by himself he will not mind saying or doing many things
which he would be ashamed of any one hearing or seeing him do?

True.

There is a principle of law and reason in him which bids him
resist, as well as a feeling of his misfortune which is forcing him to
indulge his sorrow?

True.

But when a man is drawn in two opposite directions, to and from
the same object, this, as we affirm, necessarily implies two distinct
principles in him?

Certainly.

One of them is ready to follow the guidance of the law?

How do you mean?

The law would say that to be patient under suffering is best, and that
we should not give way to impatience, as there is no knowing whether
such things are good or evil; and nothing is gained by impatience;
also, because no human thing is of serious importance, and grief stands
in the way of that which at the moment is most required.

What is most required? he asked.

That we should take counsel about what has happened, and when
the dice have been thrown order our affairs in the way which

reason deems best; not, like children who have had a fall, keeping hold of the part struck and wasting time in setting up a howl, but always accustoming the soul forthwith to apply a remedy, raising up that which is sickly and fallen, banishing the cry of sorrow by the healing art.

Yes, he said, that is the true way of meeting the attacks of fortune.

Yes, I said; and the higher principle is ready to follow this suggestion of reason?

Clearly.

And the other principle, which inclines us to recollection of our troubles and to lamentation, and can never have enough of them, we may call irrational, useless, and cowardly?

Indeed, we may.

And does not the latter—I mean the rebellious principle—furnish a great variety of materials for imitation? Whereas the wise and calm temperament, being always nearly equable, is not easy to imitate or to appreciate when imitated, especially at a public festival when a promiscuous crowd is assembled in a theatre. For the feeling represented is one to which they are strangers.

Certainly.

Then the imitative poet who aims at being popular is not by nature made, nor is his art intended, to please or to affect the principle in the soul; but he will prefer the passionate and fitful temper, which is easily imitated?

Clearly.

And now we may fairly take him and place him by the side of the painter, for he is like him in two ways: first, inasmuch as his creations have an inferior degree of truth—in this, I say, he is like him; and he is also like him in being concerned with an inferior part of the soul; and therefore we shall be right in refusing to admit him into a well-ordered State, because he awakens and nourishes and strengthens the feelings and impairs the reason. As in a city when the evil are permitted to have authority and the good are put out of the way, so in the soul of man, as we maintain, the imitative poet implants an evil constitution, for he indulges the irrational nature which has no discernment of greater and less, but thinks the same thing at one time great and at another small—he is a manufacturer of images and is very far removed from the truth.

Exactly.

But we have not yet brought forward the heaviest count in our accusation:—the power which poetry has of harming even the good (and there are very few who are not harmed), is surely an awful thing?

Yes, certainly, if the effect is what you say.

Hear and judge: The best of us, as I conceive, when we listen to a passage of Homer, or one of the tragedians, in which he represents some pitiful hero who is drawling out his sorrows in a long oration, or weeping, and smiting his breast—the best of us, you know, delight in giving way to sympathy, and are in raptures at the excellence of the poet who stirs our feelings most.

Yes, of course I know.

But when any sorrow of our own happens to us, then you may observe that we pride ourselves on the opposite quality—we would fain be quiet and patient; this is the manly part, and the other which delighted us in the recitation is now deemed to be the part of a woman.

Very true, he said.

Now can we be right in praising and admiring another who is doing that which any one of us would abominate and be ashamed of in his own person?

No, he said, that is certainly not reasonable.

Nay, I said, quite reasonable from one point of view.

What point of view?

If you consider, I said, that when in misfortune we feel a natural hunger and desire to relieve our sorrow by weeping and lamentation, and that this feeling which is kept under control in our own calamities is satisfied and delighted by the poets;—the better nature in each of us, not having been sufficiently trained by reason or habit, allows the sympathetic element to break loose because the sorrow is another's; and the spectator fancies that there can be no disgrace to himself in praising and pitying any one who comes telling him what a good man he is, and making a fuss about his troubles; he thinks that the pleasure is a gain, and why should he be supercilious and lose this and the poem too? Few persons ever reflect, as I should imagine, that from the evil of other men something of evil is communicated to themselves. And so the feeling of sorrow which has gathered strength at the sight of the misfortunes of others is with difficulty repressed in our own.

How very true!

And does not the same hold also of the ridiculous? There are jests which you would be ashamed to make yourself, and yet on the comic stage, or indeed in private, when you hear them, you are greatly amused by them, and are not at all disgusted at their unseemliness;—the case of pity is repeated;—there is a principle in human nature which is disposed to raise a laugh, and this which you once restrained by reason, because you were afraid of being thought a buffoon, is now let out again; and having stimulated the risible faculty at the theatre, you are betrayed unconsciously to yourself into playing the comic poet at home.

Quite true, he said.

And the same may be said of lust and anger and all the other affections, of desire and pain and pleasure, which are held to be inseparable from every action—in all of them poetry feeds and waters the passions instead of drying them up; she lets them rule, although they ought to be controlled, if mankind are ever to increase in happiness and virtue.

I cannot deny it.

Therefore, Glaucon, I said, whenever you meet with any of the eulogists of Homer declaring that he has been the educator of Hellas, and that he is profitable for education and for the ordering of human things, and that you should take him up again and again and get to know him and regulate your whole life according to him, we may love and honour those who say these things—they are excellent people, as far as their lights extend; and we are ready to acknowledge that Homer is the greatest of poets and first of tragedy writers; but we must remain firm in our conviction that hymns to the gods and praises of famous men are the only poetry which ought to be admitted into our State. For if you go beyond this and allow the honeyed muse to enter, either in epic or lyric verse, not law and the reason of mankind, which by common consent have ever been deemed best, but pleasure and pain will be the rulers in our State.

PAUSANIAS

2nd Century C.E.

DESCRIPTION OF GREECE

ca. 143-161 C.E.

Pausanias, a traveler and geographer of the second century, wrote *Periegesis* or *Description of Greece*, a 10-volume work describing 13 major areas of Greece.[1] These volumes, written with the detail and precision that can only come of first-hand observation, cover the Peloponnesus and parts of northern Greece. Pausanias wrote in a direct and unpretentious style with admiration for the glories of Greece, highlighting the sanctuaries, sculpture, and tombs of ancient Greece, including those of Delphi, and the legends, folklore, and history connected with these sites. Ancient Delphi was the site of the Delphic Oracle, dedicated to the god Apollo, and honored throughout the Greek world as the *omphalos*, the center of the universe. The Oracle exerted vast influence and was consulted before all major endeavors, including war. In this selection, taken from his description of Delphi, Pausanias tells of the Tripod of the Plataeans, erected to commemorate the victory of the Greek city-states over the Persian army at Plataea (*ca.* 479 B.C.E.), inscribed with the names of the 31 city-states that contributed to the victory

---

[1] Attica and Megaris, Sicyonia, Phliasia and Argolis, Laconica, Messinia, Elis, Achaea, Arcadia, Boetia, Phoces, and Corinthia

and with "maxims useful for the life of men." The three inscribed columns were removed by the Roman Emperor Constantine in the 4th century and taken to Constantinople (Istanbul).

Pausanius continues his description of a bronze statue of Homer with a slab of bearing the prediction of the Oracle, of the altar dedicated to Poseidon, and of the tomb of Neoptolemus, son of Achilles. With his travels tracing the footsteps of Homer, Pausanias recorded precise and accurate descriptions—without aesthetic, political, economic, or scientific embellishment—that provided literal roadmaps archaeological excavations of ancient Greece in the 18th and 19th centuries.

SOURCE

Pausanias. 143-161 C.E. *Description of Greece*. In *Pausanias Description of Greece*. Vol. IV, Book X. W. H. S. Jones, Trans. Cambridge: Harvard University Press, 1935; reprinted 1979. 507-511.*

DESCRIPTION OF GREECE

XXIV. Such was the course of the war. In the fore-temple at Delphi are written maxims useful for the life of men, inscribed by those whom the Greeks say were sages. These were: from Ionia, Thales of Miletus and Bias of Priene; of the Aeolians in Lesbos, Pittacus of Mitylene; of the Dorians in Asia, Cleobulus of Lindus; Solon of Athens and Chilon of Sparta; the seventh sage, according to the list of Plato, the son of Ariston, is not Periander, the son of Cypselus, but Myson of Chenae, a village on Mount Oeta. These sages, then, came to Delphi and dedicated to Apollo the celebrated maxims, "Know thyself" and "Nothing in excess."

---

* Reprinted by permission of the publishers and the Trustees of the Loeb Classical Library from PAUSANIAS VOLUME IX, Loeb Classical Library Volume 297, translated by W. H. S. Jones, Cambridge: Mass.: Harvard University Press, copyright 1935 by the President and Fellows of Harvard College. The Loeb Classical Library ® is a registered trademark of the President and Fellows of Harvard College.

So these men wrote what I have said, and you can see a bronze statue of Homer on a slab, and read the oracle that they say Homer received:—

> Blessed and unhappy, for to be both wast thou born.
> Thou seekest thy father-land; but no father-land
>   hast thou, only a mother-land.
> The island of Ios is the father-land of thy mother,
>   which will receive thee
> When thou hast died; but be on thy guard against
>   the riddle of the young children.

The inhabitants of Ios point to Homer's tomb in the island, and in another part to that of Clymene, who was, they say, the mother of Homer. But the Cyprians, who also claim Homer as their own, say that Themisto, one of their native women, was the mother of Homer, and that Euclus foretold the birth of Homer in the following verses:—

> And then in sea-girt Cyprus there will be a mighty singer,
> Whom Themisto, lady fair, shall bear in the fields,
> A man of renown, far from rich Salamis.
> Leaving Cyprus, tossed and wetted by the waves,
> The first and only poet to sing of the woes of spacious
>   Greece,
> For ever shall he be deathless and ageless.

These things I have heard, and I have read the oracles, but express no private opinion about either the age or date of Homer.

In the temple has been built an altar of Poseidon, because Poseidon too possessed in part the most ancient oracle. There are also images of two Fates; but in place of the third Fate there stand by their side Zeus, Guide of Fate, and Apollo, Guide of Fate. Here you may behold the hearth on which the priest of Apollo killed Neoptolemus, the son of Achilles. The story of the end of Neoptolemus I have told elsewhere.[1] Not far from the hearth has

---

[1] See Book IV. xvii. 4.

been dedicated a chair of Pindar. The chair is of iron, and on it they say Pindar sat whenever he came to Delphi, and there composed his songs to Apollo. Into the innermost part of the temple there pass but few, but there is dedicated in it another image of Apollo, made of gold.

Leaving the temple and turning to the left you will come to an enclosure in which is the grave of Neoptolemus, the son of Achilles. Every year the Delphians sacrifice to him as to a hero. Ascending from the tomb you come to a stone of no large size. Over it every day they pour olive oil, and at each feast they place on it unworked wool. There is also an opinion about this stone, that it was given to Cronus instead of his child, and that Cronus vomited it up again.

Coming back to the temple after seeing the stone, you come to the spring called Cassotis. By it is a wall of no great size, and the ascent to the spring is through the wall. It is said that the water of this Cassotis sinks under the ground, and inspires the women in the shrine of the god. She who gave her name to the spring is said to have been a nymph of Parnassus.

SAINT AUGUSTINE

354-430

CONFESSIONS

397 C.E.

Aurelius Augustinus, known as Augustine, was born the son of a pagan farmer in what is now Algeria, at the time, part of the Roman Empire. By the age of 32, his degenerate youth had been followed by laudable accomplishments in the imperial court in Milan, and his conversion to Christianity. Eventually he became Bishop of Hippo. His life is richly revealed in *Confessions* (the story of his soul), *Retractations* (the story of his mind), and the *Life of Augustine*, written by his friend Possidius. Augustine's life falls into three periods: the young wanderer and his gradual return to faith; the development of his doctrine of Christian philosophy; and the development of his activities as Bishop of Hippo. He became one of the main figures in the merging of the Greek philosophical tradition with Judeo-Christian religious and spiritual traditions. He acknowledges Neo-Platonism with making it possible for him to envision a non-physical, spiritual reality. His accounts of knowledge and illumination, his emphasis on intellectualism and will, and his belief in the exercise of reason have made his writings of continuing importance in Christian theology.

Confessions is a diary of a soul's search for truth in which Augustine describes his struggles with temptation and his love of God, giving advice on how to live a Christian life. He addresses enduring spiritual questions, ultimately believing that happiness is not found in transitory physical pleasure but in searching for truth beyond the material world. The first ten books of *Confessions* relate the story of his youth and early adulthood in Carthage, Rome, and Milan, and continue with his struggle against evil, his attempts to find his faith, and his ultimate conversion to Christianity. The last three books contain unrelated allegorical explanations of the Mosaic account of Creation, with prayers, meditations, and instructions now found in Christian liturgies.

Book IV, the selection below, describes his teaching at Tagaste, his mistress, his interest in astrology, and the loss of a friend that led to an analysis of grief and transience. It also relates the story of his years among the Manicheans, a Christian sect, founded by the Babylonian Mani in the 3rd century: the Manicheans developed a complicated cosmogony based on the belief in two controlling principles, one good and one evil. Augustine eventually refuted the Manicheans' belief. In his continuing search for truth, he looked to Neo-Platonism, in which the universe is regarded as eternal, God is described as a transcendent non-material being, and evil is described as a lack or a loss.

SOURCE

Augustine. 397 C.E. *Confessions*. Book IV. In Augustine and Robert Maynard Hutchins. *Confessions, The City of God, On Christian Doctrine by Saint Augustine*. Great Books of the Western World. Chicago: Encyclopedia Britannica, 1952. 19-27.*

THE CONFESSIONS

Book IV

Augustine's life from nineteen to eight and twenty; himself a Manchean, and seducing others to the same heresy; partial obedience amidst vanity

---

and sin, consulting astrologers; only partially shaken herein; loss of an early friend, who is converted by being baptized when in a swoon; reflections on grief, on real and unreal friendship, and love of fame; writes on "the fair and fit," yet cannot rightly, though God had given him great talents, since he entertained wrong notions of God; and so even his knowledge he applied ill.

[I] 1. For this space of nine years then (from my nineteenth year to my eight-and-twentieth) we lived seduced and seducing, deceived and deceiving, in divers lusts; openly, by sciences which they call "liberal"; secretly, with a false-named religion; here proud, there superstitious, everywhere vain! Here, hunting after the emptiness of popular praise, down even to theatrical applauses, and poetic prizes, and strifes for grassy garlands, and the follies of shows, and the in temperance of desires. There, desiring to be cleansed from these defilements, by carrying food to those who were called "elect" and "holy," out of which, in the workhouse of their stomachs, they should forge for us Angels and Gods, by whom we might be cleansed. These things did I follow, and practise with my friends, deceived by me and with me. Let the arrogant mock me, and such as have not been, to their soul's health, stricken and cast down by Thee, O my God; but I would still confess to Thee mine own shame in Thy praise. Suffer me, I beseech Thee, and give me grace to go over in my present remembrance the wanderings of my forepassed time, and to "offer unto Thee the sacrifice of thanksgiving."[1] For what am I to myself without Thee but a guide to mine own downfall? or what am I even at the best, but an infant sucking the milk Thou givest, and feeding upon Thee, the food that perisheth not?[2] But what sort of man is any man, seeing he is but a man? Let now the strong and the mighty laugh at us, but let us "poor and needy"[3] confess unto Thee.

---

[1] Ps. 116. 17.

[2] John, 6. 27.

[3] Ps. 74. 21.

[II] 2. In those years I taught rhetoric and, overcome by cupidity, made sale of a loquacity to overcome by. Yet I preferred (Lord, Thou knowest) honest scholars (as they are accounted), and these I, without artifice, taught artifices, not to be practised against the life of the guiltless, though sometimes for the life of the guilty. And Thou. O God, from afar perceivedst me stumbling in that slippery course, and amid much smoke sending out some sparks of faithfulness, which I shewed in that my guidance of such as loved vanity, and sought after leasing,[4] myself their companion. In those years I had one—not in that which is called lawful marriage, but whom I had found out in a wayward passion, void of understanding; yet but one, remaining faithful even to her; in whom I in my own case experienced what difference there is betwixt the self-restraint of the marriage-covenant, for the sake of issue, and the bargain of a lustful love, where children are born against their parents' will, although, once born, they constrain love.

3. I remember also, that when I had settled to enter the lists for a theatrical prize, some wizard asked me what I would give him to win: but I, detesting and abhorring such foul mysteries, answered, "Though the garland were of imperishable gold, I would not suffer a fly to be killed to gain me it." For he was to kill some living creatures in his sacrifices, and by those honours to invite the devils to favour me. But this ill also I rejected, not out of a pure love[5] for Thee, O God of my heart; for I knew not how to love Thee, who knew not how to conceive aught beyond a material brightness. And doth not a soul, sighing after such fictions, commit fornication against Thee, trust in things unreal, and feed the wind?[6] Still I would not forsooth have sacrifices offered to devils for me, to whom I was sacrificing myself by that superstition. For what else is it to feed the wind but to feed them, that is, by going astray to become their pleasure and derision?

---

[4]   Ps. 4. 2.

[5]   Cf. *City of God,* Bk. XIV. 9.

[6]   Hosea, 12. 1.

[III] 4. Those impostors then, whom they style mathematicians, I consulted without scruple; because they seemed to use no sacrifice, nor to pray to any spirit for their divinations: which art, however, Christian and true piety consistently rejects and condemns. For it is a good thing to confess unto Thee, and to say, "Have mercy upon me, heal my soul, for I have sinned against Thee";[7] and not to abuse Thy mercy for a license to sin, but to remember the Lord's words, "Behold, thou art made whole, sin no more, lest a worse thing come unto thee."[8] All which wholesome advice they labour to destroy, saying, "The cause of thy sin is inevitably determined in heaven"; and "This did Venus, or Saturn, or Mars": that man, forsooth, flesh and blood, and proud corruption, might be blameless; while the Creator and Ordainer of heaven and the stars is to bear the blame. And who is He but our God? the very sweetness and well-spring of righteousness, Who renderest "to every man according to his works":[9] and "a broken and contrite heart" wilt Thou not despise.[10]

5. There was in those days a wise man,[11] very skilful in physic, and renowned therein, who had with his own proconsular hand put the Agonistic garland upon my distempered head, but not as a physician: for this disease Thou only curest, who resistest the proud, and givest grace to the humble.[12] But didst Thou fail me even by that old man, or forbear to heal my soul? For having become more acquainted with him, and hanging assiduously and fixedly on his speech (for though in simple terms, it was vivid, lively, and earnest), when he had gathered by my discourse that I was given to the books of nativity-casters, he kindly and fatherly advised me to cast them away, and not fruitlessly bestow a care and diligence, necessary for useful things, upon these vanities; saying that he had

---

[7]   Ps. 41. 4.

[8]   John, 5. 14.

[9]   Rom. 2. 6; Matt. 16. 27.

[10]   Ps. 51. 17.

[11]   Vindicianus

[12]   I Peter 5.5; James 4. 6.

in his earliest years studied that art, so as to make it the profession whereby he should live, and that, understanding Hippocrates, he could soon have understood such a study as this; and yet he had given it over, and taken to physic, for no other reason but that he found it utterly false; and he, a grave man, would not get his living by deluding people. "But thou," saith he, "hast rhetoric to maintain thyself by, so that thou followest this of free choice, not of necessity: the more then oughtest Thou to give me credit herein, who laboured to acquire it so perfectly as to get my living by it alone." Of whom when I had demanded, how then could many true things be foretold by it, he answered me (as he could), "that the force of chance, diffused throughout the whole order of things, brought this about. For if when a man by hap-hazard opens the pages of some poet, who sang and thought of something wholly different, a verse oftentimes fell out, wondrously agreeable to the present business: it were not to be wondered at if, out of the soul of man, unconscious what takes place in it, by some higher instinct an answer should be given, by hap, not by art, corresponding to the business and actions of the demander."

6. And thus much, either from or through him, Thou conveyedst to me, and tracedst in my memory, what I might hereafter examine for myself. But at that time neither he, nor my dearest Nebridius, a youth singularly good and of a holy fear, who derided the whole body of divination, could persuade me to cast it aside, the authority of the authors swaying me yet more, and as yet I had found no certain proof (such as I sought) whereby it might without all doubt appear that what had been truly foretold by those consulted was the result of hap-hazard, not of the art of the star-gazers.

[IV] 7. In those years when I first began to teach rhetoric in my native town, I had made one my friend, but too dear to me from a community of pursuits, of mine own age, and, as myself, in the first opening flower of youth. He had grown up of a child with me, and we had been both school-fellows and play-fellows. But he was not yet my friend as afterwards, nor even then as true friendship is; for true it cannot be, unless in such as Thou cementest together, cleaving unto Thee, by that love which is shed abroad in our hearts

by the Holy Ghost, which is given unto us.[13] Yet was it but too
sweet, ripened by the warmth of kindred studies: for, from the
true faith (which he as a youth had not soundly and thoroughly
imbibed), I had warped him also to those superstitious and
pernicious fables for which my mother bewailed me. With me he
now erred in mind, nor could my soul be without him. But behold
Thou wert close on the steps of Thy fugitives, at once God of
vengeance[14] and Fountain of mercies, turning us to Thyself by
wonderful means: Thou tookest that man out of this life, when be
had scarce filled up one whole year of my friendship, sweet to me
be above all sweetness of that my life.

8. "Who can recount all Thy praises,"[15] which he hath felt
in his one self? What diddest Thou then, my God, and how
unsearchable is the abyss of Thy judgments?[16] For long, sore sick
of a fever, he lay senseless in a death-sweat; and, his recovery
being despaired of, he was baptized, unknowing; myself
meanwhile little regarding, and presuming that his soul would
retain rather what it had received of me, not what was wrought
on his unconscious body. But it proved far otherwise: for he was
refreshed, and restored. Forthwith, as soon as I could speak with
him (and I could, so soon as he was able, for I never left him, and
we hung but too much upon each other), I essayed to jest with
him, as though he would jest with me at that baptism which he
had received when utterly absent in mind and feeling, but had
now understood that he had received. But he so shrunk from me,
as from an enemy; and with a wonderful and sudden freedom
bade me, as I would continue his friend, forbear such language
to him. I, all astonished and amazed, suppressed all my emotions
till he should grow well, and his health were strong enough for
me to deal with him as I would. But he was taken away from my
phrensy [frenzy], that with Thee he might be preserved for my

---

13   Rom. 5. 5.
14   Ps. 94. 1.
15   Ps. 106. 2.
16   Ps. 36. 6; Rom. 11. 33.

comfort; a few days after, in my absence, he was attacked again by the fever, and so departed.

9. At this grief my heart was utterly darkened; and whatever I beheld was death. My native country was a torment to me, and my father's house a strange unhappiness: and whatever I had shared with him, wanting him, became a distracting torture. Mine eyes sought him everywhere, but he was not granted them; and I hated all places, for that they had not him; nor could they now tell me, "he is coming," as when he was alive and absent. I became a great riddle to myself, and I asked my soul, why she was so sad, and why she disquieted me sorely;[17] but she knew not what to answer me. And if I said. "Trust in God,"[18] she very rightly obeyed me not; because that most dear friend, whom she had lost, was, being man, both truer and better than that phantasm she was bid to trust in. Only tears were sweet to me, for they succeeded my friend in the dearest of my affections.

[V] 10. And now, Lord, these things are passed by, and time hath assuaged my wound. May I learn from Thee, Who art Truth, and approach the ear of my heart unto Thy mouth, that Thou mayest tell me why weeping is sweet to the miserable? Hast Thou, although present everywhere, cast away our misery far from Thee? And Thou abidest in Thyself, but we are tossed about in divers trials. And yet, unless we mourned in Thine ears, we should have no hope left. Whence then is sweet fruit gathered from the bitterness of life, from groaning, tears, sighs, and complaints? Doth this sweeten it, that we hope Thou hearest? This is true of prayer, for therein is a longing to approach unto Thee. But is it also in grief for a thing lost, and the sorrow wherewith I was then overwhelmed? For I neither hoped he should return to life, nor did I desire this with my tears; but I wept only and grieved. For I was miserable, and had lost my joy. Or is weeping indeed a bitter thing, and for very loathing of the things which we before enjoyed, does it then, when we shrink of them, please us?

---

[17] Ps. 42. 5.

[18] *Ibid.*

[VI] 11. But what speak I of these things? for now is no time to question, but to confess unto Thee. Wretched I was; and wretched is every soul bound by the friendship of perishable things; he is torn asunder when he loses them, and then he feels the wretchedness which he had ere yet he lost them, So was it then with me; I wept most bitterly, and found my repose in bitterness. Thus was I wretched, and that wretched life I held dearer than my friend. For though I would willingly have changed it, yet was I more unwilling to part with it than with him; yea, I know not whether I would have parted with it even for him, as is related (if not feigned) of Pylades and Orestes, that they would gladly have died for each other or together, not to live together being to them worse than death. But in me there had arisen some unexplained feeling, too contrary to this, for at once I loathed exceedingly to live, and feared to die. I suppose, the more I loved him, the more did I hate, and fear (as a most cruel enemy) death, which had bereaved me of him: and I imagined it would speedily make an end of all men, since it had power over him. Thus was it with me, I remember. Behold my heart, O my God, behold and see into me; for well I remember it, O my Hope, who cleansest me from the impurity of such affections, directing mine eyes towards Thee, and plucking my feet out of the snare.[19] For I wondered at others, subject to death, did live, since he whom I loved, as if he should never die, was dead: and I wondered yet more that myself, who was to him a second self, could live, he being dead. Well said one of his friend [sic], "Thou half of my soul": for I felt that my soul and his soul were "one soul in two bodies": and therefore was my life a horror to me, because I would not live halved. And therefore perchance I feared to die, lest he whom I had much loved should die wholly.

[VII] 12. O madness, which knowest not how to love men, like men! O foolish man that I then was, enduring impatiently the lot of man! I fretted then, sighed, wept, was distracted; had neither rest nor counsel. For I bore about a shattered and bleeding soul,

---

[19] Ps. 25. 15.

impatient of being borne by me, yet where to repose it I found
not. Not in calm groves, not in games and music, nor in fragrant
spots, nor in curious banquettings, nor in the pleasures of the bed
and the couch; nor (finally) in books or poesy, found in repose. All
things looked ghastly, yea, the very light; whatsoever was not what
he was, was revolting and hateful, except groaning and tears. For
in those alone found I a little refreshment. But when my soul was
withdrawn from them, a huge load of misery weighed me down.
To Thee, O Lord, it ought to have been raised, for Thee to lighten;
I knew it; but neither could nor would; the more since, when I
thought of Thee, Thou wert not to me any solid or substantial
thing. For Thou wert not Thyself, but a mere phantom, and my
error was my God. If I offered to discharge my load thereon, that it
might rest, it glided through the void, and came rushing down
again on me; and I had remained to myself a hapless spot, where I
could neither be, nor be from thence. For whither should my heart
flee from my heart? Whither should I flee from myself? Whither
not follow myself? And yet I fled out of my country; for so should
mine eyes less look for him, where they were not wont to see him.
And thus from Thagaste I came to Carthage.

[VIII] 13. Times lose no time; nor do they roll idly by; through
our senses they work strange operations on the mind. Behold, they
went and came day by day, and by coming and going introduced
into my mind other imaginations and other remembrances; and
little by little patched me up again with my old kind of delights,
unto which that my sorrow gave way. And yet there succeeded,
not indeed other griefs, yet the causes of other griefs. For whence
had that former grief so easily reached my very inmost soul, but
that I had poured out my soul upon the dust, in loving one that
must die, as if he would never die? For what restored and refreshed
me chiefly was the solaces of other friends, with whom I did love
what instead of Thee I loved: and this was a great fable, and
protracted lie, by whose adulterous stimulus our soul, which lay
itching in our ears, was being defiled. But that fable would not die
to me, so oft as any of my friends died. There were other things
which in them did more take my mind; to talk and jest together,

to do kind offices by turns; to read together honied [*sic*] books; to play the fool or be earnest together; to dissent at times without discontent, as a man might with his own self; and even with the seldomness of these dissentings, to season our more frequent consentings; sometimes to teach, and sometimes learn; long for the absent with impatience; and welcome the coming with joy. These and the like expressions, proceeding out of the hearts of those that loved and were loved again, by the countenance, the tongue, the eyes, and a thousand pleasing gestures, were so much fuel to melt our souls together, and out of many make but one.

[IX] 14. This is it that is loved in friends; and so loved that a man's conscience condemns itself if he love not him that loves him again, or love not again him that loves him, looking for nothing from his person but indications of his love. Hence that mourning, if one die, and darkenings of sorrows, that steeping of the heart in tears, all sweetness turned to bitterness; and upon the loss of life of the dying, the death of the living. Blessed whoso loveth Thee, and his friend in Thee, and his enemy for Thee. For he alone loses none dear to him, to whom all are dear in Him Who cannot be lost. And who is this but our God, the God that made heaven and earth,[20] and filleth them,[21] because by filling them He created them?[22] Thee none loseth, but who leaveth. And who leaveth Thee, whither goeth or whither fleeth he, but from Thee well-pleased, to Thee displeased? For where doth he not find Thy law in his own punishment? "And Thy law is truth,"[23] and truth Thou.[24]

[X] 15. "Turn us, O God of Hosts, shew us Thy countenance, and we shall be whole."[25] For whithersoever, the soul of man turns itself, unless towards Thee, it is rivetted upon sorrows,[26] yea though

---

20   Gen. 1. 1.
21   Jer. 23. 24.
22   See Bk. I. 2, 3.
23   Ps. 119. 142; John, 17. 17.
24   John, 14. 6.
25   Ps. 80. 19.
26   See Bk. IV. 13.

it is rivetted on things beautiful. And yet they, out of Thee, and out of the soul, were not, unless they were from Thee. They rise, and set; and by rising, they begin as it were to be; they grow, that they may be perfected; and perfected, they wax, old and wither; and all grow not old, but all wither. So when they rise and tend to be, the more quickly they grow that they may be, so much the more they haste not to be. This is the law of them. Thus much hast Thou allotted them, because they are portions of things, which exist not all at once, but by passing away and succeeding they together complete that universe whereof they are portions. And even thus is our speech completed by signs giving forth a sound: but this again is not perfected unless one word pass away when it hath sounded its part, that another may succeed. Out of all these things let my soul praise Thee, O God. Creator of all; yet let not my soul be rivetted unto these things with the glue of love, through the senses of the body. For they go whither they were to go, that they might not be; and they rend her with pestilent longings, because she longs to be, yet loves to repose in what she loves. But in these things is no place of repose; they abide not, they flee; and who can follow them with the senses of the flesh? yea, who can grasp them, when they are hard by? For the sense of the flesh is slow, because it is the sense of the flesh; and thereby is it bounded. It sufficeth for that it was made for; but it sufficeth not to stay things running their course from their appointed starting place to the end appointed. For in Thy Word, by which they are created, they hear their decree, "hence and hitherto."

[XI] 16. Be not foolish, O my soul, nor become deaf in the ear of thine heart with the tumult of thy folly. Hearken thou too. The Word Itself calleth thee to return: and there is the place of rest imperturbable, where love is not forsaken, if itself forsaketh not. Behold, these things pass away, that others may replace them, and so this lower universe be completed by all his parts. But do I depart any whither? saith the Word of God. There fix thy dwelling, trust there whatsoever thou hast thence, O my soul, at least now thou art tired out with vanities. Entrust Truth, whatsoever thou hast from the Truth, and thou shalt lose nothing; and thy decay shall bloom again, and all thy

diseases be healed,[27] and thy mortal parts be re-formed and
renewed, and bound around thee: nor shall they lay thee whither
themselves descend; but they shall stand fast with thee, and abide
for ever before God, Who abideth and standeth fast for ever.[28]

17. Why then be perverted and follow thy flesh? Be it converted
and follow thee. Whatever by her though hast sense of is in part;
and the whole, whereof these are parts, thou knowest not; and yet
they delight thee. But had the sense of thy flesh a capacity for
comprehending the whole, and not itself also, for thy punishment,
been justly restricted to a part of the whole, thou wouldest that
whatsoever existeth at this present should pass away, that so the
whole might better please thee.[29] For what we speak also, by the
same sense of the flesh thou hearest; yet wouldest not thou have
the syllables stay, but fly away, that others may come, and thou
hear the whole. And so ever, when any one thing is made up of
many, all of which do not exist together, all collectively would
please more than they do severally, could all be perceived collectively.
But far better than these is He who made all; and He is our God,
nor doth He pass away, for neither doth aught succeed Him.

[XII] 18. If bodies please thee, praise God on occasion of them,
and turn back thy love upon their Maker; lest in these things
which please thee, thou displease. If souls please thee, be they
loved in God: for they too are mutable, but in Him are they firmly
stablished; else would they pass, and pass away. In Him then be
they beloved; and carry unto Him along with thee what souls
thou canst, and say to them, "Him let us love, Him let us love: He
made these, nor is He far off. For He did not make them, and so
depart, but they are of Him, and in Him. See there He is, where
truth is loved. He is within the very heart, yet hath the heart
strayed from Him. Go back into your heart, ye transgressors[30] and
cleave fast to Him that made you. Stand with Him, and ye shall

---

[27]   Ps. 103. 3.

[28]   I Peter 1. 23.

[29]   See Bk. XIII. 22 below.

[30]   Isa. 66. 8.

stand fast. Rest in Him, and ye shall be at rest. Whither go ye in rough ways? Whither go ye? The good that you love is from Him; but it is good and pleasant[31] through reference to Him, and justly shall it be embittered, because unjustly is anything loved which is from Him, if He be forsaken for it. To what end then would ye still and still walk these difficult and toilsome ways? There is no rest where ye seek it. Seek what ye seek; but it is not there where ye seek. Ye seek a blessed life in the land of death; it is not there. For how should there be a blessed life, where life itself is not?"

19. But our true Life came down hither, and bore our death, and slew him, out of the abundance of His own life: and He thundered, calling aloud to us to return hence to Him into that secret place whence He came forth to us, first into the Virgin's womb, wherein He espoused the human creation, our mortal flesh, that it might not be for ever mortal, and thence "like a bridegroom coming out of his chamber, rejoicing as a giant to run his course."[32] For He lingered not, but ran, calling aloud by words, deeds, death, life, descent, ascension; crying aloud to us to return unto Him. And He departed from our eyes, that we might return into our heart, and there find Him. For He departed, and lo, He is here. He would not be long with us, yet left us not; for He departed thither, whence He never parted, "because the world was made by Him."[33] And in this world He was, and into this world He came to save sinners,[34] unto Whom my soul confesseth, and He healeth it, for it hath sinned against Him.[35] O ye sons of men, how long so slow of heart?[36] Even now, after the descent of Life to you, will ye not ascend and live? But whither ascend ye, when ye are on high, and set your mouth against the heavens?[37] Descend, that ye

---

[31] Cf. *City of God*, Bk. XI. 8.
[32] Ps. 19. 5.
[33] John, 1. 10.
[34] I Tim. 1. 15.
[35] Ps. 41. 4.
[36] Luke, 24. 25.
[37] Ps. 72. 9.

may ascend, and ascend to God. For ye have fallen, by "ascending against Him."[38] Tell them this, that they may weep in the valley of tears, and so carry them up with thee unto God; because out of His Spirit thou speakest thus unto them, if thou speakest, burning with the fire of charity.

[XIII] 20. These things I then knew not, and I loved these lower beauties, and I was sinking to the very depths, and to my friends I said, "Do we love anything but the beautiful? What then is the beautiful? And what is beauty? What is it that attracts and wins us to the things we love? For unless there were in them a grace and beauty, they could by no means draw us unto them." And I marked and perceived that in bodies themselves there was a beauty, from their forming a sort of whole, and again, another from apt and mutual correspondence, as of a part of the body with its whole, or a shoe with a foot, and the like. And this consideration sprang up in my mind, out of my inmost heart, and I wrote "on the fair and fit," I think, two or three books. Thou knowest, O Lord, for it is gone from me; for I have them not, but they are strayed from me, I know not how.

[XIV] 21. But what moved me, O Lord my God, to dedicate these books unto Hierius, an orator of Rome, whom I knew not by face, but loved for the fame of his learning which was eminent in him, and some words of his I had heard, which pleased me? But more did he please me, for that he pleased others, who highly extolled him, amazed that out of a Syrian, first instructed in Greek eloquence, should afterwards be formed a wonderful Latin orator, and one most learned in things pertaining unto philosophy. One is commended, and, unseen, he is loved: doth this love enter the heart of the hearer from the mouth of the commender? Not so. But by one who loveth is another kindled. For hence he is loved, who is commended, when the commender is believed to extol him with an unfeigned heart; that is, when one that loves him praises him.

22. For so did I then love men upon the judgment of men, not thine, O my God, in Whom no man is deceived. But yet why not

[38] Ps. 84. 6.

for qualities like those of a famous charioteer, or fighter with beasts in the theatre,[39] known far and wide by a vulgar popularity, but far otherwise, and earnestly, and so as I would be myself commended? For I would not be commended or loved, as actors are (though I myself did commend and love them), but had rather be unknown than so known; and even hated than so loved. Where now are the impulses to such various and divers kinds of loves laid up in one soul? Why, since we are equally men, do I love in another what, if I did not hate, I should not spurn and cast from myself? For it holds not that, as a good horse is loved by him who would not, though he might, be that horse, therefore the same may be said of an actor, who shares our nature. Do I then love in a man what I hate to be, who am a man? Man himself is a great deep, whose very hairs Thou numberest, O Lord, and they fall not to the ground without Thee.[40] And yet are the hairs of his head easier to be numbered than are his feelings, and the beatings of his heart.

23. But that orator was of that sort whom I loved, as wishing to be myself such; and I erred through a swelling pride, and was "tossed about with every wind,"[41] but yet was steered by Thee, though very secretly. And whence do I know, and whence do I confidently confess unto Thee, that I had loved him more for the love of his commenders than for the very things for which he was commended? Because, had he been unpraised, and these self-same men had dispraised him, and with dispraise and contempt told the very same things of him, I had never been so kindled and excited to love him. And yet the things had not been other, nor he himself other; but only the feelings of the relators. See where the impotent soul lies along, that is not yet stayed up by the solidity of truth! Just as the gales of tongues blow from the breast of the opinionative, so is it carried this way and that, driven forward and backward, and the light is overclouded to it, and the truth unseen. And lo, it is before us. And it was to me a great matter that my

---

[39] See Bk. VI. 13, below.

[40] Matt. 10. 29, 30.

[41] Eph. 4. 14.

discourse and labours should be known to that man: which should
he approve, I were the more kindled; but if he disapproved, my
empty heart, void of Thy solidity, had been wounded. And yet the
"fair and fit," whereon I wrote to him, I dwelt on with pleasure,
and surveyed it, and admired it, though none joined therein.

[XV] 24. But I saw not yet, whereon this weighty matter turned
in Thy wisdom, O Thou Omnipotent, "Who only doest wonders";[42]
and my mind ranged through corporeal forms; and "fair" I defined
and distinguished what is so in itself, and "fit" whose beauty is in
correspondence to some other thing: and this I supported by
corporeal examples. And I turned to the nature of the mind, but
the false notion which I had of spiritual things let me not see the
truth. Yet the force of truth did of itself flash into mine eyes, and
I turned away my panting soul from incorporeal substance to
lineaments, and colours, and bulky magnitudes. And, not being
able to see these in the mind, I thought I could not see my mind.
And whereas in virtue I loved peace, and in viciousness I abhorred
discord; in the first I observed an unity, but in the other, a sort of
division. And in that unity, I conceived the rational soul, and the
nature of truth and of the chief good to consist: but in this division
I miserably imagined there to be some unknown substance of
irrational life, and the nature of the chief evil, which should not
only be a substance, but real life also, and yet not derived from
Thee, O my God, of whom are all things. And yet that first I
called a Monad, as it had been a soul without sex;[43] but the latter
a Duad: anger in deeds of violence, and in flagitiousness, lust; not
knowing whereof I spake. For I had not known or learned that
neither was evil a substance, nor our soul that chief and
unchangeable good.

25. For as deeds of violence arise, if that emotion of the soul be
corrupted whence vehement action springs, stirring itself insolently
and unrulily, and lusts, when that affection of the soul is ungoverned,
whereby carnal pleasures are drunk in, so do errors and false opinions

---

[42]   Ps. 136. 4.
[43]   Or "an unintelligent soul."

defile the conversation, if the reasonable soul itself be corrupted; as it was then in me, who knew not that it must be enlightened by another light, that it may be partaker of truth, seeing itself is not that nature of truth. "For Thou shalt light my candle, O Lord my God. Thou shalt enlighten my darkness":[44] and "of Thy fulness have we all received,"[45] for "Thou art the true light that lighteth every man that cometh into the world";[46] for in Thee there is no variableness, neither shadow of change."[47]

26. But I pressed towards Thee, and was thrust from Thee, that I might taste of death: for thou "resistest the proud."[48] But what prouder than for me with a strange madness to maintain myself to be that by nature which Thou art? For whereas I was subject to change (so much being manifest to me, my very desire to become wise, being the wish, of worse to become better); yet chose I rather to imagine Thee subject to change, than myself not to be that which Thou art. Therefore I was repelled by Thee, and Thou resistedst my vain stiff-neckedness, and I imagined corporeal forms, and, myself flesh. I accused flesh; and, "a wind that passeth away," I returned not[49] to Thee, but I passed on and on to things which have no being, neither in Thee, nor in me, nor in the body. Neither were they created for me by Thy truth, but by my vanity devised out of things corporeal. And I was wont to ask Thy faithful little ones, my fellow-citizens (from whom, unknown to myself, I stood exiled)—I was wont, prating and foolishly, to ask them, "Why then doth the soul err which God created?" But I would not be asked, "Why then doth God err?" And I maintained that Thy unchangeable substance did err upon constraint, rather than confess that my changeable substance had gone astray voluntarily, and now, in punishment, lay in error.

---

[44] Ps. 18. 28.

[45] John, 1. 16.

[46] John, 1. 9.

[47] James, 1. 17.

[48] *Ibid.*, 4. 6; I Pet. 5. 5.

[49] Ps. 78. 39.

27. I was then some six or seven and twenty years old when I wrote those volumes; revolving within me corporeal fictions, buzzing in the ears of my heart, which I turned, O sweet truth, to thy inward melody, meditating on the "fair and fit," and longing to stand and hearken to Thee, and to rejoice greatly at the Bridegroom's voice,[50] but could not; for by the voices of mine own errors I was hurried abroad, and through the weight of my own pride I was sinking into the lowest pit. For Thou didst not "make me to hear joy and gladness," nor did the bones exult which were not yet humbled.[51]

[XVI] 28. And what did it profit me that, scarce twenty years old, a book of Aristotle, which they call *The Ten Predicaments,* falling into my hands (on whose very name I hung, as on something great and divine, so often as my rhetoric master of Carthage, and others, accounted learned, mouthed it with cheeks bursting with pride), I read and understood it unaided? And on my conferring with others, who said that they scarcely understood it with very able tutors, not only orally explaining it, but drawing many things in sand, they could tell me no more of it than I had learned, reading it by myself. And the book appeared to me to speak very clearly of substances, such as "man," and of their qualities, as the figure of a man, of what sort it is; and stature, how many feet high; and his relationship, whose brother he is; or where placed; or when born; or whether he stands or sits; or be shod or armed; or does or suffers anything; and all the innumerable things which might be ranged under these nine Predicaments, of which I have given some specimens, or under that chief Predicament of Substance.

29. What did all this further me, seeing it even hindered me? when, imagining whatever was, was comprehended under those ten Predicaments, I essayed in such wise to understand, O my God, Thy wonderful and unchangeable Unity also, as if Thou also hadst been subjected to Thine own greatness or beauty; so that (as in bodies) they should exist in Thee, as their subject: whereas Thou

---

[50]   John. 3. 21.

[51]   Ps. 51. 8, Vulg.

Thyself art Thy greatness and beauty; but a body is not great or fair in that it is a body, seeing that, though it were less great or fair, it should notwithstanding be a body. But it was falsehood which of Thee I conceived, not truth; fictions of my misery, not the realities of Thy Blessedness. For Thou hadst commanded, and it was done in me, that the earth should bring forth briars and thorns to me,[52] and that in the sweat of my brows I should eat my bread.[53]

30. And what did it profit me that all the books I could procure of the so-called liberal arts, I, the vile slave of vile affections, read by myself, and understood? And I delighted in them, but knew not whence came all that therein was true or certain. For I had my back to the light, and my face to the things enlightened; whence my face, with which I discerned the things enlightened, itself was not enlightened. Whatever was written, either on rhetoric, or logic, geometry, music, and arithmetic, by myself without much difficulty or any instructor, I understood, Thou knowest, O Lord my God; because both quickness of understanding, and acuteness in discerning, is Thy gift: yet did I not thence sacrifice to Thee. So then it served not to my use, but rather to my perdition, since I went about to get so good a portion of my substance[54] into my own keeping; and I kept not my strength for Thee,[55] but wandered from Thee into a far country, to spend it upon harlotries.[56] For what profited me good abilities, not employed to good uses? For I felt not that those arts were attained with great difficulty, even by the studious and talented, until I attempted to explain them to such; when he most excelled in them, who followed me not altogether slowly.

31. But what did this further me, imagining that Thou, O Lord God, the Truth, wert a vast and bright body,[57] and I a fragment

---

[52]   Isa. 32. 13.

[53]   Gen. 3. 19.

[54]   Luke, 15. 12.

[55]   Ps. 59.5, Vulg.

[56]   Luke, 15. 13.

[57]   See Bk. III. 12; Book IV. 3, 12; Bk. V. 19.

of that body? Perverseness too great! But such was I. Nor do I blush, O my God, to confess to Thee Thy mercies towards me, and to call upon Thee, who blushed not then to profess to men my blasphemies, and to bark against Thee. What profited me then my nimble wit in those sciences and all those most knotty volumes, unravelled by me without aid from human instruction; seeing I erred so foully, and with such sacrilegious shamefulness, in the doctrine of piety? Or what hindrance was a far slower wit to Thy little ones, since they departed not far from Thee, that in the nest of Thy Church they might securely be fledged, and nourish the wings of charity, by the food of a sound faith. O Lord our God, under the shadow of Thy wings let us hope;[58] protect us, and carry us. Thou wilt carry us both when little, and even to hoar hairs wilt Thou carry us;[59] for our firmness, when it is Thou, then is it firmness; but when our own, it is infirmity. Our good ever lives with Thee; from which when we turn away, we are turned aside. Let us now, O Lord, return, that we may not be overturned, because with Thee our good lives without any decay, which good art Thou; nor need we fear, lest there be no place whither to return, because we fell from it: for through our absence, our mansion fell not—Thy eternity.

---

[58] Ps. 36. 7.

[59] Isa. 46. 4.

KARL MARX

1818-1883

and

FREDERICK ENGELS

1820-1895

THE GERMAN IDEOLOGY
1845-1846

Karl Marx philosopher, social scientist, historian, and revolutionary, is considered the most influential socialist thinker of the 19th century. Largely ignored in his lifetime, his social, economic, and political ideas gained recognition after his death, when his ideas and meanings were modified for political purposes. Born in Trier, Germany, Marx received a classical education, then studied jurisprudence at Bonn and later in Berlin. He became a member of the Young Hegelians in Berlin and edited *Rheinische Zeitung*, a liberal newspaper. His articles on economic questions resulted in the closing of the newspaper by the Prussian government. In 1843, Marx emigrated to Paris, where he made contact with émigré German workers and French socialists. Here he began his lifelong partnership with Frederick Engels.

Marx first set down his Communist views in *Economic and Philosophical Manuscripts* (1844), but expelled from Paris soon thereafter, he moved to Brussels with Engels. While there he made an intensive study of the materialist conception of history. With the outbreak of revolutions in Europe in the mid-19th century, he sought refuge in London, where he remained for the rest of his life, devoted to the study of political economy.

Frederick Engels, born in Germany, served in the Army as a volunteer and then worked in his father's cotton-spinning business in Manchester, England. In 1844, he moved to Brussels, then (with Marx) to Paris and Cologne. In 1849, he took part in an uprising in South Germany, returning then to London and finally to Manchester, where he ultimately become a joint proprietor in his father's business. He retired from business in 1869.

The Communist Manifesto (1848) is Marx and Engels's best known collaboration. However, the selection here is from *The German Ideology*, written somewhat earlier (1845 and 1846) and published posthumously. The text opposes Ludwig Feuerbach's materialist and idealist outlooks, particularly his advocating of the biological foundation of human nature. In their expansive treatise, Marx and Engels laid the foundations for Marxism, providing one of their first dissertations on materialism, revolution, and communism. The basic thesis of *The German Ideology* is that human nature is socially and historically created by the conditions of one's life and the circumstances that shape and form consciousness. The link is labor.

SOURCE

Marx, Karl and Frederick Engels. 1846. "The Relation of State and Law to Property," "Conquest," and "Artistic Talent." In *The German Ideology, Part I.* C.J. [H.]. Arthur, Ed. [no Trans. given] New York: International Publishers, 1970. 79-81, 89-90, 108-109.*

---

*   Reprinted by permission of International Publishers, New York City.

THE GERMAN IDEOLOGY
PART I: FEUERBACH [EXCERPT]

The Relation of State and Law to Property

The first form of property, in the ancient world as in the Middle Ages, is tribal property, determined with the Romans chiefly by war, with the Germans by the rearing of cattle. In the case of the ancient peoples, since several tribes live together in one town, the tribal property appears as State property, and the right of the individual to it as mere "possession" which, however, like tribal property as a whole, is confined to landed property only. Real private property began with the ancients, as with modern nations, with movable property.—(Slavery and community) *(dominium ex jure Quiritum).*[1] In the case of the nations which grew out of the Middle Ages, tribal property evolved through various stages—feudal landed property, corporative movable property, capital invested in manufacture—to modern capital, determined by big industry and universal competition, i.e. pure private property, which has cast off all semblance of a communal institution and has shut out the State from any influence on the development of property. To this modern private property corresponds the modern State, which, purchased gradually by the owners of property by means of taxation, has fallen entirely into their hands through the national debt, and its existence has become wholly dependent on the commercial credit which the owners of property, the bourgeois, extend to it, as reflected in the rise and fall of State funds on the stock exchange. By the mere fact that it is a *class* and no longer an *estate*,[2] the bourgeoisie is forced to organize itself no longer locally, but nationally, and to give a general form to its mean average interest. Through the emancipation of private property from the community, the State has become a separate entity, beside and outside civil society; but it is nothing more than

---

[1]   Ownership in accordance with the law applying to full Roman citizens. [C.J.A.]

[2]   Social position or rank, especially of high order.

the form of organisation which the bourgeois necessarily adopt both for internal and external purposes, for the mutual guarantee of their property and interests. The independence of the State is only found nowadays in those countries where the estates have not yet completely developed into classes, where the estates, done away with in more advanced countries, still have a part to play, and where there exists a mixture; countries, that is to say, in which no one section of the population can achieve dominance over the others. This is the case particularly in Germany. The most perfect example of the modern State is North America. The modern French, English and American writers all express the opinion that the State exists only for the sake of private property, so that this fact has penetrated into the consciousness of the normal man.

Since the State is the form in which the individuals of a ruling class assert their common interests, and in which the whole civil society of an epoch is epitomised, it follows that the State mediates in the formation of all common institutions and that the institutions receive a political form. Hence the illusion that law is based on the will, and indeed on the will divorced from its real basis—on *free* will. Similarly, justice is in its turn reduced to the actual laws.

Civil law develops simultaneously with private property out of the disintegration of the natural community. With the Romans the development of private property and civil law had no further industrial and commercial consequences, because their whole mode of production did not alter. (Usury!)

With modern peoples, where the feudal community was disintegrated by industry and trade, there began with the rise of private property and civil law a new phase, which was capable of further development. The very first town which carried on an extensive maritime trade in the Middle Ages, Amalfi, also developed maritime law. As soon as industry and trade developed private property further, first in Italy and later in other countries, the highly developed Roman civil law was immediately adopted again and raised to authority. When later the bourgeoisie had acquired so much power that the princes took up its interests in order to overthrow the feudal nobility by means of the bourgeoisie, there began in all countries—in France in the sixteenth century—the real development of law, which in all countries except England proceeded on the basis of the Roman Codex. In England, too, Roman legal principles had to be introduced to further the development of civil law (especially in the case of movable property). (It must not be forgotten that law has just as little an independent history as religion.)

In civil law the existing property relationships are declared to be the result of the general will. The *jus utendi et abutendi* itself asserts on the one hand the fact that private property has become entirely independent of the community, and on the other the illusion that private property itself is based solely on the private will, the arbitrary disposal of the thing. In practice, the *abuti* has very definite economic limitations for the owner of private property, if he does not wish to see his property and hence his *jus abutendi* pass into other hands, since actually the thing, considered merely with reference to his will, is not a thing at all, but only becomes a thing, true property in intercourse, and independently of the law (a *relationship,* which the philosophers call an idea). This juridical illusion, which reduces law to the mere will, necessarily leads, in the further development of property relationships, to the position that a man may have a legal title to a thing without really having the thing. If, for instance, the income from a piece of land is lost owing to competition, then the proprietor has certainly his legal title to it along with the *jus utendi et abutendi.* But he can do nothing with it: he owns nothing as a landed proprietor if in addition he has not enough capital to cultivate his ground. This illusion of the jurists also explains the fact that for them, as for every code, it is altogether fortuitous that individuals enter into relationships among themselves (e.g. contracts); it explains why they consider that these relationships [can] be entered into or not at will, and that their content rests purely on the individual [free] will of the contracting parties.

Whenever, through the development of industry and commerce, new forms of intercourse have been evolved (e.g. assurance companies, etc.), the law has always been compelled to admit them among the modes of acquiring property.

[FROM PART 2 & PART 3]

Conquest

This whole interpretation of history appears to be contradicted by the fact of conquest. Up till now violence, war, pillage, murder and robbery, etc. have been accepted as the driving force of history. Here we must limit ourselves to the chief points and take, therefore, only the most striking example—the destruction of an old civilisation by a barbarous people and the resulting formation of an entirely new organisation of society. (Rome and the barbarians; feudalism and Gaul; the Byzantine Empire and the Turks.)

With the conquering barbarian people war itself is still, as indicated above, a regular form of intercourse, which is the more eagerly exploited as the increase in population together with the traditional and, for it, the only possible, crude mode of production gives rise to the need for new means of production. In Italy, on the other hand, the concentration of landed property (caused not only by buying-up and indebtedness but also by inheritance, since loose living being rife and marriage rare, the old families gradually died out and their possessions fell into the hands of a few) and its conversion into grazing-land (caused not only by the usual economic forces still operative today but by the importation of plundered and tribute-corn and the resultant lack of demand for Italian corn) brought about the almost total disappearance of the free population. The very slaves died out again and again, and had constantly to be replaced by new ones. Slavery remained the basis of the whole productive system. The plebeians, midway between freemen and slaves, never succeeded in becoming more than a proletarian rabble. Rome indeed never became more than a city; its connection with the provinces was almost exclusively political and could, therefore, easily be broken again by political events.

Nothing is more common than the notion that in history up till now it has only been a question of *taking*. The barbarians *take* the Roman Empire, and this fact of taking is made to explain the transition from the old world to the feudal system. In this taking by barbarians, however, the question is, whether the nation which is conquered has evolved industrial productive forces, as is the case with modern peoples, or whether their productive forces are based for the most part merely on their association and on the community. Taking is further determined by the object taken. A banker's fortune, consisting of paper, cannot be taken at all, without the taker's submitting to the conditions of production and intercourse of the country taken. Similarly the total industrial capital of a modern industrial country. And finally, everywhere there is very soon an end to taking, and when there is nothing more to take, you have to set about producing. From this necessity of producing, which very soon asserts itself, it follows that the form of community adopted by the settling conquerors must correspond to the stage of development of the productive forces they find in existence; or, if this is not the case from the start, it must change according to the productive forces. By this, too, is explained the fact, which people profess to have noticed everywhere in the period following the migration of the peoples, namely, that the servant was master, and that the conquerors very soon took over language, culture and manners from the conquered. The feudal system was by no means brought complete from Germany, but had its origin, as far as the conquerors were concerned, in the martial organisation of the army during the actual conquest, and this only evolved after the conquest into the feudal system proper through the action of the productive forces found in the conquered countries. To what an extent this form was determined by the productive forces is shown by the abortive attempts to realise other forms derived from reminiscences of ancient Rome (Charlemagne, etc.).

Artistic Talent

He [Stirner] imagines that the so-called organisers of labour wanted to organise the entire activity of each individual, and yet it is precisely among them that a difference is drawn between directly productive labour, which has to be organised, and labour which is not directly productive. In regard to the latter, however, it was not their view, as Sancho imagines, that each should do the work of Raphael, but that anyone in whom there is a potential Raphael should be able to develop without hindrance. Sancho imagines that Raphael produced his pictures independently of the division of labour that existed in Rome at the time. If he were to compare Raphael with Leonardo da Vinci and Titian, he would know how greatly Raphael's works of art depended on the flourishing of Rome at that time, which occurred under Florentine influence, while the works of Leonardo depended on the state of things in Florence, and the works of Titian, at a later period, depended on the totally different development of Venice. Raphael as much as any other artist was determined by the technical advances in art made before him, by the organisation of society and the division of labour in his locality, and, finally, by the division of labour in all the countries with which his locality had intercourse. Whether an individual like Raphael succeeds in developing his talent depends wholly on demand, which in turn depends on the division of labour and the conditions of human culture resulting from it.

In proclaiming the uniqueness of work in science and art, Stirner adopts a position far inferior to that of the bourgeoisie. At the present time it has already been found necessary to organise this "unique" activity. Horace Vernet would not have had time to paint even a tenth of his pictures if he regarded them as works which "only this Unique person is capable of producing." In Paris, the great demand for vaudevilles and novels brought about the organisation of work for their production, organisation which at any rate yields something better than its "unique" competitors in Germany. In astronomy, people like Arago, Herschel, Encke and Bessel considered it necessary to organise joint observations and only after that obtained some fruitful results. In historical science, it is absolutely impossible for the "Unique" to achieve anything at all, and in this field, too, the French long ago surpassed all other nations thanks to organisation of labour. Incidentally, it is self-evident that all these organisations based on modern division of labour still lead only to extremely limited results, representing a step forward only compared with the preview narrow isolation . . . .

The exclusive concentration of artistic talent in particular individuals, and its suppression in the broad mass which is bound up with this, is a consequence of division of labour. If, even in certain social conditions, everyone was an excellent painter, that would not at all exclude the possibility of each of them being also an original painter, so that here too the difference between "human" and "unique" labour amounts to sheer nonsense. In any case, with a communist organisation of society, there disappears the subordination of the artist to local and national narrowness, which arises entirely from division of labour, and also the subordination of the artist to some definite art, thanks to which he is exclusively a painter, sculptor, etc., the very name of his activity adequately expressing the narrowness of his professional development and his dependence on division of labour. In a communist society there are no painters but at most people who engage in painting among other activities.

FRIEDRICH NIETZSCHE

1844-1900

TWILIGHT OF THE IDOLS

1895

Friedrich Nietzsche, German philosopher, poet, and philologist, was born in Saxony and educated at the universities of Bonn and Leipzig. Appointed Professor of Classical Philosophy at the University of Basle, Switzerland, he resigned this position in 1879 from ill health, including migraines and poor eyesight. Nietzsche was influenced by the philosophies of Plato and Aristotle, the German philosopher Arthur Schopenhauer (1788-1860), the German composer Richard Wagner, and Darwin's theory of evolution. In the 1880s, he traveled and wrote a series of landmark philosophical works, including *Thus Spake Zarathustra, Beyond Good and Evil,* and *On the Genealogy of Morals.* In 1889, Nietzsche suffered a mental breakdown from which he never recovered.

Twilight of the Idols derives its title from Wagner's opera, *Twilight of the Gods (Götterdammerung).* Central to Nietzsche's thoughts is the affirmation of life. The essays it contains are deliberately provocative and provide a wide-ranging critique of the Greek tradition of over-emphasis on reason in the search for absolute truth. He disagrees with Heraclitus that our senses can falsify reality and claims the only "real" world is one that is perceptible to our senses. He also calls into question European cultural values and concludes that traditional philosophy and religion enervate the human capacity for realization. The basic contention of the essay is that traditional values, and especially Christianity, have lost their power in the lives of individuals and that a re-appraisal of values was neccessary. Nietzsche's "idols" are hollow beliefs, pounded out with philosophers' hammers. Nietzsche maintains that there are no universal truths and that all human behavior is motivated by the will to power— striving to extend the self, while the will-to-life affirms human identity. The will-to-power is not power over others but the power over oneself that is necessary for independence, originality, and creativity.

SOURCE

Nietzsche, Friedrich. 1895. *The Twilight of the Idols.* In *The Works of Friedrich Nietzsche.* Volume XI. Alexander Tille, Ed. Thomas Common, Trans. New York: Macmillan, 1924. 167-170, 177-179, 182-184.

THE TWILIGHT OF THE IDOLS [EXCERPTS]

How the "True World" Finally Became a Fable

History of an Error

1   The true world attainable by the wise, the pious, and the virtuous man,—he lives in it, *he embodies it.*

(Oldest form of the idea, relatively rational, simple, and convincing. Transcription of the proposition, "I, Plato, *am* the truth.")

2 The true world unattainable at present, but promised to the
wise, the pious, and the virtuous man (to the sinner who
repents).

(Progress of the idea: it becomes more refined, more
insidious, more incomprehensible,—it *becomes feminine*, it
becomes Christian.)

3 The true world unattainable, undemonstrable, and unable to
be promised; but even as conceived, a comfort, an obligation,
and an imperative.

(The old sun still, but shining only through mist and
scepticism; the idea become sublime, pale, northerly,
Koenigsbergian.)

4 The true world—unattainable? At any rate unattained. And
being unattained also *unknown*. Consequently also neither
comforting, saving, nor obligatory: what obligation could
anything unknown lay upon us?

(Grey morning. First yawning of reason. Cock-crowing of
Positivism.)

5 The "true world"—an idea neither good for anything, nor
even obligatory any longer,—an idea become useless and
superfluous; *consequently* a refuted idea: let us do away
with it!

(Full day; breakfast; return of *bon sens* and cheerfulness;
Plato blushing for shame; infernal noise of all free
intellects.)

6 We have done away with the true world: what world is left?
perhaps the seeming? . . . But no! *in doing away with the true,
we have also done away with the seeming world!*

(Noon; the moment of the shortest shadow; end of the longest
error; climax of mankind; *INCIPIT ZARATHUSHTRA.)*

8

A psychology of the artist.—To the existence of art, to the existence of any aesthetic activity or perception whatsoever, a preliminary psychological condition is indispensable, namely, *ecstasy.* Ecstasy must first have intensified the sensitiveness of the whole mechanism; until this takes place art is not realised. All kinds of ecstasy, however differently conditioned, possess this power; above all the ecstasy of sexual excitement, the oldest and most primitive form of ecstasy. In like manner the ecstasy which follows in the train of all great desires, of all strong emotions; the ecstasy of the feast, of the contest, of a daring deed, of victory, of all extreme agitation; the ecstasy of cruelty; the ecstasy in destruction; the ecstasy under certain meteorological influences—for example, spring ecstasy; or under the influence of narcotics; finally, the ecstasy of will, the ecstasy of an overcharged and surging will.—The essential thing in ecstasy is the feeling of increased power and profusion. Out of this feeling we impart to things, we *constrain* them to accept something from us, we force them by violence;—this proceeding is called *idealising.* Let us here free ourselves from a prejudice: idealising does *not* consist, as is commonly believed, in an abstraction or deduction of the insignificant or the contingent. An immense *forcing out* of principal traits is rather the decisive characteristic, so that the others thereby disappear.

9

In this condition we enrich everything out of our own profusion; what we see, and what we wish for we see enlarged, crowded, strong, and overladen with power. He who, in this condition, transforms things till they mirror his power,—till they are reflections of his perfection. This *constraint* to transform into the perfect is—art. Everything that he is not, nevertheless becomes for him a delight in himself; in art man enjoys himself as perfection. It would be allowable to imagine an opposite state of things, a specific anti-artisticalness of instinct—a mode of being which would impoverish everything, attenuate everything, make everything consumptive. In fact, history furnishes us with abundance of such anti-artists, persons with starved lives, who must necessarily lay hold of things, drain them, and make them *more emaciated*. This is the case with the genuine Christian, Pascal, for example; a Christian, who is at the same time an artist, *is not to be found*. Let no one be childish enough to refer me to the case of Raphael, or to any homeopathic Christian of the nineteenth century. Raphael said yea, he did yea; consequently Raphael was no Christian. . . .

10

What do the antithetical notions *Apollonian* and *Dionysian* (which I have introduced into aesthetics) imply, when we conceive of them both as modes of ecstasy? Apollonian ecstasy above all keeps the eye on the alert so that it acquires the faculty of vision. The painter, the sculptor, and the epic poet, are visionaries *par excellence*. In the Dionysian condition, on the other hand, the entire emotional system is excited, and has its energies augmented; so that it discharges itself simultaneously by all channels of expression, and forces the faculties of representation, of imitation, of transfiguration, of metamorphosis—all kinds of mimicry and acting—into activity at one and the same time. The essential thing is the easiness of the metamorphosis, the *incapacity to resist a* stimulus (similar to the case of certain hysterical patients, who also act *every* role at every hint). It is impossible for Dionysian man not to understand any suggestion, he overlooks no symptom of emotion, he possesses the highest manifestation of knowing and divining instinct, as also the highest development of communicative art. He assumes every external appearance, every emotion; he changes himself continually.—Music, as we understand it at present, is also a collective excitement and collective discharge of the emotions, nevertheless it is only the survival of a much wider world of emotional expression, a mere *residuum* of Dionysian histrionism. To make music possible as a separate art, several of the senses—

especially muscular sense—have here been eliminated (relatively at least, for to a certain extent all rhythm still speaks to our muscles); so that man no longer immediately imitates and gives bodily expression to every feeling. Nevertheless that is the Dionysian normal condition, at any rate the original condition: music is the slowly attained specialisation of this condition at the cost of the faculties nearest akin to it.

11

The actor, the mime, the dancer, the musician, and the lyric poet are fundamentally akin in their instincts and one in their essence, but they have gradually specialised and separated from one another—till indeed they are in contradiction. The lyric poet remained longest united with the musician; the actor remained longest connected with the dancer.—The *architect* represents neither a Dionysian, nor an Apollonian condition; here it is the great act of will, the will which removes mountains, ecstasy of strong will that is desirous of art. The most powerful men have always inspired architects; the architect has always been under the suggestion of power. In the work of architecture pride, triumph over gravity and will to power, are intended to display themselves; architecture is a sort of eloquence of power embodied in forms, sometimes persuading, even flattering and sometimes merely commanding. The highest feeling of power and security is expressed in that which has the *grand style*. Power which needs no further demonstration, which scorns to please, which answers unwillingly, which has no sense of any witness near it, which is without consciousness that there is opposition to it, which reposes in *itself*, fatalistic, a law among laws: *that* is what speaks of itself as the grand style.

19

Beautiful and ugly.—Nothing is more conditioned, let us say more *restricted*, than our sense of the beautiful. A person who would try to think of it as detached from the delight of man in man would immediately lose his footing. The "beautiful in itself" is merely an expression, not even a concept. In the beautiful, man posits himself as the standard of perfection; in select cases he worships himself in that standard. A species cannot possibly do otherwise than thus to say yea to itself. Its *lowest* instinct, that of self-maintenance and self-expansion, still radiates in such sublimities. Man believes the world itself to be overcharged with beauty,—he *forgets* that he is the cause of it. He alone has endowed it with beauty, alas! only with very human, all-too-human beauty . . . In reality man mirrors himself in things; he counts everything beautiful which reflects his likeness; the verdict "beautiful" is man's *conceit of his species.* A little suspicion may in fact whisper the question into a sceptic's ear—Is the world really beautified, just because man thinks it is? Man has *humanised* it; that is all. But nothing, nothing whatever warrants us in supposing that it is just man who furnishes the model of the beautiful. Who knows how he appears in the eyes of a higher judge of taste? Perhaps risky? perhaps even entertaining? perhaps a little arbitrary? . . . "Oh divine Dionysos, why dost thou pull mine ears?" asked Ariadne once of her philosophic lover, in one of the celebrated dialogues at Naxos. "I find a sort of humour in thine ears, Ariadne: why are they not longer?"

20

Nothing is beautiful, except man: all aesthetics rest on this *naïveté*, it is their *first* truth. Let us straightway add the second: nothing is ugly, except *degenerating* man;—the domain of aesthetic judgment is thereby limited.—Re-examined physiologically, all that is ugly weakens and afflicts man. It reminds him of deterioration, of danger, and of impotence; he actually suffers loss of power by it. The effect of ugliness can be measured by the dynamometer. Whenever man is depressed he has a sense of the proximity of something "ugly." His sense of power, his will to power, his courage, his pride—they decrease with the ugly, they increase with the beautiful. In both cases *we draw an inference,* the premises of which are accumulated in enormous fullness in instinct. The ugly is understood as a sign and symptom of degeneration; that which reminds us in the remotest manner of degeneracy prompts us to pronounce the verdict, "ugly." Every indication of exhaustion, gravity, age, or lassitude; every kind of constraint, such as cramp or paralysis; and above all the odour, the colour, and the likeness of decomposition or putrefaction, be it utterly attenuated even to a symbol:—all these things call forth a similar reaction, the evaluation "ugly." A *hatred* is there excited: whom does man hate there? There can be no doubt: the *decline of his type.* The hatred is inspired by the most profound instinct of the species; there is horror, foresight, profundity, and far-reaching vision in it—it is the profoundest of all hatreds. On account of it, art is *profound.*

24

L'art pour l'art.—The fighting against the end in art is always warfare against the *moralising* tendency in art, against its subordination to morality. *L'art pour l'art*: that is, "the devil take morality." But this very hostility betrays the domination of the prejudice. When the end of the ethical preacher and improver of mankind has been excluded from art, it does not at all follow that art in itself is without an end, without a goal, meaningless; in short, *l'art pour l'art*—a serpent which bites its own tail. "No end at all, rather than a moral end!"—thus speaks pure passion. A psychologist, on the other hand, asks, what does all art do? does it not praise? does it not glorify? does it not select? does it not bring into prominence? In each of these cases it *strengthens or weakens* certain valuations . . . Is this only a contingent matter? an accident? something with which the instinct of the artist would not at all be concerned? Or rather, is it not the pre-requisite which *enables* the artist to do something? Is his fundamental instinct directed towards art? or is it not rather directed towards the sense of art, namely, *life*? towards a *desirableness of life*?—Art is the great stimulus to life, how could art be understood as purposeless, as aimless, as *l'art pour l'art?*—A question still remains: art makes manifest also much that is ugly, harsh, and questionable in life,—does it not thereby seem to make life intolerable?—In fact there have been philosophers who gave this meaning to it: Schopenhauer taught that the whole purpose of art is "to disengage from will"; he honoured it as the great usefulness of tragedy "to dispose to resignation."—This however—I have already hinted at it—is pessimistic optics and the "evil eye";—one must appeal to artists themselves. *What of his own personality does the artist communicate to others in tragedy?* It is not precisely the fearless state of mind in presence of the frightful and the questionable which he exhibits?—This state of mind is highly desirable in itself; whoever knows it, honours it with the highest regard. He communicates it, he *is obliged* to communicate it, provided he is an artist, a genius of communication. Bravery and self-possession in presence of a powerful enemy, an awful calamity, or a problem which awakens dread—it is this *triumphal* condition which the tragic artist selects and glorifies. In presence of tragedy the martial spirit in us celebrates its Saturnalia; he who is accustomed to affliction, he who seeks affliction—*heroic* man— extols his existence with tragedy,—to him alone the tragic artist offers the draught of this sweetest cruelty.—

FRANZ BOAS

1858-1942

PRIMITIVE ART

1927

Franz Boas is one of the most influential anthropologists and ethnologists of the 19th and 20th centuries. Born in Minden, Germany, he attended the University of Heidelberg and the University of Kiel, where he studied geography. On his first field trip, in 1883-84, he studied the Eskimo tribes of the Canadian Arctic, resulting in his new interests in ethnology and anthropology. In 1899, he became a professor at Columbia University in New York, where he developed one of the foremost anthropology departments in the United States, based on rigorous methodology and the inclusion of evolution, archaeology, language, and culture in anthropology.

Primitive Art, first published in 1927, is a definitive analytical description of the fundamental aspects of primitive art. Boas's thesis is that there is a fundamental sameness of intellectual processes among all races and cultural forms of the present day. Further, he developed the theory of "historical particularism," which maintains that each culture has a unique history and that every cultural phenomenon is a result of historical and social development as well as geographical conditions. He argued against the theories of universal laws that govern how cultures operate and against the evolutionary scale, from savagery to culture as theorized in the 19th century. For Boas, cultures are too complex to be evaluated by generalizations of the evolution of developing cultures. Instead, he sought to understand cultures through their own particular histories.

Boas draws on his work with the Kwakiutl Indians of Vancouver Island and mainland British Columbia, Canada. His belief that culture is a system in which all evidence of a culture is important demands the collection of data on ethnology, physical anthropology, archaeology, linguistics, and aesthetics. The hypothesis that all institutions of a culture tend to be interrelated is known as "functional integration." Boas further added cultural relativism to anthropological theory, pointing out that all populations had complete and equally developed cultures and that the study of a culture must be conducted on the culture's own terms, not judged by Western values or aesthetics.

SOURCE

Boas, Franz. 1927. "Introduction." *Primitive Art*. New York: Dover, 1955. 9-16.*

PRIMITIVE ART

INTRODUCTION

No people known to us, however hard their lives may be, spend all their time, all their energies in the acquisition of food and shelter, nor do those who live under more favorable conditions and who are free to devote to other pursuits the time not needed for securing their sustenance occupy themselves with purely industrial work or idle away the days in indolence. Even the poorest tribes have produced work that gives to them esthetic pleasure, and those whom a bountiful nature or a greater wealth of inventions has granted freedom from care, devote much of their energy to the creation of works of beauty.

---

*   Reprinted by permission from Dover Publications, New York.

In one way or another esthetic pleasure is felt by all members of mankind. No matter how diverse the ideals of beauty may be, the general character of the enjoyment of beauty is of the same order everywhere; the crude song of the Siberians, the dance of the African Negroes, the pantomime of the Californian Indians, the stone work of the New Zealanders, the carvings of the Melanesians, the sculpture of the Alaskans appeal to them in a manner not different from that felt by us when we hear a song, when we see an artistic dance, or when we admire ornamental work, painting or sculpture. The very existence of song, dance, painting and sculpture among all the tribes known to us is proof of the craving to produce things that are felt as satisfying through their form, and of the capability of man to enjoy them.

All human activities may assume forms that give them esthetic values. The mere cry, or the word does not necessarily possess the elements of beauty. If it does so it is merely a matter of accident. Violent, unrestrained movements induced by excitement; the exertions of the chase and the movements required by daily occupations are partly reflexes or passion, partly practically determined. They have no immediate esthetic appeal. The same is true of all products of industrial activity. The daubing of paint, the whittling of wood or bone, the flaking of stone do not necessarily lead to results that compel our admiration on account of their beauty.

Nevertheless, all of them may assume esthetic values. Rhythmical movements of the body or of objects, forms that appeal to the eye, sequences of tones and forms of speech which please the ear, produce artistic effects. Muscular, visual and auditory sensations are the materials that give us esthetic pleasure and that are used in art.

We may also speak of impressions that appeal to the senses of smell, taste and touch. A composition of scents, a gastronomical repast may be called works of art provided they excite pleasurable sensations.

What then gives to the sensation an esthetic value? When the technical treatment has attained a certain standard of excellence, when the control of the processes involved is such that certain typical forms are produced, we call the process an art, and however simple the forms may be, they may be judged from the point of view of formal perfection; industrial pursuits such as cutting, carving, molding, weaving; as well as singing, dancing and cooking are capable of attaining technical excellence and fixed forms. The judgment of perfection of technical form is essentially an esthetic judgment. It is hardly possible to state objectively just where the line between artistic and pre-artistic forms should be drawn, because we cannot determine just where the esthetic attitude sets in. It seems certain, however, that wherever a definite type of movement, a definite sequence of tones or a fixed form has developed it must become a standard by which its perfection, that is, its beauty, is measured.

Such types exist among mankind the world over, and we must assume that if an unstandardized form should prove to possess an esthetic appeal for a community it would readily be adopted. Fixity of form seems to be most intimately connected with our ideas of beauty.

Since a perfect standard of form can be attained only in a highly developed and perfectly controlled technique there must be an intimate relation between technique and a feeling for beauty.

It might be said that achievement is irrelevant as long as the ideal of beauty for which the would-be artist strives is in existence, although on account of imperfect technique he may be unable to attain it. Alois Riegl expresses this idea by saying that the will to produce an esthetic result is the essence of artistic work. The truth of this assertion may be admitted and undoubtedly many individuals strive for expression of an esthetic impulse without being able to realize it. What they are striving for presupposes the existence of an ideal form which the unskilled muscles are unable to express adequately. The intuitive feeling for form must be present. So far as our knowledge of the works of art of primitive people extends the feeling for form is inextricably bound up with technical experience. Nature does not seem to present formal ideals,—that is fixed types that are imitated,—except when a natural object is used in daily life; when it is handled, perhaps modified, by technical processes. It would seem that only in this way form impresses itself upon the human mind. The very fact that the manufactures of man in each and every part of the world have pronounced style proves that a feeling for form develops with technical activities. There is nothing to show that the mere contemplation of nature or of natural

objects develops a sense of fixed form. Neither have we any proof that
a definite stylistic form develops as a product purely of the power of
the imagination of the workman, unguided by his technical experience
which brings the form into his consciousness. It is conceivable that
elementary esthetic forms like symmetry and rhythm, are not entirely
dependent upon technical activities; but these are common to all art
styles; they are not specifically characteristic of any particular region.
Without stability of form of objects, manufactured or in common
use, there is no style; and stability of form depends upon the
development of a high technique, or in a few cases on the constant use
of the same kind of natural products. When stable forms have been
attained, imaginative development of form in an imperfect technique
may set in and in this case the will to produce an esthetic result may
outrun the ability of the would-be artist. The same consideration
holds good in regard to the esthetic value of muscular movements
used in song and dance.

The manufactures of man the world over prove that the ideal
forms are based essentially on standards developed by expert techni-
cians. They may also be imaginative developments of older stan-
dardized forms. Without a formal basis the will to create something
that appeals to the sense of beauty can hardly exist.

Many works of art affect us in another way. The emotions may
be stimulated not by the form alone, but also by close associations
that exist between the form and ideas held by the people. In other
words, when the forms convey a meaning, because they recall past
experiences or because they act as symbols, a new element is added
to the enjoyment. The form and its meaning combine to elevate
the mind above the indifferent emotional state of every-day life.
Beautiful sculpture or painting, a musical composition, dramatic
art, a pantomime, may so affect us. This is no less true of primitive
art than of our own.

Sometimes esthetic pleasure is released by natural forms. The
song of a bird may be beautiful; we may experience pleasure in
viewing the form of a landscape or in viewing the movements of an
animal; we may enjoy a natural taste or smell, or a pleasant feeling;

grandeur of nature may give us an emotional thrill and the actions of animals may have a dramatic effect; all of these have esthetic values but they are not art. On the other hand, a melody, a carving, a painting, a dance, a pantomime are esthetic productions, because they have been created by our own activities.

Form, and creation by our own activities are essential features of art. The pleasure or elevation of the mind must be brought about by a particular form of sense impression, but this sense impression must be made by some kind of human activity or by some product of human activity.

It is essential to bear in mind the twofold source of artistic effect, the one based on form alone, the other on ideas associated with form. Otherwise the theory of art will be one-sided. Since the art of man, the world over, among primitive tribes as well as among civilized nations, contains both elements, the purely formal and the significant, it is not admissible to base all discussions of the manifestations of the art impulse upon the assumption that the expression of emotional states by significant forms must be the beginning of art, or that, like language, art is a form of expression. In modern times this opinion is based in part on the often observed fact that in primitive art even simple geometrical forms may possess a meaning that adds to their emotional value, and that dance, music and poetry almost always have definite meaning. However, significance of artistic form is neither universal nor can it be shown that it is necessarily older than the form.

I do not intend to enter into a discussion of the philosophical theories of esthetics, but will confine myself to a few remarks on the views of a number of recent authors who have treated art on the basis of ethnological material, and only in so far as the question is concerned whether primitive art is expressive of definite ideas.

Our views agree fundamentally with those of Fechner who recognizes the "direct" appeal of the work of art on the one side and the associated elements that give a specific tone to the esthetic effects on the other.

Wundt restricts the discussion of art to those forms in which the artistic work expresses some thought or emotion. He says, "For the psychological study art stands in a position intermediate between language and myth . . . . Thus the creative artistic work appears to us as a peculiar development of the expressive movements of the body. Gesture and language pass in a fleeting moment. In art they are sometimes given a higher significance; sometimes the fleeting movement is given a permanent form . . . All these relations are manifested principally in the relatively early, although not in the very earliest stages of artistic work in which the momentary needs of expression of thought dominate art as well as language."

Max Verworn says: "Art is the faculty to express conscious processes by means created by the artist himself in such a manner that they may be perceived by our sense organs. In this general sense language, song, music and dance are art, just as well as painting, sculpture and ornamentation. The graphic and plastic arts in the narrow sense of the term result from the ability of making conscious processes visible in permanent materials."

Richard Thurnwald accepts the view-point of Wundt when he says, "Art, however inadequate its means may be, is a means of expression that belongs to mankind. The means employed are distinct from those used in gesture, language and writing. Even when the artist is intent only upon the repetition of what he has in mind he does so with at least the subconscious purpose of communicating his ideas, of influencing others."

The same onesidedness may be recognized in Yrjö Hirn's opinion, who says: "In order to understand the art impulse as a tendency to esthetic production we must bring it into connection with some function from the nature of which the specifically artistic qualities may be derived. Such a function is to be found, we believe, in the activities of emotional expression."

It will be seen that all these authors confine their definition of art to those forms which are expressions of emotional states or of ideas, while they do not include in art the pleasure conveyed by purely formal elements that are not primarily expressive.

Ernst Grosse expresses similar views in somewhat different form. He stresses the practical purpose of artistic forms which appears to him as primary. However, he assumes that these forms, while devoted first of all to practical purposes, are intended at the same time to serve an esthetic need that is felt by the people. Thus, he says, that primitive ornament is by origin and by its fundamental nature not intended as decorative but as a practically significant mark or symbol, that is to say as expressive. If I understand him correctly this practical significance implies some kind of meaning inherent in the form.

Emil Stephan concludes from his detailed discussion of Melanesian art that technical motives offer no sufficient explanation for the origin of artistic forms (pp. 52 et seq.). He considers all ornament as representative and sees the origin of art in that unconscious mental process by which the form appears as distinct from the content of the visual impression, and in the desire to give permanence to the form (p. 51). For this reason he considers the artistic forms also as equivalents of the way in which the form appears to the primitive artist.

Alfred C. Haddon and W. H. Holmes seek the origin of all decorative art in realism. They discuss the transfer of technical forms to ornament but they see in these also results of the endeavor to reproduce realistic form, namely; technical details. Henry Balfour agrees, on the whole, with this position but he stresses also the development of decorative motives from the actual use of technical processes.

Gottfried Semper emphasizes the importance of the form as determined by the manner of use. He also stresses the influence of designs developed weaving and of their transfer upon other forms of technique, particularly upon architectural forms.

Alois Riegl is also inclined to stress the representative character of the most ancient art forms, basing his argument essentially upon the realistic paleolithic carvings and paintings. He sees the most important step forward in the attempt to show the animals in outline, on a two-dimensional surface which necessitates the substitution of an ideal line for the three-dimensional form that is given to us by every day experience. He assumes that geometric ornament developed from the treatment of the line, obtained by the process just mentioned, according to formal principles. . . .

John Cotton Dana

1856-1929

The Gloom of the Museum

1917

John Cotton Dana is widely recognized as a pioneer in museum philosophy in the 20th century. As a staff member at the Denver Public Library, he became a library innovator, instituting open stacks where patrons could browse and starting the first branch specifically for children. In 1902, he took the position of head of the Newark (New Jersey) Public Library, where his services included a branch for businessmen. In 1909, he became the founding director of the Newark Museum, where he advocated the community-based museum. During this time, he wrote the essay below, which was published as a pamphlet by the museum.

In *The Gloom of the Museum*, Dana critiques American art museums and offers his vision for the future. The gloom he refers to is in the art museum, based on European models as repositories of art collections of the wealthy. These museums, according to Dana, may evoke civic pride but they do not serve community needs or teach the ordinary visitor. Instead, the museum should be a social force in the community, collaborating with schools, libraries, and civic centers to provide life-long education. Dana also advocated the inclusion of objects of everyday life, including the applied and decorative arts, that have meaning within the community and that exemplify universal principles of design and taste. Foremost in his vision is that the museum should grow out of the needs of the community and serve the community through interpretation that educates and enlightens. Dana's theories remain relevant, continuing to be a forceful influence in the on-going debate over the purpose and missions of museums.

SOURCE

Dana, John Cotton. 1917. *The Gloom of the Museum.* In *Reinventing the Museum: Historical and Contemporary Perspectives on the Paradigm Shift.* Gail Anderson, Ed. Walnut Creek, CA: AltaMira, 2004. 13-29. (Originally published as a booklet in the Newark Museum Series, Newark NJ: Newark Museum Association/The American Association of Museums.)*

THE GLOOM OF THE MUSEUM

PROLOGUE

Today, museums of art are built to keep objects of art, and objects of art are bought to be kept in museums. As the objects seem to do their work if they are safely kept, and as museums seem to serve their purpose if they safely keep the objects, the whole thing is as useful in the splendid isolation of a distant park as in the center of the life of the community which possesses it.

Tomorrow, objects of art will be bought to give pleasure, to make manners seem more important, to promote skill, to exalt handwork, and to increase the zest of life by adding to it new interests; and these objects being bought for use will be put where the most people can most handily use them: in a museum planned for making the best use of all it contains, and placed where a majority of its community can quickly and easily visit it.

PART I: HOW THE ARTS HAVE BEEN INDUCED TO FLOURISH

The story of an art epoch in the life history of a people seems to resolve itself into something like this:

Character and circumstances lead the people into conquest. It may sound better, though it means the same, to say that character and circumstances bring out a few men of genius who lead and rule the people and take them on to conquest. The conquest means wealth, and this is true whether the conquest be of other peoples by leadership and force of arms, or of the land's natural resources and of methods of producing and using power.

Always a few gain most of the wealth and hold most of the power. The conquest being somewhat well assured, these few have leisure. They search for occupations and things and indulgences which may give them pleasure. Whatever else these occupations, objects, and indulgences may be, they must be such as the common people cannot have; for the rich and ruling class must always keep itself distinct from the lower classes in its pleasures and pastimes, just as it always did in its leadership in war and government. These distinctive recreations and diversions and admired objects of the powerful and rich have always been of about the same character. War is first choice; if not war of the higher kind in which is involved the existence of the tribe, family, city, dukedom, principality, kingdom, or nation over which the rich and powerful in question rule, then a war of petty conquest, mean in itself, but permitting some braggadocio, keeping up the clan spirit and exalting the ruling class. Lacking a vigorous and dangerous war on battlefields to engage all their activities, the rulers have often turned to hunting—to hunting in a form which nature, or special laws, or the rules of the game make somewhat dangerous; for if it does not at least seem dangerous, those who engage in it will not appear brave to the lower classes. The form of hunting chosen is usually one which is quite inaccessible to the poor and weak. Big game near home, and better still at a good distance; falconry, the right to use falcons being easily restricted to the few; fox hunting on horseback; dangerous athletic sports; and latterly automobiling, ballooning, and flying—these have all had or shall have their vogue.

Another obvious method of distinguishing their life from that of the common people has been the possession of distinctive residences beyond all need in size, number, cost, and adornment. It is through these residences that the rich and powerful have chiefly been led to become patrons of the arts. The wish to make full use of the religious habits of the ruled has often led the rich to build and adorn churches; and always, of course, the need of expensive and peculiar dress has been an occasion for calling in the aid of artisans of certain kinds. The study of literature, language, history, and the fine arts has also often been a recreating of the rich, though usually these studies have been pursued by proxy. As unusual native ability has almost always been one of the essentials to success in acquiring wealth and power, it is not strange that an occasional member of the class of the ruling rich has shown marked ability in letters and the arts, or at least in appreciation of them. But pursuit of art and letters has usually ended with little more than such a patronage of them as would bring in return ample adulation, a reputation for learning, and glorification in history.

Comparative security, then, after a series of profitable wars, finds the rich and powerful compelled to engage in expensive sports, to build large and expensive residences, and to decorate them and to adorn elaborately their own persons that there may be no lack of distinctions between themselves and the common people. The demand for architects, painters, sculptors, gold and silversmiths, ironworkers, and artisans of all kinds thus at once arises; and a demand also for teachers, poets, orators, and historians to make a pretense of love of learning.

It is worth noting here that in former days these workers produced without the intervention of machinery; that the rich have usually been ready to adopt the older methods in art productions if for any reason they were inaccessible to the poor; and that today admiration for the handmade is largely born of a desire to have something which, being unique in its kind, will impart a little of the old leisure-class exclusiveness to its owner.

The patronage of the arts, with the consequent development thereof, has varied in extent in the rise to wealth and leisure of the leaders among different peoples, as circumstances dictated, but its origin seems always to have been about the same. Whenever this patronage has appeared—whenever, that is, the demand for objects of art has arisen—the supply has been forthcoming.

Fashion among the rich has sometimes prevented the results of this patronage of art from showing themselves very plainly in the country of the rich. In our day, for example, the fashion is to import from abroad and to say that good artwork cannot be produced at home; so we have a Barbizon painting factory in Paris, makers of antiques in Italy, and a digging up of gone-by utensils and furniture in all European and Asiatic countries. These old things cost more in the first place, the tariff makes them more expensive still, and their ownership gives considerable of the ruling-class distinction. Were it to become the fashion to patronize American designers and craftsmen in all lines and to give artists and architects a free hand instead of insisting on conformity to the ancient ways as interpreted by the ignorant rich, we would have a larger art demand in America; the supply would raise prices and wages; art study would be encouraged; more men of genius, skill, and training would come here from abroad; and we would begin our own renaissance.

Those who know Mr. Veblen's delightful book on *The Theory of the Leisure Class* will see that I have borrowed from him in my statement about the character of the diversions and the conspicuous waste of the rich.

But our renaissance does not come. We have an aristocracy based on wealth, with accompanying power. This aristocracy feels the same need that aristocracies have always felt of acquiring ancient, rare, and costly objects that the possession of them may mark them as superior to the poor and weak. They find that the easiest way to acquire such objects is not to cause them to be produced by artists and artisans of their own country—America—but, as already noted, to purchase them in older countries. What had already given distinction to their owners in France, Italy, England, and Germany is seen at once to be peculiarly well fitted to give a like distinction here. Hence the products of our own people are definitely held in no esteem as honorific possessions. Art in America does not flourish.

I have used the foregoing remarks, taken from a paper published in the *Independent* seven years ago, as a preface to the essay which follows on the gloom of the museum in the hope that they will make still more self-evident the statements in the latter concerning the origin of American museums of art. The kinds of objects— ancient, costly, and imported—that the rich feel they must buy to give themselves a desired distinction are inevitably the kinds that they, as patrons and directors of museums, cause those museums to acquire. Veritably, most of our great museums look with open scorn on the products of American artists and artisans.

The peculiar sanctity of oil paint on canvas has been graciously extended in some small degree to New World products, and our great museums occasionally buy, more often receive as gifts, and still more often receive as loans for exhibition the works of American painters. But most of our richer museums of art, that in Chicago being a notable exception, follow the dictates of the rich. They very evidently do not think it is the proper function of a museum of art to promote, foster, or patronize American talent.

The new museum, for the development of which this series is designed, will hold that its first duty is to discover talent and encourage its development here at home.

The rich and powerful collect foreign things and insist that foreign things only shall be enshrined in the museum they patronize. The poor follow the rich in this thinking. The attempt to modify this state of affairs is not one that is full of hope. But the growing habit of cities to maintain their own museums will surely tend to democratize them; and if, in the beginnings of the museums that are now coming into existence, the suggestions for making them immediately and definitely useful to their founders and patrons— the public—which we find today so widely approved among museum workers are quite generally adopted, the day will soon come when many public museums will look upon the promotion of American art as one of their most important functions.

PART II: THE GLOOM OF THE MUSEUM, WITH SUGGESTIONS FOR REMOVING IT.

Prefatory Note

The art of museum construction, acquisition, and management is in its infancy. No one can say with authority how that art will be developed in the next few years. But on this much at least the public may congratulate itself: that museum authorities now feel that their respective establishments should be, above all things, attractive in a sane and homely way to the public which owns them.

Art museums of necessity have the faults of their ancestry, and these faults are so obvious that even a layman like myself may see them, and the plain statement of such of them as a layman dares to say he sees may help to move the intelligent part of the public to set to work to correct them.

Throughout this discussion I have art museums almost solely in mind.

How Museums Came to Be So Gloomily Beautiful

One need visit only a few of the older museums of art and archaeology in Europe to understand why most American museums of the same subjects are so ineffective.

In Europe, these older museums have objects of great importance to students of art, of history in general, of the history of art, of social development, and of the history of invention and discovery. Large groups of these objects were first collected many years ago by wealthy and powerful individuals: princes, kings, emperors, and members of the nobility. These collectors were usually entirely selfish in their acquisition, rarely looking beyond their own personal pleasure or the aggrandizement of their immediate families. They collected that they might possess, not that they might use, or that others might use, the things collected for the pleasure and advancement of the world at large.

As the idea of general welfare crept into and modified the government of any given country, the ruling powers of that country in many cases confiscated or purchased these collected treasures, added other purchases and gifts to them, made them so-called public collections, and deposited them for safekeeping in national and municipal buildings. These buildings were for the most part erected for other purposes than the reception and proper display of works of art and archaeology. This fact usually made it possible to install collections in them only under such conditions of space and light as prevented either logical or artistic arrangement and made both casual observation and careful study of most of the objects a burden instead of pleasure.

As the collections were of very great value—consisting usually of originals which no money could replace, which should therefore be guarded with the utmost care—the first thought in regard to them was their preservation; their utilization being a secondary and rather remote affair.

Why Museum Buildings Are Temples and Palaces

The character of the buildings which, as time went on, were here and there erected to house these collections of priceless originals, was determined by several factors. As most of the collections had found their first homes in the palaces of rulers or members of the nobility, it was quite naturally concluded that their new homes should also be in the style of the local palace or royal residences. As the things collected were objects of art, it seemed obvious that they should be housed in artistic buildings, and as for several centuries it has been difficult for architects or those having power over art collections to conceive of an artistic building save in terms of Greek or Renaissance architecture, nearly all special museum buildings imitated either the Greek temple or the Italian palace.

In Europe, therefore, we find museums to be either old buildings of the royal palace type or later constructions copying the palace or the Greek temple; containing priceless originals in all lines of art, craftsmanship, and archaeology; arranged as the characters of the several buildings compel; guarded with extreme care; dutifully visited by serious-minded tourists; and used sparingly by a small number of special students.

New America Copies the Old Europe, of Course

This, roughly speaking, was the museum idea as it embodied itself in Europe when the subject of museums began a few decades ago to be taken up seriously in America. It was inevitable that the first wish of all our museum enthusiasts should be to produce imitations of the European institutions. Those institutions were, in most cases, long established and greatly admired, and they furnished the only illustrations of the museum idea.

Moreover, collections more or less well suited to form the beginnings of art museums had been made here, after the European manner, by a few of the rich; some of these had fallen by gift or will to public use, accompanied not infrequently by the requirement that they be permanently housed in art buildings which were inevitably fashioned after the European type.

The promoters of art museums in America had no choice in the matter. The approved examples of Europe, the precedents already established in America in accordance with those examples, the unanimous votes of architects and trustees on what it is that makes a building a fit home for works of art, and the voice of so much of the general public as had ever seen or heard of European museums— all these factors united to complete the erection here of the kind of museum building which now oppresses us.

Why Museums Are Way Off in the Woods

The prevalence of the European idea of a museum determined not only the character of our museum buildings but also their location. As they must be works of art, and as temples and palaces need open space about them to display their excellences, and as space in the centers of towns is quite expensive, donors, architects, trustees, and city fathers all agreed that the art museum building should be set apart from the city proper, preferably in a park with open space about it. Distance from the center of population and the difficulty most citizens would encounter did they attempt to see the museum's contents were given no weight in comparison with the obvious advantages of display of the building's outer charms.

The Museum of Religious Gloom

A city may with perfect propriety set itself to the task of making a collection of rare and ancient original products of man's craftsmanship, spending, for example, $10,000 for a piece of tapestry, $100,000 for a painting, $30,000 for a marble statue, $20,000 for a piece of porcelain, and so on; it may add to these by gift and may place them all in a one-story, poorly lighted, marble, fireproof building set in a park remote from the city's center. But it ought to do this with a full comprehension of the fact that, while it is in so doing establishing a "Museum of Art" in the sense in which that phrase is most often used today, it is not forming an institution which will either entertain or instruct the community to an extent at all commensurate with its cost. In such an establishment the city will have an "art museum" of the kind which the citizen points out with pride to visiting friends; which appears in the advertising pamphlets of the local boards of trade; which is the recipient of an occasional painting or other work of art from a local art patron; which some strangers and a few resident women and children occasionally use to produce in themselves the maximum of fatigue with the minimum of pleasure; which will offer through the opening of loan collections a few opportunities each winter for society to display itself and demonstrate its keen aesthetic interests.

Rarity and High Price Make Things More Beautiful

The European examples which were so disastrous in their effect on the character and location of our museum buildings had an unfortunate influence also on the character and arrangement of their contents.

In the order of events in Europe, as already noted, one country after another and one city after another came into the possession of treasures of art and archaeology—priceless originals—which it was the duty of the authorities to preserve with the utmost care. Our own art museum enthusiasts, imitating their predecessors, sought also to form collections of unique and costly objects. A delusion like that which everywhere possesses the art novice as to the relative value of real oil paintings, however atrocious, and colored lithographic reproductions of paintings, however excellent, possessed those who made private art collections and those who selected and purchased objects for our museums. Art museum objects were not chosen for their beauty or for the help they might give in developing good taste in the community, but for their rarity, their likeness to objects found in European museums, and for their cost.

The older collections on the continent are naturally largely historical and archaeological. This seemed sufficient reason for making our collections of the same kind.

The wish to form collections which should illustrate the development of this or that special form of art also influenced greatly the character of our early museums.

But the wish to make them, like their European models, include a large number of things peculiar, unique, not copies, not obtainable by others, and costly, was probably the chief factor in making our museums mausoleums of curios.

The objects acquired being rare and costly, it was inevitable that they should be very carefully safeguarded, placed where they could be seen only (and that not very adequately), and never handled and examined closely.

American Museums Today

That this rough outline of recent museum history in America is fairly correct is amply demonstrated by present-day American museums themselves. They are usually housed in buildings fashioned to look like Greek temples or Renaissance palaces, which are very poorly adapted to the proper installation of collections

and very rarely well planned for growth. These buildings are set
apart from the city whose citizens they are built to serve, often in
remote parks. The objects in them are very largely second-rate
original artworks, usually with large additions of things historical
or archaeological of little art value. Many of the buildings are so
expensive to administer and to light and to heat that the managers
can keep them open to the public only a small part of the hours
when the public can best visit them. They are visited by few, that
few being made up largely of strangers passing through the city;
and the objects displayed are used for practical, everyday purposes
and are looked to for suggestions applying to daily life by a very
small number of persons, and by them very rarely.

Museum Failures Are Not Chargeable to Specific Persons

It may be said that if this development of American art
museums into remote palaces and temples—filled with objects
not closely associated with the life of the people who are asked to
get pleasure and profit from them, and so arranged and administered
as to make them seem still more remote—it may be said that if
this development has been as natural and inevitable as has been
suggested, then no one can be charged with responsibility for the
fact, and not much can be done to correct the error.

It would indeed be difficult to lay the burden of this unfortunate
line of development on the shoulders of any persons who may be
specifically named. It would be difficult also to correct the mistake
already made. No one, for example, would quite dare to suggest
(taking up the point only of location) to the citizens of Boston,
New York, Buffalo, and Cincinnati that they can much better afford,
in the long run, to move their museums into the centers of daily
movement of population and thereby secure a tenfold enlargement
of their use and influence, than they can to go on paying large
sums for their maintenance in relative idleness where they are now.

And it would be idle to attempt to persuade architects and
trustees and a public, bound to accept the architectural
conventions of their time, that when they use the outward
presentations of one-story buildings designed for housing gods

in a perpetual twilight as the peripheries of well-lighted and convenient and easily warmed and controlled spaces for the display of precious objects to thousands of visitors, they show a certain magnificent courage, but not good architectural traits, not originality, and not common sense.

But, in spite of the depressing influence of fashion and of the architectural paralysis induced by the classic burden in these matters, one may hope that all museums hereafter built need not conform to the old ideas, and that some of the museums already in existence can be so modified as to be far more useful and influential than they are today.

The Art of Museum Making in Its Infancy

The art of making museums which will be largely used by those who pay for them and will please and profit all who visit them is in its infancy. No one ventures to describe definitely the ideal American art museum. A few suggestions may at least provoke helpful discussion.

Museums Should Be Central

An art museum should be so located that it may be reached by a maximum number of persons with a minimum expenditure of time and money. It should be near the center of the city which maintains it—not its population center but its rapid transit center—and as near as possible also to its more important railway stations that strangers may visit it quickly and cheaply.

It may be said that a collection of art objects properly housed in a beautiful building gains somewhat in dignity and importance and in its power to influence beneficially those who visit it if it is set apart a little from the city's center of strenuous commercial and material life; holds itself somewhat aloof, as it were; detaches itself from the crowd; and seems to care to speak only to those whose desire for its teachings is strong enough to lead them to make some sacrifice of time and money to enjoy them.

The suggestion is a specious one. This theory of the fitness of remoteness is born of pride and satisfaction in the location and character of museums as they are. The buildings are remote and are religious or autocratic or aristocratic in style; their administrators, perhaps in part because of this very aloofness and sacrosanct environment, are inclined to look upon themselves as high priests of a peculiar cult, who may treat the casual visitor with tolerance only when he comes to worship rather than to look with open eyes and to criticize freely; and the trustees are prone to think more of their view of the proper museum atmosphere than of museum patronage, more of preservation than of utilization.

The same theory as to the preciosity which remoteness may confer, applied to art in general and carried to its logical conclusions, would forbid the expenditure of public funds or private gifts on the beautifying of streets or bridges or public buildings. Under its application, one might say that a commercial city should be built in the coldest, baldest possible style, and that beautiful façades of homes, office buildings, and factories should be erected as façades only in remote parks and boulevards, there to be solemnly visited and viewed by those who truly care to exalt their souls and purify their intellects.

The Museum Building: Some of Its Obvious Qualities

The museum building located in the city's center should satisfy the fundamental conditions of all good architecture: It should be large enough for its purpose; it should be constructed of the materials, proper in its day, which are best adapted to its form and size; it should be in harmony with its surroundings; and it should be as beautiful as the highest technique and the best taste of the time can make it.

A building of steel and concrete in a modern American city is not made an appropriate home of the fine arts by placing on its front the façade of one or the façades of half a dozen Greek temples or of 15th-century Italian palaces. It is impossible to believe that the best Greek architects, if they were the masters in good taste we suppose them to have been, would have continued to make their buildings look as though they were built of columns of stone, with huge girders and crossbeams of the same material, long after they had learned to use steel and concrete in construction.

In time we shall learn to insist that great public buildings like libraries and museums be erected as such and not as imitations of structures developed for quite other purposes, in other cities, in other times, and under limitations as to material and method by which we are no longer bound.

A modern museum building for an American city is a distinct problem in arrangement and a difficult one not to be solved by the adoption for its exterior of a type, however beautiful, which in origin and development never bore the slightest relation to the subject of museums.

It may be said that the contents of art museums are in part priceless, cannot be replaced, must be so housed as to make their destruction by fire impossible, and that, therefore, the only safe location for a museum is in a park, far from all other buildings. In reply it may be said that the high value put on many of the objects in art museums is largely fictitious, born of the rivalry of rich collectors and even of rich museums in their search for objects of honorable uniqueness; that a few students could truly feel their loss; but that as instruments of human enlightenment and happiness they are by no means priceless. Next, it may be noted that it is doubtful if any art museum authorities have yet erected a remote building on the contents of which they can get fire insurance rates as low as they could get them on the same contents housed in a fireproof building in the center of their city. There are risks in remoteness as well as safeguards. It should also be said that if a city wants a warehouse for the storage of art treasures, build it by all means; but do not encumber it with the fine, open spaces of a public park. But if it wants an institution of the newer museum type, something from which can be derived pleasure, surely, and profit if the gods permit, then let that be built where it can be easily made use of, in the city's center.

In a great city the museum building could properly be several, perhaps many, stories high, and if open space about it were quite impossible for financial reasons, light could be had from courts. Nearly all rooms would then be lighted from one side, as nearly all exhibition, study, and lecture rooms should be.

The Vast Extent of Museum Collections Leads to Obscurity

The objects gathered in art museums will continue to include the works of men's hands in all materials, for all purposes, of all countries, and for all time. Students of every form of art will continue to ask that museums include not only the products of that art when it was at the highest point of its development, but also its products in every stage of its growth and of its decline. Museums—that is, some of the large museums at least—must continue to be not only museums of many arts, but also of the histories of those arts, and therefore of archaeology and of ethnology.

But as time goes on, many collections, thus expanding naturally into other fields than that of art, will become unwieldy, overloaded with objects of interest only to the very special student, mere confusing masses of seemingly unrelated objects to the ordinary visitor. They will lose all effectiveness in what should be their special field—that of suggesting to the observer that a certain refinement of daily life is worth all it costs—and, to the would-be promoter of this refinement, that certain special methods in this, that, and the other field have been successful once and may be successful again. That is to say, art museum collections continually tend to lose the power of doing that which they were designed to do, which is to say to us that manners and feelings are important parts of life. For the objects which have to do with age-long gropings after good things will always tend to become so numerous as to hide the good things themselves.

The Undue Reverence for Oil Paint

The extreme veneration now paid by museum authorities to great paintings will surely become weaker as the possibilities of a museum's influence become better understood. Painting in oil upon canvas is not a craft that makes a strong appeal to the average man, save through the stories it tells. Its value, after all, is almost entirely pictorial. As mere pictures—which is all that they are to the average observer of ordinary intelligence, plus the interest born of their age, their history, and their cost—they each year suffer more and more from the competition of other pictures not done in oil on canvas, found in posters, in journals and newspapers, and in the cinema. In due course the oil painting will take its place in museums with other products of men's hands simply as one of the many things of high beauty and great suggestiveness produced in perfection only by men of special talent who have been able to master a difficult technique.

This fact will in time be recognized and acted upon: that the oil painting has no such close relation to the development of good taste and refinement as have countless objects of daily use. The genius and skill which have gone into the adornment and perfecting of familiar household objects will then receive the same recognition as do now the genius and skill of the painter in oils. Paintings will no longer be given an undue share of space, and on them will be expended no undue share of the museum's annual income. It is doubtful if any single change in the general principles of art museum management will do as much to enhance museum influence as will this placing of the oil painting in its proper relation with other objects.

The Subordination of Painting and the Promotion of Applied Art

If oil paintings are put in the subordinate place in which they belong, the average art museum will have much more room for the display of objects which have quite a direct bearing on the daily life of those who support it, visit either the main buildings or its branches, and make use of its collections. One need not be specific; the museum will show by originals or replicas what has been done by other people to make more convenient and attractive all the things that we use and wear and see day by day, from shoes to signposts and from table knives to hat pins. As the museum gives more space and more attention to these things, it will quite inevitably also display the objects in which its own city is particularly interested. It will have no absurd fear that it will be commercialized and debased if it shows what is being done today in the field of applied art in its own city and in other parts of the world. It will take no shame from the fact that it is handling and installing and displaying articles made by machinery for actual daily use by mere living people. One of the grotesqueries of expertness in museum work today is the reverential attention paid to products of craftsmanship which are (1) old, (2) rare, (3) high in price, (4) a little different from all others, and (5) illustrate a change in method of work or in the fashion of their time. Still more depressing is this reverence when it is accompanied, as it often is, with indifference, or scorn, or fear of commercial taint, toward products of craftsmanship which are (1) modern, (2) common, (3) not high in price, (4) a copy of the old, rare, and priceless.

What could be more ludicrous than the sight of those who, openly devoted to the worship of beauty, treat with scorn modern reproductions of old things which they have pronounced beautiful, even if they copy the old so well that only labels and microscopes can distinguish one from the other, or even if, not professing to be exact reproductions, they show originality and high skill in design, are technically quite perfect, and either disclose the taste of the time or are factors in the betterment of that taste.

Surely a function of a public art museum is the making of life more interesting, joyful, and wholesome; and surely a museum cannot very well exercise that function unless it relates itself quite closely to the life it should be influencing; and surely it cannot thus relate itself unless it comes in close contact with the material adornment of that life—its applied arts.

The necklace found on an Egyptian mummy is unique, old, and costly. But even if presented to a museum by someone of wealth and influence, it still may be hideous and it may have no suggestion whatever for the modern designer. If it has certain suggestive value in this line, it thereby becomes just as well worthy of its place in the museum as is a necklace made yesterday in a neighboring city. Being unique, it should be kept. Its origin gives it an archaeological value. But if it is admitted to a museum of art, it need not stand in the way of the display in the same museum of modern necklaces which may interest many and may give suggestion and stimulus to modern designers.

Of course, it is not the Egyptian mummy's necklace which stands in the way of the display of modern necklaces, but the spirit of curators, experts, directors, and trustees. They become enamored of rarity, of history, and, in this specific instance, of necklaces as indicative of steps in civilization. They become lost in their specialties and forget their museum. They become lost in their idea of a museum and forget its purpose. They become lost in working out their idea of a museum and forget their public. And soon, not being brought constantly in touch with the life of their community through handling and displaying that community's output in one or scores of lines, they become entirely separated from it and go on making beautifully complete and very expensive collections, but never construct a living, active, and effective institution.

Is the Department Store a Museum?

A great city department store of the first class is perhaps more like a good museum of art than are any of the museums we have yet established. It is centrally located; it is easily reached; it is open to all at all the hours when patrons wish to visit it; it receives all courteously and gives information freely; it displays its most attractive and interesting objects and shows countless others on request; its collections are classified according to the knowledge and needs of its patrons; it is well lighted; it has convenient and inexpensive rest rooms; it supplies guides free of charge; it advertises itself widely and continuously; and it changes its exhibits to meet daily changes in subjects of interest, changes of taste in art, and the progress of invention and discovery.

A department store is not a good museum, but so far are museums from being the active and influential agencies they might be that they may be compared with department stores and not altogether to their advantage.

The Museum as the Teacher and Advertiser

To make itself alive, a museum must do two things: It must teach and it must advertise. As soon as it begins to teach, it will of necessity begin to form an alliance with present teaching agencies, the public schools, the colleges and universities, and the art institutions of all kinds. It is only by bearing in mind the history of its development and the part that imitation has played in that development that one can understand how American communities have been able to establish, build up, and maintain great collections of works of art, beautifully and expensively housed and administered, which yet have almost no cooperative relations with all the other educational and social-betterment institutions of the same communities. Teaching tends to become dogmatic. Dogmatism in art is injurious, but museum teaching need not be dogmatic. Indeed, museums might well be less dogmatic than they now are. They buy high-priced paintings and spend vast sums for rare brocades, pottery, ancient wood carvings, and whatnot, and then set these (with an ample air of assurance of wisdom which may very well be called dogmatic) before their constituents, saying, "Look, trust the expert, and admire." Far less dogmatic would it be to set side by side in a case ancient and rare modern and commercial pottery, and say, "Here are what some call the fine products of the potter's art when it was at its best in Italy long ago, and here are products of the potters of America today. You will find a comparative study of the two very interesting."

Would there be anything debasing in such an apposition? Would it be less dogmatic than is nearly all museum presentation of itself today?

By no right in reason whatever is a museum a mere collection of things, save by right of precedent. Yet precedent has so ruled in this field that our carefully organized museums have little more power to influence their communities than has a painting which hangs on the wall of some sanctuary, a sanctuary which few visit and they only to wonder as they gaze and to depart with the proud consciousness that they have seen. Some of the best of our museums, spending many thousands per year on administration and many other thousands on acquisitions, are now pluming themselves on the fact that they employ one—only one—person to make their collections more interesting to the thousands who visit them; that they have a hall in which during a winter a few lectures are given; and that they publish a bulletin recording their progress in piling up treasures, and catalogues which are as devoid of human interest as a perfect catalogue can be.

Museums of the future will not only teach at home, they will travel abroad through their photographs, their textbooks, and their periodicals. Books, leaflets, and journals—which will assist and supplement the work of teachers and will accompany, explain, and amplify the exhibits which art museums will send out—will all help to make museum expenditures seem worthwhile.

Why Not Branch Museums?

Museums will soon make themselves more effective through loan exhibits and through branches.

The museum is in most cases so remote from the city's center that even if it were to rival in attractiveness the theater, the cinema, and the department store, the time and money it takes to reach it would bar most from ever paying it a visit. It should establish branches, large and small, as many as funds permit, in which could be seen a few of the best things in one and another field that genius and skill have produced; in which could be seen the products of some of the city's industries, placed beside those of other cities, of other countries, and of other times; in which thousands of the citizens could each day see—at the cost of a few minutes only of their time—a few at least of the precious objects which their money has been used to collect.

Even though the main museum building is centrally situated, the need of branches—in a large city, at least—is quite obvious. The small branch would be more effective in the appeal it could make to many visitors than the main building could ever be. A half hour in the presence of one fine painting, a dozen Greek vases (with perhaps a few of other times and countries for comparison), one great piece of sculpture—each of these with ample descriptive notes and leaflets—would arouse more genuine feeling and a deeper interest than an aimless stroll through rooms full of the world's best art products.

These branches need not be in special buildings. Often, a single room conveniently located would serve as well as, or even better than, an elaborate and forbidding structure. How the idea would be worked out in detail no one can say. Apparently it has never been tried. But there seems to be no reason other than that found in precedent why the art treasures of a city—its own property, bought by itself to illuminate and broaden and make more enjoyable the life of its citizens—should rest always in the splendid isolation of that remote temple or palace erected for them.

Museum Objects May Be Lent

Art museums frequently borrow collections of objects and show them temporarily. Why do they not more often reverse the process?

More than 20 years ago, a self-constituted committee of women established in Massachusetts what was in effect a library art league. With the aid of the libraries which joined the league, they brought together a large number of interesting collections, chiefly of pictures of many kinds and dealing with many subjects, which traveled about and were shown at one library after another. For many years the University of the State of New York has been sending out from Albany collections of pictures to be exhibited in the libraries of the state and in other proper institutions.

Groups of museums, notably the group now operating under the direction of the Federation of Arts, have long been borrowing and successively showing collections of paintings, engravings, pottery, bronzes, and other objects. The Newark Library has prepared or arranged several exhibits of art and handicraft which have been shown in a total of more than 100 American cities. The American Museum of Natural History lends annually thousands of specially prepared exhibits to the schools of New York and vicinity. The Commercial Museums of Philadelphia prepare collections for the schools of the whole state of Pennsylvania. In St.

Louis, an educational museum—geographical, scientific, and industrial, maintained by the board of education—lends many thousands of objects and collections each year to the schools of the city. In Germany, there go forth each year from a central bureau in Hagen many carefully prepared exhibitions of objects of art and handicraft gathered from the best workshops in the empire; and the South Kensington museum has been lending objects to towns and cities in Great Britain for many years.

In spite of all these good examples of the possibilities for helpfulness which lie in loan collections shown for brief periods in each of a score of cities or in each of a hundred schools of the same city, the habit of lending subjects from and by museums of art is almost unknown in this country.

Even the youngest and most modest of museums—unless it is of the purely mortuary type, housed in a temple, complete in all its appointments, installed for all time according to the museum laws of its founders and hastening to its destined end of disuse— even such a museum has objects which would find a hitherto useless life crowned with good works were they lent freely to schools, libraries, art schools, civic centers, and whatnot in the town to which they belong.

Museums of science are sending their exhibits to their patrons, old and young. It is quite evident that art museums will soon follow their example.

The art museums are just now greatly concerned over the question of how they shall make themselves of value to the young people of their respective communities. It is plain enough that it is impossible in a large city for the young people to make the journey to the central museum times enough to gain more than the most fleeting of impressions. They have not the money for car fares, they must go in crowds and teachers must accompany the crowds, and school time for this is lacking, and if they were to go times enough to get any enduring lessons from their visits, they would crowd the central building to the doors.

Why not take the museum to the young people? Public branches can serve the adults; and collections, groups, single objects, and photographs and other pictures can easily be placed in school houses, and surely soon will be.

Do We Need Museums at All?

I have ventured to mention the great department stores in the same sentence with museums of art. No sooner is the comparison made than other suggestive comparisons come to mind. The dealer in paintings has his art gallery, always convenient, open to all without charge, with exhibitions constantly changing. Dealers in works of art in general seem to approach even nearer to the museum ideal. Then on the industrial side we find that every factory and workshop is a museum in action, and, if it produces beautiful objects, is a living exhibit of arts and crafts.

Stores are each year more attractive and more informing; each year factories are more humanely and rationally managed, are more inviting and more informing, and are more freely open to interested visitors under reasonable restrictions. Each year the printing press produces better and cheaper illustrations of artworks of every kind, with a descriptive letter press which grows each year not only more ample but also more direct and simple. And each year the cinema reproduces for us more faithfully the activities of men in all lines of work and in all countries and makes it easier for us all to understand what books and journals try to tell us through text and pictures.

This question then arises: Does a world which is supplied by mere trade and industry with convenient storehouses of the world's products old and new, the best as well as the poorest, with industrial exhibits in factories of every kind, and with pictures and texts of amazing beauty and suggestiveness—does a world having all these things need the art museum at all?

The Museum as the Public's Friend and Guide

The question just asked answers itself at once, of course. Save for the very young, the opportunities for self-education offered by the street, the store, the factory, the movie, and the all-pervasive page of print are quite ample. Any boy or girl who will can gain an excellent education without the ministration of the school. But, on the whole, in spite of its manifest deficiencies, it seems wise to maintain the school and promote education through it.

Just so with those refinements of human nature—those betterments of manner and feeling, which I have ventured to name as good things which art museums exist to promote—these refinements may be attained by any, save the very young, who will attend thereto and will diligently use, to that end, the materials always at hand in dress, architecture, shop window, nature, and the ever-present picture and printed page. But in spite of the infinity of ever-present opportunity for everyone's education in the refinement of life and the enrichment of the leisure hour, it has seemed wise to establish and maintain the museum of art.

I have tried to show that this museum has been so absorbed in one aspect of its work that it has left untouched its more important and pressing duties. It has built itself an elaborate and costly home, beautiful after the fashion of its time and the taste of its community. In this home it has gathered the rare, the curious, the beautiful, and always, when possible, the unique and costly. So doing it has paid its debt to history and archaeology, has gained for its city a certain passing and rather meretricious distinction, and has given a select few an opportunity to pursue their study of fashion in taste, in ornament, and in technique.

Now seems to come the demand that the museum serve its people in the task of helping them to appreciate the high importance of manner, to hold by the laws of simplicity and restraint, and to broaden their sympathies and multiply their interests.

ROLAND BARTHES

1915-1980

"TOYS"

1957

Roland Barthes, writer, literary critic, and academic, is one of the most important intellectual figures of post-World War II France. He is known for his influential theories and observations in semiology, the study of signs and symbols, and how they are used in literature. Barthes studied the classics, grammar, and philosophy at the University of Paris, graduating in 1943. After teaching French at universities in Romania and Egypt, he went to work at the Centre National de la Recherche Scientifique. In 1976, he became the first person to hold the chair of literary semiology at the Collège de France. He was also a founder of the Groupe Théâtral Antique in Paris and the magazine *Théâtre Populaire*. Barthes died in a car accident in 1980.

Mythologies, one of Barthes's earliest works, is a compilation of his articles on a variety of topics. He describes *Mythologies* as having "a double theoretical framework: on the one hand, an ideological critique bearing on the language of so-called mass-culture; on the other, a first attempt to analyze semiologically the mechanics of the language" (Preface to the 1970 edition). In the articles in *Mythologies,* Barthes sets out to show how mass culture is significant through an inspection of the meanings of popular cultural artifacts

and practices. In doing so, he examines how they
utilitarian functions as well as implied and impo.
These myths of everyday life are based on illusion an.

SOURCE

Barthes, Roland. 1957. "Toys." In *Mythologies*. Annette Lavers,
Trans. (Editions du Seuil, Paris). New York: Hill and Wang,
1972. 53-55.*

TOYS

French toys: one could not find a better illustration of the
fact that the adult Frenchman sees the child as another self. All
the toys one commonly sees are essentially a microcosm of the
adult world; they are all reduced copies of human objects, as if in
the eyes of the public the child was, all told, nothing but a smaller
man, a homunculus to whom must be supplied objects of his
own size.

Invented forms are very rare: a few sets of blocks, which appeal
to the spirit of do-it-yourself, are the only ones which offer
dynamic forms. As for the others, French toys always mean
something, and this something is always entirely socialized,
constituted by the myths or the techniques of modem adult life:
the Army, Broadcasting, the Post Office, Medicine (miniature
instrument-cases, operating theatres for dolls), School, Hair-Styling
(driers for permanent-waving), the Air Force (Parachutists),
Transport (trains, Citroëns, Vedettes, Vespas, petrol-stations),
Science (Martian toys).

The fact that French toys literally prefigure the world of adult
functions obviously cannot but prepare the child to accept them
all, by constituting for him, even before he can think about it, the

alibi of a Nature which has at all times created soldiers, postmen and Vespas. Toys here reveal the list of all the things the adult does not find unusual: war, bureaucracy, ugliness, Martians, etc. It is not so much, in fact, the imitation which is the sign of an abdication, as its literalness: French toys are like a Jivaro [South American Indian] head, in which one recognizes, shrunken to the size of an apple, the wrinkles and hair of an adult. There exist, for instance, dolls which urinate; they have an oesophagus, one gives them a bottle, they wet their nappies [diapers]; soon, no doubt, milk will turn to water in their stomachs. This is meant to prepare the little girl for the causality of house-keeping, to 'condition' her to her future role as mother. However, faced with this world of faithful and complicated objects, the child can only identify himself as owner, as user, never as creator; he does not invent the world, he uses it: there are, prepared for him, actions without adventure, without wonder, without joy. He is turned into a little stay-at-home householder who does not even have to invent the mainsprings of adult causality; they are supplied to him ready-made: he has only to help himself, he is never allowed to discover anything from start to finish. The merest set of blocks, provided it is not too refined, implies a very different learning of the world: then, the child does not in any way create meaningful objects, it matters little to him whether they have an adult name; the actions he performs are not those of a user but those of a demiurge [a powerful creative force]. He creates forms which walk, which roll, he creates life, not property: objects now act by themselves, they are no longer an inert and complicated material in the palm of his hand. But such toys are rather rare: French toys are usually based on imitation, they are meant to produce children who are users, not creators.

The bourgeois status of toys can be recognized not only in their forms, which are all functional, but also in their substances. Current toys are made of a graceless material, the product of chemistry, not of nature. Many are now molded from complicated mixtures; the plastic material of which they are made has an appearance at once gross and hygienic, it destroys all the pleasure, the sweetness, the humanity of touch. A sign which fills one with consternation is the gradual disappearance of wood, in spite of its being an ideal material because of its firmness and its softness, and the natural warmth of its touch. Wood removes, from all the forms which it supports, the wounding quality of angles which are too sharp, the chemical coldness of metal. When the child handles it and knocks it, it neither vibrates nor grates, it has a sound at once muffled and sharp. It is a familiar and poetic substance, which does not sever the child from close contact with the tree, the table, the floor. Wood does not wound or break down; it does not shatter, it wears out, it can last a long time, live with the child, alter little by little the relations between the object and the hand. If it dies, it is in dwindling, not in swelling out like those mechanical toys which disappear behind the hernia of a broken spring. Wood makes essential objects, objects for all time. Yet there hardly remain any of these wooden toys from the Vosges, these fretwork farms with their animals, which were only possible, it is true, in the days of the craftsman. Henceforth, toys are chemical in substance and colour; their very material introduces one to a coenaesthesis of use, not pleasure. These toys die in fact very quickly, and once dead, they have no posthumous life for the child.

VINE DELORIA, JR.

1933-

GOD IS RED

1994

Vine Deloria, Jr., academic, historian, and prolific author, is a member of the Standing Rock Sioux. Since the 1960s, he has been one of the most outspoken and influential advocates of Native American affairs, serving as executive director of the National Congress of American Indians and a chair of the Repatriation Committee of the National Museum of the American Indian, a group integral to the legislation of the Native American Graves Protection and Repatriation Act (Public Law 101-601). He has promoted Native American cultural nationalism and worked for the greater understanding of Native American history and philosophy. Deloria holds a master's degree in theology and a J.D. from the University of Colorado where he is professor emeritus of history. Among his many books are *Custer Died for Your Sins: An Indian Manifesto* (1969), *Behind the Trail of Broken Treaties: An Indian Declaration of Independence* (1974), *The Metaphysics of Modern Existence* (1979), *American Indians, American Justice* (1983), *Aggressions of Civilization: Federal Indian Policy Since the 1880s* (1984), and *Red Earth, White Lies: Native Americans and the Myth of Scientific Fact* (1995). In 1996, he was awarded the Native Writers' Circle of the Americas Lifetime Achievement Award.

In "Sacred Places and Moral Responsibility," Deloria calls attention to the role that spaces and places have on religious perceptions. His examination is based on the belief that humans are part of the fabric of life that constitutes the natural world and that the world is endangered by misuse and destruction wrought by technology. Native American philosophy is based on the need to live with the land rather than trying to dominate or exploit it. He further compares and contrasts the concept of sacred land of Native Americans with historic sites such as the Gettysburg Battlefield that have been deemed sacred in the American psyche. Another kind of sacred place, according to Deloria's thesis, is the holy place, sites where the Higher Powers have revealed themselves to humans, a phenomenon found worldwide.

SOURCE

Deloria, Jr., Vine. 1973. "Chapter 16: Sacred Places and Moral Responsibility." In *God is Red: A Native View of Religion*. Golden, Colorado: Fulcrum Publishing, 1994. 267-282.*

GOD IS RED

Chapter 16: Sacred Places and Moral Responsibility

When the tribes were forced from their aboriginal homelands and confined to small reservations, many of the tribal religious rituals were prohibited by the BIA in the 1870s and 1880s because of an inordinately large number of Christian zealots as Indian agents. We read in chapter 14 how traditional people had to adopt various subterfuges so that their religious life could be continued. Some tribes shifted their ceremonial year to coincide with the whites' holidays and conducted their most important rituals on national holidays and Christian feast days, explaining to curious whites that they were simply honoring George Washington and celebrating Christmas and Easter.

Many shrines and holy places were located far away from the new reservation homelands, but because they were not being exploited economically or used by settlers, it was not difficult for small parties of people to go into the mountains or to remote lakes and buttes and conduct ceremonies without interference from non-Indians.

Since World War II, this situation has changed dramatically. We have seen a greatly expanding national population, the introduction of corporate farming practices that have placed formerly submarginal lands under cultivation, more extensive mining and timber industry activities, and a greatly expanded recreation industry—all of which have severely impacted the use of public lands in the United States. Few rural areas now enjoy the isolation of half a century ago, and as multiple use of lands increased, many of the sacred sites that were on public lands were threatened by visitors and subjected to new uses. Tribal religious leaders were often able to work out informal arrangements with federal and state agencies to allow them access to these places for religious purposes. But as the personnel changed in state and federal agencies, a new generation of bureaucrats, catering to developers, recreation interest, and the well-established economic groups who have always used public lands for a pittance, began to restrict Indian access to sacred sites by establishing increasingly narrow rules and regulations for managing public lands.

In 1978, in a symbolic effort to clarify the status of traditional religious practices and practitioners, Congress passed a joint Resolution entitled the American Indian Religious Freedom Act. This act declared that it was the policy of Congress to protect and preserve the inherent right of American Indians to believe, express, and practice their traditional religions. The resolution identified the problem as one of a "lack of knowledge or the insensitive and inflexible enforcement of Federal policies and regulations." Section 2 of the resolution directed the president to require the various federal departments to evaluate their policies and procedures, report back to Congress on the results of their survey, and make recommendations for legislative actions.[1]

Many people assumed that this resolution clarified the federal

---

[1]   92 Stat 469, U.S.C. §1996.

attitude toward traditional religions, and it began to be cited in litigation involving the construction of dams, roads, and the management of federal lands. Almost unanimously, however, the federal courts have since ruled that the resolution did not protect or preserve the right of Indians to practice their religion and conduct ceremonies at sacred sites on public lands.[2] Some courts even hinted darkly that any formal recognition of the existence of tribal practices would be tantamount to establishing a state religion,[3] an interpretation that, upon analysis, is a dreadful misreading of American history and the Constitution and may have been an effort to inflame anti-Indian feelings.

A good example for making this claim was the 1988 Supreme Court decision in the *Lyng v. Northwest Indian Cemetery Protective Association* case that involved protecting the visitation rights of the traditional religious leaders of three tribes to sacred sites in the Chimney Rock area of the Six Rivers National Forest in Northern California. The Forest Service proposed to build a 6-mile paved road that would have opened part of the area to commercial logging. This area, known by three Indian tribes as the "High

---

[2] See *Wilson v. Block,* 708 F 2d. (D.C.Cir 1983). Hopi and Navajo sacred sites and shrines on San Francisco peak were destroyed by the U.S. Forest Service to make room for a new ski lift. In *Fools Crow v. Cullet,* 706 F. 2d 856 (8th Cir 1983) the court upheld intrusions by the U.S. Park Service on Sioux vision quest use of Bear Butte. In *Badoni v. Higginson,* 638 F. 2d 172 (10th Cir 1980) the court allowed the destruction of a Navajo sacred site at Rainbow Bridge in the Grand Canyon area.

[3] The majority decision in *Lyng* even suggested that to recognize traditional Indian religious freedom would make it seem as if the Indians owned the federal lands.

No disrespect for these practices is implied when one notes that such beliefs could easily require de facto beneficial ownership of some rather spacious tracts of public property. Even without anticipating future cases, the diminution of the government's property rights, and the concomitant subsidy of the Indian religion, would in this case be far from trivial . . . 108 S. Ct. 1319, 1327 (1988)

Country," was the center of their religious and ceremonial life. The lower federal courts prohibited the construction of the road on the grounds that it would have made religious ceremonial use of the are[a] impossible. Before the Supreme Court could hear the appeal, Congress passed the California Wilderness Act that made the question of constructing the road moot for all practical purposes. But the Supreme Court insisted on hearing the appeal of the Forest Service and deciding the religious issues. It turned the tribes down flat, ruling that the Free Exercise clause did not prevent the government from using its property in any way it saw fit and in effect rolling back the religious use of the area completely.

Most troubling about the Supreme Court's decision was the insistence on analyzing tribal religions within the same conceptual framework as western organized religions. Justice O'Connor observed,

> A broad range of government activities—from social welfare programs to foreign aid to conservation projects—will always be considered essential to the spiritual well-being of some citizens, often on the basis of sincerely held religious beliefs. Others will find the very same activity deeply offensive, and perhaps incompatible with their own search for spiritual fulfillment and with the tenets of their religion.[4]

Thus, ceremonies and rituals that had been performed for thousands of years were treated as if they were popular fads or simply matters of personal preference based upon the erroneous assumption that religion was only a matter of individual aesthetic choice.

Justice Brennan's dissent vigorously attacked this spurious line of reasoning, outlining with some precision the communal aspect of the tribal religions and their relationship to the mountains. But his argument failed to gather support within the Court. Most

---

[4] At 1327

observers of the Supreme Court were simply confounded at the majority's conclusion that suggested that destroying a religion "did not unduly burden it" and that no constitutional protections were available to the Indians.[5]

When informed of the meaning of this decision, most people have shown great sympathy for the traditional religious people. At the same time, they have had great difficulty understanding why it is so important that these ceremonies be held, that they be conducted only at certain locations, and that they be held in secrecy and privacy. This lack of understanding highlights the great gulf that exists between traditional Western thinking about religion and the Indian perspective. It is the difference between individual conscience and commitment (Western) and communal tradition (Indian), these views can only be reconciled by examining them in a much broader historical and geographical context.

Justice Brennan attempted to make this difference clear when he observed, "Although few tribal members actually made medicine at the most powerful sites, the entire tribe's welfare hinges on the success of individual practitioner."[6] More than that, however, the "world renewal" ceremonies conducted by the tribes were done on behalf of the earth and all forms of life. To describe these ceremonies as if they were comparable to Oral Roberts seeking funds or Jimmy Swaggart begging forgiveness for his continuing sexual misconduct or Justice O'Connor's matters of community aesthetic preference is to miss the point entirely. In effect, the Court declared that

---

[5]   Justice Brennan's dissent makes this point specifically,

The Court today, however, ignores *Roy's* emphasis on the internal nature of the government practice at issue there, and instead construes that case as further support for the proposition that governmental action that does not coerce conduct inconsistent with religious faith simply does not implicate the concerns of the Free Exercise Clause. That such a reading is wholly untenable, however, is demonstrated by the cruelly surreal result it produces here: *governmental action that will virtually destroy a religion is nevertheless deemed not to 'burden' that religion.* (at 1337) (Emphasis added.)

[6]   At 1332

Indians cannot pray for the planet or for other people and other forms of life in the manner required by their religion.

Two contradictory responses seem to characterize the non-Indian attitudes toward traditional tribal religions. Some people want the traditional healers to share their religious beliefs in the same manner that priests, rabbis, and ministers expound publicly the tenets of their denominations. Other people feel that Indian ceremonials are simply remnants of primitive life and should be abandoned. Neither perspective understands that Indian tribes are communities in ways that are fundamentally different than other American communities and organizations. Tribal communities are wholly defined by the family relationships; the non-Indian communities are defined primarily by residence, by an arbitrary establishment of political jurisdiction, or by agreement with generally applicable sets of intellectual beliefs. Ceremonial and ritual knowledge is possessed by everyone in the Indian community, although only a few people may actually be chosen to perform these acts. Authorization to perform ceremonies comes from higher spiritual powers and not by certification through an institution or any formal organization.

A belief in the sacredness of lands in the non-Indian context may become the preferred belief of an individual or group of people based on their experiences or on an intensive study of preselected evidence. But this belief becomes the subject of intense criticism and does not, except under unusual circumstances, become an operative principle in the life and behavior of the non-Indian group. The same belief, when seen in the Indian context, is an integral part of the experiences of the people—past, present, and future. The idea does not become a bone of contention among the people for even if someone does not have the experience or belief in the sacredness of lands, he or she accords tradition the respect that it deserves. Indians who have never visited certain sacred sites nevertheless know of these places from the community knowledge, and they intuit this knowing to be an essential part of their being.

Justice Brennan, in countering the arguments raised by Justice

O'Connor that any recognition of the sacredness of certain sites would allow traditional Indian religions to define the use of all public lands, suggested that the burden of proof be placed on the traditional people to demonstrate why some sites are central to their practice and other sites, while invoking a sense of reverence, are not as important. This requirement is not unreasonable, but it requires a willingness on the part of non-Indians and the courts to entertain different ideas about the nature of religion—ideas which until the present have not been a part of their experience or understanding.

If we were to subject the topic of the sacredness of lands to a Western rational analysis, fully recognizing the such an analysis is merely for our convenience in discussion and does not represent the nature of reality, we would probably find four major categories of description. Some of these categories are overlapping because some groups might not agree with the description of certain sites in the categories in which other Indians would place them. Nevertheless, it is the principle of respect for the sacred that is important.

The first and most familiar kind of sacred lands are places to which we attribute sanctity because the location is a site where, within our own history, something of great importance has taken place. Unfortunately, many of these places are related to instances of human violence. Gettysburg National Cemetery is a good example of this kind of sacred land. Abraham Lincoln properly noted that we cannot hallow the Gettysburg battlefield because others, the men who fought there, had already consecrated it by giving "that last full measure of devotion." We generally hold these places sacred because people did there what we might one day be required to do—give our lives in a cause we hold dear. Wounded Knee, South Dakota, has become such a place for many Indians where a band of Sioux Indians were massacred. On the whole, however, the idea of regarding a battlefield as sacred was entirely foreign to most tribes because they did not see war as a holy enterprise. The Lincoln Memorial in Washington, D.C., might be an example of a nonmartial location, and, although Justice

O'Connor felt that recognizing the sacredness of land and location might inspire an individual to have a special fondness for this memorial, it is important to recognize that we should have some sense of reverence in these places.

Every society needs these kinds of sacred places because they help to instill a sense of social cohesion in the people and remind them of the passage of generations that have brought them to the present. A society that cannot remember and honor its past is in peril of losing its soul. Indians, because of our considerably longer tenure on this continent, have many more sacred places than do non-Indians. Many different ceremonies can be and have been held at these locations; there is both an exclusivity and an inclusiveness, depending upon the occasion and the ceremony. In this classification the site is all important, but it is sanctified each time ceremonies are held and prayers offered.

A second category of sacred lands has a deeper, more profound sense of the sacred. It can be illustrated in Old Testament stories that have become the foundation of three world religions. After the death of Moses, Joshua led the Hebrews across the River Jordan into the Holy Land. On approaching the river with the Ark of the Covenant, the waters of the Jordan "rose up" or parted and the people, led by the Ark, crossed over on "dry ground," which is to say they crossed without difficulty. After crossing, Joshua selected one man from each of the Twelve Tribes and told him to find a large stone. The twelve stones were then placed together in a monument to mark the spot where the people had camped after having crossed the river successfully. When asked about this strange behavior, Joshua then replied, "That this may be a sign among you, that when your children ask their fathers in time to come, saying 'What mean ye by these stones?' Then you shall answer them: That the waters of Jordan were cut off before the Ark of the Covenant of the Lord, when it passed over Jordan."[7]

In comparing this site with Gettysburg, we must understand

---

[7]   Joshua 4:6-7

a fundamental difference. Gettysburg is made sacred by the actions of men. It can be described as exquisitely dear to us, but it is not a location where we have perceived that something specifically other than ourselves is present, something mysteriously religious in the proper meaning of those words has happened or been made manifest. In the crossing of the River Jordan, the sacred or higher powers have appeared in the lives of human beings. Indians would say something holy has appeared in an otherwise secular situation. No matter how we might attempt to explain this event in later historical, political, or economic terms, the essence of the event is that the sacred has become a part of our experience.

Some of the sites that traditional religious leaders visit are of this nature. Buffalo Gap at the southeastern edge of the Black Hills of South Dakota marks the location where the buffalo emerged each spring to begin the ceremonial year of the Plains Indians, and it has this aspect of sacred /secular status. It may indeed be the starting point of the Great Race that determined the primacy between two-legged and four-legged creatures at the beginning of the world. Several mountains in New Mexico and Arizona mark places where the Pueblo, Hopi, and Navajo peoples completed their migrations, were told to settle, or where they first established their spiritual relationships with bear, deer, eagle, and other peoples who participate in the ceremonials.

Every identifiable region has sacred places peculiar to its geography and as we extend the circle geographically from any point in North America, we begin to include an ever-increasing number of sacred sites. Beginning in the American Southwest we must include the Apache, Ute, Comanche, Kiowa, and other tribes as we move away from the Pueblo and Navajo lands. These lands would be sacred to some tribes but secular to the Pueblo, Hopi, and Navajo. The difference would be in the manner of revelation and what the people experienced. There is immense particularity in the sacred and it is not a blanket category to be applied indiscriminately. Even east of the Mississippi, though many places have been nearly obliterated, people retain knowledge of these sacred sites. Their sacredness does not depend on human occupancy but on the stories that describe the revelation that enabled human beings to experience the holiness there.

In the religious world of most tribes, birds, animals, and plants compose the "other peoples" of creation. Depending on the ceremony, various of these "peoples" participate in human activities. If Jews and Christians see the action of a deity at sacred places in the Holy Land and in churches and synagogues, traditional Indian people experience spiritual activity as the whole of creation becomes active participants in ceremonial life. Because the relationship with the "other peoples" is so fundamental to the human community, most traditional practitioners are reluctant to articulate the specific elements of either the ceremony or the locations. Because some rituals involve the continued prosperity of the "other peoples," discussing the nature of the ceremony would violate the integrity of these relationships. Thus, traditional people explain that these ceremonies are being held for "all our relatives" but are reluctant to offer any further explanations. It is these ceremonies in particular that are now to be denied protection under the Supreme Court rulings.

It is not likely that non-Indians have had many of these kinds of religious experiences, particularly because most churches and synagogues have special rituals that are designed to cleanse the buildings so that their services can be held there untainted by the natural world. Non-Indians have simply not been on this continent very long; their families have rarely settled in one place for any period of time so that no profound relationship with the environment has been possible. Additionally, non-Indians have engaged in the senseless killing of wildlife and utter destruction of plant life. It is unlikely that they would have understood efforts by other forms of life to communicate with humans. Although, some non-Indian families who have lived continuously in isolated rural areas tell stories about birds and animals similar to the traditions of many tribes indicating that lands and the "other peoples" do seek intimacy with our species.

The third kind of sacred lands are places of overwhelming holiness where the Higher Powers, on their own initiative, have revealed Themselves to human beings. Again, we can illustrate this in the Old Testament narrative. Prior to his journey to Egypt, Moses spent his time herding his father-in-law's sheep on or near Mount Horeb. One day he took the flock to the far side of the mountain and to his amazement saw a bush burning with fire but not being consumed by it. Approaching this spot with the usual curiosity of a person accustomed to the outdoor life, Moses was startled when the Lord spoke to him from the bush, warning "Draw not hither; put off thy shoes from thy feet, for the place where on thou standest is holy ground."[8]

This tradition tells us that there are places of unquestionable, inherent sacredness on this earth, sites that are holy in and of themselves. Human societies come and go on this earth and any prolonged occupation of a geographical region will produce shrines and sacred sites discerned by the occupying people, but there will always be a few sites at which the highest spirits dwell. The stories that explain the sacred nature of these locations will frequently provide startling parallels to the account about the burning bush. One need only look at the shrines of present-day Europe. Long before Catholic or Protestant churches were built in certain places, other religions had established shrines and temples of that spot. These holy places are locations where people have always gone to communicate and commune with higher spiritual powers.

This phenomenon is worldwide and all religions find that these places regenerate people and fill them with spiritual powers. In the Western Hemisphere these places, with few exceptions, are known only by American Indians. Bear Butte, Blue Lake, and the High Places in the *Lyng* case are all well known locations that are sacred in and of themselves. People have been commanded to perform ceremonies at these holy places so that the earth and all its forms of life might survive and prosper. Evidence of this moral responsibility that sacred places command has come through the testimony of traditional people when they have tried to explain to non-Indians at various times in this century—in court, in conferences, and in conversations—that they must perform certain ceremonies

---

[8]   Exodus 3:5

at specific times and places in order that the sun may continue to shine, the earth prosper, and the stars remain in the heavens. Tragically, this attitude is interpreted by non-Indians as indicative of the traditional leader's personal code or philosophy and is not seen as a simple admission of a moral duty.

Skeptical non-Indians, and representatives of other religions seeking to discredit tribal religions, have sometimes deliberately violated some of these holy places with no ill effects. They have then come to believe that they have demonstrated the false nature of Indian beliefs. These violations reveal a strange non-Indian belief in a form of mechanical magic that is touchingly adolescent, a belief that an impious act would, or could trigger an immediate response from the higher spiritual powers. Surely these impious acts suggest a deity who jealously guards his or her prerogatives and wreaks immediate vengeance for minor transgressions—much as some Protestant sects have envisioned God and much as an ancient astronaut (see chapter 9) wanting to control lesser beings might act.

It would be impossible for the thoughtless or impious acts of one species to have an immediate drastic effort on the earth. The cumulative effect of continuous secularity, however, poses a different kind of danger. Long-standing prophecies tell us of the impious people who would come here, defy the creator, and cause the massive destruction of the planet. Many traditional people believe that we are now quite near that time. The cumulative evidence of global warming, acid rain, the disappearance of amphibians, overpopulation, and other products of civilized life certainly testify to the possibility of these prophecies being correct.

Of all the traditional ceremonies extant and actively practiced at the time of contact with non-Indians, ceremonies derived from or related to these holy places have the highest retention rate because of their extraordinary planetary importance. Ironically, traditional people have been forced to hold these ceremonies under various forms of subterfuge and have been abused and imprisoned for doing them. Yet the ceremonies have very little to do with individual or tribal prosperity. Their underlying theme is one of gratitude expressed by human beings on behalf of all forms of life. They act to complete and renew the entire and complete cycle of life, ultimately including the whole cosmos present in its specific realizations, so that in the last analysis one might describe ceremonials as the cosmos becoming thankfully aware of itself.

Having used Old Testament examples to show the objective presence of the holy places, we can draw additional conclusions about the nature of these holy places from the story of the Exodus. Moses did not demand that the particular location of the burning bush become a place of worship for his people, although there was every reason to suppose that he could have done so. Lacking information, we must conclude that the holiness of this place precluded its use as a shrine. If Moses had been told to perform annual ceremonies at that location during specific days or times of the year, world history would have been entirely different.

Each holy site contains its own revelation. This knowledge is not the ultimate in the sense that Near Eastern religions like to claim the universality of their ideas. Traditional religious leaden tell us that in many of the ceremonies new messages are communicated to them. The ceremonies enable humans to have continuing relationships with higher spiritual powers so that each bit of information is specific to the time, place, and circumstances of the people. No revelation can be regarded as universal because times and conditions change.

The second and third kinds of sacred lands result from two distinctly different forms of sacred revelations where the sacred is actively involved in secular human activities and where the sacred takes the initiative to chart out a new historical course for humans. Because there are higher spiritual powers who can communicate with people, there has to be a fourth category of sacred lands. People must always be ready to experience new revelations at new locations. If this possibility did not exist, all deities and spirits would be dead. Consequently, we always look forward to the revelation of new sacred places and ceremonies. Unfortunately, some federal courts irrationally and arbitrarily circumscribe this universal aspect of religion by insisting that traditional religious practitioners

restrict their identification of sacred locations to places that were
historically visited by Indians, implying that at least for the federal
courts, God is dead.

In denying the possibility of the continuing revelation of the
sacred in our lives, federal courts, scholars, and state and federal
agencies refuse to accord credibility to the testimony of religious
leaders. They demand evidence that a ceremony or location has
always been central to the beliefs and practices of an Indian tribe
and impose exceedingly rigorous standards of proof on Indians
who appear before them. This practice allows the Supreme Court
to command what should not to be done, it lets secular institutions
rule on the substance of religious belief and practice. Thus, courts
will protect a religion that shows every symptom of being dead
but will create formidable barriers if it appears to be alive. Justice
Scalia made this posture perfectly clear when he announced in
Smith, that it would be unconstitutional to ban the casting of
"statues that are used for worship purposes" or to prohibit bowing
down before a golden calf.

We live in time and space and receive most of our signals about
proper behavior from each other and the environment around us.
Under these circumstances, the individual and the group *must* both
have some kind of sanctity if we are to have a social order at all. By
recognizing the various aspects of the sacredness of lands as we
have described, we place ourselves in a realistic context in which
the individual and the group can cultivate and enhance the sacred
experience. Recognizing the sacredness of lands on which previous
generations have lived and died is the foundation of all other
sentiment. Instead of denying this dimension of our emotional
lives, we should be setting aside additional places that have
transcendent meaning. Sacred sites that higher spiritual powers
have chosen for manifestation enable us to focus our concerns on
the specific form of our lives. These places remind us of our unique
relationship with the spiritual forces that govern the universe and
call us to fulfill our religious vocations. These kinds of religious
experiences have shown us something of the nature of the universe

by an affirmative manifestation of themselves and this knowledge illuminates everything else that we know.

The nature of tribal religion brings contemporary America a new kind of legal problem. Religious freedom has existed as a matter of course in America *only* when religion has been conceived as a set of objective beliefs. This condition is actually not freedom at all because it would be exceedingly difficult to read minds and determine what ideas were being entertained at the time. So far in American history religious freedom has not involved the consecration and setting aside of lands for religious purposes or allowing sincere but highly divergent behavior by individuals and groups. The issue of sacred lands, as we have seen was successfully raised in the case of the Taos Pueblo people. Nevertheless, a great deal more remains to be done to guarantee Indian people the right to practice their own religion.

A number of other tribes have sacred sanctuaries in lands that have been taken by the government for purposes other than religion. These lands must be returned to the respective Indian tribes for their ceremonial purposes. The greatest number of Indian shrines are located in New Mexico and here the tribal religions have remained comparatively strong. Cochiti Pueblo needs some 24,000 acres of land for access to and use of religious shrines in what is now Bandelier National Monument. The people also have shrines in the Tetilla Peak area. San Juan Pueblo has also been trying to get lands returned for religious purposes. Santa Clara Pueblo requested the Indian Claims Commission to set aside 30,000 acres of the lands that have religious and ceremonial importance to its people but are presently in the hands of the National Forest Service and Atomic Energy Commission.

In Arizona the Hopi people have a number of shrines that are of vital importance to their religion. Traditionals regard the Black Mesa area as sacred, but it is being leased to Peabody Coal by the more assimilative tribal council. The San Francisco Peaks within the Coconino National Forest are sacred became they are believed to be the homes of the Kachinas who play a major part in the Hopi ceremonial system. The Navajo have a number of sacred mountains now under federal ownership. Mount Taylor in the Cibola National Forest, Blanca Peak in southern Colorado, Hesperus Peak in the San Juan National Forest, Huerfano Mountain on public domain lands, and Oak Creek canyon in the Coconino National Forest are all sites integral to the Navajo tradition. Part of the Navajo religion involves the "mountain chant" that describes the seven sacred mountains and a sacred lake located within these mountains. The Navajo believe their ancestors arose from this region at the creation. Last, but certainly not least, is the valiant struggle now being waged by the Apache people to prevent the University of Arizona from building several telescopes on Mount Graham in southern Arizona.

In other states several sacred sites we are under threat of exploitation. The Forest Service is proposing to construct a major parking lot and observation platform at the Medicine Wheel site near Powell, Wyoming, that is sacred to many tribes from Montana, the Dakotas, and Wyoming. Because the only value of this location is its relationship to traditional Indian religions that need isolation and privacy, it seems ludicrous to pretend that making it accessible to more tourists and subject to increasing environmental degradation is enhancing it. The Badger Two Medicine area of Montana, where oil drilling has been proposed, is a sacred area for traditional Blackfeet who live in the vicinity. The Pipestone Quarry in southwestern Minnesota was confiscated from the Yankton Sioux in the closing decades of the last century when some missionaries pressure the federal government to eliminate Indian access to this important spot.

Finally, there is the continuing struggle over the Black Hills of South Dakota. Many Americans are now aware of this state thanks to the success of the movie *Dances with Wolves* that not only depicted the culture of the Sioux Indians but also filled the screen with the magnificent landscape of the northern Great Plains. Nineteen ninety-one was a year of great schizophrenia and strange anomalies in South Dakota. Local whites shamelessly capitalized on the success of the movie at the same time they were frothing at the mouth over the continuing efforts of the Sioux people to get the federal lands in the Black Hills returned to them. Governor George

Mickelson announced a "Year of Reconciliation" that simply became twelve months of symbolic maneuvering for publicity and renewal of political images. When some of the Sioux elders suggested that the return of Bear Butte near Sturgis would be a concrete step toward reconciliation, non-Indians were furious that reconciliation might require them to make good-faith effort to heal the wounds from a century of conflict.

The question that must be addressed in the issue of sacred lands is the extent to which the tribal religions can be maintained if sacred lands are restored. Would restoration of the sacred Pipestone Quarry result in more people seeking to follow the traditional religious life or would it result in continued use of the stone for tourism and commercial purposes? A small group of Sioux people have made a living during this century from making ashtrays and decorative carvings from this sacred rock; they refuse to stop their exploitation. A major shift in focus is needed by traditional Sioux people to prepare to reconsecrate the quarry and return to the old ways of reverence.

A very difficult task lies ahead for the people who continue to believe in the old tribal religions. In the past, these traditions have been ridiculed by disbelievers, primarily missionaries and social scientists. Today injuries nearly as grievous we visited on traditional religions by the multitude of non-Indians who seek entrance and participation in ceremonies and rituals. Many of these non-Indians blatantly steal symbols, prayers and teaching by laying claim to alleged offices in tribal religions. Most non-Indians see in tribal religions the experiences and reverence that are missing in their own heritage. No matter how hard they try, they always reduce the teachings and ceremonies to a complicated word game and ineffectual gestures. Lacking communities and extended families, they are unable to put the religion into practice.

Some major efforts must be made by the Indians of this generation to demonstrate the view of the world that their tradition teaches has an integrity of its own and represents a sensible and respectable perspective of the world and a valid means of interpreting experiences. There are many new studies that seem to confirm certain tribal practices as reasonable and sometimes even as sophisticated techniques for handling certain kinds of problems. It might be sufficient to show that these patterns of behavior are indicative of a consistent attitude toward the world and includes the knowledge that everything is alive and related.

Sacred places are the foundation of all other beliefs and practices because they represent the presence of the sacred in our lives. They properly inform us that we are not larger than nature and that we have responsibilities to the rest of the natural world that transcend our own personal desires and wishes. This lesson must be learned by each generation; unfortunately the technology of industrial society always leads us in the other direction. Yet it is certain that as we permanently foul our planetary nest, we shall have to learn a most bitter lesson. There probably is not sufficient time for the non-Indian population to understand the meaning of sacred lands and incorporate the idea into their lives and practices. We can but hope that some protection can be afforded these sacred places before the world becomes wholly secular and is destroyed.

Part II

Shapes: Narrative

NARRATIVE

No one can resist a good story. Perhaps even it is one of the identifying marks of the species to organize our perceptions through narrative. A narrative is basically the story of an action with a beginning, middle, and an end, and told or narrated, rather than presented by actors on a stage. This action does not have to be told from beginning to end—in fact, most stories are NOT told in chronological order. Horace's *Ars Poetica* instructs poets to start stories *in medias res*, "in the middle of things," not *ab ovo*, or "from the egg." Horace is wittily referring to the way Homer starts the *Iliad* with a fight—not on the battlefield but in council—nine years into the Trojan War. The egg reference takes us back to the birth of Helen, after the rape of Leda by Zeus in the form of a swan (another story), and Helen is called by some storytellers the cause of the Trojan War.

But that is not Homer's story, and one of the endless attractions of stories is that the way they are told, the point of view that shapes or frames the story, is as important as the events and characters. Homer's point of view is not particularly concerned with the causes of the war—Helen or something else—but with the effects of Achilleus's anger at Agamemnon's slighting of his contribution to the siege of Troy. Homer's story is not an attempt to provide a history or an explanation of the conflict between the Greeks and Trojans, although archeologists discovered that many of the details in Homer's epic have a historical validity once denied the poem. Homer wants to tell the story from the point of view of Achilleus's struggle with his sense of honor and his duty to his comrades, and the choice between a short life with fame, or a long life of relative obscurity. Even though Homer's tale involves ancient heroes and a conflict we know very little about (outside his poem), over two millennia later we are enthralled with it.

The great stories enthrall us because they enable us see ourselves in a new way, whether it is through Dante's medieval allegory of one man's search for the right path after losing his way in the middle of a dark wood in the *Divine Comedy*, or Cervantes's early seventeenth-century comic tale of *Don Quixote*, a man whose obsessive reading leads him to substitute the world of chivalric romance for the much less attractive one that he lives in. Both of these works have not only entranced readers, but have inspired artists and composers to create works that reflect their response to these great narratives. These responses are revealing, because great stories cannot be reduced to a plot summary, or an analysis: the best response may be another work of art. Art, and music, and literature may be the only way of presenting some truths that are central to the human experience. In this way, a great story has to be experienced, to be heard just like music, or seen, like visual art. We are entertained and instructed—the *dulce et utile* ("sweet and useful") that Horace states is the hallmark of good literature—and are led to understand more completely who we are—as a species and individually. Some of these characters or figures represent struggles that humans of all times have had, and they have become enduring types of human identity. The psychologist Karl Jung coined the term archetypes for literary characters that have this special resonance, but that is yet another story in the long and wonderful list of what you want to read next.

James A. Koger, Ph.D.
Professor of English

THE EPIC OF GILGAMESH

ca. 2500-1500 B.C.E.

ANONYMOUS

The Epic of Gilgamesh is a story of adventure, travel, morality, and the search for knowledge. The world's first recorded epic, dating from the third millennium B.C.E., it pre-dates the *Iliad* and *Odyssey* of Homer by at least 1500 years. The epic tells of the legendary king of Uruk in ancient Mesopotamia (present day Iraq). Evidence exists that Gilgamesh was an historical figure from ca. 2600 B.C.E., when he was the fifth ruler in Uruk's First Dynasty. Through reverence for his status as a warrior and a diplomat and his charismatic demeanor, his story most probably became intertwined with mythology and local stories of heroic action. Gilgamesh is the greatest of the Mesopotamian heroes, and like later Greek heroes, he is described a demigod (part god and part man), whose tragedy lies in the eternal battle between divine will and human destiny. From his mother, the goddess Ninsun, he inherited strength; from his semi-divine father Lugalbanda, he inherited mortality. Portrayed in Mesopotamian sculpture as a powerful bearded warrior who struggles with lions, bulls, and monsters, his human failing was his weakness for and harassment of women, to the extent that the people raised a cry of grievance to the goddess Araru.

Enlil (or Ellil), the protector of the city Nippur, was the powerful and aggressive warrior god who, in duality, manifested in violent storms and brought about the growth of crops. Enlil controlled the fate of Gilgamesh. Enkidu, the wild animal-like man created from clay by Araru to oppose Gilgamesh, was the opposite of the hero in every way. Gilgamesh and Enkidu grappled and so impressed one another that Enkidu became Gilgamesh's companion in a great adventure and the search to obliterate evil from the world.

In "The Forest Journey," Gilgamesh and Enkidu set out to the forest of the west to find and kill the ferocious monster Humbaba (or Huwawa), who had been made guardian of the forest by Enlil. "The Forest Journey" can be interpreted on various levels—as history, adventure, and allegory. On the historical level, the forest, probably in northern Syria, was inhabited by tribes who fought to protect the cedars that were a source of timber for the construction of cities. As an adventure, it is the story of two heroes who seek fame in the face of untold obstacles. As an allegory, Humbaba represents the concept of evil that all humankind encounters and must overcome for civilization to continue. Gilgamesh and Enkidu triumph over evil, but because they have used the power and weapons of Shamash to destroy the agent of Enlil, they will suffer the consequences.

Source

Anonymous. *ca.* 2500-1500 B.C.E. "The Forest Journey." In *The Epic of Gilgamesh: An English Version with an Introduction.* Sandars, N. K., Trans. Baltimore: Penguin Books, 1964. 68-73.*

The Epic of Gilgamesh

2: The Forest Journey

ENLIL of the mountain, the father of the gods, had decreed the destiny of Gilgamesh. So Gilgamesh dreamed and Enkidu said, 'The meaning of the dream is this. The father of the gods has given

---

you kingship, such is your destiny, everlasting life is not your destiny. Because of this do not be sad at heart, do not be grieved or oppressed. He has given you power to bind and to loose, to be the darkness and the light of mankind. He has given you unexampled supremacy over the people, victory in battle from which no fugitive returns, in forays and assaults from which there is no going back. But do not abuse this power, deal justly with your servants in the palace, deal justly before Shamash.'

The lord Gilgamesh turned his thoughts to the Country of the Living; on the Land of Cedars the Lord Gilgamesh reflected. He said to his servant Enkidu, 'I have not established my name stamped on brick as my destiny decreed; therefore I will go to the country where the cedar is felled. I will set up my name in the place where the names of famous men are written, and where no man's name is yet written I will raise a monument to the gods.'

The eyes of Enkidu were full of tears and his heart was sick. He sighed bitterly and Gilgamesh met his eye and said, 'My friend, why do you sigh so bitterly?' But Enkidu opened his mouth and said, 'I am weak, my arms have lost their strength, the cry of sorrow sticks in my throat. Why must you set your heart on this enterprise?' Gilgamesh answered Enkidu, 'Because of the evil that is in the land, we will go to the forest and destroy the evil; for in the forest lives Humbaba whose name is "Hugeness," a ferocious giant.' But Enkidu sighed bitterly and said, 'When I went with the wild beasts ranging through the wilderness I discovered the forest; its length is ten thousand leagues in every direction. Enlil has appointed Humbaba to guard it and armed him in sevenfold terrors, terrible to all flesh is Humbaba. When he roars it is like the torrent of the storm, his breath is like fire, and his jaws are death itself. He guards the cedars so well that when the wild heifer stirs in the forest, though she is sixty leagues distant, he hears her. What man would willingly walk into that country and explore its depths? I tell you, weakness overpowers whoever goes near it: It is not an equal struggle when one fights with Humbaba; he is a great warrior, Gilgamesh, the watchman of the forest never sleeps.'

Gilgamesh replied: 'Where is the man who can clamber to heaven? Only the gods live for ever with glorious Shamash, but as

for us men, our days are numbered, our occupations are a breath
of wind. How is this, already you are afraid! I will go first although
I am your lord, and you may safely call out, "Forward, there is
nothing to fear!" Then if I fall I leave behind me a name that
endures; men will say of me, "Gilgamesh has fallen in fight with
ferocious Humbaba." Long after the child has been born in my
house, they will say it, and remember.' Enkidu spoke again to
Gilgamesh, 'O my lord, if you will enter that country, go first to
the hero Shamash, tell the Sun God, for the land is his. The country
where the cedar is cut belongs to Shamash.'

Gilgamesh took up a kid, white without spot, and a brown
one with it; he held them against his breast, and he carried them
into the presence of the sun. He took in his hand his silver sceptre
and he said to glorious Shamash, 'I am going to that country, O
Shamash, I am going; my hands supplicate, so let it be well with
my soul and bring me back to the quay of Uruk. Grant, I beseech,
your protection, and let the omen be good.' Glorious Shamash
answered, 'Gilgamesh, you are strong, but what is the Country of
the Living to you?'

'O Shamash, hear me, hear me, Shamash, let my voice be heard.
Here in the city man dies oppressed at heart, man perishes with
despair in his heart. I have looked over the wall and I see the bodies
floating on the river, and that will be my lot also. Indeed I know it
is so, for whoever is tallest among men cannot reach the heavens,
and the greatest cannot encompass the earth. Therefore I would
enter that country: because I have not established my name stamped
on brick as my destiny decreed, I will go to the country where the
cedar is cut. I will set up my name where the names of famous
men are written; and where no man's name is written I will raise a
monument to the gods.' The tears ran down his face and he said,
'Alas, it is a long journey that I must take to the Land of Humbaba.
If this enterprise is not to be accomplished, why did you move me,
Shamash, with the restless desire to perform it? How can I succeed
if you will not succour me? If I die in that country I will die without
rancour, but if I return I will make a glorious offering of gifts and
of praise to Shamash.'

So Shamash accepted the sacrifice of his tears; like the compassionate man he showed him mercy. He appointed strong allies for Gilgamesh, sons of one mother and stationed them in the mountain caves. The great winds he appointed: the north wind, the whirlwind, the storm and the icy wind, the tempest and the scorching wind. Like vipers, like dragons, like a scorching fire, like a serpent that freezes the heart, a destroying flood and the lightnings' fork, such were they and Gilgamesh rejoiced.

He went to the forge and said, 'I will give orders to the armourers; they shall cast us our weapons while we watch them.' So they gave orders to the armourers and the craftsmen sat down in conference. They went into the groves of the plain and cut willow and box-wood; they cast for them axes of nine score pounds, and great swords they cast with blades of six score pounds each one, with pommels and hilts of thirty pounds. They cast for Gilgamesh the axe 'Might of Heroes' and the bow of Anshan; and Gilgamesh was armed and Enkidu; and the weight of the arms they carried was thirty score pounds.

The people collected and the counsellors in the streets and in the market-place of Uruk; they came through the gate of seven bolts and Gilgamesh spoke to them in the market-place: 'I, Gilgamesh, go to see that creature of whom such things are spoken, the rumour of whose name fills the world. I will conquer him in his cedar wood and show the strength of the sons of Uruk, all the world shall know of it. I am committed to this enterprise: to climb the mountain, to cut down the cedar, and leave behind me an enduring name.' The counsellors of Uruk, the great market, answered him, 'Gilgamesh, you are young, your courage carries you too far, you cannot know what this enterprise means which you plan. We have heard that Humbaba is not like men who die, his weapons are such that none can stand against them; the forest stretches for ten thousand leagues in every direction; who would willingly go down to explore its depths? As for Humbaba, when he roars it is like the torrent of the storm, his breath is like fire and his jaws are death itself. Why do you crave to do this thing, Gilgamesh? It is no equal struggle when one fights with Humbaba.'

When he heard these words of the counsellors Gilgamesh looked at his friend and laughed, 'How shall I answer them; shall I say I am afraid of Humbaba, I will sit at home all the rest of my days?' Then Gilgamesh opened his mouth again and said to Enkidu, 'My friend, let us go to the Great Palace, to Egalmah, and stand before Ninsun the queen. Ninsun is wise with deep knowledge, she will give us counsel for the road we must go.' They took each other by the hand as they went to Egalmah, and they went to Ninsun the great queen. Gilgamesh approached, he entered the palace and spoke to Ninsun. 'Ninsun, will you listen to me; I have a long journey to go, to the Land of Humbaba, I must travel an unknown road and fight a strange battle. From the day I go until I return, till I reach the cedar forest and destroy the evil which Shamash abhors, pray for me to Shamash.'

Ninsun went into her room, she put on a dress becoming to her body, she put on jewels to make her breast beautiful, she placed a tiara on her head and her skirts swept the ground. Then she went up to the altar of the Sun, standing upon the roof of the palace; she burnt incense and lifted her arms to Shamash as the smoke ascended: 'O Shamash, why did you give this restless heart to Gilgamesh, my son; why did you give it? You have moved him and now he sets out on a long journey to the Land of Humbaba, to travel an unknown road and fight a strange battle. Therefore from the day that he goes till the day he returns, until he reaches the cedar forest, until he kills Humbaba and destroys the evil thing which you, Shamash, abhor, do not forget him; but let the dawn, Aya your dear bride, remind you always, and when day is done give him to the watchman of the night to keep him from harm.' Then Ninsun the mother of Gilgamesh extinguished the incense, and she called to Enkidu with this exhortation: 'Strong Enkidu, you are not the child of my body, but I will receive you as my adopted son; you are my other child like the foundlings they bring to the temple. Serve Gilgamesh as a foundling serves the temple and the priestess who reared him. In the presence of my women, my votaries and hierophants, I declare it.' Then she placed the amulet for a pledge round his neck, and she said to him, 'I entrust my son to you; bring him back to me safely.'

HERODOTUS

484-425/420 B.C.E.

THE HISTORY

440 B.C.E.

Herodotus, born as a Persian subject in the colony of Halicarnassus, Asia Minor, is now considered the "father of history," by virtue of *The History*, the first example of unified historical prose narrative based on strict chronology and causation. A member of a wealthy family, Herodotus was exiled from Halicarnassus for taking part in a conspiracy against Persian rule. He spent time on Samos and traveled in Europe, Africa along the Nile, and Asia Minor, including Babylonia and Syria, all the while collecting material. He later took part in the liberation of Halicarnassus.

Herodotus used personal observation and Homeric devices to capture the attention of his intended audience. His introduction and lengthy digressions serve as footnotes and citations to the narrative through which he relates events and the dramatic speeches that provide further explanation. According to legend, he read his work to the assembled gods at Olympia; the nine books of *The History* were honored with the names of the nine Muses.

The first books of *The History* deal with the history and cultures of ancient peoples. The later books document the 5th-century B.C.E. wars between Greece and Persia, the western and eastern centers of what was then assumed to be the world. His accounts traces the conflict back to mythical times. In Book VIII, "Urania," Herodotus continues his narrative of Xerxes, the Persian king, and his ill-fated invasion of Greece. Xerxes's advance was halted at Athens in a battle at sea. The Persian army, beset with hunger and disease, retreated to Asia for the second time in ten years. The Greeks celebrated by making offerings to the gods, building monuments, and distributing the spoils of war.

After the vast loot was dispersed to the Greeks, each man voted first for himself as having shown the most merit in war and second for Themistocles, who had provoked the battle at sea and who ultimately received the most nominations for the prize of valor. But envy hindered a final decision and the assembled Greeks sailed home to Athens without awarding the prize. Themistocles went to Lacedaemon in Sparta, in the hope of being honored there, and was given a crown of olive and the most beautiful chariot in Sparta. On his return to Athens, however, the merit of his honor was questioned by one of his enemies, who claimed it was the fame of Athens that won him honor.

SOURCE

Herodotus. 440 B.C.E. *The History.* Book VIII,"Urania" (§§ 113-125). Henry Cary, Trans. (Baehr text). London: Routledge, 1892. 435-439.

THE HISTORY

§113. The army with Xerxes having stayed a few days after the sea-fight, marched back into Boeotia[1] by the same way, for it appeared to Mardonius [Xerxes's general], both that he should escort the king, and that the season of the year was unfit for military operations; and that it would be better to winter in Thessaly,[2] and to make an attempt on the Peloponnesus early in the spring. When

---

[1]   Central area of ancient Greece

[2]   Greek city-state

he arrived in Thessaly, Mardonius there selected, first, all the Persians who are called Immortals, except Hydarnes their general, for he declared he would not leave the king; after these, out of the rest of the Persians, the cuirassiers,[3] and the body of a thousand horse, and the Medes, Sacae, Bactrians, and Indians, both infantry and cavalry; he chose these whole nations; but from the rest of the allies he selected a few, choosing such as were of a good stature, or by whom he knew some gallant action had been performed. Amongst them, he chose the greatest part of the Persians, who wore necklaces and bracelets; next to them, the Medes; these were not less numerous than the Persians, but were inferior in strength. Thus the whole together, with the cavalry, made up the number of three hundred thousand.

§114. At this time, while Mardonius was selecting his army, and Xerxes was in Thessaly, an oracle came to the Lacedaemonians[4] from Delphi, *admonishing them* to demand satisfaction of Xerxes for the death of Leonidas, and to accept whatever should be given by him. Accordingly, the Spartans immediately despatched a herald as quickly as possible, who when he overtook the whole army still in Thessaly, having come into the presence of Xerxes, spoke as follows: "King of the Medes, the Lacedaemonians and Heraclidae of Sparta demand of you satisfaction for blood, because you have slain their king, while protecting Greece." But he laughing, and having waited a considerable time, as Mardonius happened to be standing near him, pointed to him, and said, "This Mardonius, then, shall give them such satisfaction as they deserve." The herald, having accepted the omen, went away.

§115. Xerxes, having left Mardonius in Thessaly, himself marched in all haste to the Hellespont; and arrived at the place of crossing in forty-five days, bringing back no part of his army so to speak. Wherever, and among whatever nation, they happened to be marching, they seized and consumed their corn; but if they found no fruit, overcome by hunger, they eat up the herbage that

---

3   mounted soldiers wearing armor

4   Spartans

sprung up from the ground, and stripped off the bark of trees and gathered leaves, both from the wild and cultivated, and left nothing; this they did from hunger, But a pestilence and dysentery falling on the army, destroyed them on their march. Such of them as were sick, Xerxes left behind, ordering the cities through which he happened to be passing, to take care of and feed them: some in Thessaly, others at Siris of Paeonia, and in Macedonia. Here having left the sacred chariot of Jupiter, when he marched against Greece, he did not receive it back, as he returned; for the Paeonians having given it to the Thracians, when Xerxes demanded it back, said that the mares had been stolen, as they were feeding, by the upper Thracians, who dwell round the sources of the Strymon.

§116. There the king of the Bisaltae and of the Crestonian territory, a Thracian, perpetrated a most unnatural deed: he declared that he would not willingly be a slave to Xerxes, but went up to the top of Mount Rhodope, and enjoined his sons not to join the expedition against Greece. They, however, disregarding his prohibition, from a desire to see the war, served in the army with the Persian; but when they all returned safe, being six in number, their father had their eyes put out for this disobedience; and they met with this recompence.

§117. The Persians, when in their march from Thrace[5] they arrived at the passage, in great haste crossed over the Hellespont[6] to Abydos in their ships; for they found the rafts no longer stretched across, but broken up by a storm. While detained there, they got more food than on their march, and having filled themselves immoderately, and changed their water, a great part of the army that survived, died: the rest with Xerxes reached Sardis.[7]

§118. This different account is also given, that when Xerxes in his retreat from Athens arrived at Eïon on the Strymon, from thence he no longer continued his journey by land, but committed the army to Hydarnes to conduct to the Hellespont, and himself going

---

[5]   An empire north of Greece

[6]   Dardanelles, the strait between the Aegean Sea and the Sea of Marmara

[7]   ancient kingdom of Lydia in Asia Minor

on board a Phoenician ship passed over to Asia: that during his voyage a violent and tempestuous wind from the Strymon overtook him; and then, for the storm increased in violence, the ship being overloaded, so that many of the Persians, who accompanied Xerxes were on the deck, thereupon the king becoming alarmed, and calling aloud, asked the pilot if there were any hope of safety for them; and he said: "There is none, sire, unless we get rid of some of those many passengers." It is further related, that Xerxes, having heard this answer said: "O Persians, now let some among you show his regard for the king, for on you my safety seems to depend." That he spoke thus; and that they, having done homage, leapt into the sea; and that the ship being lightened, thus got save to Asia. *It is added*, that Xerxes immediately after he landed, did as follows: he presented the pilot with a golden crown, because he had saved the king's life; but ordered his head to be struck off, because he had occasioned the loss of many Persians.

§119. This latter story is told of the return of Xerxes, but appears to me not at all deserving of credit, either in other respects, nor as to this loss of the Persians; for if this speech had been made by the pilot to Xerxes, I should not find one opinion in ten thousand to deny that the king would have acted thus: that he would have send down into the hold of the ship those who were on deck, since they were Persians, and Persians of high rank, and would have thrown into the sea a number of rowers, who were Phoenicians, equal to that of the Persians. He, however, as I have before related, proceeding on the march with the rest of the army, returned to Asia.

§120. This also is a strong proof: it is known that Xerxes reached Abdera on his way back, and made an alliance of friendship with the people, and presented them with a golden scymetar,[8] and a gold embroidered tiara. And as the Abderites themselves say, saying what is by no means credible to me, he there for the first time loosened his girdle in his flight from Athens, as being at length in a place of safety. Abdera is situated nearer to the Hellespont than

---

[8]   scimitar: a saber

the Strymon and Eïon, whence they say he embarked on board the ship.

§121. Meanwhile the Greeks, finding they were not able to reduce Andros,[9] turned to Carystus, and having ravaged their country, returned to Salamis.[10] In the first place, then, they set apart first-fruits for the gods, and among other things, three Phoenician triremes;[11] one to be dedicated at the Isthmus, which was there in my time; a second at Sunium, and the third to Ajax, there at Salamis. After that, they divided the booty, and sent the first-fruits to Delphi, from which a statue was made, holding the beak of a ship in its hand, and twelve cubits in height; it stands in the place where is the golden statue of Alexander the Macedonian.

§122. The Greeks, having sent first-fruits to Delphi, inquired of the god in the name of all, if he had received sufficient and acceptable first-fruits: he answered, that from the rest of the Greeks he had, but not from the Æginetae;[12] of them he demanded an offering on account of their superior valour in the sea-fight at Salamis. The Æginetae, being informed of this, dedicated three golden stars, which are placed on a brazen mast in the corner, very near the bowl of Croesus.[13]

§123. After the division of the booty, the Greeks sailed to the Isthmus, for the purpose of conferring the palm of valour upon him among the Greeks who had proved himself most deserving throughout the war. When the generals, having arrived, distributed the ballots at the altar of Neptune,[14] selecting the first and second out of all; thereupon every one gave his vote for himself, each thinking himself the most valiant; but with respect to the second place, the majority concurred in selecting Themistocles. They,

---

9   island near Greece

10   ancient city on island of Cyprus

11   ancient galleys having three banks of oars

12   citizens of an ancient state in southeast Greece

13   King Croesus of Lydia became proverbial for his wealth and the prosperity of his kingdom

14   god of the sea

therefore, had but one vote, whereas Themistocles had a great majority for the second honour.

§124. Though the Greeks, out of envy, would not determine this matter, but returned to their several countries without coming to a decision; yet Themistocles was applauded and extolled throughout all Greece, as being by far the wisest man of the Greeks. But because, although victorious, he was not honoured by those who fought at Salamis, he immediately afterwards went to Lacedaemon, hoping to be honoured there. The Lacedaemonians received him nobly, and paid him the greatest honours. They gave the prize of valour to Eurybiades, a crown of olive; and of wisdom and dexterity to Themistocles, to him also a crown of olive. And they presented him with the most magnificent chariot in Sparta; and having praised him highly, on his departure, three hundred chosen Spartans, the same that are called knights, escorted him as far as the Tegean boundaries. He is the only man that we know of whom the Spartans escorted on his journey.

§125. When he arrived at Athens, from Lacedaemon, thereupon Timodemus of Aphidnae, who was one of Themistocles' enemies, though otherwise a man of no distinction, became mad through envy, reproached Themistocles, alleging against him his journey to Lacedaemon; and that the honours he received from the Lacedaemonians were conferred on account of Athens, and not for his own sake. But he, as Timodemus did not cease to repeat the same thing, said: "The truth is, neither should I, were I a Belbinite, have been thus honoured by the Spartans; nor would you, fellow, were you an Athenian." So far, then, this occurred.

BHAGAVAD GITA, THE SONG CELESTIAL

400 B.C.E.

ANONYMOUS

Bhagavad Gîtâ is the non-sectarian doctrine of universal truth associated with Hinduism's scripture of Sanâtana Dharma. It narrates the quest for moral and spiritual growth, focusing on self-knowledge. Hinduism instructs that all lives, human and non-human, are sacred; non-violence (Ahimsa) is fundamental to this belief. The message of the *Bhagavad Gîtâ* arises out of Arjuna's unwillingness to do his duty as a warrior—to destroy and kill. The resulting discourse between Krishna, the Supreme Lord, and Arjuna, his devotee, takes place on the battlefield of Kurukshetra near New Delhi, *ca.* 3100 B.C.E., as recorded in the epic *Mahâbhârata*.

Krishna advises Arjuna to fight, while Arjuna is torn between duties—to fight for his ancestral kingdom of the Pândavs or to accept defeat in the name of peace and non-violence. Thus, Arjuna's personal struggle becomes a universal struggle between self-inquiry and self-knowledge. In Chapter XI: Arjuna becomes enlightened but thinks others may not accept Krishna as the cause of all causes. In order to prove Krishna's divinity, Arjuna entreats Krishna to reveal his universal form. Arjuna comes to realize that Krishna is speaking only for Arjuna's personal his illumination and that this is happening to him by Krishna's grace. He is now convinced that Krishna is present in everyone's heart—Krishna is the source of everything.

SOURCE

Anonymous. 400 B.C.E. *Bhagavad Gita, The Song Celestial.* "Chapter XI: Vision of the Deity as the Soul of the Universe." Mohini M. Chatterji, Ed. and Trans. Boston: Ticknor, 1887. 169-179.

BHAGAVAD GÎTÂ, THE SONG CELESTIAL

Chapter XI: Vision of the Deity as the Soul of the Universe

THE Blessed Lord having declared, in the last chapter, that he holds the whole universe by one portion of his power, Arjuna begs to be favored with a vision of the way in which the Deity by His unsearchable power supports the whole universe; and his prayer is granted. In reality the Deity has no form; what prophets and pure-souled devotees see is the reflection, so to speak, of the incomprehensible Divine Majesty on the spiritual perception of man. Arjuna's vision recalls the visions of Moses, Isaiah, Ezekiel, and Saint John. The mysterious and symbolical import of these spiritual experiences is not perceived by the spiritually blind, who in consequence fall into the most degrading superstitions.

ARJUNA *said*:

1. By the words supreme, and relating to the mystery of the Spirit, by thee spoken, has this, my delusion, been removed.

2. By me have been heard from thee in full the origin and end of things, O thou with eyes like the lotus-leaf, as also the exhaustless majesty.

3. O Supreme God, it is even as thou flayest of thyself. I long to see thy Divine form, O Supreme Spirit.

4. O Lord, if thou thinkest it possible to be seen by me, then show me, O King of all mystics, thy exhaustless Self.

THE BLESSED LORD *spoke*:

5. O son of Prithâ, behold my forms, by hundreds and by thousands, of many varieties, divine, and of many colors, and with many limbs.

6. Behold the Vasus, the Rudras, the Açvins, and also the Maruts, O son of Bharata; behold many and wonderful things never seen before.

7. Here, in my body, behold to-day, O Gudâkeça, the whole universe, animate and inanimate, in one place contained, and every other thing that thou wishest to see.

8. But thou art not able to see Me with these thine own eyes. I shall give thee the eye divine; behold my power as God.

SANJAYA *said*:

9. O King, having said this, Hari the lord of great and mysterious power, showed to the son of Prithâ the Supreme form Divine.

The Deity has no form in reality, but by reason of His unsearchable powers He appears to have infinity of forms and attributes. Among such forms, that seen by Arjuna is the highest.

10. With many mouths and eyes, with many marvels, with many divine ornaments, with many divine weapons raised,

11. Wearing divine garlands, and garments, with divine perfumes and ornaments, full of what is wonderful to all, the universe-faced infinite Lord.

12. The splendor of that great Soul may haply be likened to the radiance of a thousand suns risen at once in the heavens.

13. Then Pându's son beheld, seated in one place, in the body of the God of gods, the whole universe, in many forms varied.

14. Then Dhananjaya, overcome with wonder, and hair standing on end with joy, bowing down with his head to the Deity, spoke with joined palms.

ARJUNA *said*:

15. O God, in thy body I behold all the gods, the assemblage of things of every kind, the lord Brahmâ seated on his lotus-seat, and all of the sages and uragas[1] divine.

16. I behold thee on all sides, with infinite forms, with many arms, stomachs, mouths, and eyes. O Lord of the universe, O Universe-formed, thy end, nor middle, nor again thy beginning do I see.

17. Thee, with diadem, mace, and discus, the mass of splendor, on all sides refulgent, do I behold, so difficult to behold, immeasurable, on all thy sides the majesty of burning fire and sun.

18. Thou art the exhaustless, supreme goal of knowledge; thou art the supreme support of this universe; thou art changeless, the protector of the unchanging law of righteousness; thou art the Eternal Spirit,—this is my faith.

19. Devoid of beginning, middle, and end, with power infinite, with infinite numbers of arms, with sun and moon as eyes, I behold thee, with burning-fire-mouth, and with thy majesty oppressing the universe.

20. Heaven and earth and space between are filled by thee alone, as also the sides, every one. Seeing this thy marvellous form of terror, the worlds three are afflicted, O thou great Soul.

21. This concourse of gods enters into thee, and some in fear I chant praise with joined palms, the assemblage of great sages and perfect beings, saying "Svasti," behold and glorify thee with perfect hymns.

22. The Rudras, the Adityas, the Vasus, and they called the Sâdhyas, the Viçvadevas, the Açvins, the Maruts, and the Ushmapâs the Gandharvas, the Yakshas, the Asuras, and the assemblage of the Siddhas all behold thee in wonder.[2]

---

[1] "Uragas" are an order of celestial beings who possess great wisdom, usually understood to be in some way connected with serpents.

[2] These various groups are all orders of celestial beings.

23. O Thou of mighty arms, beholding thy form immense, with many mouths and eyes, with many arms, thighs, and feet, many stomachs and many twisted tusks, all beings are trembling with fear, and so am I.

24. Seeing thee, sky-touching, with many resplendent limbs, with gaping mouths, my heart oppressed with terror, I know not self-possession nor can I gain calmness of spirit, O Vishnu.

25. Beholding thy faces like the fire of destruction, and frightful to behold, owing to tusks, neither do I know the points of heaven, nor had I gained peace. Be gracious, O Lord of gods, O Support of the universe.

26. All these sons of Dhritarâshtra, together with this assemblage of the rulers of earth, Bhîshma, Drona, as also Karna, together with the chief among warriors on our side,

27. Impetuously are rushing into thy mouths, terrible and preternatural owing to the tusks. Some are seen, caught between thy teeth, with their heads crushed.

28. As the many-watered rush of rivers flows ever towards the ocean, so these heroes of this mortal sphere enter into thy mouths, on all sides burning.

29. As moths, with impetuosity excited, enter for destruction into the flaming fire, even so do these creatures, for destruction, enter into thy mouths with collected impetuosity.

30. Whilst swallowing on all sides, with flaming mouths, thou relishest all these creatures assembled filling the whole universe with thy splendor, thy cruel flames oppress with heat, O Vishnu.

31. Declare unto me who is this terrible form of thine. Salutation to thee, O Greatest of gods! Be gracious! I seek to know thee, the primeval; I know not thy doing.

THE BLESSED LORD *spoke*:

32. Time I am, in fulness, the consumer of creatures, here at work for the destruction of creatures. Besides thee, the warriors in these divisions shall not be.

33. Therefore stand thou up, gain fame; conquering enemies, enjoy foeless empire; even before, by me they have been slain; be thou but the instrument, O thou both-handed.

34. Drona, Bhîsma and Jayadratha, Karna, as well as the other heroic warriors, by me slain, conquer thou; lose not heart, fight; thou art the conqueror of enemies in war.

SANJAYA *said:*

35. Hearing these words of Keçava, with palms joined and in tremor, bowing down to Krishna, again spoke the diademed hero with faltering voice, again and again frightened and bowing down.

ARJUNA *said*:

36. Verily it is so, O Hrishikeça; by thy glorification the universe rejoices and shows love to thee; the evil spirits, frightened, flee in all directions, and all the assembled perfect men bow down to thee.

37. O Great soul, why should they not bow down to thee, greater even than Brahmâ, the first maker, O Eternal, O Lord of gods, O Abode of the universe. Thou art the aught and naught, the exhaustless essence that is beyond.

38. Thou art the primeval God, the ancient Spirit; thou art the supreme place of extinction of this universe; thou art the knower, thou art the known, as also the supreme abode; O thou infinite-formed, by thee this universe is filled.

39. The gods, Wind, Death, Fire, Water, and Moon, the ancient progenitor thou art, as also the great-grand-father. Salutation, salutation be unto thee, thousand-fold and again and again salutation, salutation unto thee!

40. Salutation in the east, and salutation also behind, O thou All; salutation in all directions; thou art of infinite valor and immeasurable power; thou pervadest all things and hence art All.

41. By me, not knowing this thy majesty, whatever lowering to thee has been said, either in thoughtlessness or in love,—such as, "O Krishna, O Yadu's son, O friend,"

42. And whatever unmeet treatment thou hast received in walking, bed, seat, and eating, for the purpose of jest, whether in thy presence or absence,—this I beg thee, the immeasurable, to forgive.

43. Of this universe, animate and inanimate, thou art the father and the object of adoration, the greatest of the great. There is none

equal unto thee, how can there be a superior, O Thou with majesty unimaged in the three worlds?

44. The bowing down, and holding the body so low, thee, O Lord, I Pray for grace; forgive, O Lord, as forgives the father the son, the friend the friend, and the lover the beloved.

45. Having seen what was never seen before, I am joyful, and yet my heart is afflicted with terror; show me that form, O God, be gracious, O Lord of gods and abode of the universe.

46. With diadem and mace in thy hand, I desire to see thee as before. O Thou of a thousand arms, of that form with four arms become Thou, O Universe-formed.

The Blessed Lord *spoke*:

47. By me, full of grace, this my supreme form, all-refulgent, all-embracing, infinite primeval, that has been shown to thee by my mysterious power, has not before been seen by any other.

48. Neither by study of Vedas, nor the practical knowledge of sacrifices, nor through gifts, nor works, nor frightful austerities, thus in form am able to be seen by any but thee, O best of Kuru's sons.

Thou hast seen me in this form only through my grace, and no one not similarly favored can ever see this form.

49. Let there be no affliction for thee, nor down-heartedness; having thus seen this, my form of terror, this my previous form, behold again, with fear departed and joyous in heart.

Sanjaya *said*:

50. Then Vâsudeva, who thus speaking showed again his proper form to Arjuna. The great soul comforted him, the frightened one, by again becoming gentle-formed.

Arjuna *said*:

51. O Janârdana, having seen this thy gentle and human form, I am now become peaceful at heart and self-possessed.

THE BLESSED LORD *spoke*:

52. This my form, whose sight is so hard to obtain, that thou hast seen, even the gods are ever desirous of the sight of this form.

53. As seen by thee, I may not thus be seen by the study of the Vedas, nor by austere practices, nor by the making of gifts, nor by acts of worship.

54. By self-identifying devotion, indeed, as thus I may be known and seen in truth and entered into.

55. He that works but for me, for whom I am the supreme goal, who is devoted to me, devoid of zest in things,[3] and devoid of hostility, comes to me, O Pându's son.

> Thus ends chapter the eleventh, called the "Vision of the Deity as the Soul of the Universe" in the blessed Bhagavad Gîtâ, the sacred lore, the divine wisdom, the book of divine union, the colloquy between the blessed Krishna and Arjuna, and contained in the Bhîshma Parvan of the blessed Mahâbhârata, which is a collection of one hundred thousand verses by Vyâsa.

Salutation to Krishna
by devotion to whom is attainable the vision of his universe-form,
which even the gods long in vain to see.

---

[3] That is, being ready at any moment to part with the things of this world for the sake of the Lord.

FRANCESCO PETRARCH

1304-1374

"THE ASCENT OF MOUNT VENTOUX"

1336

Francesco Petrarch was born in Arezzo to a family in exile. In 1311, Petrarch's family moved to Pisa and, later, followed the Holy See to Avignon. Petrarch began his studies in Montpelier and in 1320 began to study law in Bologna. In 1326, he turned to the study of the classics, finishing his Minor Orders of the Catholic Church in 1330. He spent the remainder of his life in service to the Church, undertaking ambassadorial and diplomatic missions throughout Europe. In 1336, he began to compile *Rerum vulgarium fragmenta*. At the time of his death in 1374, it contained 366 poems and sonnets, many about his love for the mysterious Laura, believed to be Laura de Noves, the wife of Hugues II de Sade. Petrarch had two illegitimate children by two women, a son Giovanni who died of the plague in 1361 and a daughter Francesca. In 1340, Petrarch received invitations from Rome and Paris to accept the crown of poet laureate; in Rome, he called for the rebirth of classical wisdom and poetry. In keeping with his interest in the classics, he developed the idea of the laurel as a symbol of poetic immortality.

Petrarch spent many years traveling in service to the Church—his letters compare his travels with the spiritual journey. In 1343, Petrarch's brother became a Carthusian[1] monk, an event that caused Petrarch's re-examination of his faith. The result was *Secretum*, three imaginary conversations with St. Augustine. He also began to keep his own letters to, among others, kings, popes, and the ghost of Homer. The letter here selected, "The Ascent of Mount Ventoux," is considered a milestone of the new Humanistic spirit that marked the Renaissance. His motive is to see the view. Yet in a greater sense, it records allegorically a spiritual journey of "human contemplation" and the search for truth.

SOURCE

Petrarch, Francesco. 1336. "The Ascent of Mount Ventoux." In *Petrarch: The First Modern Scholar and Man of Letters.* James Harvey Robinson, Ed. and Trans. New York: Putnam, 1898. 307-320.

THE ASCENT OF MOUNT VENTOUX

A good deal has been written about Petrarch's famous ascent of Mount Ventoux. Körting assuredly exaggerates its significance when he declares it "an epoch-making deed" which would by itself substantiate Petrarch's title to be called the first modern man. The reader will observe that, however modern may have been the spirit in which the excursion was undertaken, the relapse into mediæval perversity was speedy and complete. As we shall find, Petrarch had no sooner reached the top than he bethought himself of his Augustine, before whose stern dictum the wide landscape quickly lost its fascination. [-JHR.]

---

[1] an order of austere, contemplative monks

The Ascent of Mount Ventoux.
To Dionisio da Borgo San Sepolcro.[2]

To-day I made the ascent of the highest mountain in this region, which is not improperly called Ventosum [windy]. My only motive was the wish to see what so great an elevation had to offer. I have had the expedition in mind for many years; for, as you know, I have lived in this region from infancy, having been cast here by that fate which determines the affairs of men. Consequently the mountain, which is visible from a great distance, was ever before my eyes, and I conceived the plan of some time doing what I have at last accomplished to-day. The idea took hold upon me with especial force when, in re-reading Livy's *History of Rome*, yesterday, I happened upon the place where Philip of Macedon, the same who waged war against the Romans, ascended Mount Hæmus in Thessaly, from whose summit he was able, it is said, to see two seas, the Adriatic and the Euxine. Whether this be true or false I have not been able to determine, for the mountain is too far away, and writers disagree. Pomponius Mela, the cosmographer—not to mention others who have spoken of this occurrence—admits its truth without hesitation; Titus Livius, on the other hand, considers it false. I, assuredly, should not have left the question long in doubt, had that mountain been as easy to explore as this one. Let us leave this matter one side, however, and return to my mountain here,—it seems to me that a young man in private life may well be excused for attempting what an aged king could undertake without arousing criticism.

When I came to look about for a companion I found, strangely enough, that hardly one among my friends seemed suitable, so rarely do we meet with just the right combination of personal tastes and characteristics, even among those who are dearest to us. This one was too apathetic, that one over-anxious; this one too

---

[2]   This letter, written when Petrarch was about thirty-two years old, is addressed to an Augustinian monk and professor of divinity and philosophy in the University of Paris.

slow, that one too hasty; one was too sad, another over-cheerful; one more simple, another more sagacious, than I desired. I feared this one's taciturnity and that one's loquacity. The heavy deliberation of some repelled me as much as the lean incapacity of others. I rejected those who were likely to irritate me by a cold want of interest, as well as those who might weary me by their excessive enthusiasm. Such defects, however grave, could be borne with at home, for charity suffereth all things, and friendship accepts any burden; but it is quite otherwise on a journey, where every weakness becomes much more serious. So, as I was bent upon pleasure and anxious that my enjoyment should be unalloyed, I looked about me with unusual care, balanced against one another the various characteristics of my friends, and without committing any breach of friendship I silently condemned every trait which might prove disagreeable on the way. And would you believe it?— I finally turned homeward for aid, and proposed the ascent to my only brother, who is younger than I, and with whom you are well acquainted. He was delighted and gratified beyond measure by the thought of holding the place of a friend as well as of a brother.

At the time fixed we left the house, and by evening reached Malaucène, which lies at the foot of the mountain, to the north. Having rested there a day, we finally made the ascent this morning, with no companions except two servants; and a most difficult task it was. The mountain is a very steep and almost inaccessible mass of stony soil. But, as the poet has well said, "Remorseless toil conquers all." It was a long day, the air fine. We enjoyed the advantages of vigour of mind and strength and agility of body, and everything else essential to those engaged in such an undertaking, and so had no other difficulties to face than those of the region itself. We found an old shepherd in one of the mountain dales, who tried, at great length, to dissuade us from the ascent, saying that some fifty years before he had, in the same ardour of youth, reached the summit, but had gotten for his pains nothing except fatigue and regret, and clothes and body torn by the rocks and briars. No one, so far as he or his companions knew, had ever tried the ascent before or after him. But his counsels increased rather than diminished our desire to proceed, since youth is suspicious of warnings. So the old man, finding that his efforts were in vain, went a little way with us, and pointed out a rough path among the rocks, uttering many admonitions, which he continued to send after us even after we had left him behind. Surrendering to him all such garments or other possessions as might prove burdensome to us, we made ready for the ascent, and started off at a good pace. But, as usually happens, fatigue quickly followed upon our excessive exertion, and we soon came to a halt at the top of a certain cliff. Upon starting on again we went more slowly, and I especially advanced along the rocky way with a more deliberate step. While my brother chose a direct path straight up the ridge, I weakly took an easier one which really descended. When I was called back, and the right road was shown me, I replied that I hoped to find a better way round on the other side, and that I did not mind going farther if the path were only less steep. This was just an excuse for my laziness; and when the others had already reached a considerable height I was still wandering in the valleys. I had failed to find an easier path, and had only increased the distance and difficulty of the ascent. At last I became disgusted with the intricate way I had chosen, and resolved to ascend without more ado. When I reached my brother, who, while waiting for me, had had ample opportunity for rest, I was tired and irritated. We walked along together for a time, but hardly had we passed the first spur when I forgot about the circuitous route which I had just tried, and took a lower one again. Once more I followed an easy, roundabout path through winding valleys, only to find myself soon in my old difficulty. I was simply trying to avoid the exertion of the ascent; but no human ingenuity can alter the nature of things, or cause anything to reach a height by going down. Suffice it to say that, much to my vexation and my brother's amusement, I made this same mistake three times or more during a few hours.

After being frequently misled in this way, I finally sat down in a valley and transferred my winged thoughts from things corporeal to the immaterial, addressing myself as follows:—"What thou hast repeatedly experienced to-day in the ascent of this mountain, happens to thee, as to many, in the journey toward the blessed life. But this is not so readily perceived by men, since the motions of the body are obvious and external while those of the soul are invisible and hidden. Yes, the life which we call blessed is to be sought for on a high eminence, and strait is the way that leads to it. Many, also, are the hills that lie between, and we must ascend, by a glorious stairway, from strength to strength. At the top is at once the end of our struggles and the goal for which we are bound. All wish to reach this goal, but, as Ovid says, 'To wish is little; we must long with the utmost eagerness to gain our end.' Thou certainly dost ardently desire, as well as simply wish, unless thou deceivest thyself in this matter, as in so many others. What, then, doth hold thee back? Nothing, assuredly, except that thou wouldst take a path which seems, at first thought, more easy, leading through low and worldly pleasures. But nevertheless in the end, after long wanderings, thou must perforce either climb the steeper path, under the burden of tasks foolishly deferred, to its blessed culmination, or lie down in the valley of thy sins, and (I shudder to think of it!), if the shadow of death overtake thee, spend an eternal night amid constant torments." These thoughts stimulated both body and mind in a wonderful degree for facing the difficulties which yet remained. Oh, that I might traverse in spirit that other road for which I long day and night, even as to-day I overcame material obstacles by my bodily exertions! And I know not why it should not be far easier, since the swift immortal soul can reach its goal in the twinkling of an eye, without passing through space, while my progress to-day was necessarily slow, dependent as I was upon a failing body weighed down by heavy members.

One peak of the mountain, the highest of all, the country people call "Sonny," why, I do not know, unless by antiphrasis, as I have sometimes suspected in other instances; for the peak in question would seem to be the father of all the surrounding ones. On its top is a little level place, and here we could at last rest our tired bodies.

Now, my father, since you have followed the thoughts that spurred me on in my ascent, listen to the rest of the story, and

devote one hour, I pray you, to reviewing the experiences of my
entire day. At first, owing to the unaccustomed quality of the air
and the effect of the great sweep of view spread out before me, I
stood like one dazed. I beheld the clouds under our feet, and what
I had read of Athos and Olympus seemed less incredible as I myself
witnessed the same things from a mountain of less fame. I turned
my eyes toward Italy, whither my heart most inclined. The Alps,
rugged and snow-capped, seemed to rise close by, although they
were really at a great distance; the very same Alps through which
that fierce enemy of the Roman name once made his way, bursting
the rocks, if we may believe the report, by the application of vinegar.
I sighed, I must confess, for the skies of Italy, which I beheld rather
with my mind than with my eyes. An inexpressible longing came
over me to see once more my friend and my country. At the same
time I reproached myself for this double weakness, springing, as it
did, from a soul not yet steeled to manly resistance. And yet there
were excuses for both of these cravings, and a number of
distinguished writers might be summoned to support me.

Then a new idea took possession of me, and I shifted my thoughts
to a consideration of time rather than place. "To-day it is ten years
since, having completed thy youthful studies, thou didst leave
Bologna. Eternal God! In the name of immutable wisdom, think
what alterations in thy character this intervening period has beheld!
I pass over a thousand instances. I am not yet in a safe harbour
where I can calmly recall past storms. The time may come when I
can review in due order all the experiences of the past, saying with
St. Augustine, 'I desire to recall my foul actions and the carnal
corruption of my soul, not because I love them, but that I may the
more love thee, O my God.' Much that is doubtful and evil still
clings to me, but what I once loved, that I love no longer. And yet
what am I saying? I still love it, but with shame, but with heaviness
of heart. Now, at last, I have confessed the truth. So it is. I love, but
love what I would not love, what I would that I might hate. Though
loath to do so, though constrained, though sad and sorrowing, still
I do love, and I feel in my miserable self the truth of the well known
words, 'I will hate if I can; if not, I will love against my will.' Three

years have not yet passed since that perverse and wicked passion which had a firm grasp upon me and held undisputed sway in my heart began to discover a rebellious opponent, who was unwilling longer to yield obedience. These two adversaries have joined in close combat for the supremacy, and for a long time now a harassing and doubtful war has been waged in the field of my thoughts."

Thus I turned over the last ten years in my mind, and then, fixing my anxious gaze on the future, I asked myself, "If, perchance, thou shouldst prolong this uncertain life of thine for yet two lustres, and shouldst make an advance toward virtue proportionate to the distance to which thou hast departed from thine original infatuation during the past two years, since the new longing first encountered the old, couldst thou, on reaching thy fortieth year, face death, if not with complete assurance, at least with hopefulness, calmly dismissing from thy thoughts the residuum of life as it faded into old age?"

These and similar reflections occurred to me, my father. I rejoiced in my progress, mourned my weaknesses, and commiserated the universal instability of human conduct. I had well-nigh forgotten where I was and our object in coming; but at last I dismissed my anxieties, which were better suited to other surroundings, and resolved to look about me and see what we had come to see. The sinking sun and the lengthening shadows of the mountain were already warning us that the time was near at hand when we must go. As if suddenly wakened from sleep, I turned about and gazed toward the west. I was unable to discern the summits of the Pyrenees, which form the barrier between France and Spain; not because of any intervening obstacle that I know of but owing simply to the insufficiency of our mortal vision. But I could see with the utmost clearness, off to the right, the mountains of the region about Lyons, and to the left the bay of Marseilles and the waters that lash the shores of Aigues Mortes, altho' all these places were so distant that it would require a journey of several days to reach them. Under our very eyes flowed the Rhone.

While I was thus dividing my thoughts, now turning my attention to some terrestrial object that lay before me, now raising my soul, as I had done my body, to higher planes, it occurred to me to look into my copy of St. Augustine's *Confessions*, a gift that I owe to your love, and that I always have about me, in memory of both the author and the giver. I opened the compact little volume, small indeed in size, but of infinite charm, with the intention of reading whatever came to hand, for I could happen upon nothing that would be otherwise than edifying and devout. Now it chanced that the tenth book presented itself. My brother, waiting to hear something of St. Augustine's from my lips, stood attentively by. I call him, and God too, to witness that where I first fixed my eyes it was written: "And men go about to wonder at the heights of the mountains, and the mighty waves of the sea, and the wide sweep of rivers, and the circuit of the ocean, and the revolution of the stars, but themselves they consider not." I was abashed, and, asking my brother (who was anxious to hear more), not to annoy me, I closed the book, angry with myself that I should still be admiring earthly things who might long ago have learned from even the pagan philosophers that nothing is wonderful but the soul, which when great itself, finds nothing great outside itself. Then, in truth, I was satisfied that I had seen enough of the mountain; I turned my inward eye upon myself, and from that time not a syllable fell from my lips until we reached the bottom again. Those words had given me occupation enough, for I could not believe that it was by a mere accident that I happened upon them. What I had there read I believed to be addressed to me and to no other remembering that St. Augustine had once suspected the same thing in his own case, when, on opening the book of the Apostle, as he himself tells us, the first words that he saw there were, "Not in rioting and drunkenness, not in chambering and wanton-ness, not in strife and envying. But put ye on the Lord Jesus Christ, and make not provision for the flesh, to fulfil the lusts thereof."

The same thing happened earlier to St. Anthony, when he was listening to the Gospel where it is written, "If thou wilt be perfect, go and sell that thou hast, and give to the poor, and thou shalt have treasure in heaven: and come and follow me." Believing this scripture to have been read for his especial benefit, as his biographer

Athanasius says, he guided himself by its aid to the Kingdom of Heaven. And as Anthony on hearing these words waited for nothing more, and as Augustine upon reading the Apostle's admonition sought no farther, so I concluded my reading in the few words which I have given. I thought in silence of the lack of good counsel in us mortals, who neglect what is noblest in ourselves, scatter our energies in all directions, and waste ourselves in a vain show, because we look about us for what is to be found only within. I wondered at the natural nobility of our soul, save when it debases itself of its own free will, and deserts its original estate, turning what God has given it for its honour into dishonour. How many times, think you, did I turn back that day, to glance at the summit of the mountain, which seemed scarcely a cubit high compared with the range of human contemplation,—when it is not immersed in the foul mire of earth? With every downward step I asked myself this: If we are ready to endure so much sweat and labour in order that we may bring our bodies a little nearer heaven, how can a soul struggling toward God, up the steeps of human pride and human destiny, fear any cross or prison or sting of fortune? How few, I thought, but are diverted from their path by the fear of difficulties or the love of ease! How happy the lot of those few, if any such there be! It is of them, assuredly, that the poet was thinking, when he wrote:

> Happy the man who is skilled to understand
> Nature's hid causes; who beneath his feet
> All terrors casts, and death's relentless doom,
> And the loud roar of greedy Acheron.

How earnestly should we strive, not to stand on mountain-tops, but to trample beneath us those appetites which spring from earthly impulses.

With no consciousness of the difficulties of the way, amidst these preoccupations which I have so frankly revealed, we came, long after dark, but with the full moon lending us its friendly light, to the little inn which we had left that morning before dawn.

The time during which the servants have been occupied in preparing our supper, I have spent in a secluded part of the house, hurriedly jotting down these experiences on the spur of the moment lest, in case my task were postponed, my mood should change on leaving the place, and so my interest in writing flag.

You will see, my dearest father, that I wish nothing to be concealed from you, for I am careful to describe to you not only my life in general but even my individual reflections. And I beseech you, in turn, to pray that these vague and wandering thoughts of mine may some time become firmly fixed, and, after having been vainly tossed about from one interest to another, may direct themselves at last toward the single, true, certain, and everlasting good.

MALAUCÈNE, April 26.

MIGUEL DE CERVANTES

1547-1616

THE HISTORY OF DON QUIXOTE

1605 and 1615

Miguel de Cervantes Saavedra, a Spanish writer of poems, plays, and romances, is regarded by many to be the most important figure in Spanish literature as well as one of enormous impact in all literatures of Western culture. His most famous work is *El ingeniso hidalgo Don Quixote de la Mancha (The Ingenious Gentleman Don Quixote de La Mancha)* excerpted here though written in the early 17th century was recently produced very successfully as a Broadway musical, *Man of La Mancha*. *Don Quixote* is considered by some to be the first and greatest modern novel; it is a seminal work, which has continued to enrich literature, art, music, and dance.

According to tradition, Cervantes conceived of the idea for *Don Quixote* while in prison in Argamasilla in La Mancha, following a dispute with members of the local populace. A satire on chivalry, the novel was an immediate success and was soon translated into English and French, moving Cervantes to a preeminent position as a writer. *Don Quixote* mocks the novels of chivalry that glorified the ideals of constancy, bravery, and loyalty, with their stereotypical plots, heroic battles, and virtuous maidens. Set against the panorama of 17th century Spanish society, *Don Quixote* also a model of the picaresque novel, a story of a roving scoundrel (*picaro*) who engages in a series of adventures. First published in two parts in 1605 and 1615, it has since passed through many printings and pirated editions.

As evident here in Chapter 1, Don Quixote, in an attempt to show his contemporaries their failure to maintain the old system, tries to be an example of chivalry, morality, honor, and heroism. But he is neither understood by his contemporaries nor understanding of the new ways of society. The mediator is the self-motivated Sancho Panza. The conflict reaches an impasse when Don Quixote refuses to face facts. He clings to his dreams and chivalric ideals, no matter how preposterous his adventures. The novel ends when sanity returns and he renounces chivalry. In the process Don Quixote ceases to exist and the character dies, for he cannot live in a world whose values are so different from his own.

On one level, *Don Quixote* is a parody of the popular novels of Cervantes's time. On another, it portrays an historic code of honor threatened by war and the religious zealotry of the Inquisition, inundated with the riches of explorations and colonization, and stratified by a class structure based on nobility and property. On this level, the character of Don Quixote symbolizes the search for wisdom, integrity, and truth in a world where these values seem doomed.

Source

Saavedra, Miguel de Cervantes.1605 and 1615. *The History of Don Quixote.* "Part I. Chapter I." J.W. Clark, Ed. Charles Jarvis, Trans. New York: Hogarth, n.d. 1-5.

The History of Don Quixote

Chapter 1:
The Quality and Way of Living of the Renowned Don Quixote de la Mancha

At a certain village in La Mancha, of which I cannot remember the name, there lived not long ago one of those old-fashioned gentlemen who are never without a lance upon a rack, an old target, a lean horse, and a greyhound. Soup, more frequently of mutton than of beef, minced meats on most nights, lentiles on Fridays, griefs and groans on Saturdays, and a pigeon extraordinary on Sundays, consumed three-quarters of his revenue; the rest was laid out in a doublet of fine cloth, velvet breeches, with slippers of the same for holidays; and a suit of the very best homespun, which he bestowed on himself for working days. His whole family was a housekeeper something turned of forty, a niece not twenty, and a man that served him in the house and in the field, and could saddle a horse and handle the pruning-hook. The master himself was nigh fifty years of age, of a hale and strong complexion, lean-bodied, and thin-faced, an early riser and a lover of hunting. Some say his surname was Quixada, or Quesada (for authors differ in this particular); however, we may reasonably conjecture he was called Quixada (*i e.*, lantern-jaws), though this concerns us but little, provided we keep strictly to the truth in every point of this history.

You must know, then, that when our gentleman had nothing to do (which was almost all the year round), he passed his time in reading books of knight-errantry, which he did with that application and delight, that at last he in a manner wholly left off his country sports, and even the care of his estate: nay, he grew so strangely besotted with these amusements, that he sold many acres of arable land to purchase books of that kind, by which means he collected as many of them as were to be had; but, among them all, none pleased him like the works of the famous Feliciano de Sylva; for the clearness of his prose, and those intricate expressions with which it is interlaced, seemed to him so many pearls of eloquence, especially when he came to read the challenges, and the amorous addresses, many of them in this extraordinary style: "The reason of your unreasonable usage of my reason, does so enfeeble my reason, that I have reason to expostulate with your beauty." And this, "The sublime heavens, which with your divinity divinely fortify you with the stars, and fix you the deserver of the desert that is deserved by your grandeur." These, and such like expressions, strangely puzzled the poor gentleman's understanding, while he was breaking his brain to unravel their meaning, which Aristotle himself could never have found, though he should have been raised from the dead for that very purpose.

He did not so well like those dreadful wounds which Don Belianis gave and received; for he considered that all the art of surgery could never secure his face and body from being strangely disfigured with scars. However, he highly commended the author for concluding his book with a promise to finish that unfinishable adventure; and many times he had a desire to put pen to paper, and faithfully and literally finish it himself; which he had certainly done, and doubtless with good success, had not his thoughts been wholly engrossed in much more important designs.

He would often dispute with the curate of the parish, a man of learning, that had taken his degrees at Siguenza, who was the better knight, Palmerin of England, or Amadis de Gaul; but Master Nicholas, the barber of the same town, would say that none of them could compare with the Knight of the Sun; and that if any one came near him, it was certainly Don Galaor, the brother of Amadis de Gaul; for he was a man of a most commodious temper, neither was he so finical, nor such a puling, whining lover as his brother; and as for courage; he was not a jot behind him.

In fine, he gave himself up so wholly to the reading of romances, that a-nights he would pore on until it was day, and a-days he would read on until it was night; and thus by sleeping little, and reading much, the moisture of his brain was exhausted to that degree that at last he lost the use of his reason. A world of disorderly notions, picked out of his books, crowded into his imagination; and now his head was full of nothing but enchantments, quarrels, battles, challenges, wounds, complaints, amours, torments, and abundance of stuff and impossibilities; insomuch that all the fables and fantastical tales which he read seemed to him now as true as the most authentic histories. He would say that the Cid Ruy Diaz was a very brave knight, but not worthy to stand in competition with the Knight of the Burning Sword, who, with a single back-stroke, had cut in sunder two fierce and mighty giants. He liked yet better Bernardo del Carpio, who, at Roncesvalles, deprived of life the enchanted Orlando having lifted him from the ground, and choked him in the air, as Hercules did Antaeus, the son of the Earth.

As for the giant Morgante, he always spoke very civil things of him; for though he was one of that monstrous brood who ever were intolerably proud and brutish, he still behaved himself like a civil and well-bred person.

But of all men in the world he admired Rinaldo of Montalban, and particularly his sallying out of his castle to rob all he met; and then again his carrying away the idol of Mahomet, which was all massy gold, as the history says; but he so hated that traitor Galadon, that for the pleasure of kicking him handsomely, he would have given up his housekeeper; nay, and his niece into the bargain.

Having thus lost his understanding, he unluckily stumbled upon the oddest fancy that ever entered into a madman's brain; for now he thought it convenient and necessary, as well for the increase of his own honour, as the service of the public, to turn knight-errant, and roam through the whole world, armed cap-a-pie, and mounted on his steed, in quest of adventures; that thus imitating those knight-errants of whom he had read, and following their course of life, redressing all manner of grievances, and exposing himself to danger on all occasions, at last, after a happy conclusion of his enterprises, he might purchase everlasting honour and renown. Transported with these agreeable delusions, the poor gentleman already grasped in imagination the imperial sceptre of Trebizonde, and, hurried away by his mighty expectations, he prepares with all expedition to take the field.

The first thing he did was to scour a suit of armour that had belonged to his great-grandfather, and had lain time out of mind carelessly rusting in a corner; but when he had cleaned and repaired it as well as he could, he perceived there was a material piece wanting; for, instead of a complete helmet, there was only a single head-piece. However, his industry supplied that defect; for with some pasteboard he made a kind of half-beaver, or vizor, which, being fitted to the head-piece, made it look like an entire helmet.

Then, to know whether it were cutlass-proof, he drew his sword, and tried its edge upon the pasteboard vizor; but with the very first stroke he unluckily undid in a moment what he had been a whole week a-doing. He did not like its being broke with so much ease, and therefore, to secure it from the like accident, he made it anew, and fenced it with thin plates of iron, which he fixed on the inside of it so artificially that at last he had reason to be satisfied with the solidity of the work; and so, without any farther experiment, he resolved it should pass to all intents and purposes for a full and sufficient helmet.

In the next place, he went to view his horse, and though the animal had more blemishes than limbs, being a worse jade than Gonela's, *qui tantum pellis et ossa fuit*, his master thought that neither Alexander's Bucephalus, nor the Cid's Babieca, could be compared with him. He was four days considering what name to give him; for, as he argued with himself, there was no reason that a horse bestrid by so famous a knight, and withal so excellent in himself, should not be distinguished by a particular name; and therefore he studied to give him such a one as should demonstrate as well what kind of horse he had been before his master was a knight-errant, as what he was now; thinking it but just, since the owner changed his profession, that the horse should also change his title, and be dignified with another; a good big word, such a one as should fill the mouth, and seem consonant with the quality and profession of his master. And thus after many names which he devised, rejected, changed, liked, disliked, and pitched upon again, he concluded to call him Rozinante; a name, in his opinion, lofty, sounding, and significant of what he had been before, and also of what he was now: in a word, a horse before, or above, all the vulgar breed of horses in the world.

When he had thus given his horse a name so much to his satisfaction, he thought of choosing one for himself; and having seriously pondered on the matter eight whole days more, at last he determined to call himself Don Quixote. Whence the author of this most authentic history draws this inference, that his right name was Quixada, and not Quesada, as others obstinately pretend.

And observing that the valiant Amadis, not satisfied with the bare appellation of Amadis, added to it the name of his country, that it might grow more famous by his exploits, and so styled himself Amadis de Gaul; so he, like a true lover of his native soil, resolved to call himself Don Quixote de la Mancha; which addition, to his thinking, denoted very plainly his parentage and country, and consequently would fix a lasting honour on that part of the world.

And now, his armour being scoured, his headpiece improved to a helmet, his horse and himself new named, he perceived he wanted nothing but a lady, on whom he might bestow the empire of his heart; for he was sensible that a knight-errant without a mistress was a tree without either fruit or leaves, and a body without a soul. "Should I," said he to himself, "by good or ill fortune, chance to encounter some giant, as it is common in knight-errantry, and happen to lay him prostrate on the ground, transfixed with my lance, or cleft in two, or, in short, overcome him, and have him at my mercy, would it not be proper to have some lady to whom I may send him as a trophy of my valour? Then when he comes into her presence, throwing himself at her feet, he may thus make his humble submission:—'Lady, I am the giant Caraculiambro, lord of the island of Malindrania, vanquished in single combat by that never-deservedly enough extolled knight-errant Don Quixote de la Mancha, who has commanded me to cast myself most humbly at your feet, that it may please your honour to dispose of me according to your will.'" Oh! how elevated was the knight with the conceit of this imaginary submission of the giant; especially having withal bethought himself of a person on whom he might confer the title of his mistress! which, it is believed, happened thus:—Near the place where he lived, dwelt a good, likely country lass, for whom he had formerly had a sort of an inclination, though, it is believed, she never heard of it, nor regarded it in the least. Her name was Aldonza Lorenzo, and this was she whom he thought he might entitle to the sovereignty of his heart; upon which he studied to find her out a new name, that might have some affinity with her old one, and yet at the same time sound somewhat like that of a princess, or lady of quality; so at last he resolved to call her Dulcinea, with the addition of del Toboso, from the place where she was born; a name, in his opinion, sweet, harmonious, extraordinary, and no less significative than the others which he had devised.

PART III

SHAPES: DRAMA

DRAMA

Drama is a powerful path to self-knowledge and also teaches us about the people and places of past and present societies. Drama is living literature—it shows us the visual and aural conflict between opposing forces or people. We can identify with characters in dramatic literature, their struggles and desires, as they are acted out in front of us. Shakespeare's Hamlet gives advice to the Players about dramatic truth: "whose end, both at the first and now, was and is, to hold, as 'twere, the mirror up to nature . . ." (*Hamlet*, III. ii).

Drama reflects society, both past and present. In the truth we observe on stage we can be enlightened as we look at the serious nature of ourselves and others. Or we may be entertained, and perhaps even laugh at ourselves, as we recognize or imagine our foibles.

Most importantly, drama is best experienced by a communal body—the audience—bound together in the ephemeral images, words, and emotions as a theatrical piece unfolds before our eyes, ears, and hearts. We must remember that plays are written to be performed. Through the live event, and the circle of energy and communication that is created between the actors on stage and the audience, drama becomes a powerful event that may leave a deep, lasting memory, and one that may lead us, whether individually or as a group, to a higher sense of purpose.

We apply this dramatic truth to our own, real-life situations. We seek out the truth in our studies of the past and present. Drama, ever-changing as a mirror of society, may also move us forward, as human beings continue to crave and seek out higher truths in ourselves and truth in our collaborations and actions with others.

Jeffrey K. Wittman
Professor of Theatre

ARISTOTLE

384-322 B.C.E.

POETICS

350 B.C.E.

Aristotle, referred to by medieval scholars simply as "the Philosopher," was born in Stagira in northern Greece, the son of Nichomachus, the court physician to the Macedonian royal family. Aristotle first trained in medicine but in 367 went to Athens to study philosophy with Plato. He stayed at Plato's Academy until about 347. Aristotle opposed some of Plato's teachings, so when Plato died, Aristotle was not appointed head of the Academy. Leaving Athens, he spent some time traveling in Asia Minor (now Turkey) and its islands. He returned to Macedonia in 338 to tutor Alexander the Great. After Alexander conquered Athens, Aristotle returned to Athens to set up the Lyceum, where he worked until Alexander's death, when Athens rebelled against Macedonian rule and Aristotle's political situation became precarious. To avoid being put to death, he fled to the island of Euboea, where he died soon after.

Aristotle is said to have written 150 philosophical treatises. The 30 that survive touch on philosophical problems ranging from physics to aesthetics to politics. Fundamental to his theories was the inherent human desire for knowledge, as evidenced by the gratification resulting from the assimilation of information through the senses. Aristotle made the classical statement on Greek tragedy in his *Poetics*, a work which has had a profound influence on succeeding generations of poets, dramatists, critics, and philosophers. The word *poetieo* ultimately derives from the Greek word *poesis*, meaning to create or produce. While Plato regarded art with contempt, since at best art was an imitation of an imitation and thus far removed form the truth, Aristotle believed that art dealt with the universal and, in imitating nature, communicated much truth about nature. In *Poetics,* Aristotle presented a clear contrast between history and poetry; he also analyzed epic, tragedy, and comedy as forms of dramatic literature.

SOURCE

Aristotle. 350 B.C.E. *Poetics.* In *Aristotle's Theory of Poetry and Fine Art, with a Critical Text and Translation of The Poetics.* S.H. Butcher, Ed. and Trans. London: Macmillan, 1907. 7-111.

POETICS

I. 'Imitation' the common principle of the Arts of Poetry

I propose to treat of Poetry in itself and of its various kinds, noting the essential quality of each; to inquire into the structure of the plot as requisite to a good poem; into the number and nature of the parts of which a poem is composed; and similarly into whatever else falls within the same inquiry. Following, then, the order of nature, let us begin with the principles which come first.

Epic poetry and Tragedy, Comedy also and Dithyrambic poetry, and the music of the flute and of the lyre in most of their forms, are all in their general conception modes of imitation. They differ, however, from one another in three respects,—the medium, the objects, the manner or mode of imitation, being in each case distinct.

For as there are persons who, by conscious art or mere habit, imitate and represent various objects through the medium of colour and form, or again by the voice; so in the arts above mentioned, taken as a whole, the imitation is produced by rhythm, language, or 'harmony,' either singly or combined.

Thus in the music of the flute and of the lyre, 'harmony' and rhythm alone are employed; also in other arts, such as that of the shepherd's pipe, which are essentially similar to these. In dancing, rhythm alone is used without 'harmony'; for even dancing imitates character, emotion, and action, by rhythmical movement.

There is another art which imitates by means of language alone, and that either in prose or verse—which verse, again, may either combine different metres or consist of but one kind—but this has hitherto been without a name. For there is no common term we could apply to the mimes of Sophron and Xenarchus and the Socratic dialogues on the one hand; and, on the other, to poetic imitations in iambic, elegiac, or any similar metre. People do, indeed, add the word 'maker' or 'poet' to the name of the metre, and speak of elegiac poets, or epic (that is, hexameter) poets, as if it were not the imitation that makes the poet, but the verse that entitles them all indiscriminately to the name. Even when a treatise on medicine or natural science is brought out in verse, the name of poet is by custom given to the author; and yet Homer and Empedocles have nothing in common but the metre, so that it would be right to call the one poet, the other physicist rather than poet. On the same principle, even if a writer in his poetic imitation were to combine all metres, as Chaeremon did in his Centaur, which is a medley composed of metres of all kinds, we should bring him too under the general term poet. So much then for these distinctions.

There are, again, some arts which employ all the means above mentioned,—namely, rhythm, tune, and metre. Such are Dithyrambic and Nomic poetry, and also Tragedy and Comedy; but between them the difference is, that in the first two cases these means are all employed in combination, in the latter, now one means is employed, now another. Such, then, are the differences of the arts with respect to the medium of imitation.

II. The Objects of Imitation

Since the objects of imitation are men in action, and these men must be either of a higher or a lower type (for moral character mainly answers to these divisions, goodness and badness being the distinguishing marks of moral differences), it follows that we must represent men either as better than in real life, or as worse, or as they are. It is the same in painting. Polygnotus depicted men as nobler than they are, Pauson as less noble, Dionysius drew them true to life.

Now it is evident that each of the modes of imitation above mentioned will exhibit these differences, and be come a distinct kind in imitating objects that are thus distinct. Such diversities may be found even in dancing, flute-playing, and lyre-playing. So again in language, whether prose or verse unaccompanied by music. Homer, for example, makes men better than they are; Cleophon as they are; Hegemon the Thasian, the inventor of parodies, and Nicochares, the author of the Deiliad, worse than they are. The same thing holds good of Dithyrambs and Nomes; here too one may portray different types, as Timotheus and Philoxenus differed in representing their Cyclopes. The same distinction marks off Tragedy from Comedy; for Comedy aims at representing men as worse Tragedy as better than in actual life.

III. The Manner of Imitation

There is still a third difference—the manner in which each of these objects may be imitated. For the medium being the same, and the objects the same, the poet may imitate by narration—in which case he can either take another personality as Homer does, or speak in his own person, unchanged—or he may present all his characters as living and moving before us.

These, then, as we said at the beginning, are the three differences which distinguish artistic imitation,—the medium, the objects, and the manner. So that from one point of view, Sophocles is an imitator of the same kind as Homer—for both imitate higher types of character; from another point of view, of the same kind as Aristophanes—for both imitate persons acting and doing. Hence, some say, the name of 'drama' is given to such poems, as representing action. . . .

[*Aristotle here recounts arguments among Greek over regional claims to various names of dramatic forms.*]

IV. The Origin and Development of Poetry

Poetry in general seems to have sprung from two causes, each of them lying deep in our nature. First, the instinct of imitation is implanted in man from childhood, one difference between him and other animals being that he is the most imitative of living creatures; and through imitation he learns his earliest lessons; and no less universal is the pleasure felt in things imitated. We have evidence of this in the facts of experience. Objects which in themselves we view with pain, we delight to contemplate when reproduced with minute fidelity: such as the forms of the most ignoble animals and of dead bodies. The cause of this again is, that to learn gives the liveliest pleasure, not only to philosophers but to men in general; whose capacity, however, of learning is more limited. Thus the reason why men enjoy seeing a likeness is, that in contemplating it they find themselves learning or inferring, and saying perhaps, 'Ah, that is he.' For if you happen not to have seen the original, the pleasure will be due not to the imitation as such, but to the execution, the colouring, or some such other cause.

Imitation, then, is one instinct of our nature. Next, there is the instinct for 'harmony' and rhythm, metres being manifestly sections of rhythm. Persons, therefore, starting with this natural gift developed by degrees their special aptitudes, till their rude improvisations gave birth to Poetry.

Poetry now diverged in two directions, according to the individual character of the writers. The graver spirits imitated noble actions, and the actions of good men. The more trivial sort imitated tile actions of meaner persons, at first composing satires, as the former did hymns to the gods and the praises of famous men. A poem of the satirical kind cannot indeed be put down to any author earlier than Homer; though many such writers probably there were. But from Homer onward, instances can be cited,—his own Margites, for example, and other similar compositions. The appropriate metre was also here introduced; hence the measure is still called the iambic or lampooning measure, being that in which people lampooned one another. Thus the older poets were distinguished as writers of heroic or of lampooning verse.

As, in the serious style, Homer is pre-eminent among poets, for he alone combined dramatic form with excellence of imitation, so he too first laid down the main lines of Comedy, by dramatising the ludicrous instead of writing personal satire. His Margites bears the same relation to Comedy that the Iliad and Odyssey do to Tragedy. But when Tragedy and Comedy came to light, the two classes of poets still followed their natural bent: the lampooners became writers of Comedy, and the Epic poets were succeeded by Tragedians, since the drama was a larger and higher form of art.

Whether Tragedy has as yet perfected its proper types or not; and whether it is to be judged in itself, or in relation also to the audience,—this raises another question. Be that as it may, Tragedy—as also Comedy—was at first mere improvisation. The one originated with the leaders of the Dithyramb, the other with those of the phallic songs, which are still in use in many of our cities. Tragedy advanced by slow degrees; each new element that showed itself was in turn developed. Having passed through many changes, it found its natural form, and there it stopped.

Aeschylus first introduced a second actor; he diminished the importance of the Chorus, and assigned the leading part to the dialogue. Sophocles raised the number of actors to three, and added scene-painting. Moreover, it was not till late that the short plot was discarded for one of greater compass, and the grotesque diction of the earlier satyric form for the stately manner of Tragedy. The iambic measure then replaced the trochaic tetrameter, which was originally employed when the poetry was of the satyric order, and had greater affinities with dancing. Once dialogue had come in, Nature herself discovered the appropriate measure. For the iambic is, of all measures, the most colloquial: we see it in the fact that conversational speech runs into iambic lines more frequently than into any other kind of verse; rarely into hexameters, and only when we drop the colloquial intonation. The additions to the number of 'episodes' or acts, and the other improvements of which tradition tells, must be taken as already described; for to discuss them in detail would, doubtless, be a large undertaking.

V. Definition of the Ludicrous, and a brief sketch of the rise of Comedy

Comedy is, as we have said, an imitation of characters of a lower type,—not, however, in the full sense of the word bad, the Ludicrous being merely a subdivision of the ugly. It consists in some defect or ugliness which is not painful or destructive. To take an obvious example, the comic mask is ugly and distorted, but does not imply pain.

The successive changes through which Tragedy passed, and the authors of these changes, are well known, whereas Comedy has had no history, because it was not at first treated seriously. It was late before the Archon granted a comic chorus to a poet; the performers were till then voluntary. Comedy had already taken definite shape when comic poets, distinctively so called, are heard of. Who introduced masks, or prologues, or increased the number of actors,—these and other similar details remain unknown. As for the plot, it came originally from Sicily; but of Athenian writers Crates was the first who, abandoning the 'iambic' or lampooning form, generalised his themes and plots.

Epic poetry agrees with Tragedy in so far as it is an imitation in verse of characters of a higher type. They differ, in that Epic poetry admits but one kind of metre, and is narrative in form. They differ, again, in their length: for Tragedy endeavours, as far as possible, to confine itself to a single revolution of the sun, or but slightly to exceed this limit; whereas the Epic action has no limits of time. This, then, is second point of difference; though at first the same freedom was admitted in Tragedy as in Epic poetry.

Of their constituent parts some are common to both, some peculiar to Tragedy. Whoever, therefore, knows what is good or bad Tragedy, knows also about Epic poetry: for all the elements of

an Epic poem are found in Tragedy, but the elements of a Tragedy
are not all found in the Epic poem.

VI. Definition of Tragedy

Of the poetry which imitates in hexameter verse, and of
Comedy, we will speak hereafter. Let us now discuss Tragedy,
resuming its formal definition, as resulting from what has been
already said.

Tragedy, then, is an imitation of an action that is serious,
complete, and of a certain magnitude; in language embellished
with each kind of artistic ornament, the several kinds being found
in separate parts of the play; in the form of action, not of narrative;
through pity and fear effecting the proper purgation of these
emotions. By 'language embellished,' I mean language into which
rhythm, 'harmony,' and song enter. By 'the several kinds in separate
parts,' I mean, that some parts are rendered through the medium
of verse alone, others again with the aid of song.

Now as tragic imitation implies persons acting, it necessarily
follows, in the first place, that Spectacular equipment will be a
part of Tragedy. Next, Song and Diction, for these are the medium
of imitation. By 'Diction' I mean the mere metrical arrangement
of the words: as for 'Song,' it is a term whose sense every one
understands.

Again, Tragedy is the imitation of an action; and an action
implies personal agents, who necessarily possess certain distinctive
qualities both of character and thought; for it is by these that we
qualify actions themselves, and these—thought and character—
are the two natural causes from which actions spring, and on actions
again all success or failure depends. Hence, the Plot is the imitation
of the action:—for by plot I here mean the arrangement of the
incidents. By Character I mean that in virtue of which we ascribe
certain qualities to the agents. Thought is required wherever a
statement is proved, or, it may be, a general truth enunciated.
Every Tragedy, therefore, must have six parts, which parts determine
its quality—namely, Plot, Character, Diction, Thought, Spectacle,
Song. Two of the parts constitute the medium of imitation, one

the manner, and three the objects of imitation. And these complete the list. These elements have been employed, we may say, by the poets to a man; in fact, every play contains Spectacular elements as well as Character, Plot, Diction, Song, and Thought.

But most important of all is the structure of the incidents. For Tragedy is an imitation, not of men, but of an action and of life, and life consists in action, and its end is a mode of action, not a quality. Now character determines men's qualities, but it is by their actions that they are happy or the reverse. Dramatic action, therefore, is not with a view to the representation of character; character comes in as subsidiary to the actions. Hence the incidents and the plot are the end of a tragedy; and the end is the chief thing of all. Again, without action there cannot be a tragedy; there may be without character. The tragedies of most of our modern poets fail in the rendering of character; and of poets in general this is often true. It is the same in painting; and here lies the difference between Zeuxis and Polygnotus. Polygnotus delineates character well: the style of Zeuxis is devoid of ethical quality. Again, if you string together a set of speeches expressive of character, and well finished in point of diction and thought, you will not produce the essential tragic effect nearly so well as with a play which, however deficient in these respects, yet has a plot and artistically constructed incidents. Besides which, the most powerful elements of emotional interest in Tragedy—Peripeteia or Reversal of the Situation, and Recognition scenes—are parts of the plot. A further proof is, that novices in the art attain to finish of diction and precision of portraiture before they can construct the plot. It is the same with almost all the early poets.

The Plot, then, is the first principle, and, as it were, the soul of a tragedy: Character holds the second place. A similar fact is seen in painting. The most beautiful colours, laid on confusedly, will not give as much pleasure as the chalk outline of a portrait. Thus Tragedy is the imitation of an action, and at the agents mainly with a view to the action.

Third in order is Thought,—that is, the faculty of saying what is possible and pertinent in given circumstances. In the case of oratory, this is the function of the political art and of the art of rhetoric: and so indeed the older poets make their characters speak the language of civic life; the poets of our time, the language of the rhetoricians. Character is that which reveals moral purpose, showing what kind of things a man chooses or avoids. Speeches, therefore, which do not make this manifest, or in which the speaker does not choose or avoid anything whatever, are not expressive of character. Thought, on the other hand, is found where something is proved to be or not to be, or a general maxim is enunciated.

Fourth among the elements enumerated comes Diction; by which I mean, as has been already said, the expression of the meaning in words; and its essence is the same both in verse and prose.

Of the remaining elements Song holds the chief place among the embellishments

The Spectacle has, indeed, an emotional attraction of its own, but, of all the parts, it is the least artistic, and connected least with the art of poetry. For the power of Tragedy, we may be sure, is felt even apart from representation and actors. Besides, the production of spectacular effects depends more on the art of the stage machinist than on that of the poet.

VII. The Plot must be a Whole

These principles being established, let us now discuss the proper structure of the Plot, since this is the first and most important part of Tragedy.

Now, according to our definition, Tragedy is an imitation of an action that is complete, and whole, and of a certain magnitude; for there may be a whole that is wanting in magnitude. A whole is that which has a beginning, a middle, and an end. A beginning is that which does not itself follow anything by causal necessity, but after which something naturally is or comes to be. An end, on the contrary, is that which itself naturally follows some other thing, either by necessity, or as a rule, but has nothing following it. A middle is that which follows something as some other thing follows it. A well constructed plot, therefore, must neither begin nor end at haphazard, but conform to these principles.

Again, a beautiful object, whether it be a living organism or any whole composed of parts, must not only have an orderly arrangement of parts, but must also be of a certain magnitude; for beauty depends on magnitude and order. Hence a very small animal organism cannot be beautiful ; for the view of it is confused, the object being seen in an almost imperceptible moment of time. Nor, again, can one of vast size be beautiful; for as the eye cannot take it all in at once, the unity and sense of the whole is lost for the spectator; as for instance there were one a thousand miles long. As, therefore, in the case of animate bodies and organisms a certain magnitude is necessary, and a magnitude which may be easily embraced in one view; so in the plot, a certain length is necessary, and a length which can be easily embraced by the memory. The limit of length in relation to dramatic competition and sensuous presentment, is no part of artistic theory. For had it been the rule for a hundred tragedies to compete together, the performance would have been regulated by the water-clock,—as indeed we are told was formerly done. But the limit as fixed by the nature of the drama itself is this:—the greater the length, the more beautiful will the piece be by reason of its size, provided that the whole be perspicuous. And to define the matter roughly, we may say that the proper magnitude is comprised within such limits, that the sequence of events, according to the law o probability or necessity, will admit of a change from bad fortune to good, or from good fortune to bad.

VIII. The Plot must be a Unity

Unity of plot does not, as some persons think, consist in the unity of the hero. For infinitely various are the incidents in one man's life which cannot be reduced to unity; and so, too, there are man actions of one man out of which we cannot make one action. Hence the error, as it appears, of all poets who have composed a Heracleid, a Theseid, or other poems of the kind. They imagine that as Heracles was one man, the story of Heracles must also be a unity. But Homer, as in all else he is of surpassing merit, here too—whether from art or natural genius—seems to have happily discerned the truth. In composing the Odyssey he did not include all of the adventures of Odysseus—such as his wound on Parnassus, or his feigned madness at the mustering of the host between which there was no necessary or probable connexion: but he made the Odyssey, and likewise the Iliad, to centre round an action that in our sense of the word is one. As therefore, in the other imitative arts, the imitation is one when the object imitated is one, so the plot, being an imitation of an action, must imitate one action and that a whole, the structural union of the parts being such that, if any one of them is displaced or removed, the whole will be disjointed and disturbed. For a thing whose presence or absence makes no visible difference, is not an organic part of the whole.

IX. Dramatic Unity

It is, moreover, evident from what has been said, that it is not the function of the poet to relate what has happened, but what may happen,—what is possible according to the law of probability or necessity. The poet and the historian differ not by writing in verse or a prose. The work of Herodotus might he put into verse, and it would still be a species of history, with metre no less than without it. The true difference is at one relates what has happened, the other what may happen. Poetry, therefore, is a more philosophical and a higher thing than history: for poetry tends to express universal, history the particular. By the universal I mean how a person of a certain type will on occasion speak or act, according to the law of probability or necessity; and it is this universality at which poetry in the names she attaches to the personages. The particular is—for example—what Alcibiades did or suffered. In Comedy this is already apparent: for here the poet first constructs the plot on the lines of probability, and then inserts characteristic names;—unlike the lampooners who write about particular individuals. But tragedians still keep to real names, the reason being that what is possible is credible: what has not happened a we do not at once feel sure to be possible: but what has happened is manifestly possible: otherwise it would not have happened. Still there are some tragedies in which there are only one or two well known names, the rest being fictitious. In others, none are well known,—as in Agathon's Antheus, where incidents and names alike are fictitious, and yet they give none the less pleasure. We must not, therefore, at all costs keep to the received legends, which are the usual subjects of Tragedy. Indeed, it would be absurd to attempt it; for even subjects that are known are known only to a few, and yet give pleasure to all. It clearly follows that the poet or 'maker' should be the maker of plots rather than of verses; since he is a poet because he imitates, and what he imitates are actions. And even if be chances to take an historical subject, he is none the less a poet; for there is no reason why some events that have actually happened should not conform to the law of the probable and possible, and in virtue of that quality in them he is their poet or maker.

Of all plots and actions the epeisodic are the worst. I call a plot 'epeisodic' in which the episodes or acts succeed one another without probable or necessary sequence. Bad poets compose such pieces by their own fault, good poets, to please the players; for, as they write show pieces for competition, they stretch the plot beyond its capacity, and are often forced to break the natural continuity.

But again, Tragedy is an imitation not only of a complete action, but of events terrible and pitiful. Such an effect is best produced when the events come on us by surprise; and the effect is heightened when, at the same time, they follow as cause and effect. The tragic wonder will then be greater than if they happened of themselves or by accident; for even coincidences are most striking when they have an air of design. We may stance the statue of Mitys at Argos, which fell upon his murderer while he was a spectator at a festival, and killed him. Such events seem not to be due to mere chance. Plots, therefore, constructed on these principles are necessarily the best.

X. Definitions of Simple and Complex Plots

Plots are either Simple or Complex, for the actions in real life, of which the plots are an imitation, obviously show a similar distinction. An action which is one and continuous in the sense above defined, I call Simple, when the change of fortune takes place without Reversal of the Situation and without Recognition.

A Complex action is one in which the change is accompanied by such Reversal, or by Recognition, or by both. These last should arise from the internal structure of the plot, so that what follows should be the necessary or probable result of the preceding action. It makes all the difference whether any given event is a case of *propter hoc* or *post hoc*.

XI. Reversal of the Situation, Recognition, and Tragic or disastrous Incident defined and explained

Reversal of the Situation is a change by which the action veers round to its opposite, subject always to our rule of probability or necessity. Thus in the Oedipus, the messenger comes to cheer Oedipus and free him from his alarms about his mother, but by revealing who he is, he produces the opposite effect. Again in the Lynceus, Lynceus is being led away to is death, and Danans goes with him, meaning to slay him; but the outcome of the action is, that Danaus is killed and Lynceus saved.

Recognition, as the name indicates, is a change from ignorance to knowledge, producing love or hate between the persons destined by the poet for good or bad fortune. The best form of recognition is coincident with a Reversal of the Situation, as in the Oedipus. There ore indeed other forms. Even inanimate things of the most trivial kind may sometimes be objects of recognition. Again, we may recognise or discover whether a person has done a thing or not. But the recognition which is most intimately connected with the plot and action is, as we have said, the recognition of persons. This recognition, combined with Reversal, will produce either pity or fear; and actions producing these effects are those which, by our definition, Tragedy represents. Moreover, it is upon such situations that the issues of good or had fortune will depend. Recognition, then, being between persons, it may happen that one person only is recognised by the other—when the latter is already known—or it may be necessary that the recognition should be on both sides. Thus Iphigeina is revealed to Orestes by the sending of the letter;

but another act of recognition is required to make Orestes known to Iphigenia.

Two parts, then, of the Plot—Reversal of the Situation and Recognition—turn upon surprises. A third part is the Tragic Incident. The Tragic Incident is a destructive or painful action, such as death on the stage, bodily agony, wounds and the like.

XII. The 'quantitative parts' of Tragedy defined

[The parts of Tragedy which must be treated as elements of the whole have been already mentioned. We now come to the quantitative parts—the separate parts into which Tragedy is divided—namely, Prologue, Episode, Exodos, Choric song; this last being divided into Parodos and Stasimon. These are common to all plays: peculiar to some are the songs of actors from the stage and the Commoi.

The Prologos is that entire part of a tragedy which a precedes the Parodos of the Chorus. The Episode is that entire part of a tragedy which is between complete choric songs. The Exodos is that entire part of a tragedy which has no choric song after it. Of the Choric part the Parodos is the first undivided utterance of the Chorus: the Stasimon is a Choric ode without anapaests or trochaic tetrameters: the Commos is a joint lamentation of Chorus and actors. The parts of Tragedy which must be treated as elements of the whole have been already mentioned. The quantitative parts—the separate parts into which it is divided—are here enumerated.—S.E.B.]

XIII. What constitutes Tragic Action

As the sequel to what has already been said, we must proceed to consider what the poet should aim at, and what he should avoid, in constructing his plots; and by what means the specific effect of Tragedy will be produced.

A perfect tragedy should, as we have seen, be arranged not on the simple but on the complex plan. It should, moreover, imitate actions which excite pity and fear, this being the distinctive mark of tragic imitation. It follows plainly, in the first place, that the change of fortune presented must not be the spectacle of a virtuous man brought from prosperity to adversity: for this moves neither pity nor fear; it merely shocks us. Nor, again, that of a bad man passing from adversity to prosperity: for nothing can be more alien to the spirit of Tragedy; it possesses no single tragic quality; it neither satisfies the moral sense nor calls forth pity or fear. Nor, again, should the downfall of the utter villain be exhibited. A plot of this kind would, doubtless, satisfy the moral sense, but it would inspire neither pity nor fear; for pity is aroused by unmerited misfortune, fear by the misfortune of a mail like ourselves. Such an event, therefore, will be neither pitiful nor terrible. There remains, then, the character between these two extremes,—that of a man who is not eminently good and just, yet whose misfortune is brought about not by vice or depravity, but by some error or frailty. He must be one who is highly renowned and prosperous,—a personage like Oedipus, Thyestes, or other illustrious men of such families.

A well constructed plot should, therefore, be single in its issue, rather than double as some maintain. The change of fortune should be not from bad to good, but, reversely, from good to bad. It should come about as the result not of vice, but of some great error or frailty, in a character either such as we have described, or better rather than worse. The practice of the stage bears out our view. At first the poets recounted any legend that came in their way. Now, the best tragedies are founded on the story of a few houses,—on the fortunes of Alcmaeon, Oedipus, Orestes, Meleager, Thyestes, Telephus, and those others who have done or suffered something terrible. A tragedy, then, to be perfect according to the rules of art should be of this construction. Hence they are in error who censure Euripides just because he follows this principle in his plays, many of which end unhappily. It is, as we have said, the right ending. The best proof is that on the stage and in dramatic competition, such plays, if well worked out, are the most tragic in effect; and Euripides, faulty though he may be in the general management of his subject, yet is felt to be the most tragic of the poets.

In the second rank comes the kind of tragedy which some place first. Like the Odyssey, it has a double thread of plot, and also an opposite catastrophe for the good and for the bad. It is accounted the best because of the weakness of the spectators; for the poet is guided in what he writes by the wishes of his audience. The pleasure, however, thence derived is not the true tragic pleasure. It is proper rather to Comedy, where those who, in the piece, are the deadliest enemies—like Orestes and Aegisthus—quit the stage as friends at the close, and no one slays or is slain.

XIV. The tragic emotions of pity and fear should spring out of the Plot itself

Fear and pity may be aroused by spectacular means; but they may also result from the inner structure of the piece, which is the better way, and indicates a superior poet. For the plot ought to be so constructed that, even without the aid of the eye, he who hears the tale told will thrill with horror and melt to pity at what takes place. This is the impression we should receive from hearing the story of the Oedipus. But to produce this effect by the mere spectacle is a less artistic method, and dependent on extraneous aids. Those who employ spectacular means to create a sense not of the terrible but only of the monstrous, are strangers to the purpose of Tragedy; for we must not demand of Tragedy any and every kind of pleasure, but only that which is proper to it. And since the pleasure which the poet should afford is that which comes from pity and fear through imitation, it is evident that this quality must be impressed upon the incidents.

Let us then determine what are the circumstances which strike us as terrible or pitiful.

Actions capable of this effect must happen between persons who are either friends or enemies or indifferent to one another. If an enemy kills an enemy, there is nothing to excite pity either in the act or the intention,—except so far as the suffering in itself is pitiful. So again with indifferent persons. But when the tragic incident occurs between those who are near or dear to one another—

if, for example, a brother kills, or intends to kill, a brother, a son his father, a mother her son, a son his mother, or any other deed of the kind is done—these are the situations to be looked for by the poet. He may not indeed destroy the framework of the received legends—the fact, for instance, that Clytemnestra was slain by Orestes and Eriphyle by Alcmaeon—but he ought to show invention of his own, and skillfully handle the traditional material. Let us explain more clearly what is meant by skilful handling.

The action may be done consciously and with knowledge of the persons, in the manner of the older poets. It is thus too that Euripides makes Medea slay her children. Or, again, the deed of horror may be done, but done in ignorance, and the tie of kinship or friendship be discovered afterwards. The Oedipus of Sophocles is an example. Here, indeed, the incident is outside drama proper; but cases occur where it falls within the action of the play: one may cite the Alcmaeon of Astydamas, or Telegonus in the Wounded Odysseus. Again, there is a third case,—<to be about to act with knowledge the persons and then not to act. The fourth case is> when some one is about to do an irreparable deed through ignorance, and makes the discovery before it is done. These are the only possible ways. For the deed must either be done or not done,—and that wittingly or unwittingly. But of all these ways, to be about to act knowing the persons, and then not to act, is thee worst. It is shocking without being tragic, for no disaster follows. It is, therefore, never, or very rarely, found in poetry. One instance, however, is in the Antigone, where Haemon threatens to kill Creon. The next and better way is that the deed should be perpetrated. Still better, that it should be perpetrated in ignorance, and the discovery made afterwards. There is then nothing to shock us, while the discovery produces a startling effect. The last case is the best, as when in the Cresphontes Merope is about to slay her son, but, recognising who he is, spares his life. So the Iphigenia, the sister recognises the brother just in time. Again in the Helle, the son recognises the mother went on the point of giving her up. This, then, is why a few families only, as has been already observed, furnish the subjects of tragedy. It was not art, but happy chance, that led poets to look for such situations and so impress the tragic quality upon their plots. They are compelled, therefore, to have recourse to those houses whose history contains moving incidents like these.

Enough has now been said concerning the structure of the incidents, and the proper constitution of the plot.

XV. The element of Character in Tragedy

In respect of Character there are four things to be aimed at. First, and most important, it must be good. Now any speech or action that manifests moral purpose of any kind will be expressive of character: the character will be good if the purpose is good. This rule is relative to each class. Even a woman may be good, and also a slave; though the woman may be said to be an inferior being, and the slave quite worthless. The second thing to aim at is propriety. There is a type of manly valour; but valour in a woman, or unscrupulous cleverness, is in inappropriate. Thirdly, character must be true to life: for this is a distinct thing from goodness and propriety, as here described. The fourth point is consistency: for though the subject of the imitation, who suggested the type, be inconsistent, still he must be consistently inconsistent. As an example of motiveless degradation of character, we s have Menelaus in the Orestes: of character indecorous and inappropriate, the lament of Odysseus in the Scylla, and the speech of Melanippe: of inconsistency, the Iphigenia at Aulis,—for Iphigenia the suppliant in no way resembles her later self.

As in the structure of the plot, so too in the portraiture of character, the poet should always aim either at the necessary or the probable. Thus a person of a given character should speak or act in a given way, by the rule either of necessity or of probability; just as this event should follow that by necessity or probable sequence. It is therefore evident that the unraveling of the plot, no less than the complication, must arise out of the plot itself, it must not be brought about by the *Deus ex Machina*—as in the Medea, or in the Return of the Greeks in the Iliad. The *Deus ex Machina* should be employed only for events external to the drama,—for antecedent or subsequent events, which lie beyond the range of human knowledge, and which require to be reported or foretold; for to the gods we ascribe the power of seeing all things. Within the action there must be nothing irrational. If the irrational cannot be excluded, it should be outside the scope of the tragedy. Such is the irrational element in the Oedipus of Sophocles.

Again, since Tragedy is an imitation of persons who are above the common level, the example of good portrait-painters should be followed. They, while reproducing the distinctive form of the original, make a likeness which is true to life and yet more beautiful. So too the poet, in representing men who are irascible or indolent, or have other defects of character, should preserve the type and yet ennoble it. In this way Achilles is portrayed by Agathon and Homer.

These then are rules the poet should observe. Nor should he neglect those appeals to the senses, which, though not among the essentials, are the concomitants of poetry; for here too there is much room for error. But of this enough has been said in the published treatises.

XVI. Recognition: its various kinds, with examples

What Recognition is has been already explained. We will now enumerate its kinds.

First, the least artistic form, which, from poverty of wit, is most commonly employed—recognition by signs. Of these some are congenital,—such as 'the spear which the earth-born race bear on their bodies,' or the stars introduced by Carcinus in his Thyestes. Others are acquired after birth; and of these sonic are bodily marks, as scars; some external tokens, as necklaces, or the little ark in the Tyro by which the discovery is effected. Even these admit of more or less skillful treatment. Thus in the recognition of Odysseus by his scar, the discovery is made in one way by the nurse, in another by the herdsman. The use of tokens for the express purpose of proof—and, indeed, any formal proof with or without tokens—is a less artistic mode of recognition. A better kind is that which comes about by a turn of incident, as in the Bath Scene in the Odyssey.

Next come the recognitions invented at will by the poet, and on that account wanting in art. For example, Orestes in the Iphigenia reveals the fact that he is Orestes. She, indeed, makes herself known by the letter; but he, by speaking himself, and saying what the poet, not what the plot requires. This, therefore, is nearly allied to the fault above mentioned:—for Orestes might as well have brought tokens with him. Another similar instance is the 'voice of the shuttle' in the Tereus of Sophocles.

The third kind depends on memory when the sight of some object awakens a feeling: as in the Cyprians of Dicaeogenes, where the hero breaks into tears on seeing the picture; or again in the 'Lay of Alcinous,' where Odysseus, hearing the minstrel play the lyre, recalls the past and weeps; and hence the recognition.

The fourth kind is by process of reasoning. Thus in the Choëphori:—'Some one resembling me has come: no one resembles me but Orestes: therefore Orestes has come . . . .' [*Other examples given here.*]

XVII. Practical rules for the Tragic Poet

In constructing the plot and working it out with the proper diction, the poet should place the scene, as far as possible, before his eyes. In this way, seeing everything with the utmost vividness, as if he were spectator of the action, he will discover what is in keeping with it, and be most unlikely to overlook inconsistencies. The need of such a rule is shown by the fault found in Carcinus. Amphiaraus was on his way from the temple. This fact escaped the observation of one who did not see the situation. On the stage, however, the piece failed, the audience being offended at the oversight.

Again, the poet should work out his play, to the best of his power, with appropriate gestures; for those who feel emotion are most convincing through natural sympathy with the characters they represent; and one who is agitated storms, one who is angry rages, with the most life-like reality. Hence poetry implies either a happy gift of nature or a strain of madness. In the one case a man can take the mould of any character; in the other, he is lifted out of his proper self.

As for the story, whether the poet takes it ready made or constructs it for himself, he should first sketch its general outline, and then fill in the episodes and amplify in detail. The general plan may be illustrated by the Iphigenia. A young girl is sacrificed; she disappears mysteriously from the eyes of those who sacrificed her; she is transported to another country, where the custom is to offer up all strangers to the goddess. To this ministry she is appointed. Some time later her own brother chances to arrive. The fact that the oracle for some reason ordered him to go there, is outside the general plan of the play. The purpose, again, of his coming is outside the action proper. However, he comes, he is seized, and, when on the point of being sacrificed, reveals who he is. The mode of recognition may be either that of Euripides or of Polyidus, in whose play he exclaims very naturally:—'So it was not my sister only, but I too, who was doomed to be sacrificed'; and by that remark he is saved.

After this, the names being once given. it remains to fill in the episodes. We must see that they are relevant to the action. In the case of Orestes, for example, there is the madness which led to his capture, and deliverance by means of the purificatory rite. In drama, time episodes are short, but it is these that give extension to Epic poetry. Thus the story of the Odyssey can be stated briefly. A certain man is absent from home for many years: he is jealously watched by Poseidon, and left desolate. Meanwhile his home is in a wretched plight—suitors are wasting his subsistence and plotting against his son. At length, tempest-tost, he himself arrives; he makes certain persons acquainted with him; he attacks the suitors with his own hand, and is himself preserved while he destroys them. This is the essence of the plot; the rest is episode.

XVIII. Further rules for the Tragic Poet

Every tragedy falls into two parts,—Complication and Unravelling or *Dénouement*. Incidents extraneous to the action are frequently combined with a portion of the action proper, to form the Complication; the rest is the Unravelling. By the Complication I mean all that extends from the beginning of the action and the part which marks the turning-point to good or bad fortune. The Unravelling is that which extends from the beginning of the change to the end. Thus, the Lynceus of Theodectes, the Complication consists of the incidents presupposed in the drama, the seizure of the child, and then again * * <The Unravelling> extends from the accusation of murder to the end.

There are four kinds of Tragedy, the Complex, depending entirely on the Reversal of the Situation and Recognition; the Pathetic (where the motive is passion),—such as the tragedies on Ajax and Ixion; the Ethical (where the motives are ethical),—such as the Phthiotides and the Peleus. The fourth kind is the Simple. <We here exclude the purely spectacular element>, exemplified by the Phorcides, the Prometheus, and scenes laid in Hades. The poet should endeavor, if possible, to combine all poetic merits; or failing that, the greatest number and those the most important; the more so, in face of the cavilling criticism of the day. For whereas there have hitherto been good poets, each in his own branch, the critics now expect one man to surpass all others in their several lines of excellence.

In speaking of a tragedy as the same or different, the best test to take is the plot. Identity exists where the Complication and Unravelling are the same. Many poets tie the knot well, but unravel it ill. Both arts, however, should always be mastered.

Again, the poet should remember what has been often said, and not make a Tragedy into an Epic structure. By an Epic structure I mean one with a multiplicity of plots: as if, for instance, you were to make a tragedy out of the entire story of the Iliad. In the Epic poem, owing to its length, each part assumes its proper magnitude. In the drama the result is far from answering to the poet's expectation. The proof is that the poets who have dramatized the whole story of the Fall of Troy, instead of selecting portions, like Euripides; or who have taken the whole tale of Niobe, and not a part of her story, like Aeschylus, either fail utterly or meet with poor success on the stage. Even Agathon has been known to fail from this one defect. In his Reversals of the Situation, however, he shows a marvellous skill in the effort to hit the popular taste,—to produce a tragic effect that satisfies the moral sense. This effect is produced when the clever rogue, like Sisyphus, is outwitted, or the brave villain defeated. Such an event is probable in Agathon's sense of the word: 'it is probable,' he says, 'that many things should happen contrary to probability.'

The Chorus too should be regarded as one of the actors; it should be an integral part of the whole, and share in the action, in the manner not of Euripides but of Sophocles. As for the later poets, their choral songs pertain as little to the subject of the piece as to that of any other tragedy. They are, therefore, sung as mere interludes,—a practice first begun by Agathon. Yet what difference is there between introducing such choral interludes, and transferring a speech, or even a whole act, from one play to another?

XIX. Thought, or the Intellectual element, and Diction in Tragedy

It remains to speak of Diction and Thought, the other parts of Tragedy having been already discussed. Concerning Thought, we may assume what is said in the Rhetoric, to which inquiry the subject more strictly belongs. Under Thought is included every effect which has to be produced by speech, the subdivisions being,—proof and refutation; the excitation of the feelings, such as pity, fear, anger, and the like; the suggestion of importance or its opposite. Now, it is evident that the dramatic incidents must be treated from the same points of view as the dramatic speeches, when the object is to evoke the sense of pity, fear, importance, or probability. The only difference is, that the incidents should speak for themselves without verbal exposition; while the effects aimed at in speech should be produced by the speaker, and as a result of the speech. For what were the business of a speaker, if the Thought were revealed quite apart from what he says?

Next, as regards Diction. One branch of the inquiry treats of the Modes of Expression. But this province of knowledge belongs to the art of Delivery and to the masters of that science. It includes, for instance,—what is a command, a prayer, a narrative, a threat, a question, an answer, and so forth. To know or not to know these things involves no serious censure upon the poet's art. For who can admit the fault imputed to Homer by Protagoras,—that in the words, 'Sing, goddess, of the wrath,' he gives a command under the idea that he utters a prayer? For to tell some one to do a thing or not to do it is, he says, a command. We may, therefore, pass this over as an inquiry that belongs to another art, not to poetry.

XX. Diction, or Language in general
[*This section discusses the sounding of words.*]

XXI. Poetic Diction
[*More about kinds of words.*]

XXII. How Poetry combines elevation of language with perspicuity
The perfection of style is to be clear without being mean. [*More about types of verbal figures.*]

XXIII. Epic Poetry
As to that poetic imitation which is narrative in form and employs a single metre, the plot manifestly ought, as in a tragedy, to be constructed on dramatic principles. It should have for its subject a single action, whole and complete, with a beginning, a middle, and an end. It will thus resemble a living organism in all its unity, and produce the please proper to it. It will differ in structure from historical compositions, which of necessity present not a single action, but a single period, and all that happened within that period to one person or to many, little connected together as the events may be. [*Aristotle furnishes examples from the work of Homer.*]

XXIV. Further points of agreement with Tragedy
Again, Epic poetry must have as many kinds as Tragedy: it must be simple, or complex, or 'ethical,' or 'pathetic.' The parts also, with the exception of song and spectacle, are the same; for it requires Reversals of the Situation, Recognitions, and Tragic incidents. Moreover, the thoughts and the diction must be artistic.

In all these respects Homer is our earliest and sufficient model. Indeed each of his poems has a twofold character. The Iliad is at once simple and 'pathetic,' and the Odyssey complex (for Recognition scenes run through it), and at the same time 'ethical.' Moreover, in diction and thought he is supreme.

Epic poetry differs from Tragedy in the scale on which it is constructed, and in its metre. As regards scale or length, we have already laid down an adequate limit: the beginning and the end must be capable of being brought within a single view. This condition will be satisfied by poems on a smaller scale than the old epics, and answering in length to the group of tragedies presented at a single sitting.

Epic poetry has, however, a great—a special—capacity for enlarging its dimensions, and we can see the reason. In Tragedy we cannot imitate several lines of actions carried on at one and the same time; we must ourselves to the action on the stage and the part taken by the players. But in Epic poetry, owing to the narrative form, many events simultaneously transacted presented; and these, if relevant to the subject, add mass and dignity to the poem. The Epic has here advantage, and one that conduces to grandeur of effect, to diverting the mind of the hearer, and relieving the story with varying episodes. For sameness of incident soon produces satiety, and makes tragedies fail on the stage.

As for the metre, the heroic measure has proved its fitness by the test of experience. If a narrative poem in any other metre or in many metres were now composed, it would be found incongruous. For of all measures the heroic is the stateliest and the most massive; and hence it most readily admits rare words and metaphors, which is another point in which the narrative form of imitation stands alone. On the other hand, the iambic and the trochaic tetrameter are stirring measures, the latter being akin to dancing, the former expressive of action. Still more absurd would it be to mix together different metres, as was done by Chaeremon. Hence no one has ever composed a poem on a great scale in any other than heroic verse. Nature herself, as we have said, teaches the choice of the proper measure.

Homer, admirable in all respects, has the special merit of being the only poet who rightly appreciates the part he should take himself. The poet should speak as little as possible in his own person, for it is not this that makes him an imitator. Other poets appear themselves upon the scene throughout, and imitate but little and rarely. Homer, after a few prefatory words, at once brings in a man or woman, or other personage; none of them wanting in characteristic qualities, but each with a character of his own.

The element of the wonderful is admitted in Tragedy. The irrational, on which the wonderful depends for its chief effects, has wider scope in Epic poetry, because there the person acting is not seen. Thus, the pursuit of Hector would be ludicrous if placed upon the stage—the Greeks standing still arid not joining in the pursuit, and Achilles waving them back. But in the Epic poem the absurdity passes unnoticed. Now the wonderful is pleasing: as may be inferred from the fact that, in telling a story, every one adds something startling of his own, knowing that his hearers like it. It is Homer who has chiefly taught other poets the art of telling lies skillfully. The secret of it lies in a fallacy. For, assuming that if one thing is or becomes, a second is or becomes, men imagine that, if the second is, the first likewise is or becomes. But this is a false inference. Hence, where the first thing is untrue, it is quite unnecessary, provided the second be true, to add that the first is or has become. For the mind, knowing the second to be true, falsely infers the truth of the first. There is an example of this in the Bath Scene of the Odyssey.

Accordingly, the poet should prefer probable Impossibilities to improbable possibilities. The tragic plot must not be composed of irrational parts. Everything irrational should, if possible. be excluded; or, at all events it should lie outside the action of the play (as, in the Oedipus, the hero's ignorance as to the manner of Laius' death); Not within the drama,—as in the Electra, the messenger's account of the Pythian games; or, as in the Mysians, the man who has come from Tegea to Mysia and is still speechless. The plea that otherwise the plot would have been ruined, is ridiculous; such a plot should not be the first instance be constructed. But once the irrational has been introduced and an air of likelihood imparted to it, we must accept it in spite of the absurdity. Take even the irrational incidents in the Odyssey, where Odysseus is left upon the shore of Ithaca. How intolerable even these might have been would be apparent if an inferior poet were to treat the subject. As it is, the absurdity is veiled by the poetic charm with which the poet invests it.

The diction should be elaborated in the pauses of the action, where there is no expression of character or thought. For, conversely, character and thought are merely obscured by a diction that is over brilliant.

XXV. Critical Objections brought against Poetry, and the principles on which they are to be answered

With respect to critical difficulties and their solutions, the number and nature of the sources from which they may be drawn may be thus exhibited.

The poet being an imitator, like a painter or any other artist, must of necessity imitate one of three objects,—things as they were or are, things as they are said or thought to be, or things as they ought to be. The vehicle of expression is language,—either current terms or, it may be, rare words or metaphors. There are so many modifications of language, which we concede to the poets. Add to this, that the standard of correctness is not the same in poetry and politics, any more than in poetry and any other art. Within the art of poetry itself there are two kinds of faults,—those which touch its essence, and those which are accidental. If a poet has chosen to imitate something, <but has imitated it incorrectly> through want of capacity, the error is inherent in the poetry. But if the failure is due to a wrong choice—if he has represented a horse as throwing out both his off legs at once, or introduced technical inaccuracies in medicine, for example, or in any other art—the error is not essential to the poetry. These are the points of view from which we should consider and answer the objections raised by the critics.

First as to matters which concern the poet's own art. If he describes the impossible, he is guilty of error; but the error may be justified, if the end of the art be thereby attained (the end being that already mentioned),—if, that is, the effect of this or any other part of the poem is thus rendered more striking. A case in point is the pursuit of Hector. If however, the end might have been as well, or better, attained without violating the special rules of the poetic art, the error is not justified: for every kind of error should, if possible, be avoided.

Again, does the error touch the essentials of the poetic art, or some accident of it? For example,—not to know that a hind has no hours is a less serious matter than to paint it inartistically.

Further, if it be objected that the description is not true to fact, the poet may perhaps reply,—'But the objects are as they ought to be:' just as Sophocles said the he drew men as they ought to be; Euripides, as they are. In this way the objection may be met. If, however, the representation be of neither kind, the poet may answer,—'This is how men say the thing is.' This applies to tales about the gods. It may well be that these stories are not higher than fact nor yet true to fact: they are, very possibly, what Xenophanes says of them. But anyhow, 'this is what is said.' Again, a description may be no better than the fact: 'still, it was the fact;' as in the passage about the arms: 'Upright upon their butt-ends stood the spears.' This was the custom then, as it is among the Illyrians.

Again, in examining whether what has been said or done by some one is poetically right or not, we must not look merely to the particular act or saying, and ask whether it is poetically good or bad. We must also consider by whom it is said or done, to whom, when, in whose interest, or for what end; whether, for instance, it be to secure a greater good, or avert a greater evil. . . .

[Aristotle talks about errors in language use]

. . . Thus, there are five sources from which critical objections are drawn. Things are censured either as impossible, or irrational, or morally hurtful, or contradictory, or contrary to artistic correctness.

The answers should be sought under the twelve heads above mentioned.

XXVI. A general estimate of the comparative worth of Epic Poetry and Tragedy

The question may be raised whether the Epic or Tragic mode of imitation is the higher. If the more refined art is the higher, and the more refined in every case is that which appeals to the better sort of audience, the art which imitates anything and everything is manifestly most unrefined. The audience is supposed to be too dull to comprehend unless something of their own is thrown in by the performers, who therefore indulge in restless movements. . . . [*Examples of bad artistic performance follow*]. . . . Tragic art, then, as a whole, stands to Epic in the same relation as the younger to the elder actors. So we are told that Epic poetry is addressed to a cultivated audience, who do not need gesture; Tragedy, to an inferior public. Being then unrefined, it is evidently the lower of the two.

Now, in the first place, this censure attaches not to the poetic but to the histrionic art; for gesticulation may be equally overdone in epic recitation, as by Sosistratus, or in lyrical competition, as by Mnasitleus the Opuntian. Next, all action is not to be condemned—any more than all dancing—but only that of bad performers. Such was the fault found in Callippides, as also in others of our own day, who are censured for representing degraded women. Again, Tragedy like Epic poetry produces its effect even without action; it reveals its power by mere reading. If then, in all other respects it is superior, this fault, we say, is not inherent in it.

And superior it is, because it has all the epic elements—it may even use the epic metre—with the music and spectacular effects as important accessories; and these produce the most vivid of impression in reading as well as representation. Moreover, the art attains its end within narrower limits for the concentrated effect is more pleasurable than one which is spread over a long time and is diluted. What, for example, would be the effect the Oedipus of Sophocles, if it were cast into a form as long as the Iliad? Once more, the Epic imitation has less unity; as is shown by this, that any Epic poem will furnish subjects for several tragedies. Thus if the story adopted by the poet has a strict unity, it must either be concisely told and appear truncated; or, it conform to the Epic canon of length, it must seem weak and watery. <Such length implies some loss of unity, > if, I mean, the poem is constructed out of several actions, like the Iliad and the Odyssey, which have many such parts, each with a certain magnitude of its own. Yet these poems are as perfect as possible in structure, each is, in the highest degree attainable, an imitation of single action.

If, then, Tragedy is superior to Epic poetry in all these respects, and, moreover, fulfils its specific function better as an art—for each art ought to produce, not any chance pleasure, but the pleasure proper to it, as already stated—it plainly follows that Tragedy is the higher art, as attaining its end more perfectly. . . .

ARISTOPHANES

ca. 456-380 B.C.E.

LYSISTRATA

401 B.C.E.

The Greek poet and comic dramatist Aristophanes lived most of his life during the Peloponnesian War (between Athens and Sparta). Little is known of his life but his education suggests that his family was of some wealth. What we know of the author is his wit, invention, and skillful use of language. Eleven of the 44 plays by Aristophanes have survived. In ancient Greece, comic plays were performed annually in Athens at the City Dionysia (the festival dedicated to Dionysus, the god of wine and ecstatic liberation), in which five poets competed for prizes and distinction, each producing one play. Although Aristophanes wrote comedy that is often rather ribald, his plays dealt with serious themes. His satire targeted prominent politicians (including Pericles), social foibles, philosophers, and other poets.

Lysistrata is the third and concluding play of Aristophanes's war and peace series, written to protest the corruption of public morality brought about by the imperialism which led to the war. *Lysistrata* was first staged to promote peaceful coexistence between Athens and Sparta in 411 B.C.E., shortly after the destruction of the Athenian army and navy by Sparta. *Lysistrata* was one of few opportunities to laugh at war, but following the war, such productions were no longer allowed. The theme of *Lysistrata* is that of women's efforts to bring about peace where men had failed. In the twenty-first year of the war, the women of Athens, led by Lysistrata and supported by women delegates from other Greek city-states, take matters into their own hands. To force the men to stop the war, Lysistrata hatches a scheme—the women, in self-denial, will refuse all sexual favors until the men have reached terms of peace. The campaign also includes the women seizing the Acropolis and its state treasury, where they fight old men for possession of the citadel. Before long, the plan is effective. Peace is reached and the play ends with the celebratory festivities of the Athenians and Spartans. Amid the play's hilarious comedy are serious issues brought out by Aristophanes's double chorus, one of women and one of old men: Lysistrata talks passionately of the many who have died in the war and the old men lament that there are no longer any young men to take their places when they die.

SOURCE

Aristophanes. *ca.* 401 B.C.E. *Lysistrata*. In *Aristophanes, with the Translation of Benjamin Bickley Rogers: In Three Volumes*. Vol. III. New York: Putnam, 1924.

LYSISTRATA

The Persons of the drama.

LYSISTRATA

CALONICE

MYRRHINE

LAMPITO

STRATYLLIS, etc.

CHORUS of Women.

MAGISTRATE

CINESIAS

SPARTAN HERALD

ENVOYS

ATHENIANS
Porter, Market Idlers, etc.
CHORUS of old Men.

LYSISTRATA *stands alone with the Propylaea at her back.*

LYSISTRATA: If they were trysting for a Bacchanal,
                A feast of Pan or Colias or Genetyllis,
                The tambourines would block the rowdy streets,
                But now there's not a woman to be seen
                Except—ah, yes—this neighbour of mine yonder.

Enter CALONICE.

LYSISTRATA: Good day Calonice.
CALONICE: Good day Lysistrata.
                But what has vexed you so? Tell me, child.
                What are these black looks for? It doesn't suit you
                To knit your eyebrows up glumly like that.
LYSISTRATA: Calonice, it's more than I can bear,
                I am hot all over with blushes for our sex.
                Men say we're slippery rogues—
CALONICE: And aren't they right?
LYSISTRATA: Yet summoned on the most tremendous business
                For deliberation, still they snuggle in bed.
CALONICE: My dear, they'll come. It's hard for women, you know,
                To get away. There's so much to do.
                Husbands to be patted and put in good tempers:
                Servants to be poked out: children washed
                Or soothed with lullays or fed with mouthfuls of
                    pap.
LYSISTRATA: But I tell you, here's a far more weighty object.
CALONICE: What is it all about, dear Lysistrata,
                That you've called the women hither in a troop?
                What kind of an object is it?
LYSISTRATA: A tremendous thing!

CALONICE: And long?

LYSISTRATA: Indeed, it may be very lengthy.

CALONICE: Then why aren't they here?

LYSISTRATA: No man's connected with it;
If that was the case, they'd soon come fluttering along.
No, no. It concerns an object I've felt over
And turned this way and that for sleepless nights.

CALONICE: It must be fine to stand such long attention.

LYSISTRATA: So fine it comes to this—Greece saved by Woman!

CALONICE: By Woman? Wretched thing, I'm sorry for it.

LYSISTRATA: Our country's fate is henceforth in our hands:
To destroy the Peloponnesians root and branch—

CALONICE: What could be nobler!

LYSISTRATA: Wipe out the Boeotians—

CALONICE: Not utterly. Have mercy on the eels!*

LYSISTRATA: But with regard to Athens, note I'm careful
Not to say any of these nasty things;
Still, thought is free . . . . But if the women join us
From Peloponnesus and Boeotia, then
Hand in hand we'll rescue Greece.

CALONICE: How could we do
Such a big wise deed? We women who dwell
Quietly adorning ourselves in a back-room
With gowns of lucid gold and gawdy toilets
Of stately silk and dainty little slippers . . . .

LYSISTRATA: These are the very armaments of the rescue.
These crocus-gowns, this outlay of the best myrrh,
Slippers, cosmetics dusting beauty, and robes
With rippling creases of light.

CALONICE: Yes, but how?

LYSISTRATA: No man will lift a lance against another—

CALONICE: I'll run to have my tunic dyed crocus.

LYSISTRATA: Or take a shield—

CALONICE: I'll get a stately gown.

LYSISTRATA: Or unscabbard a sword—

---

*   The Boeotian eels were highly esteemed delicacies in Athens.

CALONICE: Let me buy a pair of slippers.
LYSISTRATA: Now, tell me, are the women right to lag?
CALONICE: They should have turned birds, they should have grown
             wings and flown.
LYSISTRATA: My friend, you'll see that they are true Athenians:
             Always too late. Why, there's not a woman
             From the shoreward demes arrived, not one from Salamis.
CALONICE: I know for certain they awoke at dawn,
             And got their husbands up if not their boat sails.
LYSISTRATA: And I'd have staked my life the Acharnian dames
             Would be here first, yet they haven't come either!
CALONICE: Well anyhow there is Theagenes' wife
             We can expect—she consulted Hecate.
             But look, here are some at last, and more behind them.
             See . . . where are they from?
CALONICE: From Anagyra they come.
LYSISTRATA: Yes, they generally manage to come first.

                      Enter MYRRHINE.

MYRRHINE: Are we late, Lysistrata? . . . What is that?
             Nothing to say?
LYSISTRATA: I've not much to say for you,
             Myrrhine, dawdling on so vast an affair.
MYRRHINE: I couldn't find my girdle in the dark.
             But if the affair's so wonderful, tell us, what is it?
LYSISTRATA: No, let us stay a little longer till
             The Peloponnesian girls and the girls of Boeotia
             Are here to listen.
MYRRHINE: That's the best advice.
             Ah, there comes Lampito.

                      Enter LAMPITO.

LYSISTRATA: Welcome, Lampito!
             Dear Spartan girl with a delightful face,

	Washed with the rosy spring, how fresh you look
	In the easy stride of your sleek slenderness,
	Why you could strangle a bull!
LAMPITO:	I think I could.
	It's frae exercise and kicking high behint.*
LYSISTRATA:	What lovely breasts to own!
LAMPITO:	Oo . . . your fingers
	Assess them, ye tickler, wi' such tender chucks
	I feel as if I were an altar-victim.
LYSISTRATA:	Who is this youngster?
LAMPITO:	A Boeotian lady.
LYSISTRATA:	There never was much undergrowth in Boeotia,
	Such a smooth place, and this girl takes after it.
CALONICE:	Yes, I never saw a skin so primly kept.
LYSISTRATA:	This girl?
LAMPITO:	A sonsie open-looking jinker!
	She's a Corinthian.
LYSISTRATA:	Yes, isn't she
	Very open, in some ways particularly.
LAMPITO:	But who's garred this Council o' Women to meet here?
LYSISTRATA:	I have.
LAMPITO:	Propound then what you want o' us.
MYRRHINE:	What is the amazing news you have to tell?
LYSISTRATA:	I'll tell you, but first answer one small question.
MYRRHINE:	As you like.
LYSISTRATA:	Are you not sad your children's fathers
	Go endlessly off soldiering afar
	In this plodding war? I am willing to wager
	There's not one here whose husband is at home.
CALONICE:	Mine's been in Thrace, keeping an eye on Eucrates
	For five months past.

---

* The translator has put the speech of the Spartan characters in Scotch
dialect, which is related to English about as was the Spartan dialect to the
speech of Athens. The Spartans, in their character, anticipated the shrewd,
canny, uncouth Scotch highlander of modern times.

MYRRHINE: And mine left me for Pylos
                 Seven months ago at least.

LAMPITO: And as for mine
                 No sooner has he slipped out frae the line
                 He straps his shield and he's snickt off again.

LYSISTRATA: And not the slightest glitter of a lover!
                 And since the Milesians betrayed us, I've not seen
                 The image of a single upright man
                 To be a marble consolation to us.
                 Now will you help me, if I find a means
                 To stamp the war out.

MYRRHINE: By the two Goddesses, Yes!
                 I will though I've to pawn this very dress
                 And drink the barter-money the same day.

CALONICE: And I too though I'm split up like a turbot
                 And half is hackt off as the price of peace.

LAMPITO: And I too! Why, to get a peep at the shy thing
                 I'd clamber up to the tip-top o' Taygetus.

LYSISTRATA: Then I'll expose my mighty mystery.
                 O women, if we would compel the men
                 To bow to Peace, we must refrain—

MYRRHINE: From what?
                 O tell us!

LYSISTRATA: Will you truly do it then?

MYRRHINE: We will, we will, if we must die for it.

LYSISTRATA: We must refrain from every depth of love . . . .
                 Why do you turn your backs? Where are you going?
                 Why do you bite your lips and shake your heads?
                 Why are your faces blanched? Why do you weep?
                 Will you or won't you, or what do you mean?

MYRRHINE: No, I won't do it. Let the war proceed.

CALONICE: No, I won't do it. Let the war proceed.

LYSISTRATA: You too, dear turbot, you that said just now
                 You didn't mind being split right up in the least?

CALONICE: Anything else? O bid me walk in fire

But do not rob us of that darling joy.
What else is like it, dearest Lysistrata?

LYSISTRATA: And you?

MYRRHINE: O please give me the fire instead.

LYSISTRATA: Lewd to the least drop in the tiniest vein,
Our sex is fitly food for Tragic Poets,
Our whole life's but a pile of kisses and babies.
But, hardy Spartan, if you join with me
All may be righted yet. O help me, help me.

LAMPITO: It's a sair, sair thing to ask of us, by the Twa,
A lass to sleep her lane and never fill
Love's lack except wi' makeshifts . . . But let it be.
Peace maun be thought of first.

LYSISTRATA: My friend, my friend!
The only one amid this herd of weaklings.

CALONICE: But if—which heaven forbid—we should refrain
As you would have us, how is Peace induced?

LYSISTRATA: By the two Goddesses, now can't you see
All we have to do is idly sit indoors
With smooth roses powdered on our cheeks,
Our bodies burning naked through the folds
Of shining Amorgos' silk, and meet the men
With our dear Venus-plats plucked trim and neat.
Their stirring love will rise up furiously,
They'll beg our arms to open. That's our time!
We'll disregard their knocking, beat them off
And they will soon be rabid for a Peace.
I'm sure of it.

LAMPITO: Just as Menelaus, they say,
Seeing the bosom of his naked Helen
Flang down the sword.

CALONICE: But we'll be tearful fools
If our husbands take us at our word and leave us.

LYSISTRATA: There's only left then, in Pherecrates' phrase,
To flay a skinned dog—flay more our flayed desires.

CALONICE: Bah, proverbs will never warm a celibate.
               But what avail will your scheme be if the men
               Drag us for all our kicking on to the couch?
LYSISTRATA: Cling to the doorposts.
CALONICE: But if they should force us?
LYSISTRATA: Yield then, but with a sluggish, cold indifference.
               There is no joy to them in sullen mating.
               Besides we have other ways to madden them;
               They cannot stand up long, and they've no delight
               Unless we fit their aim with merry succour.
CALONICE: Well if you must have it so, we'll all agree.
LAMPITO: For us I ha' no doubt. We can persuade
               Our men to strike a fair an' decent Peace,
               But how will ye pitch out the battle-frenzy
               O' the Athenian populace?
LYSISTRATA: I promise you
               We'll wither up that curse.
LAMPITO: I don't believe it.
               Not while they own ane trireme oared an' rigged,
               Or a' those stacks an' stacks an' stacks o' siller.
LYSISTRATA: I've thought the whole thing out till there's no flaw.
               We shall surprise the Acropolis today:
               That is the duty set the older dames.
               While we sit here talking, they are to go
               And under pretence of sacrificing, seize it.
LAMPITO: Certie, that's fine; all's warking for the best.
LYSISTRATA: Now quickly, Lampito, let us tie ourselves
               To this high purpose as tightly as the hemp of words
               Can knot together.
LAMPITO: Set out the terms in detail
               And we'll a' swear to them.
LYSISTRATA: Of course . . . Well then
               Where is our Scythianess? Why are you staring?
               First lay the shield, boss downward, on the floor
CALONICE: But, Lysistrata,
               What is this oath that we're to swear?

LYSISTRATA: What oath!
In Aeschylus they take a slaughtered sheep
And swear upon a buckler. Why not we?

CALONICE: O Lysistrata, Peace sworn on a buckler!

LYSISTRATA: What oath would suit us then?

CALONICE: Something burden bearing
Would be our best insignia . . . . A white horse!
Let's swear upon its entrails.

LYSISTRATA: A horse indeed!

CALONICE: Then what will symbolise us?

LYSISTRATA: This, as I tell you—
First set a great dark bowl upon the ground
And disembowel a skin of Thasian wine,
Then swear that we'll not add a drop of water.

LAMPITO: Ah, what aith could clink pleasanter than that!

LYSISTRATA: Bring me a bowl then and a skin of wine.

CALONICE: My dears, see what a splendid bowl it is;
I'd not say No if asked to sip it off.

LYSISTRATA: Put down the bowl. Lay hands, all, on the victim.
Skiey Queen who givest the last word in arguments,
And thee, O Bowl, dear comrade, we beseech:
Accept our oblation and be propitious to us.

CALONICE: What healthy blood, la, how it gushes out!

LAMPITO: An' what a leesome fragrance through the air.

LYSISTRATA: Now, dears, if you will let me, I'll speak first.

CALONICE: Only if you draw the lot, by Aphrodite!

LYSISTRATA: So, grasp the brim, you, Lampito, and all.
You, Calonice, repeat for the rest
Each word I say. Then you must all take oath
And pledge your arms to the same stem conditions—

LYSISTRATA: To husband or lover I'll not open arms

CALONICE: *To husband or lover I'll not open arms*

LYSISTRATA: Though love and denial may enlarge his charms.

CALONICE: *Though love and denial may enlarge his charms.*
O, O, my knees are failing me, Lysistrata!

LYSISTRATA: But still at home, ignoring him, I'll stay,

CALONICE: *But still at home, ignoring him, I'll stay,*
LYSISTRATA: Beautiful, clad in saffron silks all day.
CALONICE: *Beautiful, clad in saffron silks all day.*
LYSISTRATA: If then he seizes me by dint of force,
CALONICE: *If then he seizes me by dint of force,*
LYSISTRATA: I'll give him reason for a long remorse.
CALONICE: *I'll give him reason for a long remorse.*
LYSISTRATA: I'll never lie and stare up at the ceiling,
CALONICE: *I'll never lie and stare up at the ceiling,*
LYSISTRATA: Nor like a lion on all fours go kneeling.
CALONICE: *Nor like a lion on all fours go kneeling.*
LYSISTRATA: If I keep faith, then bounteous cups be mine.
CALONICE: *If I keep faith, then bounteous cups be mine.*
LYSISTRATA: If not, to nauseous water change this wine.
CALONICE: *If not, to nauseous water change this wine.*
LYSISTRATA: Do you all swear to this?
MYRRHINE: We do, we do.
LYSISTRATA: Then I shall immolate the victim thus.
She drinks.
CALONICE: Here now, share fair, haven't we made a pact?
Let's all quaff down that friendship in our turn.
LAMPITO: Hark, what caterwauling hubbub's that?
LYSISTRATA: As I told you,
The women have appropriated the citadel.
So, Lampito, dash off to your own land
And raise the rebels there. These will serve as hostages,
While we ourselves take our places in the ranks
And drive the bolts right home.
CALONICE: But won't the men
March straight against us?
LYSISTRATA: And what if they do?
No threat shall creak our hinges wide, no torch
Shall light a fear in us; we will come out
To Peace alone.
CALONICE: That's it, by Aphrodite!
As of old let us seem hard and obdurate.

LAMPITO *and some go off; the others go up into the*
Acropolis. Chorus of OLD MEN *enter to attack the*
captured Acropolis.

Make room, Draces, move ahead; why your shoulder's chafed, I see,
With lugging uphill these lopped branches of the olive-tree.
How upside-down and wrong-way-round a long life sees things grow.
Ah, Strymodorus, who'd have thought affairs could tangle so?

> The women whom at home we fed,
> Like witless fools, with fostering bread,
> Have impiously come to this—
> They've stolen the Acropolis,
> With bolts and bars our orders flout
>   And shut us out.

Come, Philurgus, bustle thither; lay our faggots on the ground,
In neat stacks beleaguering the insurgents all around;
And the vile conspiratresses, plotters of such mischief dire,
Pile and burn them all together in one vast and righteous pyre:
Fling with our own hands Lycon's wife to fry in the thickest fire.
By Demeter, they'll get no brag while I've a vein to beat!
Cleomenes himself was hurtled out in sore defeat.

> His stiff-backed Spartan pride was bent.
> Out, stripped of all his arms, he went:
> A pigmy cloak that would not stretch
> Or hide his rump (the draggled wretch),
> Six sprouting years of beard, the spilth
>   Of six years' filth.

That was a siege! Our men were ranged in lines of seventeen deep
Before the gates, and never left their posts there, even to sleep.
Shall I not smite the rash presumption then of foes like these,
Detested both of all the gods and of Euripides—
Else, may the Marathon-plain not boast my trophied victories!

Ah, now, there's but a little space
To reach the place!
A deadly climb it is, a tricky road
With all this bumping load:
A pack-ass soon would tire. . . .
How these logs bruise my shoulders! further still
Jog up the hill,
And puff the fire inside,
Or just as we reach the top we'll find it's died.
   Ough, phew!
   I choke with the smoke.

Lord Heracles, how acrid-hot
Out of the pot
This mad-dog smoke leaps, worrying me
And biting angrily. . . .
'Tis Lemnian fire that smokes,
Or else it would not sting my eyelids thus. . . .
Haste, all of us;
Athene invokes our aid.
Laches, now or never the assault must be made!
   Ough, phew!
   I choke with the smoke.

Thanked be the gods! The fire peeps up and crackles as it should.
Now why not first slide off our backs these weary loads of wood
And dip a vine-branch in the brazier till it glows, then straight
Hurl it at the battering-ram against the stubborn gate?
If they refuse to draw the bolts in immediate compliance,
We'll set fire to the wood, and smoke will strangle their defiance.
Phew, what a spluttering drench of smoke! Come, now from off
  my back. . . .
Is there no Samos-general to help me to unpack?
Ah there, that's over! For the last time now it's galled my shoulder.
Flare up thine embers, brazier, and dutifully smoulder,
To kindle a brand, that I the first may strike the citadel.

Aid me, Lady Victory, that a triumph-trophy may tell
How we did anciently this insane audacity quell!

Chorus of WOMEN.

What's that rising yonder? That ruddy glare, that smoky skurry?
O is it something in a blaze? Quick, quick, my comrades, hurry

      Nicodice, helter-skelter!
      Or poor Calyce's in flames
      And Cratylla's stifled in the welter.
      O these dreadful old men
      And their dark laws of hate!

There, I'm all of a tremble lest I turn out to be too late.
I could scarcely get near to the spring though I rose before dawn,
What with tattling of tongues and rattling of pitchers in one jostling
    din

      With slaves pushing in! . . .
      Still here at last the water's drawn
      And with it eagerly I run
      To help those of my friends who stand
      In danger of being burned alive.
      For I am told a dribbling band
      Of greybeards hobble to the field,
      Great faggots in each palsied hand,
      As if a hot bath to prepare,
      And threatening that out they'll drive

These wicked women or soon leave them charring into ashes there.
O Goddess, suffer not, I pray, this harsh deed to be done,
But show us Greece and Athens with their warlike acts repealed!

      For this alone, in this thy hold,
      Thou Goddess with the helm of gold,

We laid hands on thy sanctuary,
Athene.... Then our ally be
And where they cast their fires of slaughter
Direct our water!

STRATYLLIS: (*caught*):   Let me go!

WOMEN: You villainous old men, what's this you do?
No honest man, no pious man, could do such
        things as you.

MEN: Ah ha, here's something most original, I have no doubt:
A swarm of women sentinels to man the walls without.

WOMEN: So then we scare you, do we? Do we seem a fearful host?
You only see the smallest fraction mustered at this post.

MEN: Ho, Phaedrias, shall we put a stop to all these
        chattering tricks?
Suppose that now upon their backs we splintered
these our sticks?

WOMEN: Let us lay down the pitchers, so our bodies will be free,
In case these lumping fellows try to cause some injury.

MEN. O hit them hard and hit again and hit until they
        run away,
And perhaps they'll learn, like Bupalus, not to have
too much to say.

WOMEN: Come on, then—do it! I won't budge, but like a dog
        I'll bite
At every little scrap of meat that dangles in my sight.

MEN: Be quiet, or I'll bash you out of any years to come.

WOMEN: Now you just touch Stratyllis with the topjoint of
        your thumb.

MEN: What vengeance can you take if with my fists your
        face I beat?

WOMEN: I'll rip you with my teeth and strew your entrails at
        your feet.

MEN: Now I appreciate Euripides' strange subtlety:
Woman is the most shameless beast of all the beasts that be.

WOMEN: Rhodippe, come, and let's pick up our waterjars
        once more.

MEN:	Ah cursed drab, what have you brought this water hither for?
WOMEN:	What is our fire for then, you smelly corpse? Yourself to burn?
MEN:	To build a pyre and make your comrades ready for the urn.
WOMEN:	And I've the water to put out your fire immediately.
MEN:	What, you put out my fire?
WOMEN:	Yes, sirrah, as you soon will see.
MEN:	I don't know why I hesitate to roast you with this flame.
WOMEN:	If you have any soap you'll go off cleaner than you came.
MEN:	Cleaner, you dirty slut?
WOMEN:	A nuptial-bath in which to lie!
MEN:	Did you hear that insolence?
WOMEN:	I'm a free woman, I.
MEN:	I'll make you hold your tongue.
WOMEN:	Henceforth you'll serve in no more juries.
MEN:	Burn off her hair for her.
WOMEN:	Now forward, water, quench their furies!
MEN:	O dear, O dear!
WOMEN:	So . . . was it hot?
MEN:	Hot! . . . Enough, O hold,
WOMEN:	Watered, perhaps you'll bloom again—why not?
MEN:	Brrr, I'm wrinkled up from shivering with cold.
WOMEN:	Next time you've fire you'll warm yourself and leave us to our lot.

MAGISTRATE *enters with attendant* SCYTHIANS

MAGISTRATE: Have the luxurious rites of the women glittered
Their libertine show, their drumming tapped out crowds,
The Sabazian Mysteries summoned their mob,
Adonis been wept to death on the terraces,
As I could hear the last day in the Assembly?
For Demostratus—let bad luck befoul him—
Was roaring, "We must sail for Sicily,"

While a woman, throwing herself about in a dance
Lopsided with drink, was shrilling out "Adonis,
Woe for Adonis." Then Demostratus shouted,
"We must levy hoplites at Zacynthus,"
And there the woman, up to the ears in wine,
Was screaming "Weep for Adonis" on the house-top,
The scoundrelly politician, that lunatic ox,
Bellowing bad advice through tipsy shrieks:
Such are the follies wantoning in them.

MEN: O if you knew their full effrontery!
All of the insults they've done, besides sousing us
With water from their pots to our public disgrace
For we stand here wringing our clothes like grown-
    up infants.

MAGISTRATE: By Poseidon, justly done! For in part with us
The blame must lie for dissolute behaviour
And for the pampered appetites they learn.
Thus grows the seedling lust to blossoming:
We go into a shop and say, "Here, goldsmith,
You remember the necklace that you wrought my wife;
Well, the other night in fervour of a dance
Her clasp broke open. Now I'm off for Salamis;
If you've the leisure, would you go tonight
And stick a bolt-pin into her opened clasp."
Another goes to a cobbler, a soldierly fellow,
Always standing up erect, and says to him,
"Cobbler, a sandal-strap of my wife's pinches her,
Hurts her little toe in a place where she's sensitive.
Come at noon and see if you can stretch out wider
This thing that troubles her, loosen its tightness."
And so you view the result. Observe my case—
I, a magistrate, come here to draw
Money to buy oar-blades, and what happens?
The women slam the door full in my face.
But standing still's no use. Bring me a crowbar,

And I'll chastise this their impertinence.
What do you gape at, wretch, with dazzled eyes?
Peering for a tavern, I suppose.
Come, force the gates with crowbars, prise them apart!
I'll prise away myself too . . .   (LYSISTRATA *appears*)

LYSISTRATA: Stop this banging.
I'm coming of my own accord. . . . Why bars?
It is not bars we need but common sense.

MAGISTRATE: Indeed, you slut! Where is the archer now?
Arrest this woman, tie her hands behind.

LYSISTRATA: If he brushes me with a finger, by Artemis,
The public menial, he'll be sorry for it.

MAGISTRATE: Are you afraid? Grab her about the middle.
Two of you then, lay hands on her and end it.

CALONICE: By Pandrosos! if your hand touches her
I'll spread you out and trample on your guts.

MAGISTRATE: My guts! Where is the other archer gone?
Bind that minx there who talks so prettily.

MYRRHINE: By Phosphor, if your hand moves out her way
You'd better have a surgeon somewhere handy.

MAGISTRATE: You too! Where is that archer? Take that woman.
I'll put a stop to these surprise-parties.

STRATYLLIS: By the Tauric Artemis, one inch nearer
My fingers, and it's a bald man that'll be yelling.

MAGISTRATE: Tut tut, what's here? Deserted by my archers . . . .
But surely women never can defeat us;
Close up your ranks, my Scythians. Forward at them.

LYSISTRATA: By the Goddesses, you'll find that here await you
Four companies of most pugnacious women
Armed cap-a-pie from the topmost louring curl
To the lowest angry dimple.

MAGISTRATE: On, Scythians, bind them.

LYSISTRATA: On, gallant allies of our high design,
Vendors of grain-eggs-pulse-and-vegetables,
Ye garlic-tavern-keepers of bakeries,

Strike, batter, knock, hit, slap, and scratch our foes,
Be finely imprudent, say what you think of them . . . .
Enough! retire and do not rob the dead.

MAGISTRATE: How basely did my archer-force come off.

LYSISTRATA: Ah, ha, you thought it was a herd of slaves
You had to tackle, and you didn't guess
The thirst for glory ardent in our blood.

LYSISTRATA: By Apollo, I know well the thirst that heats you—
Especially when a wine-skin's close.

MEN: You waste your breath, dear magistrate, I fear, in
        answering back.
What's the good of argument with such a
        rampageous pack?
Remember how they washed us down (these very
        clothes I wore)
With water that looked nasty and that smelt so even more.

WOMEN: What else to do, since you advanced too dangerously nigh.
If you should do the same again, I'll punch you in
        the eye.
Though I'm a stay-at-home and most a quiet life enjoy,
Polite to all and every (for I'm naturally coy),
Still if you wake a wasps' nest then of wasps you
        must beware.

MEN: How may this ferocity be tamed? It grows too great
        to bear.
Let us question them and find if they'll perchance declare
        The reason why they strangely dare
        To seize on Ganaos' citadel,
        This eyrie inaccessible,
        This shrine above the precipice,
        The Acropolis.
Probe them and find what they mean with this idle
        talk; listen, but watch they don't try to deceive.
You'd be neglecting your duty most certainly if now
        this mystery unplumbed you leave.

MAGISTRATE: Women there! Tell what I ask you, directly . . . .
Come, without rambling, I wish you to state

What's your rebellious intention in barring up thus
    on our noses our own temple-gate.

LYSISTRATA: To take first the treasury out of your management,
    and so stop the war through the absence of gold.

MAGISTRATE: Is gold then the cause of the war?

LYSISTRATA: Yes, gold caused it and miseries more, too many to
    be told.

'Twas for money, and money alone, that Pisander
    with all of the army of mob-agitators

Raised up revolutions. But, as for the future, it
    won't be worth while to set up to be traitors.

Not an obol they'll get as their loot, not an obol! while
    we have the treasure-chest in our command.

MAGISTRATE: What then is that you propose?

LYSISTRATA: Just this—merely to take the
    exchequer henceforth in hand.

MAGISTRATE: The exchequer!

LYSISTRATA: Yes, why not? Of our capabilities you have had
    various clear evidences.

Firstly remember we have always administered
    soundly the budget of all home-expenses.

mAGISTRATE: But this matter's different.

LYSISTRATA: How is it different?

MAGISTRATE: Why, it deals chiefly with war-time supplies.

LYSISTRATA: But we abolish war straight by our policy.

MAGISTRATE: What will you do if emergencies arise?

LYSISTRATA: Face them our own way.

MAGISTRATE: What *you* will?

LYSISTRATA: Yes *we* will!

MAGISTRATE: Then there's no help for it: we're all destroyed.

LYSISTRATA: No, willy-nilly you must be safeguarded.

MAGISTRATE: What madness is this?

LYSISTRATA: Why, it seems you're annoyed.
    It must be done, that's all.

MAGISTRATE: Such awful oppression never,
    O never in the past yet I bore.

LYSISTRATA: You must be saved, sirrah—that's all there is to it.

MAGISTRATE: If we don't want to be saved?
LYSISTRATA: All the more.
MAGISTRATE: Why do you women come prying and meddling in matters of state touching war-time and peace?
LYSISTRATA: That I will tell you.
MAGISTRATE: O tell me or quickly I'll—
LYSISTRATA: Hearken awhile and from threatening cease.
MAGISTRATE: I cannot, I cannot; it's growing too insolent.
WOMEN: Come on; you've far more than we have to dread.
MAGISTRATE: Stop from your croaking, old carrion-crow there . . . Continue.
LYSISTRATA: Be calm then and I'll go ahead.
All the long years when the hopeless war dragged along, we, unassuming, forgotten in quiet,
Endured without question, endured in our loneliness all your incessant child's antics and riot.
Our lips we kept tied, though aching with silence, though well all the while in our silence we knew
How wretchedly everything still was progressing by listening dumbly the daylong to you.
For always at home you continued discussing the war and its politics loudly, and we
Sometimes would ask you, our hearts deep with sorrowing, though we spoke lightly, though happy to see,
"What's to be inscribed on the side of the Treaty-stone?
What, dear, was said in the Assembly today?"
"Mind your own business," he'd answer me growlingly, "hold your tongue, woman, or else go away."
And so I would hold it.
WOMEN: I'd not be silent for any man living on earth, no, not I!
MAGISTRATE: Not for a staff?
LYSISTRATA: Well, so I did nothing but sit in the house, feeling dreary, and sigh,
While ever arrived some fresh tale of decisions more foolish by far and presaging disaster.

Then I would say to him, "O my dear husband, why
    still do they rush on destruction the faster?"
At which he would look at me sideways, exclaiming,
    "Keep for your web and your shuttle your care,
Or for some hours hence your cheeks will be sore and
    hot; leave this alone, war is Man's sole affair!"

MAGISTRATE: By Zeus, but a man of fine sense, he.

LYSISTRATA: How sensible?

You dotard, because he at no time had lent
His intractible ears to absorb from our counsel one
    temperate word of advice, kindly meant?
But when at the last in the streets we heard shouted
    (everywhere ringing the ominous cry)
"Is there no one to help us, no saviour in Athens?"
    and,"No, there is no one," come back in reply.
At once a convention of all wives through Hellas
    here for a serious purpose was held,
To determine how husbands might yet back to wisdom
    despite their reluctance in time be compelled.
Why then delay any longer? It's settled. For the
    future you'll take up our old occupation.
Now in turn you're to hold tongue, as we did, and
    listen while we show the way to recover the nation.

MAGISTRATE: *You* talk to *us*! Why, you're mad. I'll not stand it.

LYSISTRATA: Cease babbling, you fool; till I end, hold your tongue.

MAGISTRATE: If I should take orders from one who wears veils,
    may my neck straightaway be deservedly wrung.

LYSISTRATA: O if that keeps pestering you,
    I've a veil here for your hair,
    I'll fit you out in everything
    As is only fair.

CALONICE: Here's a spindle that will do.

MYRRHINE: I'll add a wool-basket too.

LYSISTRATA: Girdled now sit humbly at home,
    Munching beans, while you card wool and comb.
    For war from now on is the Women's affair.

WOMEN.

Come then, down pitchers, all,
And on, courageous of heart,
In our comradely venture
Each taking her due part.
I could dance, dance, dance, and be fresher after,
I could dance away numberless suns,
To no weariness let my knees bend.
Earth I could brave with laughter,
Having such wonderful girls here to friend.
O the daring, the gracious, the beautiful ones!
Their courage unswerving and witty
                    Will rescue our city.

O sprung from the seed of most valiant-wombed grandmothers,
    scions of savage and dangerous nettles!
Prepare for the battle, all. Gird up your angers. Our way the wind
    of sweet victory settles.

LYSISTRATA: O tender Eros and Lady of Cyprus, some flush of
                    beauty I pray you devise
              To flash on our bosoms and, O Aphrodite, rosily
                    gleam on our valorous thighs!
              Joy will raise up its head through the legions warring
                    and all of the far-serried ranks of mad-love
              Bristle the earth to the pillared horizon, pointing in
                    vain to the heavens above.
              I think that perhaps then they'll give us our title—
                    Peace-makers.
MAGISTRATE: What do you mean? Please explain.
LYSISTRATA: First, we'll not see you now flourishing arms about
              into the Marketing-place clang again.
WOMEN: No, by the Paphian.
LYSISTRATA: Still I can conjure them as past where
              the herbs stand or crockery's sold Like Corybants
              jingling (poor sots) fully armoured, they noisily
              round on their promenade strolled.

MAGISTRATE: And rightly; that's discipline, they—

LYSISTRATA: But what's sillier than to go on an errand of buying a fish
Carrying along an immense Gorgon-buckler instead
    of the usual platter or dish?
A phylarch I lately saw, mounted on horse-back,
    dressed for the part with long ringlets and all,
Stow in his helmet the omelet bought steaming
    from an old woman who kept a food—stall.
Nearby a soldier, a Thracian, was shaking wildly his
    spear, like Tereus in the play,
To frighten a fig-girl while unseen the ruffian filched
    from her fruit-trays the ripest away.

MAGISTRATE: How, may I ask, will your rule re-establish order and
justice in lands so tormented?

LYSISTRATA: Nothing is easier.

MAGISTRATE: Out with it speedily—what is this plan
that you boast you've invented?

LYSISTRATA: If, when yarn we are winding, it chances to tangle, then,
    as perchance you may know, through the skein
This way and that still the spool we keep passing till
    it is finally clear all again:
So to untangle the War and its errors, ambassadors
    out on all sides we will send
This way and that, here, there and round about—
    soon you will find that the War has an end.

MAGISTRATE: So with these trivial tricks of the household,
    domestic analogies of threads, skeins and spools,
You think that you'll solve such a bitter complexity,
    unwind such political problems, you fools!

LYSISTRATA: Well, first as we wash dirty wool so's to cleanse it, so
    with a pitiless zeal we will scrub
Through the whole city for all greasy fellows; burrs
    too, the parasites, off we will rub.
That verminous plague of insensate place-seekers
    soon between thumb and forefinger we'll crack.
All who inside Athens' walls have their dwelling into
    one great common basket we'll pack.

Disenfranchised or citizens, allies or aliens, pell-mell
   the lot of them in we will squeeze.
Till they discover humanity's meaning . . . . As for
   disjointed and far colonies,
Them you must never from this time imagine as
   scattered about just like lost hanks of wool.
Each portion we'll take and wind in to this centre,
   inward to Athens each loyalty pull,
Till from the vast heap where all's piled together at
   last can be woven a strong Cloak of State.

MAGISTRATE: How terrible is it to stand here and watch them
   carding and winding at will with our fate,
Witless in war as they are.

LYSISTRATA: What of us then, who ever in
   vain for our children must weep
Borne but to perish afar and in vain?

MAGISTRATE: Not that, O let that one memory sleep!

LYSISTRATA: Then while we should be companioned still merrily,
   happy as brides may, the livelong night,
Kissing youth by, we are forced to lie single . . . .
   But leave for a moment our pitiful plight,
It hurts even more to behold the poor maidens
   helplessly wrinkling in staler virginity.

MAGISTRATE: Does not a man age?

LYSISTRATA: Not in the same way. Not as a woman grows
   withered, grows he.
He, when returned from the war, though grey-
   headed, yet if he wishes can choose out a wife.
But she has no solace save peering for omens,
   wretched and lonely the rest of her life.

MAGISTRATE: But the old man will often select—

LYSISTRATA: O why not finish and die?
A bier is easy to buy,
A honey-cake I'll knead you with joy,
This garland will see you are decked.

CALONICE: I've a wreath for you too.

MYRRHINE: I also will fillet you.

LYSISTRATA: What more is lacking? Step aboard the boat.
See, Charon shouts ahoy.
You're keeping him, he wants to shove afloat.

MAGISTRATE: Outrageous insults! Thus my place to flout!
Now to my fellow-magistrates I'll go
And what you've perpetrated on me show.

LYSISTRATA: Why are you blaming us for laying you out?
Assure yourself we'll not forget to make
The third day offering early for your sake.

MAGISTRATE *retires,* LYSISTRATA *returns within.*

OLD MEN.

All men who call your loins your own, awake at last, arise
And strip to stand in readiness. For as it seems to me
Some more perilous offensive in their heads they now devise.

    I'm sure a Tyranny
    Like that of Hippias
    In this I detect. . . .
    They mean to put us under
    Themselves I suspect,
    And that Laconians assembling
    At Cleisthenes' house have played
    A trick-of-war and provoked them
    Madly to raid
    The Treasury, in which term I include
    The pay for my food.

    For is it not preposterous
    They should talk this way to us
    On a subject such as battle!
And, women as they are, about bronze bucklers dare to prattle—
Make alliance with the Spartans—people I for one

Like very hungry wolves would always most sincerely shun . . . .
>   Some dirty game is up their sleeve,
>   I believe.
Tyranny, no doubt . . . but they won't catch me, that I know.
>   Henceforth on my guard I'll go,
A sword with myrtle-branches wreathed for ever in my hand,
And under arms in the Public Place I'll take my watchful stand,
Shoulder to shoulder with Aristogeiton. Now my staff I'll draw
>   And start at once by knocking that shocking
>   Hag upon the jaw.

WOMEN.

Your own mother will not know you when you get back to the town.
But first, my friends and allies, let us lay these garments down,
And all ye fellow-citizens, hark to me while I tell
>   What will aid Athens well.
>   Just as is right, for I
>   Have been a sharer
>   In all the lavish splendour
>   Of the proud city.
>   I bore the holy vessels
>   At seven, then
>   I pounded barley
>   At the age of ten,
>   And clad in yellow robes,
>   Soon after this,
>   I was Little Bear to
>   Brauronian Artemis;
>   Then neckletted with figs,
>   Grown tall and pretty,
>   I was a Basket-bearer,
>   And so it's obvious I should
>   Give you advice that I think good,
>   The very best I can.
It should not prejudice my voice that I'm not born a man,
If I say something advantageous to the present situation.

For I'm taxed too, and as a toll provide men for the nation.
　　While, miserable greybeards, you,
　　　　It is true,
Contribute nothing of any importance whatever to our needs;
　　　　But the treasure raised against the Medes
You've squandered, and do nothing in return, save that you make
Our lives and persons hazardous by some imbecile mistake.
What can you answer? Now be careful, don't arouse my spite,
Or with my slipper I'll take you napping, faces slapping
　　　　Left and right.

MEN.
　　What villainies they contrive!
　　Come, let vengeance fall,
　　You that below the waist are still alive,
　　Off with your tunics at my call—
　　Naked, all.
　　For a man must strip to battle like a man.
No quaking, brave steps taking, careless what's ahead, whiteshoed,
　　in the nude, onward bold,
　　　　All ye who garrisoned Leipsidrion of old . . . .
　　　　Let each one wag
　　　　As youthfully as he can,
　　　　And if he has the cause at heart
　　　　Rise at least a span.

　　We must take a stand and keep to it,
　　For if we yield the smallest bit
　　　　To their importunity.
Then nowhere from their inroads will be left to us immunity.
But they'll be building ships and soon their navies will attack us,
As Artemisia did, and seek to fight us and to sack us.
　　　　And if they mount, the Knights they'll rob
　　　　Of a job,
For everyone knows how talented they all are in the saddle,
　　　　Having long practised how to straddle;

No matter how they're jogged there up and down, they're never thrown.
Then think of Myron's painting, and each horse-backed Amazon
In combat hand-to-hand with men. . . . Come, on these women fall,
     And in pierced wood-collars let's stick quick
     The necks of one and all.

        WOMEN.
     Don't cross me or I'll loose
     The Beast that's kennelled here. . . .
     And soon you will be howling for a truce,
     Howling out with fear.
     But my dear,
Strip also, that women may battle unhindered. . . .
But you, you'll be too sore to eat garlic more, or one black bean, I
   really mean, so great's my spleen, to kick you black and blue
     With these my dangerous legs.
     I'll hatch the lot of you,
     If my rage you dash on,
     The way the relentless Beetle
     Hatched the Eagle's eggs.

     Scornfully aside I set
     Every silly old-man threat
     While Lampito's with me.
Or dear Ismenia, the noble Theban girl. Then let decree
Be hotly piled upon decree; in vain will be your labours,
You futile rogue abominated by your suffering neighbours.
     To Hecate's feast I yesterday went—
     Off I sent
To our neighbours in Boeotia, asking as a gift to me
     For them to pack immediately
That darling dainty thing . . . a good fat eel I meant of course;
But they refused because some idiotic old decree's in force.
O this strange passion of decrees nothing on earth can check,
Till someone puts a foot out tripping you, and slipping you
     Break your neck.

LYSISTRATA *enters in dismay.*

WOMEN:	Dear Mistress of our martial enterprise,
	Why do you come with sorrow in your eyes?
LYSISTRATA:	O 'tis our naughty femininity,
	So weak in one spot, that hath saddened me.
WOMEN:	What's this? Please speak.
LYSISTRATA:	Poor women! O so weak!
WOMEN:	What can it be? Surely your friends may know.
LYSISTRATA:	Yea, I must speak it though it hurt me so.
WOMEN:	Speak; can we help? Don't stand there mute in need.
LYSISTRATA:	I'll blurt it out then—our women's army's mutinied.
WOMEN:	O Zeus!
LYSISTRATA:	What use is Zeus to our anatomy?
	Here is the gaping calamity I meant:
	I cannot shut their ravenous appetites
	A moment more now. They are all deserting.
	The first I caught was sidling through the postern
	Close by the Cave of Pan: the next hoisting herself
	With rope and pulley down: a third on the point
	Of slipping past: while a fourth malcontent, seated
	or instant flight to visit Orsilochus
	On bird-back, I dragged off by the hair in time. . . .
	They are all snatching excuses to sneak home.
	Look, there goes one. . . . Hey, what's the hurry?
1st WOMAN:	I must get home. I've some Milesian wool
	Packed wasting away, and moths are pushing through it.
LYSISTRATA:	Fine moths indeed, I know. Get back within.
1st WOMAN:	By the Goddesses, I'll return instantly.
	I only want to stretch it on my bed.
LYSISTRATA:	You shall stretch nothing and go nowhere either.
1st WOMAN:	Must I never use my wool then?
LYSISTRATA:	If needs be.
2nd WOMAN:	How unfortunate I am! O my poor flax!
	It's left at home unstript.
LYSISTRATA:	So here's another

	That wishes to go home and strip her flax.
	Inside again!
2nd WOMAN:	No, by the Goddess of Light,
	I'll be back as soon as I have flayed it properly.
LYSISTRATA:	You'll not flay anything. For if you begin
	There'll not be one here but has a patch to be flayed.
3rd WOMAN:	O holy Eilithyia, stay this birth
	Till I have left the precincts of the place!
LYSISTRATA:	What nonsense is this?
3rd WOMAN:	I'll drop it any minute.
LYSISTRATA:	Yesterday you weren't with child.
3rd WOMAN:	But I am today.
	O let me find a midwife, Lysistrata.
	O quickly!
LYSISTRATA:	Now what story is this you tell?
	What is this hard lump here?
3rd WOMAN:	It's a male child.
LYSISTRATA:	By Aphrodite, it isn't. Your belly's hollow,
	And it has the feel of metal . . . . Well, I soon can see.
	You hussy, it's Athene's sacred helm,
	And you said you were with child.
3rd WOMAN:	And so I am.
LYSISTRATA:	Then why the helm?
3rd WOMAN:	So if the throes should take me
	Still in these grounds I could use it like a dove
	As a laying-nest in which to drop the child.
LYSISTRATA:	More pretexts! You can't hide your clear intent,
	And anyway why not wait till the tenth day
	Meditating a brazen name for your brass brat?
WOMAN:	And I can't sleep a wink. My nerve is gone
	Since I saw that snake-sentinel of the shrine.
WOMAN:	And all those dreadful owls with their weird hooting!
	Though I'm wearied out, I can't close an eye.
LYSISTRATA:	You wicked women, cease from juggling lies.
	You want your men. But what of them as well?
	They toss as sleepless in the lonely night,

I'm sure of it. Hold out awhile, hold out,
But persevere a teeny-weeny longer.
An oracle has promised Victory
If we don't wrangle. Would you hear the words?

WOMEN: Yes, yes, what is it?

LYSISTRATA: Silence then, you chatterboxes.
Here—
Whenas the swallows flocking in one place from the hoopoes
Deny themselves love's gambols any more,
All woes shall then have ending and great Zeus the Thunderer
Shall put above what was below before.

WOMEN: Will the men then always be kept under us?

LYSISTRATA: *But if the swallows squabble among themselves and fly away*
Out of the temple, refusing to agree,
Then The Most Wanton Birds in all the World
They shall be named for ever. That's his decree.

WOMEN: It's obvious what it means.

LYSISTRATA: Now by all the gods
We must let no agony deter from duty,
Back to your quarters. For we are base indeed,
My friends, if we betray the oracle.

                          She goes out.

OLD MEN.

I'd like to remind you of a fable they used to employ,
When I was a little boy:
How once through fear of the marriage-bed a young man,
Melanion by name, to the wilderness ran,
          And there on the hills he dwelt.
          For hares he wove a net
          Which with his dog he set—
          Most likely he's there yet.
For he never came back home, so great was the fear he felt.
          I loathe the sex as much as he,
          And therefore I no less shall be
          As chaste as was Melanion.

MAN: Grann'am, do you much mind men?

WOMEN: Onions you won't need, to cry.

MAN: From my foot you shan't escape.

WOMAN: What thick forests I espy.
So much Myronides' fierce beard
And thundering black back were feared,
That the foe fled when they were shown—
Brave he as Phormion.

WOMEN

Well, I'll relate a rival fable just to show to you
A different point of view:
There was a rough-hewn fellow, Timon, with a face
That glowered as through a thorn-bush in a wild, bleak place.
He too decided on flight,
This very Furies' son,
All the world's ways to shun
And hide from everyone,
Spitting out curses on all knavish men to left and right.
But though he reared this hate for men,
He loved the women even then,
And never thought them enemies.

WOMAN: O your jaw I'd like to break.

MAN: That I fear do you suppose?

WOMAN: Learn what kicks my legs can make.

MAN: Raise them up, and you'll expose—

WOMAN: Nay, you'll see there, I engage,
All is well kept despite my age,
And tended smooth enough to slip
From any adversary's grip.

LYSISTRATA appears.

LYSISTRATA: Hollo there, hasten hither to me.
Skip fast along.

WOMAN: What is this? Why the noise?

LYSISTRATA:	A man, a man! I spy a frenzied man!
	He carries Love upon him like a staff.
	O Lady of Cyprus, and Cythera, and Paphos,
	I beseech you, keep our minds and hands to the oath.
WOMAN:	Where is he, whoever he is?
LYSISTRATA:	By the Temple of Chloe,
WOMAN:	Yes, now I see him, but who can he be?
LYSISTRATA:	Look at him. Does anyone recognise his face?
MYRRHINE:	I do. He is my husband, Cinesias.
LYSISTRATA:	You know how to work. Play with him, lead him on,
	Seduce him to the cozening-point—kiss him, kiss him,
	Then slip your mouth aside just as he's sure of it,
	Ungirdle every caress his mouth feels at
	Save that the oath upon the bowl has locked.
MYRRHINE:	You can rely on me.
LYSISTRATA:	I'll stay here to help
	In working up his ardor to its height
	Of vain magnificence. . . . The rest to their quarters.

Enter CINESIAS.

CINESIAS:	Who is this that stands within our lines?
LYSISTRATA:	A man?
CINESIAS:	Too much a man!
LYSISTRATA:	Then be off at once.
CINESIAS:	Who are you that thus eject me?
LYSISTRATA:	Guard for the day.
CINESIAS:	By all the gods, then call Myrrhine hither.
LYSISTRATA:	So, call Myrrhine hither! Who are you?
CINESIAS:	I am her husband Cinesias, son of Anthros.
LYSISTRATA:	Welcome, dear friend! That glorious name of yours
	Is quite familiar in our ranks. Your wife
	Continually has it in her mouth.
	She cannot touch an apple or an egg
	But she must say, "This to Cinesias!"
CINESIAS:	O is that true?

LYSISTRATA: By Aphrodite, it is.
                 If the conversation strikes on men, your wife
                 Cuts in with, "All are boobies by Cinesias.
CINESIAS: Then call her here.
LYSISTRATA: And what am I to get?
CINESIAS: This, if you want it . . . See, what I have here.
                 But not to take away.
LYSISTRATA: Then I'll call her.
CINESIAS: Be quick, be quick. All grace is wiped from life
                 Since she went away. O sad, sad am I
                 When there I enter on that loneliness,
                 And wine is unvintaged of the sun's flavour.
                 And food is tasteless. But I've put on weight.
MYRRHINE: I love him O so much! but he won't have it.
(above)   Don't call me down to him.
CINESIAS: Sweet little Myrrhine!
                 What do you mean? Come here.
MYRRHINE: O no I won't.
                 Why are you calling me? You don't want me.
CINESIAS: Not want you! with this week-old strength of love.
MYRRHINE: Farewell.
CINESIAS: Don't go, please don't go, Myrrhine.
                 At least you'll hear our child. Call your mother, lad.
CHILD: Mummy . . . mummy . . . mummy!
CINESIAS: There now, don't you feel pity for the child?
                 He's not been fed or washed now for six days.
MYRRHINE: I certainly pity him with so heartless a father.
CINESIAS: Come down, my sweetest, come for the child's sake.
MYRRHINE: A trying life it is to be a mother!
                 I suppose I'd better go.   *She comes down.*
CINESIAS: How much younger she looks,
                 How fresher and how prettier! Myrrhine,
                 Lift up your lovely face, your disdainful face;
                 And your ankle . . . let your scorn step out its worst;
                 It only rubs me to more ardor here.
MYRRHINE: *(playing with the child)*

You're as innocent as he's iniquitous.

Let me kiss you, honey-petling, mother's darling.

CINESIAS: How wrong to follow other women's counsel
And let loose all these throbbing voids in yourself
As well as in me. Don't you go throb-throb?

MYRRHINE: Take away your hands.

CINESIAS: Everything in the house
Is being ruined.

MYRRHINE: I don't care at all.

CINESIAS: The roosters are picking all your web to rags.
Do you mind that?

MYRRHINE: Not I.

CINESIAS: What time we've wasted
We might have drenched with Paphian laughter, flung
On Aphrodite's Mysteries. O come here.

MYRRHINE: Not till a treaty finishes the war.

CINESIAS: If you must have it, then we'll get it done.

MYRRHINE: Do it and I'll come home. Till then I am bound.

CINESIAS: Well, can't your oath perhaps be got around?

MYRRHINE: No . . . no . . . still I'll not say that I don't love you.

CINESIAS: You love me! Then dear girl, let me also love you.

MYRRHINE: You must be joking. The boy's looking on.

CINESIAS: Here, Manes, take the child home! . . . There, he's gone.
There's nothing in the way now. Come to the point.

MYRRHINE: Here in the open! In plain sight?

CINESIAS: In Pan's cave.
A splendid place.

MYRRHINE: Where shall I dress my hair again
Before returning to the citadel?

CINESIAS: You can easily primp yourself in the Clepsydra.

MYRRHINE: But how can I break my oath?

CINESIAS: Leave that to me,
I'll take all risk.

MYRRHINE: Well, I'll make you comfortable.

CINESIAS: Don't worry. I'd as soon lie on the grass.

MYRRHINE: No, by Apollo, in spite of all your faults

I won't have you lying on the nasty earth.

(From here MYRRHINE *keeps on going off to fetch things.)*

CINESIAS: Ah, how she loves me.

MYRRHINE: Rest there on the bench,
While I arrange my clothes. O what a nuisance,
I must find some cushions first.

CINESIAS: Why some cushions?
Please don't get them!

MYRRHINE: What? The plain, hard wood?
Never, by Artemis! That would be too vulgar.

CINESIAS: Open your arms!

MYRRHINE: No. Wait a second.

CINESIAS: O . . .
Then hurry back again.

MYRRHINE: Here the cushions are.
Lie down while I—O dear! But what a shame,
You need more pillows.

CINESIAS: I don't want them, dear.

MYRRHINE: But I do.

CINESIAS: Thwarted affection mine,
They treat you just like Heracles at a feast
With cheats of dainties, O disappointing arms!

MYRRHINE: Raise up your head.

CINESIAS: There, that's everything at last.

MYRRHINE: Yes, all.

CINESIAS: Then run to my arms, you golden girl.

MYRRHINE: I'm loosening my girdle now. But you've not forgotten?
You're not deceiving me about the Treaty?

CINESIAS: No, by my life, I'm not.

MYRRHINE: Why, you've no blanket.

CINESIAS: It's not the silly blanket's warmth but yours I want.

MYRRHINE: Never mind. You'll soon have both. I'll come
straight back.

CINESIAS: The woman will choke me with her coverlets.

MYRRHINE: Get up a moment.

CINESIAS: I'm up high enough.

MYRRHINE: Would you like me to perfume you?

CINESIAS:	By Apollo, no!
MYRRHINE:	By Aphrodite, I'll do it anyway.
CINESIAS:	Lord Zeus, may she soon use up all the myrrh.
MYRRHINE:	Stretch out your hand. Take it and rub it in.
CINESIAS:	Hmm, it's not as fragrant as might be; that is,
	Not before it's smeared. It doesn't smell of kisses.
MYRRHINE:	How silly I am: I've brought you Rhodian scents.
CINESIAS:	It's good enough, leave it, love.
MYRRHINE:	You must be jesting.
CINESIAS:	Plague rack the man who first compounded scent!
MYRRHINE:	Here, take this flask.
CINESIAS:	I've a far better one.
	Don't tease me, come here, and get nothing more.
MYRRHINE:	I'm coming . . . I'm just drawing off my shoes . . .
	You're sure you will vote for Peace?
CINESIAS:	I'll think about it.

She runs off.

I'm dead: the woman's worn me all away.
She's gone and left me with an anguished pulse.

MEN.

Baulked in your amorous delight
How melancholy is your plight.
With sympathy your case I view;
For I am sure it's hard on you.
What human being could sustain
his unforeseen domestic strain,
     And not a single trace
Of willing women in the place!

CINESIAS:	O Zeus, what throbbing suffering!
MEN:	She did it all, the harlot, she
	With her atrocious harlotry.
WOMEN:	Nay, rather call her darling-sweet.
MEN:	What, sweet? She's a rude, wicked thing.
CINESIAS:	A wicked thing, as I repeat.

O Zeus, O Zeus,
Canst Thou not suddenly let loose

Some twirling hurricane to tear
Her flapping up along the air
And drop her, when she's whirled around,
          Here to the ground
Neatly impaled upon the stake
That's ready upright for her sake.

He goes out.

Enter SPARTAN HEARLD.
The MAGISTRATE *comes* forward.

HEARLD: Where gabs the Senate an' the Prytanes?
           I've fetcht despatches for them.
MAGISTRATE: Are you a man
           Or a monstrosity?
HEARLD: My scrimp-brained lad,
           I'm a herald, as ye see, who hae come frae Sparta
           Anent a Peace.
MAGISTRATE: Then why do you hide that lance
           That sticks out under your arms?
HERALD: I've brought no lance.
MAGISTRATE: Then why do you turn aside and hold your cloak
           So far out from your body? Is your groin swollen
           With stress of travelling?
HERALD: By Castor, I'll swear
           The man is wud.
MAGISTRATE: Indeed, your cloak is wide,
           My rascal fellow.
HERALD: But I tell ye No!
           Enow o' fleering!
MAGISTRATE: Well, what is it then?
HERALD: It's my despatch cane.
MAGISTRATE: Of course—a Spartan cane!
           But speak right out. I know all this too well.
           re new privations springing up in Sparta?

HERALD:	Och, hard as could be: in lofty lusty columns
	Our allies stand united. We maun get Pellene.
MAGISTRATE:	Whence has this evil come? Is it from Pan?
HERALD:	No. Lampito first ran asklent, then the ithers
	Sprinted after her example, and blocked, the hizzies,
	Their wames unskaithed against our every fleech.
MAGISTRATE:	What did you do?
HERALD:	We are broken, and bent double,
	Limp like men carrying lanthorns in great winds
	About the city. They winna let us even
	Wi' lightest neif skim their primsie pretties
	Till we've concluded Peace-terms wi' a' Hellas.
MAGISTRATE:	So the conspiracy is universal;
	This proves it. Then return to Sparta. Bid them
	Send envoys with full powers to treat of Peace;
	And I will urge the Senate here to choose
	Plenipotentiary ambassadors,
	As argument adducing this connection.
HERALD:	I'm off. Your wisdom nane could contravert.
	They retire.
MEN:	There is no beast, no rush of fire, like woman so untamed.
	She calmly goes her way where even panthers would be shamed.
WOMEN:	And yet you are fool enough, it seems, to dare to war with me,
	When for your faithful ally you might win me easily.
MEN:	Never could the hate I feel for womankind grow less.
WOMEN:	Then have your will. But I'll take pity on your nakedness,
	For I can see just how ridiculous you look, and so
	Will help you with your tunic if close up I now may go.
MEN:	Well, that, by Zeus, is no scoundrel-deed, I frankly will admit.
	I only took them off myself in a scoundrel raging-fit.
WOMEN:	Now you look sensible, and that you're men no one could doubt.

	If you were but good friends again, I'd take the insect out
	That hurts your eye.
MEN:	Is that what's wrong? That nasty bitie thing.
	Please squeeze it out, and show me what it is that
	makes this sting.
	It's been paining me a long while now.
WOMEN:	Well I'll agree to that,
	Although you're most unmannerly. O what a giant gnat.
	Here, look! It comes from marshy Tricorysus, I can tell.
MEN:	O thank you. It was digging out a veritable well.
	Now that it's gone, I can't hold back my tears. See
	how they fall.
WOMEN:	I'll wipe them off, bad as you are, and kiss you after all.
MEN:	I won't be kissed.
WOMEN:	O yes, you will. Your wishes do not matter.
MEN:	O botheration take you all! How you cajole and flatter.
	A hell it is to live with you; to live without, a hell:
	How truly was that said. But come, these enmities
	let's quell.
	You stop from giving orders and I'll stop from doing wrong.
	So let's join ranks and seal our bargain with a choric song.

CHORUS.

Athenians, it's not our intention
To sow political dissension
By giving any scandal mention;
But on the contrary to promote good feeling in the state
By word and deed. We've had enough calamities of late.

So let a man or woman but divulge
They need a trifle, say,
Two minas, three or four,
I've purses here that bulge.
There's only one condition made
(Indulge my whim in this I pray)—
When Peace is signed once more,
On no account am I to be repaid.

And I'm making preparation
For a gay select collation
With some youths of reputation.
I've managed to produce some soup and they're slaughtering
for me
A sucking-pig: its flesh should taste as tender as could be.
I shall expect you at my house today.
To the baths make an early visit,
And bring your children along;
Don't dawdle on the way.
Ask no one; enter as if the place
Was all your own—yours henceforth is it.
If nothing chances wrong,
The door will then be shut bang in your face.

The SPARTAN AMBASSADORS *approach.*

CHORUS: Here come the Spartan envoys with long, worried beards.
               Hail, Spartans how do you fare?
                                        Did anything new arise?
SPARTANS: No need for a clutter o' words. Do ye see our condition?
CHORUS: The situation swells to greater tension.
               Something will explode soon.
SPARTANS: It's awfu' truly.
               But come, let us wi' the best speed we may
               Scribble a Peace.
CHORUS: I notice that our men
               Like wrestlers poised for contest, hold their clothes
               Out from their bellies. An athlete's malady!
               Since exercise alone can bring relief.
ATHENIANS: Can anyone tell us where Lysistrata is?
               There is no need to describe our men's condition,
               It shows up plainly enough.
CHORUS: It's the same disease.
               Do you feel a jerking throbbing in the morning?
ATHENIANS: By Zeus, yes! In these straits I'm racked all through.

                Unless Peace is soon declared, we shall be driven
                In the void of women to try Cleisthenes.

CHORUS: Be wise and cover those things with your tunics.
                Who knows what kind of person may perceive you?

ATHENIANS: By Zeus, you're right.

SPARTANS: By the Twa Goddesses,
                Indeed ye are. Let's put our tunics on.

ATHENIANS: Hail O my fellow-sufferers, hail Spartans.

SPARTANS: O hinnie darling, what a waefu' thing
                If they had seen us wi' our lunging waddies!

ATHENIANS: Tell us then, Spartans, what has brought you here?

SPARTANS: We come to treat o' Peace.

ATHENIANS: Well spoken there!
                And we the same. Let us call out Lysistrata
                Since she alone can settle the Peace-terms.

SPARTANS: Call out Lysistratus too if ye don't mind.

CHORUS: No indeed. She hears your voices and she comes.

Enter LYSISTRATA.

                Hail, Wonder of all women! Now you must be in turn
                Hard, shifting, clear, deceitful, noble, crafty, sweet, and stern.
                The foremost men of Hellas, smitten by your fascination,
                Have brought their tangled quarrels here for your
                    sole arbitration.

LYSISTRATA: An easy task if their love's raging home-sickness
                Doesn't start trying out how well each other
                Will serve instead of us. But I'll know at once
                If they do. O where's that girl, Reconciliation?
                Bring first before me the Spartan delegates,
                And see you lift no rude or violent hands—
                None of the churlish ways our husbands used.
                But lead them courteously, as women should.
                And if they grudge fingers, guide them by other methods,
                And introduce them with ready tact. The Athenians
                Draw by whatever offers you a grip.

Now, Spartans, stay here facing me. Here you,
Athenians. Both hearken to my words.
I am a woman, but I'm not a fool.
And what of natural intelligence I own
Has been filled out with the remembered precepts
My father and the city-elders taught me.
First I reproach you both sides equally
That when at Pylae and Olympia,
At Pytho and the many other shrines
That I could name, you sprinkle from one cup
The altars common to all Hellenes, yet
You wrack Hellenic cities, bloody Hellas
With deaths of her own sons, while yonder clangs
The gathering menace of barbarians.

ATHENIANS: We cannot hold it in much longer now.

LYSISTRATA: Now unto you, O Spartans, do I speak.
Do you forget how your own countryman,
Pericleidas, once came hither suppliant
Before our altars, pale in his purple robes,
Praying for an army when in Messenia
Danger growled, and the Sea-god made earth quaver.
Then with four thousand hoplites Cimon marched
And saved all Sparta. Yet base ingrates now,
You are ravaging the soil of your preservers.

ATHENIANS: By Zeus, they do great wrong, Lysistrata.

SPARTANS: Great wrang, indeed. O! What a luscious wench!

LYSISTRATA: And now I turn to the Athenians,
Have you forgotten too how once the Spartans
In days when you wore slavish tunics, came
And with their spears broke a Thessalian host
And all the partisans of Hippias?
They alone stood by your shoulder on that day.
They freed you, so that for the slave's short skirt
You should wear the trailing cloak of liberty.

SPARTANS: I've never seen a nobler woman anywhere.

ATHENIANS: Nor I one with such prettily jointing hips.

LYSISTRATA: Now, brethren twined with mutual benefactions,
Can you still war, can you suffer such disgrace?
Why not be friends? What is there to prevent you?

SPARTANS: We're agreed, gin that we get this tempting Mole.

LYSISTRATA: Which one?

SPARTANS: That ane we've wanted to get into,
O for sae lang . . . Pylos, of course.

ATHENIANS: By Poseidon,
Never!

LYSISTRATA: Give it up.

ATHENIANS: Then what will we do?
We need that ticklish place united to us—

LYSISTRATA: Ask for some other lurking-hole in return.

ATHENIANS: Then, ah, we'll choose this snug thing here, Echinus,
Shall we call the nestling spot? And this backside haven,
These desirable twin promontories, the Maliac,
And then of course these Megarean Legs.

SPARTANS: Not that, O surely not that, never that.

LYSISTRATA: Agree! Now what are two legs more or less?

ATHENIANS: I want to strip at once and plough my land.

SPARTANS: And mine I want to fertilize at once.

LYSISTRATA: And so you can, when Peace is once declared.
If you mean it, get your allies' heads together
And come to some decision.

ATHENIANS: What allies?
There's no distinction in our politics:
We've risen as one man to this conclusion;
Every ally is jumping-mad to drive it home.

SPARTANS: And ours the same, for sure.

ATHENIANS: The Carystians first!
I'll bet on that.

LYSISTRATA: I agree with all of you.
Now off, and cleanse yourselves for the Acropolis,
For we invite you all in to a supper
From our commissariat baskets. There at table

You will pledge good behaviour and uprightness;
Then each man's wife is his to hustle home.
ATHENIANS: Come, as quickly as possible.
SPARTANS: As quick as ye like.
              Lead on.
ATHENIANS: O Zeus, quick, quick, lead quickly on.

They hurry off.

CHORUS.

Broidered stuffs on high I'm heaping,
Fashionable cloaks and sweeping
Trains, not even gold gawds keeping.
Take them all, I pray you, take them all (I do not care)
And deck your children—your daughter, if the Basket she's to bear.
Come, everyone of you, come in and take
Of this rich hoard a share.
Nought's tied so skilfully
But you its seal can break
And plunder all you spy inside.
I've laid out all that I can spare,
And therefore you will see
Nothing unless than I you're sharper-eyed.
If lacking corn a man should be
While his slaves clamour hungrily
And his excessive progeny,
Then I've a handfull of grain at home which is always to be had,
And to which in fact a more-than-life-size loaf I'd gladly add.
Then let the poor bring with them bag or sack
And take this store of food.
Manes, my man, I'll tell
To help them all to pack
Their wallets full. But O take care.
I had forgotten; don't intrude,
Or terrified you'll yell.
My dog is hungry too, and bites—beware!

Some LOUNGERS *from the Market with torches approach the*
Banqueting hall.
The PORTER *bars their entrance.*

1st MARKET-LOUNGER: Open the door.
PORTER: Here move along.
1st MARKET-LOUNGER: What's this?
      You're sitting down. Shall I singe you with my torch?
      That's vulgar! O I couldn't do it . . . yet
      If it would gratify the audience,
      I'll mortify myself.
2nd MARKET-LOUNGER: And I will too.
      We'll both be crude and vulgar, yes we will.
PORTER: Be off at once now or you'll be wailing
      Dirges for your hair. Get off at once,
      And see you don't disturb the Spartan envoys
      Just coming out from the splendid feast they've had.

The banqueters begin to come out.

1st ATHENIAN: I've never known such a pleasant banquet before,
      And what delightful fellows the Spartans are.
      When we are warm with wine, how wise we grow.
2nd ATHENIAN: That's only fair, since sober we're such fools.
      This is the advice I'd give the Athenians—
      See our ambassadors are always drunk.
      For when we visit Sparta sober, then
      We're on the alert for trickery all the while
      So that we miss half of the things they say,
      And misinterpret things that were never said,
      And then report the muddle back to Athens.
      But now we're charmed with each other. They might cap
      With the Telamon-catch instead of the Cleitagora,
      And we'd applaud and praise them just the same;
      We're not too scrupulous in weighing words.
PORTER: Why, here the rascals come again to plague me,
      Won't you move on, you sorry loafers there!

LOUNGER: Yes, by Zeus, they're already coming out.

SPARTANS: Now hinnie dearest, please tak' up your pipe
              That I may try a spring an' sing my best
              In honour o' the Athenians an' oursels.

ATHENIANS: Aye, take your pipe. By all the gods, there's nothing
              Could glad my heart more than to watch you dance.

                        SPARTANS.

                       Mnemosyne,
          Let thy fire storm these younkers,
          O tongue wi' stormy ecstasy
                   My Muse that knows
          Our deeds and theirs, how when at sea
          Their navies swooped upon
          The Medes at Artemision—
          Gods for their courage, did they strike
          Wrenching a triumph frae their foes;
                   While at Thermopylae
          Leonidas' army stood: wild-boars they were like
                   Wild-boars that wi' fierce threat
                   Their terrible tusks whet;
          The sweat ran streaming down each twisted face,
                   Faem blossoming i' strange petals o' death
                        Panted frae mortal breath,
          The sweat drenched a' their bodies i' that place,
          For the hurly-burly o' Persians glittered more
                   Than the sands on the shore.

          Come, Hunting Girl, an' hear my prayer—
          You whose arrows whizz in woodlands, come an' bless
                   This Peace we swear.
          Let us be fenced wi' agelong amity,
          O let this bond stick ever firm through thee
                   In friendly happiness.
          Henceforth no guilefu' perjury be seen!
                   O hither, hither O
                   Thou wildwood queen.

LYSISTRATA: Earth is delighted now, peace is the voice of earth.
Spartans, sort out your wives: Athenians, yours.
Let each catch hands with his wife and dance his joy,
Dance out his thanks, be grateful in music,
And promise reformation with his heels.

ATHENIANS: O Dancers, forward. Lead out the Graces,
       Call Artemis out;
Then her brother, the Dancer of Skies,
       That gracious Apollo.
       Invoke with a shout
       Dionysus out of whose eyes
Breaks fire on the maenads that follow;
And Zeus with his flares of quick lightning, and call
       Happy Hera, Queen of all,
And all the Daimons summon hither to be
       Witnesses of our revelry
And of the noble Peace we have made,
       Aphrodite our aid.
       Io Paieon, Io, cry—
       For victory, leap!
       Attained by me, leap!
       Euoi Euoi Euai Euai.

SPARTANS: Piper, gie us the music for a new sang.

Leaving again lovely lofty Taygetus
Hither O Spartan Muse, hither to greet us,
And wi' our choric voice to raise
To Amyclean Apollo praise,
And Tyndareus' gallant sons whose days
Alang Eurotas' banks merrily pass,
An' Athene o' the House o' Brass.

Now the dance begin;
Dance, making swirl your fringe o' woolly skin,
While we join voices
To hymn dear Sparta that rejoices
I' a beautifu' sang,
An' loves to see
Dancers tangled beautifully,
For the girls i' tumbled ranks
Alang Eurotas' banks
Like wanton fillies thrang,
Frolicking there
An' like Bacchantes shaking the wild air
To comb a giddy laughter through the hair,
Bacchantes that clench thyrsi as they sweep
To the ecstatic leap.

An' Helen, Child o' Leda, come
Thou holy, nimble, gracefu' Queen,
Lead thou the dance, gather thy joyous tresses up i' bands
An' play like a fawn. To madden them, clap thy hands,
And sing praise to the warrior goddess templed i' our lands,
Her o' the House o' Brass

WILLIAM SHAKESPEARE

1564-1616

OTHELLO

1604

Othello is unique among Shakespeare's tragedies in its intensity: it hurtles breathlessly through time toward its tragic climax without one moment of comic relief. It begins in darkness and ends in darkness, with all of the potential of its human treasures totally lost by the play's end. In five acts, Othello's feelings for Desdemona change from sweet adoration "O, my soul's joy . . . My soul hath her content so absolute/ That not another comfort like to this / Succeeds in unkown fate" (II.i.180,190-192) to distrust, hatred, and anger vengeful enough for him to strangle her before our very eyes, uttering "O perjured woman! Thou dost stone my heart, . . . Out strumpet!" (V. ii. 67, 81). The audience is left amazed at how such changes could have taken place in the mind of an otherwise estimable, gentle statesman and warrior.

In the scene excerpted here (III.iii), we watch Iago—dubbed by critics as the play's "motiveless malignancy" but also Othello's right-hand man in war—manipulate Othello's mind. The scene opens with Desdemona promising Othello's lieutenant Cassio that she will try to lessen Othello's anger with him for participating in a drunken brawl (actually engineered by Iago) the night before. Feeding on Othello's susceptibility to jealousy, Iago implies that Desdemona is unfaithful to Othello with Cassio, so every friendly intercession she makes on behalf of Cassio to Othello ironically damns her in Othello's mind. Yet, Othello is still not convinced. He demands "ocular proof" which Iago stages using a handkerchief that belongs to Desdemona, stolen by his wife Emilia, Desdemona's maid. Iago gives it to Othello claiming he has obtained it from the bedroom of Cassio. By the time Iago claims, "such a handkerchief—I am sure it was your wife's—did I today see Cassio wipe his beard with," Othello has lost all faith in Desdemona's fidelity.

Iago is all subtlety and calculation while the great warrior Othello has become vulnerable, driven purely by passion and pride. How Othello sees himself influences how he views Desdemona's love, for how could she, a "supersubtle Venetian," *love* one such as he, older, made coarse by lengthy military service to Venice, and less physically attractive than Cassio? At the same time, how could she *betray* one such as he, a famous, magnificent, powerful, warrior, to whom Venice owes much? Jealousy, the play's famous "green-eyed monster," seems to motivate both powerful male characters. In this scene, we watch Iago pour poisonous thoughts into Othello's mind and transform him from a lover into a monster. Othello's magnificent mind, represented through the fine poetry Shakespeare gives him at the beginning of the play, degenerates from III.iii forward, until at the end of the play, his eloquence is lost in overwhelming rage and grief.

Part of the impact of *Othello* emanates from its dramatization of a search for truth and the revelation of how easily compromised supposedly "empirical" or "objective" proof can be.

SOURCE

William Shakespeare.1604. *Othello.* Act III, Scene iii. In *Shakespeare's Tragedy of Othello, The Moore of Venice.* Wm. J. Rolfe, Ed. New York: Harper, 1886. 88-101.

OTHELLO

[*The action in this scene takes place on the island of Cyprus where Othello's troops are gathering. His new wife, Desdemona, has recently joined him from her home in Venice. There has been a drunken brawl among the soldiers the night before. While we have watched Iago stage the whole incident, Cassio appears to be at fault and has been dismissed from his much sought-after position as Othello's lieutenant.*]

SCENE III. *THE GARDEN OF THE CASTLE*

Enter Desdemona Cassio, and Emilia.

Desdemona. Be thou assur'd, good Cassio, I will do
All my abilities in thy behalf.

Emilia. Good madam, do; I warrant it grieves my husband [Iago],
As if the cause were his.

Desdemona. O, that's an honest fellow.—Do not doubt, Cassio,
But I will have my lord and you again
As friendly as you were.

Cassio.   Bounteous madam,
Whatever shall become of Michael Cassio,
He's never anything but your true servant.

Desdemona. I know 't; I thank you. You do love my lord [Othello]:
You have known him long; and be you well assur'd
He shall in strangeness stand no farther off
Than in a politic distance.

Cassio.   Ay, but, lady,
That policy may either last so long,
Or feed upon such nice and waterish diet,
Or breed itself so out of circumstance,
That, I being absent and my place supplied,
My general will forget my love and service.

Desdemona. Do not doubt that; before Emilia here
I give thee warrant of thy place. Assure thee,
If I do vow a friendship, I'll perform it

To the last article: my lord shall never rest;
I'll watch him tame and talk him out of patience;
His bed shall seem a school, his board a shrift;
I'll intermingle everything he does
With Cassio's suit. Therefore be merry, Cassio;
For thy solicitor shall rather die
Than give thy cause away.
    Emilia. Madam, here comes my lord.
    Cassio. Madam, I'll take my leave.
    Desdemona. Why, stay, and hear me speak.
    Cassio. Madam, not now. I am very ill at ease,
Unfit for mine own purposes.
    Desdemona. Well, do your discretion.   [*Exit Cassio.*

          Enter Othello *and* Iago
    Iago. Ha? I like not that.
    Othello. What dost thou say?
    Iago. Nothing, my lord; or if—I know not what.
    Othello. Was not that Cassio parted from my wife?
    Iago. Cassio, my lord! No, sure, I cannot think it,
That he would steal away so guilty-like,
Seeing you coming.
    Othello.   I do believe 'twas he.
    Desdemona. How now, my lord!
I have been talking with a suitor here,
A man that languishes in your displeasure.
    Othello. Who is 't you mean?
    Desdemona. Why, your lieutenant, Cassio. Good my lord,
If I have any grace or power to move you,
His present reconciliation take;
For if he be not one that truly loves you,
That errs in ignorance and not in cunning,
I have no judgment in an honest face.
I prithee, call him back.
    Othello.   Went he hence now?
    Desdemona. Ay, sooth; so humbled
That he hath left part of his grief with me,

To suffer with him. Good love, call him back.

Othello. Not now, sweet Desdemona; some other time.

Desdemona. But shall 't be shortly?

Othello.   The sooner, sweet, for you.

Desdemona. Shall 't be to-night at supper?

Othello.   No, not to-night.

Desdemona. To-morrow dinner, then?

Othello.   I shall not dine at home;
I meet the captains at the citadel.

Desdemona. Why, then, to-morrow night, or Tuesday morn;
On Tuesday noon, or night; on Wednesday morn:
I prithee, name the time, but let it not
Exceed three days. In faith, he's penitent;
And yet his trespass, in our common reason—
Save that, they say, the wars must make examples
Out of her best—is not almost a fault
To incur a private check. When shall he come?
Tell me, Othello; I wonder in my soul,
What you would ask me that I should deny,
Or stand so mammering on. What? Michael Cassio,
That came a-wooing with you, and so many a time,
When I have spoke of you dispraisingly,
Hath ta'en your part,—to have so much to do
To bring him in! Trust me, I could do much—

Othello. Prithee, no more: Let him come when he will;
I will deny thee nothing.

Desdemona. Why, th'is is not a boon;
'Tis as I should entreat you wear your gloves,
Or feed on nourishing dishes, or keep you warm,
Or sue to you to do a peculiar profit
To your own person: nay, when I have a suit
Wherein I mean to touch your love indeed,
It shall be full of poise and difficult weight,
And fearful to be granted.

Othello.   I will deny thee nothing;
Whereon, I do beseech thee, grant me this,

To leave me but a little to myself.

Desdemona. Shall I deny you? no; farewell, my lord.

Othello. Farewell, my Desdemona; I'll come to thee straight.

Desdemona. Emilia, come.—Be as your fancies teach you;
Where'er you be, I am obedient.

[*Exeunt Desdemona and Emilia.*

Othello. Excellent wretch! Perdition catch my soul,
But I do love thee! And when I love thee not,
Chaos is come again.

Iago. My noble lord—

Othello.   What dost thou say, Iago?

Iago. Did Michael Cassio, when you wooed my lady,
Know of your love?

Othello. He did, from first to last; why dost thou ask?

Iago. But for a satisfaction of my thought;
No further harm.

Othello.   Why of thy thought, Iago?

Iago. I did not think he had been acquainted with her.

Othello. O, yes, and went between us very oft.

Iago. Indeed?

Othello. Indeed! ay, indeed; discern'st thou aught in that?
Is he not honest?

Iago. Honest, my lord!

Othello.   Honest! ay, honest.

Iago. My lord, for aught I know.

Othello. What dost thou think?

Iago.   Think, my lord!

Othello.   Think, my lord!
By heaven, he echoes me,
As if there were some monster in his thought
Too hideous to be shown.—Thou dost mean something.
I heard thee say even now, thou lik'dst not that,
When Cassio left my wife: what didst not like?
And when I told thee he was of my counsel
In my whole course of wooing, thou criedst "Indeed!"
And didst contract and purse thy brow together,

As if thou then hadst shut up in thy brain
Some horrible conceit. If thou dost love me,
Show me thy thought.
    Iago. My lord, you know I love you.
    Othello.   I think thou dost;
And, for I know thou'rt full of love and honesty,
And weigh'st thy words before thou giv'st them breath,
Therefore these stops of thine fright me the more;
For such things in a false disloyal knave
Are tricks of custom, but in a man that's just
They're close dilations, working from the heart
That passion cannot rule.
    Iago.   For Michael Cassio,
I dare be sworn I think that he is honest.
    Othello. I think so too.
    Iago.   Men should be what they seem;
Or those that be not, would they might seem none!
    Othello. Certain, men should be what they seem.
    Iago. Why, then, I think Cassio's an honest man.
    Othello. Nay, yet there's more in this.
I prithee, speak to me as to thy thinkings,
As thou dost ruminate, and give thy worst of thoughts
The worst of words.
    Iago.   Good my lord, pardon me;
Though I am bound to every act of duty,
I am not bound to that all slaves are free to.
Utter my thoughts? Why, say they are vile and false,—
As where's that palace whereinto foul things
Sometimes intrude not? Who has that breast so pure,
But some uncleanly apprehensions
Keep leets and law-days, and in sessions sit
With meditations lawful?
    Othello. Thou dost conspire against thy friend, Iago,
If thou but think'st him wrong'd and mak'st his ear
A stranger to thy thoughts.
    Iago.   I do beseech you—

Though I perchance am vicious in my guess,
As, I confess, it is my nature's plague
To spy into abuses, and oft my jealousy
Shapes faults that are not—that your wisdom yet,
From one that so imperfectly conceits,
Would take no notice, nor build yourself a trouble
Out of his scattering and unsure observance.
It were not for your quiet nor your good,
Nor for my manhood, honesty, and wisdom,
To let you know my thoughts.
    Othello.   What dost thou mean?
    Iago. Good name in man and woman, dear my lord,
Is the immediate jewel of their souls.
Who steals my purse steals trash; 'tis something, nothing;
'Twas mine, 'tis his, and has been slave to thousands;
But he that filches from me my good name
Robs me of that which not enriches him
And makes me poor indeed.
    Othello. By heaven, I'll know thy thoughts.
    Iago. You cannot, if my heart were in your hand;
Nor shall not, whilst 'tis in my custody.
    Othello. Ha!
    Iago.   O, beware, my lord, of jealousy;
It is the green-eyed monster which doth mock
The meat it feeds on: that cuckold lives in bliss
Who, certain of his fate, loves not his wronger;
But, O, what damned minutes tells he o'er
Who dotes, yet doubts, suspects, yet strongly loves!
    Othello. O misery!
    Iago. Pour and content is rich, and rich enough;
But riches fineless is as poor as winter
To him that ever fears he shall be poor.
Good heaven, the souls of all my tribe defend
From jealousy!
    Othello.   Why, why is this?
Think'st thou I'd make a life of jealousy,

To follow still the changes of the moon
With fresh suspicions? No; to be once in doubt
Is once to be resolv'd: exchange me for a goat,
When I shall turn the business of my soul
To such exsufflicate and blown surmises,
Matching thy inference. 'Tis not to make me jealous
To say my wife is fair, feeds well, loves company,
Is free of speech, sings, plays, and dances well;
Where virtue is, these are more virtuous:
Nor from mine own weak merits will I draw
The smallest fear or doubt of her revolt;
For she had eyes, and chose me. No, Iago!
I'll see before I doubt; when I doubt, prove:
And on the proof there is no more but this,—
Away at once with love or jealousy!
    Iago. I am glad of it, for now I shall have reason
To show the love and duty that I bear you
With franker spirit; therefore, as I am bound,
Receive it from me. I speak not yet of proof.
Look to your wife; observe her well with Cassio;
Wear your eyes thus, not jealous nor secure:
I would not have your free and noble nature
Out of self-bounty, be abus'd. Look to 't.
I know our country disposition well:
In Venice they do let God see the pranks
They dare not show their husbands; their best conscience
Is not to leave 't undone, but keep 't unknown.
    Othello. Dost thou say so?
    Iago. She did deceive her father, marrying you;
And when she seem'd to shake and fear your looks,
She lov'd them most.
    Othello.   And so she did.
    Iago.   Why, go to, then;
She that, so young, could give out such a seeming,
To seel her father's eyes up close as oak—
He thought 'twas witchcraft—but I am much to blame;
I humbly do beseech you of your pardon

For too much loving you.
    Othello.   I am bound to thee for ever.
    Iago. I see this hath a little dash'd your spirits.
    Othello. Not a jot, not a jot.
    Iago.   I' faith, I fear it has.
I hope you will consider what is spoke
Comes from my love. But I do see you're mov'd:
I am to pray you not to strain my speech
To grosser issues nor to larger reach
Than to suspicion.
    Othello. I will not.
    Iago.   Should you do so, my lord,
My speech should fall into such vile success
As my thoughts aimed not. Cassio's my worthy friend—
My lord, I see you're mov'd.
    Othello. No, not much mov'd.
I do not think but Desdemona's honest.
    Iago. Long live she so! And long live you to think so!
    Othello. And yet, how nature erring from itself—
    Iago. Ay, there's the point; as—to be bold with you—
Not to affect many proposed matches
Of her own clime, complexion, and degree,
Whereto we see in all things nature tends—
Foh! one may smell in such a will most rank,
Foul disproportion, thoughts unnatural.—
But pardon me; I do not in position
Distinctly speak of her, though I may fear
Her will, recoiling to her better judgment,
May fall to match you with her country forms
And happily repent.
    Othello.   Farewell, farewell:
If more thou dust perceive, let me know more;
Set on thy wife to observe: Leave me, Iago.
    Iago. [*Going*] My lord, I take my leave.
    Othello. Why did I marry? This honest creature doubtless
Sees and knows more, much more, than he unfolds.
    Iago. [*returning*] My Lord, I would I might entreat your honor

To scan this thing no farther; leave it to time.
Though it be fit that Cassio have his place,
For, sure, he fills it up with great ability,
Yet, if you please to hold him off awhile,
You shall by that perceive him and his means.
Note if your lady strain his entertainment
With any strong or vehement importunity;
Much will be seen in that. In the mean time,
Let me be thought too busy in my fears—
As worthy cause I have to fear I am—
And hold her free, I do beseech your honor.
    Othello. Fear not my government.
    Iago. I once more take my leave.   [*Exit.*
    Othello. This fellow's of exceeding honesty,
And knows all qualities, with a learned spirit,
Of human dealings. If I do prove her haggard,
Though that her jesses were my dear heart strings,
I'd whistle her off and let her down the wind,
To prey at fortune. Haply, for I am black
And have not those soft parts of conversation
That chamberers have, or for I am declin'd
Into the vale of years,—yet that's not much—
She's gone. I am abus'd, and my relief
Must be to loathe her. O curse of marriage,
That we can call these delicate creatures ours,
And not their appetites! I had rather be a toad,
And live upon the vapor of a dungeon,
Than keep a corner in the thing I love
For others' uses. Yet, 'tis the plague of great ones;
Prerogativ'd are they less than the base;
'Tis destiny unshunnable, like death;
Even then this forked plague is fated to us
When we do quicken.—Desdemona comes.

             Enter Desdemona *and* Emilia.
If she be false, O, then heaven mocks itself!

I'll not believe 't.

Desdemona. How now, my dear Othello!
Your dinner, and the generous islanders
By you invited, do attend your presence.

Othello. I am to blame.

Desdemona.   Why do you speak so faintly?
Are you not well?

Othello. I have a pain upon my forehead here.

Desdemona. Faith, that's with watching; 't will away again:
Let me but bind it hard, within this hour
It will be well.

Othello. Your napkin is too little;

[*He puts the handkerchief from him; and it drops.*]
Let it alone. Come, I'll go in with you.

Desdemona. I am very sorry that you are not well.

[*Exeunt Othello and Desdemona.*

Emilia. I am glad I have found this napkin.
This was her first remembrance from the Moor:
My wayward husband hath a hundred times
Woo' me to steal it; but she so loves the token,
For he conjur'd her she should ever keep it,
That she reserves it evermore about her
To kiss and talk to. I'll have the work ta'en out,
And give 't Iago: what he will do with it
Heaven knows, not I;
I nothing but to please his fantasy.

Enter Iago.

Iago. How now! what do you here alone?

Emilia. Do not you chide; I have a thing for you.

Iago. You have a thing for me? It is a common thing—

Emilia. Ha!

Iago. To have a foolish wife.

Emilia. O, is that all? What will you give me now
For that same handkerchief?

Iago.   What handkerchief?
Emilia. What handkerchief!
Why, that the Moor first gave to Desdemona;
That which so often you did bid me steal.
    Iago. Hast stol'n it from her?
    Emilia. No, faith; she let it drop by negligence,
And, to th' advantage, I, being here, took 't up.
Look, here it is.
    Iago.   A good wench; give it me.
    Emilia. What will you do with 't, that you have been so earnest
To have me filch it?
    Iago. [*Snatching it*] Why, what is that to you?
    Emilia. If it be not for some purpose of import,
Give 't me again; poor lady, she'll run mad
When she shall lack it.
    Iago. Be not acknown on 't; I have use for it.
Go, leave me.   [*Exit Emilia.*
I will in Cassio's lodging lose this napkin,
And let him find it. Trifles light as air
Are to the jealous confirmations strong
As proofs of holy writ; this may do something.
The Moor already changes with my poison;
Dangerous conceits are in their natures poisons,
Which at the first are scarce found to distaste,
But with a little act upon the blood
Burn like the mines of sulfur.—I did say so.
Look where he comes!

Enter Othello
Not poppy, nor mandragora,
Nor all the drowsy syrups of the world,
Shall ever medicine thee to that sweet sleep
Which thou ow'dst yesterday.
    Othello.   Ha! Ha! false to me?
    Iago. Why, how now, General? No more of that.
    Othello. Avaunt! be gone! thou hast set me on the rack.
I swear 'tis better to be much abus'd

Than but to know 't a little.

    Iago. How now, my lord!

    Othello. What sense had I of her stolen hours of lust?
I saw 't not, thought it not, it harmed not me:
I slept the next night well, fed well, was free and merry;
I found not Cassio's kisses on her lips:
He that is robb'd, not wanting what is stol'n,
Let him not know 't, and he's not robbed at all.

    Iago. I am sorry to hear this.

    Othello. I had been happy if the general camp,
Pioners and all, had tasted her sweet body,
So I had nothing known. O, now, for ever
Farewell the tranquil mind! farewell content!
Farewell the plumed troop, and the big wars
That makes ambition virtue! O, farewell!
Farewell the neighing steed, and the shrill trump,
The spirit-stirring drum, the ear-piercing fife,
The royal banner, and all quality,
Pride, pomp, and circumstance of glorious war!
And, O you mortal engines, whose rude throats
The immortal Jove's dread clamors counterfeit,
Farewell! Othello's occupation's gone!

    Iago. Is 't possible, my lord?

    Othello. Villain, be sure thou prove my love a whore,
Be sure of it: Give me the ocular proof;
Or, by the worth of mine eternal soul,
Thou hadst been better have been born a dog
Than answer my wak'd wrath!

    Iago.   Is 't come to this?

    Othello. Make me to see 't; or at the least so prove it,
That the probation bear no hinge nor loop
To hang a doubt on, or woe upon thy life!

    Iago. My noble lord,—

    Othello. If thou dost slander her and torture me,
Never pray more; abandon all remorse;
On horror's head horrors accumulate;

Do deeds to make heaven weep, all earth amaz'd;
For nothing canst thou to damnation add
Greater than that.
    Iago.   O grace! O heaven forgive me!
Are you a man? have you a soul or sense?
God be wi' you; take mine office. O wretched fool,
That liv'st to make thine honesty a vice!
O monstrous world! Take note, take note, O world,
To be direct and honest is not safe.
I thank you for this profit; and from hence
I'll love no friend, sith love breeds such offense.
    Othello. Nay, stay; thou shouldst be honest.
    Iago. I should be wise, for honesty's a fool,
And loses that it works for.
    Othello.   By the world,
I think my wife be honest, and think she is not;
I think that thou art just, and think thou art not.
I'll have some proof. Her name, that was as fresh
As Dian's visage, is now begrim'd and black
As mine own face. If there be cords, or knives,
Poison, or fire, or suffocating streams,
I'll not endure it. Would I were satisfied!
    Iago. I see, sir, you are eaten up with passion;
I do repent me that I put it to you.
You would be satisfied?
    Othello.   Would! nay, and I will.
    Iago. And may: but how? how satisfied, my lord?
If imputation and strong circumstances,
Which lead directly to the door of truth,
Will give you satisfaction, you may have 't.
    Othello. Give me a living reason she's disloyal.
    Iago. I do not like the office;
But, sith I am enter'd in this cause so far,
Prick'd to 't by foolish honesty and love,
I will go on. I lay with Cassio lately;
And, being troubled with a raging tooth,

I could not sleep.
There are a kind of men so loose of soul,
That in their sleeps will mutter their affairs;
One of this kind is Cassio.
In sleep I heard him say 'Sweet Desdemona,
Let us be wary, let us hide our loves;'
And then, sir, would he gripe and wring my hand,
Cry 'O sweet creature!' and then kiss me hard,
As if he pluck'd up kisses by the roots
That grew upon my lips; and sigh'd, and then
Cried, 'Cursed fate that gave thee to the Moor!'
   Othello. O monstrous! monstrous!
   Iago.   Nay, this was but his dream.
   Othello. But this denoted a foregone conclusion;
'Tis a shrewd doubt, though it be but a dream.
   Iago. And this may help to thicken other proofs
That do demonstrate thinly.
   Othello.   I'll tear her all to pieces!
   Iago. Nay, yet he wise: yet we see nothing done;
She may be honest yet. Tell me but this,
Have you not sometimes seen a handkerchief
Spotted with strawberries in your wife's hand?
   Othello. I gave her such a one. 'Twas my first gift.
   Iago. I know not that; but such a handkerchief—
I am sure it was your wife's—did I to-day
See Cassio wipe his beard with.
   Othello.   If it be that—
   Iago. If it be that, or any that was hers,
It speaks against her with the other proofs.
   Othello. O, that the slave had forty thousand lives!
One is too poor, too weak for my revenge.
Now do I see 't is true. Look here, Iago,
All my fond love thus do I blow to heaven.
'T is gone.
Arise, black vengeance, from the hollow hell!
Yield up, O love, thy crown and hearted throne

To tyrannous hate! Swell, bosom, with thy fraught,
For 'tis of aspics' tongues!
    Iago.   Yet be content.
    Othello. O, blood, blood, blood!
    Iago. Patience, I say; your mind perhaps may change.
    Othello. Never, Iago. Like to the Pontic sea,
Whose icy current and compulsive course
Ne'er feels retiring ebb, but keeps due on
To the Propontic and the Hellespont,
Even so my bloody thoughts with violent pace
Shall ne'er look back, ne'er ebb to humble love,
Till that a capable and wide revenge
Swallow them up. Now, by yond marble heaven,   [*Kneels.*
In the due reverence of a sacred vow
I here engage my words,
    Iago. Do not rise yet.—   [*Kneels.*
Witness, you ever-burning lights above,
You elements that clip us round about,
Witness that here Iago doth give up
The execution of his wit, hands, heart,
To wrong'd Othello's service! Let him command,
And to obey shall be in me remorse,
What bloody business ever.   [*They rise.*
    Othello.   I greet thy love,
Not with vain thanks, but with acceptance bounteous,
And will upon the instant put thee to 't.
Within these three days let me hear thee say
That Cassio's not alive.
    Iago. My friend is dead; 'T is done at your request:
But let her live.
    Othello.   Damn her, lewd minx! O, damn her, damn her!
Come, go with me apart; I will withdraw,
To furnish me with some swift means of death
For the fair devil. Now art thou my lieutenant.
    Iago. I am your own forever.   [*Exeunt.*

GEORGE BERNARD SHAW

1856-1950

Caesar and Cleopatra
1898

Irishman George Bernard Shaw, the son of a failed merchant and a professional singer, was educated in Dublin. In 1876, to find work in journalism and writing he moved to London, where he also became involved in progressive politics. As one of the founders of the Fabian Society, he dedicated much of his work to making Britain a socialist state. The Fabian Society was later instrumental in founding the London School of Economics and Britain's Labour Party. In 1904, Shaw became affiliated with the experimental Court Theatre in London, where ten of his plays were produced in the subsequent years. Royalties from his plays and marriage to a wealthy woman gave him financial independence and power, which he used to work to end dramatic censorship and to establish a subsidized national theater. World War I, to Shaw, represented the last vestiges of 19th-century imperialism. He voiced his opposition to the war in a series of articles, *Common Sense About The War,* that were a disaster for his reputation. After the war, he returned to playwriting and rebuilt his reputation with *Back to Methuselah*

(1923) and *Saint Joan* (1925). In 1925, he was awarded the Nobel Prize for Literature. For the rest of his life, he was a celebrity who traveled and remained involved with politics. Beneficiaries of his estate were the National Gallery of Ireland, the British Museum, and the Royal Academy of Dramatic Arts, all of which are still supported by royalties from his plays.

Caesar and Cleopatra (1898) was written prior to Shaw's commercial and critical success. A three-act comedy, it portrays a Caesar and Cleopatra vastly different from those made famous by Shakespeare's tragic giants. Shakespeare's plays focus on human strength and weakness; Shaw sees the characters in terms of individual responsibility, human pettiness, and comic foibles. His Caesar is balding and middle-aged and his Cleopatra juvenile, ineffectual, and dominated by her slave/nurse, Ftatateeta. Caesar sets out to educate Cleopatra about her political responsibilities (not entirely successfully). When Cleopatra imperiously orders the murder of Pothinus, who is plotting against her, she initiates the cycle of murder and revenge warned against by Caesar. Act II is noteworthy for its discussion of the burning of the library of Alexandria, equivalent, in the words of Theodotus, to the "burning of the memory of mankind."

Shavian drama is marked by its relentless criticism of England and British cultural values, delivered by surprising mixtures of serious, provocative opinion leavened by irony, wit, and whimsy. Shaw wanted his audiences to be amused while they were being lessoned in their lack of social responsibility, unquestioning appropriation of English cultural identity, and general character weakness. *Caesar and Cleopatra* provides a delicious example of his work.

SOURCE

Shaw, George Bernard. 1900. *Caesar and Cleopatra*. Act II. In *Three Plays for Puritans*. New York: Brentano's, 1906. 190-197.

CAESAR AND CLEOPATRA

ACT II

Alexandria. A hall on the first floor of the Palace, ending in a loggia approached by two steps. Through the arches of the loggia, the Mediterranean can be seen, bright in the morning sun. The clean lofty walls, painted with a procession of the Egyptian theocracy, presented in profile as flat ornament, and the absence of mirrors, sham perspectives, stuffy upholstery and textiles, make the place handsome, wholesome, simple and cool, or, as a rich English manufacturer would express it, poor, bare, ridiculous and unhomely. For Tottenham Court Road civilization is to this Egyptian civilization as glass bead and tattoo civilization is to Tottenham Court Road.

The young king Ptolemy Dionysus (aged ten) is at the top of the steps, on his way in through, the loggia, led by his guardian Pothinus, who has him by the hand. The court is assembled to receive him. It is made up of men and women (some of the women being officials) of various complexions and races, mostly Egyptian; some of them, comparatively fair, from lower Egypt; some, much darker, from upper Egypt, with a few, Greeks and Jews. Prominent in a group on Ptolemy's right hand is Theodotus, Ptolemy's tutor. Another group on Ptolemy's left, is headed by Achillas, the general of Ptolemy's troops. Theodotus is a little old man, whose features are as cramped and wizened as his limbs, except his tall straight forehead, which occupies more space than all the rest of his face. He maintains an air of magpie keenness and profundity, listening to what the others say with the sarcastic vigilance of a philosopher listening to the exercises of his disciples. Achillas is a tall handsome man of thirty-five, with a fine black beard curled like the coat of a poodle. Apparently, not a clever man, but distinguished and dignified. Pothinus is a vigorous man of fifty, a eunuch, passionate, energetic and quick witted, but of common mind and character; impatient and unable to control his temper. He has fine tawny hair, like fur. Ptolemy, the King, looks much older than an English boy of ten; but he has the childish air, the habit of being in leading strings, the mixture of impotence and petulance, the appearance of being excessively washed, combed and dressed by other hands, which is exhibited by court-bred princes of all ages.

All receive the King with reverences. He comes down the steps to a chair of state, which stands a little to his right, the only seat in the hall. Taking his place before it, he looks nervously for instructions to Pothinus, who places himself at his left hand.

POTHINUS. The King of Egypt has a word to speak.

THEODOTUS *(in a squeak which he makes impressive by sheer self-opinionativeness).* Peace for the King's word!

PTOLEMY *(without any vocal inflexions: he is evidently repeating a lesson).* Take notice of this all of you. I am the firstborn son of Auletes the Flute Blower who was your King. My sister Berenice drove him from his throne and reigned in his stead but—but *(he hesitates)*—

POTHINUS *(stealthily prompting).*—but the gods would not suffer—

PTOLEMY. Yes—the gods would not suffer—not suffer *(he stops; then, crestfallen)* I forget what the gods would not suffer.

THEODOTUS. Let Pothinus, the King's guardian, speak for the King.

POTHINUS *(suppressing his impatience with difficulty).* The King wished to say that the gods would not suffer the impiety of his sister to go unpunished.

PTOLEMY *(hastily).* Yes: I remember the rest of it. *(He resumes his monotone.)* Therefore the gods sent a stranger, one Mark Antony, a Roman captain of horsemen, across the sands of the desert and he set my father again upon the throne. And my father took Berenice my sister and struck her head off. And now that my father is dead yet another of his daughters, my sister Cleopatra, would snatch the kingdom from me and reign in my place. But the gods would not suffer *(Pothinus coughs admonitorily)*—the gods—the gods would not suffer—

POTHINUS *(prompting)*—will not maintain—

PTOLEMY. Oh yes—will not maintain such iniquity, they will give her head to the axe even as her sister's. But with the help of the witch Ftatateeta she hath cast a spell on the Roman Julius

Caesar to make him uphold her false pretence to rule in Egypt. Take notice then that I will not suffer—that I will not suffer— *(pettishly, to Pothinus)* What is it that I will not suffer?

POTHINUS *(suddenly exploding with all the force and emphasis of political passion).* The King will not suffer a foreigner to take from him the throne of our Egypt. *(A shout of applause.)* Tell the King, Achillas, how many soldiers and horsemen follow the Roman?

THEODOTUS. Let the King's general speak!

ACHILLAS. But two Roman legions, O King. Three thousand soldiers and scarce a thousand horsemen.

The court breaks into derisive laughter; and a great chattering begins, amid which Rufio, a Roman officer, appears in the loggia. He is a burly, black bearded man of middle age, very blunt, prompt and rough, with small clear eyes, and plump nose and cheeks, which, however, like the rest of his flesh, are in ironhard condition.

RUFIO *(from the steps).* Peace, ho! *(The laughter and chatter cease abruptly.)* Caesar approaches!

THEODOTUS *(with much presence of mind).* The King permits the Roman commander to enter!

Caesar, plainly dressed, but wearing an oak wreath to conceal his baldness, enters from the loggia, attended by Britannus, his secretary, a Briton, about forty, tall, solemn, and already slightly bald, with a heavy, drooping, hazel-colored moustache trained so as to lose its ends in a pair of trim whiskers. He is carefully dressed in blue, with portfolio, inkhorn, and reed pen at his girdle. His serious air and sense of the importance of the business in his hand is in marked contrast to the kindly interest of Caesar, who looks at the scene, which is new to him, with the frank curiosity of a child, and then turns to the King's chair: Britannus and Rufio posting themselves near the steps at the other side.

CAESAR *(looking at Pothinus and Ptolemy).* So you are the King. Dull work at your age, eh? *(To Pothinus)* Your servant, Pothinus. *(He turns away unconcernedly and comes slowly along the middle of the hall, looking from side to side at the courtiers until he reaches Achillas.)* And this gentleman?

THEODOTUS. Achillas, the King's general.

CAESAR *(turning to Theodotus).* And you, sir, are—?

THEODOTUS. Theodotus, the King's tutor.

CAESAR. You teach men how to be kings. Theodotus. That is very clever of you. *(Looking at the gods on the walls as he turns away from Theodotus and goes up again to Pothinus).* And this place?

POTHINUS. The council chamber of the chancellors of the King's treasury, Caesar.

CAESAR. Ah! That reminds me. I want some money.

POTHINUS. The King's treasury is poor, Caesar.

CAESAR. Yes: I notice that there is but one chair in it.

RUFIO *(shouting gruffly)*. Bring a chair there, some of you, for Caesar.

PTOLEMY *(rising shyly to offer his chair)*. Caesar—

CAESAR *(kindly)*. No, no, my boy: that is your chair of state. Sit down.

He makes Ptolemy sit down again. Meanwhile Rufio, looking about him, sees in the nearest corner an image of the god Ra, represented as a seated man with the head of a hawk. Before the image is a bronze tripod, about as large as a three-legged stool, with a stick of incense burning on it. Rufio, with Roman resourcefulness and indifference to foreign superstitions, promptly seizes the tripod; shakes off the incense; blows away the ash; and dumps it down behind Caesar, nearly in the middle of the hall.

RUFIO. Sit on that, Caesar.

A shiver runs through the court, followed by a hissing whisper of Sacrilege!

CAESAR *(seating himself)*. Now, Pothinus, to business. I am badly in want of money.

BRITANNUS *(disapproving of these informal expressions)*. My master would say that there is a lawful debt due to Rome by Egypt, contracted by the King's deceased father to the Triumvirate; and that it is Caesar's duty to his country to require immediate payment.

CAESAR *(blandly)*. Ah, I forgot. I have not made my companions known here. Pothinus: this is Britannus, my secretary. He is an islander from the western end of the world, a day's voyage from Gaul. *(Britannus bows stiffly.)* This gentleman is Rufio, my comrade in arms. *(Rufio nods.)* Pothinus: I want 1,600 talents.

The courtiers, appalled, murmur loudly, and Theodotus and Achillas appeal mutely to one another against so monstrous a demand.

POTHINUS *(aghast)*. Forty million sesterces! Impossible. There is not so much money in the King's treasury.

CAESAR *(encouragingly)*. Only sixteen hundred talents, Pothinus. Why count it in sesterces? A sestertius is only worth a loaf of bread.

POTHINUS. And a talent is worth a racehorse. I say it is impossible. We have been at strife here, because the king's sister Cleopatra falsely claims his throne. The King's taxes have not been collected for a whole year.

CAESAR. Yes they have, Pothinus. My officers have been collecting them all the morning. *(Renewed whisper and sensation, not without some stifled laughter, among the courtiers.)*

RUFIO *(bluntly)*. You must pay, Pothinus. Why waste words? You are getting off cheaply enough,

POTHINUS *(bitterly)*. Is it possible that Caesar, the conqueror of the world, has time to occupy himself with such a trifle as our taxes?

CAESAR. My friend: taxes are the chief business of a conqueror of the world.

POTHINUS. Then take warning, Caesar. This day, the treasures of the temples and the gold of the King's treasury shall be sent to the mint to be melted down for our ransom in the sight of the people. They shall see us sitting under bare walls and drinking from wooden cups. And their wrath be on your head, Caesar, if you force us to this sacrilege!

CAESAR. Do not, fear, Pothinus: the people know how well wine tastes in wooden cups. In return for your bounty, I will settle this dispute about the throne for you, if you will. What say you?

POTHINUS. If I say no, will that hinder you?

RUFIO *(defiantly)*. No.

CAESAR. You say the matter has been at issue for a year, Pothinus. May I have ten minutes at it?

POTHINUS. You will do your pleasure, doubtless.

CAESAR. Good! But first, let us have Cleopatra here.

THEODOTUS. She is not in Alexandria: she is fled into Syria.

CAESAR. I think not. *(To Rufio)* Call Totateeta.

RUFIO *(calling)*. Ho there, Teetatota.

Ftatateeta enters the loggia and stands arrogantly at the top of the steps.

FTATATEETA. Who pronounces the name of Ftatateeta, the Queen's chief nurse?

CAESAR. Nobody can pronounce it, Tota, except yourself. Where is your mistress?

Cleopatra who is hiding, behind Ftatateeta, peeps out at them, laughing. Caesar rises.

CAESAR. Will the Queen favor us with her presence for a moment?

CLEOPATRA *(pushing Ftatateeta aside and standing haughtily on the brink of the steps).* Am I to behave like a Queen?

CAESAR. Yes.

Cleopatra immediately comes down to the chair of state; seizes Ptolemy and drags him out of his seat; then takes his place in the chair. Ftatateeta seats herself on the step of the loggia, and sits there, watching the scene with sibylline intensity.

PTOLEMY *(mortified, and struggling with his tears).* Caesar: this is how she treats me always. If I am a king why is she allowed to take everything from me?

CLEOPATRA. You are not to be King, you little cry-baby. You are to be eaten by the Romans.

CAESAR *(touched by Ptolemy's distress).* Come here, my boy, and stand by me.

Ptolemy goes over to Caesar, who, resuming his seat on the tripod, takes the boy's hand to encourage him. Cleopatra, furiously jealous, rises and glares at them.

CLEOPATRA *(with flaming cheeks).* Take your throne: I don't want it. *(She flings away from the chair, and approaches Ptolemy, who shrinks from her.)* Go this instant and sit down in your place.

CAESAR. Go, Ptolemy. Always take a throne when it is offered to you.

RUFIO. I hope you will have the good sense to follow your own advice when we return to Rome, Caesar.

Ptolemy slowly goes back to the throne, giving Cleopatra a wide berth, in evident fear of her hands. She takes his place beside Caesar.

CAESAR. Pothinus—

CLEOPATRA *(interrupting him)*. Are you not going to speak to me?

CAESAR. Be quiet. Open your mouth again before I give you leave; and you shall be eaten.

CLEOPATRA. I am not afraid. A queen must not be afraid. Eat my husband there, if you like: he is afraid.

CAESAR *(starting)*. Your husband! What do you mean?

CLEOPATRA *(pointing to Ptolemy)*. That little thing.

The two Romans and the Briton stare at one another in amazement.

THEODOTUS. Caesar: you are a stranger here, and not conversant with our laws. The kings and queens of Egypt may not marry except with their own royal blood. Ptolemy and Cleopatra are born king and consort just as they are born brother and sister.

BRITANNUS *(shocked)*. Caesar: this is not Proper.

THEODOTUS *(outraged)*. How!

CAESAR *(recovering his self-possession)*. Pardon him. Theodotus: he is a barbarian, and thinks that the customs of his tribe and island are the laws of nature.

BRITANNUS. On the contrary, Caesar, it is these Egyptians who are, barbarians; and you wrong to encourage them. I say it is a scandal.

CAESAR. Scandal or not, my friend, it opens the gate of peace. (He *rises and addresses Pothinus seriously*) Pothinus: hear what I propose.

RUFIO. Hear Caesar there.

CAESAR. Ptolemy and Cleopatra shall reign jointly in Egypt.

ACHILLAS. What of the King's younger brother and Cleopatra's younger sister?

RUFIO *(explaining)*. There is another little Ptolemy, Caesar: so they tell me.

CAESAR. Well, the little Ptolemy can marry the other sister; and we will make them both a present of Cyprus.

POTHINUS *(impatiently)*. Cyprus is of no use to anybody.

CAESAR. No matter: you shall have it for the sake of peace.

BRITANNUS *(unconsciously anticipating a later statesman)*. Peace with honor, Pothinus.

POTHINUS *(mutinously)*. Caesar: be honest. The money you demand is the price of our freedom. Take it; and leave us to settle our own affairs.

THE BOLDER COURTIERS *(encouraged by Pothinus's tone and Caesar's quietness)*. Yes, yes. Egypt for the Egyptians!

The conference now becomes an altercation, the Egyptians becoming more and more heated. Caesar remains unruffled but Rufio grows fiercer and doggeder, and Britannus haughtily indignant.

RUFIO *(contemptuously)*. Egypt for the Egyptians! Do you forget that there is a Roman army of occupation here, left by Aulus Gabinius when he set up your toy king for you?

ACHILLAS *(suddenly asserting himself)*. And now under my command. I am the Roman general here, Caesar.

CAESAR *(tickled by the humor of the situation)*. And also the Egyptian general, eh?

POTHINUS *(triumphantly)*. That is so, Caesar.

CAESAR *(to Achillas)*. So you can make war on the Egyptians in the name of Rome, and on the Romans—on me, if necessary—in the name of Egypt?

ACHILLAS. That is so. Caesar.

CAESAR. And which side are you on at present, if I may presume to ask, general?

ACHILLAS. On the side of the right and of the gods.

CAESAR. Hm! How many men have you?

ACHILLAS. That will appear when I take the field.

RUFIO *(truculently)*. Are your men Romans? If not, it matters not how many there are, provided you are no stronger than 500 to ten.

POTHINUS. It is useless to try to bluff us, Rufio. Caesar has been defeated before and may be defeated again. A few weeks ago Caesar was flying for his life before Pompey: a few months hence he may be flying, for his life before Cato and Juba of Numidia, the African King.

ACHILLAS *(following up Pothinus's speech menacingly)*. What can you do with 4,000 men?

THEODOTUS *(following up Achillas's speech with a raucous squeak).* And without money? Away with you.

ALL THE COURTIERS *(shouting fiercely and crowding towards Caesar).* Away with you. Egypt for the Egyptians! Begone.

Rufio bites his beard, too angry to speak. Caesar sits as comfortably as if he were at breakfast, and the cat were clamoring for a piece of Finnan-haddie.

CLEOPATRA. Why do you let them talk to you like that, Caesar? Are you afraid?

CAESAR. Why, my dear, what they say is quite true.

CLEOPATRA. But if you go away, I shall not be Queen.

CAESAR. I shall not go away until you are Queen.

POTHINUS. Achillas: if you are not a fool, you will take that girl whilst she is under your hand.

RUFIO *(daring them).* Why not take Caesar as well, Achillas?

POTHINUS *(retorting the defiance with interest).* Well said, Rufio. Why not?

RUFIO. Try, Achillas. *(Calling)* Guard there.

The loggia immediately fills with Caesar's soldiers, who stand, sword in hand, at the top of the steps waiting the word to charge from their centurion, who carries a cudgel. For a moment the Egyptians face them proudly: then they retire sullenly to their former places.

BRITANNUS. You are Caesar's prisoners, all of you.

CAESAR *(benevolently).* Oh no, no, no, By no means. Caesar's guests, gentlemen.

CLEOPATRA. Won't you cut their heads off?

CAESAR. What! Cut off your brother's head?

CLEOPATRA Why not? He would cut off mine, if he got the chance. Wouldn't you, Ptolemy?

PTOLEMY *(pale and obstinate).* I would. I will, too, when I grow up.

Cleopatra is rent by a struggle between her newly-acquired dignity as a queen, and a strong impulse to put out her tongue at him. She takes no part in the scene which follows, but watches it with curiosity and wonder, fidgeting with the restlessness of a child, and sitting down on Caesar's tripod when he rises.

POTHINUS. Caesar: if you attempt to detain us—

RUFIO. He will succeed, Egyptian: make up your mind to that. We hold the palace, the beach, and the eastern harbor. The road to Rome is open; and you shall travel it if Caesar chooses.

CAESAR (*courteously*). I could do no less, Pothinus, to secure the retreat of my own soldiers. I am accountable for every life among them. But you are free to go. So are all here, and in the palace.

RUFIO (*aghast at this clemency*). What! Renegades and all?

CAESAR (*softening the expression*). Roman army of occupation and all, Rufio.

POTHINUS (*desperately*). Then I make a last appeal to Caesar's justice. I shall call a witness to prove that but for us, the Roman army of occupation, led by the greatest soldier in the world, would now have Caesar at its mercy. (*Calling through the loggia*) Ho, there, Lucius Septimius (*Caesar starts, deeply moved*): if my voice can reach you, come forth and testify before Caesar.

CAESAR (*shrinking*). No, no.

THEODOTUS. Yes, I say. Let the military tribune bear witness.

Lucius Septimius, a clean shaven, trim athlete of about 40, with symmetrical features, resolute mouth, and handsome, thin Roman nose, in the dress of a Roman officer, comes in through the loggia and confronts Caesar, who hides his face with his robe for a moment; then, mastering himself, drops it, and confronts the tribune with dignity.

POTHINUS. Bear witness, Lucius Septimius. Caesar came hither in pursuit of his foe. Did we shelter his foe?

LUCIUS. As Pompey's foot touched the Egyptian shore, his head fell by the stroke of my sword.

THEODOTUS (*with viperish relish*). Under the eves of his wife and child! Remember that, Caesar! They saw it from the ship he had just left. We have given you a full and sweet measure of vengeance.

CAESAR (*with horror*). Vengeance!

POTHINUS. Our first gift to you, as your galley came into the roadstead, was the head of your rival for the empire of the world. Bear witness Lucius Septimius: is it not so?

LUCIUS. It is so. With this hand, that slew Pompey, I placed his head at the feet of Caesar.

CAESAR. Murderer! So would you have slain Caesar, had Pompey been victorious at Pharsalia.

LUCIUS. Woe to the vanquished, Caesar! When I served Pompey, I slew as good men as he, only because he conquered them. His turn came at last.

THEODOTUS *(flatteringly)*. The deed was not yours, Caesar, but ours—nay, mine; for it was done by my counsel. Thanks to us, you keep your reputation for clemency, and have your vengeance too.

CAESAR. Vengeance! Vengeance!! Oh, if I could stoop to vengeance, what would I not exact from you as the price of this murdered man's blood. *(They shrink back, appalled and disconcerted.)* Was he not my son-in-law, my ancient friend, for 20 years the master of great Rome, for 30 years the compeller of victory? Did not I, as a Roman, share his glory? Was the Fate that forced us to fight for the mastery of the world, of our making? Am I Julius Caesar, or am I a wolf, that you fling to me the grey head of the old soldier, the laurelled conqueror, the mighty Roman, treacherously struck down by this callous ruffian, and then claim my gratitude for it! *(To Lucius Septimius)* Begone: you fill me with horror.

LUCIUS *(cold and undaunted)*. Pshaw! you have seen severed heads before, Caesar, and severed right hands too, I think; some thousands of them, in Gaul, after you vanquished Vercingetorix. Did you spare him, with all your clemency? Was that vengeance?

CAESAR. No, by the gods! would that it had been! Vengeance at least is human. No, I say: those severed right hands, and the brave Vercingetorix basely strangled in a vault beneath the Capitol, were *(with shuddering satire)* a wise severity, a necessary protection to the commonwealth, a duty of statesmanship—follies and fictions ten times bloodier than honest vengeance! What a fool was I then! To think that men's lives should be at the mercy of such fools! *(Humbly)* Lucius Septimius, pardon me: why should the slayer of Vercingetorix rebuke the slayer of Pompey? You are free to go with the rest. Or stay if you will: I will find a place for you in my service.

LUCIUS. The odds are against you, Caesar. I go. *(He turns to go out through the loggia.)*

Rufio (*full of wrath at seeing his prey escaping*). That means that he is a Republican.

Lucius (*turning defiantly on the loggia steps*). And what are you?

Rufio. A Caesarian, like all Caesar's soldiers.

Caesar (*courteously*). Lucius: believe me, Caesar is no Caesarian. Were Rome a true republic, then were Caesar the first of Republicans. But you have made your choice. Farewell.

Lucius. Farewell. Come, Achillas, whilst there is yet time.

Caesar, seeing that Rufio's temper threatens to get the worse of him, puts his hand on his shoulder and brings him down the hall out of harm's way, Britannus accompanying them and posting himself on Caesar's right hand. This movement brings the three in a little group to the place occupied by Achillas, who moves haughtily away and joins Theodotus on the other side. Lucius Septimius goes out through the soldiers in the loggia. Pothinus, Theodotus and Achillas follow him with the courtiers, very mistrustful of the soldiers, who close up in their rear and go out after them, keeping them moving without much ceremony. The King is left in his chair, piteous, obstinate, with twitching face and fingers. During these movements Rufio maintains an energetic grumbling, as follows:—

Rufio (*as Lucius departs*). Do you suppose he would let us go if he had our heads in his hands?

Caesar. I have no right to suppose that his ways are any baser than mine.

Rufio. Psha!

Caesar. Rufio: if I take Lucius Septimius for my model, and become exactly like him, ceasing to be Caesar, will you serve me still?

Britannus. Caesar: this is not good sense. Your duty to Rome demands that her enemies should be prevented from doing further mischief. (*Caesar, whose delight in the moral eye-to-business of his British secretary is inexhaustible, smiles indulgently.*)

Rufio. It is no use talking to him, Britannus: you may save your breath to cool your porridge. But mark this, Caesar. Clemency is very well for you; but what is it for your soldiers, who have to fight to-morrow the men you spared yesterday? You may give what orders you please; but I tell you that your next victory will be a massacre, thanks to your clemency. I, for one, will take no prisoners. I will kill my enemies in the field; and then you can preach as much clemency as you please: I shall never have to fight them again. And now, with your leave, I will see these gentry off the premises. *(He turns to go.)*

CAESAR *(turning also and seeing Ptolemy).* What! have they left the boy alone! Oh shame, shame!

RUFIO *(taking Ptolemy's hand and making him rise).* Come, your majesty!

PTOLEMY *(to Caesar, drawing away his hand from Rufio).* Is he turning me out of my palace?

RUFIO *(grimly).* You are welcome to stay if you wish.

CAESAR *(kindly).* Go, my boy. I will not harm you; but you will be safer away, among your friends. Here you are in the lion's mouth.

PTOLEMY *(turning to go).* It is not the lion I fear, but *(looking at Rufio)* the jackal. *(He goes out through the loggia.)*

CAESAR *(laughing approvingly).* Brave boy!

CLEOPATRA *(jealous of Caesar's approbation, calling after Ptolemy).* Little silly. You think that very clever.

CAESAR. Britannus: attend the King. Give him in charge to that Pothinus fellow. *(Britannus goes out after Ptolemy.)*

RUFIO *(pointing to Cleopatra).* And this piece of goods? What is to be done with her? However, I suppose I may leave that to you. *(He goes out through the loggia.)*

CLEOPATRA *(flushing suddenly and turning on Caesar).* Did you mean me to go with the rest?

CAESAR *(a little preoccupied, goes with a sigh to Ptolemy's chair, whilst she waits for his answer with red cheeks and clenched fists).* You are free to do just as you please, Cleopatra.

CLEOPATRA. Then you do not care whether I stay or not?

CAESAR *(smiling).* Of course I had rather you stayed.

CLEOPATRA. Much, much rather?

CAESAR *(nodding).* Much, much rather.

CLEOPATRA. Then I consent to stay, because I am asked. But I do not want to, mind.

CAESAR. That is quite understood. *(Calling)* Totateeta.

Ftatateeta, still seated, turns her eyes on him with a sinister expression, but does not move.

CLEOPATRA *(with a splutter of laughter)*. Her name is not Totateeta: it is Ftatateeta. *(Calling)* Ftatateeta. *(Ftatateeta instantly rises and comes to Cleopatra.)*

CAESAR *(stumbling over the name)*. Tfatafeeta will forgive the erring tongue of a Roman. Tota: the Queen will hold her state here in Alexandria. Engage women to attend upon her; and do all that is needful.

FTATATEETA. Am I then the mistress of the Queen's household?

CLEOPATRA *(sharply)*. No: I am the mistress of the Queen's household. Go and do as you are told, or I will have you thrown into the Nile this very afternoon, to poison the poor crocodiles.

CAESAR *(shocked)*. Oh no, no.

CLEOPATRA. Oh yes, yes. You are very sentimental, Caesar; but you are clever; and if you do as I tell you, you will soon learn to govern.

Caesar, quite dumbfounded by this impertinence, turns in his chair and stares at her. Ftatateeta, smiling grimly, and showing a splendid set of teeth, goes, leaving them alone together.

CAESAR. Cleopatra: I really think I must eat you, after all.

CLEOPATRA *(kneeling beside him and looking at him with eager interest, half real, half affected to show how intelligent she is)*. You must not talk to me now as if I were a child.

CAESAR. You have been growing up since the Sphinx introduced us the other night: and you think you know more than I do already.

CLEOPATRA *(taken down, and anxious to justify herself)*. No: that would be very silly of me: of course I know that. But—*(suddenly)* are you angry with me?

CAESAR. No.

CLEOPATRA *(only half believing him)*. Then why are you so thoughtful?

CAESAR *(rising)*. I have work to do, Cleopatra.

CLEOPATRA *(drawing back)*. Work! *(Offended)* You are tired of talking to me; and that is your excuse to get away from me.

CAESAR *(sitting down again to appease her).* Well, well: another minute. But then—work!

CLEOPATRA. Work! what nonsense! You must remember that you are a king now: I have made you one. Kings don't work.

CAESAR. Oh! Who told you that, little kitten? Eh?

CLEOPATRA. My father was King of Egypt, and he never worked. But he was a great king, and cut off my sister's head because she rebelled against him and took the throne from him.

CAESAR. Well: and how did he get his throne back again?

CLEOPATRA *(eagerly, her eyes lighting up).* I will tell you. A beautiful young man, with strong round arms, came over the desert with many horsemen, and slew my sister's husband and gave my father back his throne. *(Wistfully)* I was only twelve then. Oh, I wish he would come again, now that I am a queen. I would make him my husband.

CAESAR. It might be managed, perhaps; for it was I who sent that beautiful young man to help your father.

CLEOPATRA *(enraptured).* You know him!

CAESAR *(nodding).* I do.

CLEOPATRA. Has he come with you? *(Caesar shakes his head: she is cruelly disappointed.)* Oh, I wish he had, I wish he had. If only I were a little older; so that he might not think me a mere kitten, as you do! But perhaps that is because you are old. He is many, many years younger than you, is he not?

CAESAR *(as if swallowing a pill).* He is somewhat younger.

CLEOPATRA. Would he be my husband, do you think, if I asked him?

CAESAR. Very likely.

CLEOPATRA. But I should not like to ask him. Could you not persuade him to ask me—without knowing that I wanted him to?

CAESAR *(touched by her innocence of the beautiful young man's character).* My poor child!

CLEOPATRA. Why do you say that as if you were sorry for me? Does he love anyone else?

CAESAR. I am afraid so.

CLEOPATRA *(tearfully).* Then I shall not be his first love.

CAESAR. Not quite the first. He is greatly admired by women.

CLEOPATRA. I wish I could be the first. But if he loves me, I will make him kill all the rest. Tell me: is he still beautiful? Do his strong round arms shine in the sun like marble?

CAESAR. He is in excellent condition—considering how much he eats and drinks.

CLEOPATRA. Oh, you must not say common, earthly things about him; for I love him. He is a god.

CAESAR. He is a great captain of horsemen, and swifter of foot than any other Roman.

CLEOPATRA. What is his real name?

CAESAR *(puzzled).* His real name?

CLEOPATRA. Yes. I always call him Horus, because Horus is the most beautiful of our gods. But I want to know his real name.

CAESAR. His name is Mark Antony.

CLEOPATRA *(musically).* Mark Antony, Mark Antony, Mark Antony! What a beautiful name! *(She throws her arms round Caesar's neck.)* Oh, how I love you for sending him to help my father! Did you love my father very much?

CAESAR. No, my child; but your father, as you say, never worked. I always work. So when he lost his crown he had to promise me 16,000 talents to get it back for him.

CLEOPATRA. Did he ever pay you?

CAESAR. Not in full.

CLEOPATRA. He was quite right: it was too dear. The whole world is not worth 16,000 talents.

CAESAR. That is perhaps true, Cleopatra. Those Egyptians who work paid as much of it as he could drag from them. The rest is still due. But as I most likely shall not get it, I must go back to my work. So you must run away for a little and send my secretary to me.

CLEOPATRA *(coaxing).* No: I want to stay and hear you talk about Mark Antony.

CAESAR. But if I do not get to work, Pothinus and the rest of them will cut us off from the harbor; and then the way from Rome will be blocked.

CLEOPATRA. No matter: I don't want you to go back to Rome.

CAESAR. But you want Mark Antony to come from it.

CLEOPATRA *(springing up)*. Oh yes, yes, yes: I forgot. Go quickly and work, Caesar; and keep the way over the sea open for my Mark Antony. *(She runs out through the loggia, kissing her hand to Mark Antony across the sea.)*

CAESAR *(going briskly up the middle of the hall to the loggia steps)*. Ho, Britannus. *(He is startled by the entry of a wounded Roman soldier, who confronts him from the upper step.)* What now?

SOLDIER. *(pointing to his bandaged head)*. This, Caesar; and two of my comrades killed in the market place.

CAESAR *(quiet, but attending)*. Ay. Why?

SOLDIER. There is an army come to Alexandria, calling itself the Roman army.

CAESAR. The Roman army of occupation. Ay?

SOLDIER. Commanded by one Achillas.

CAESAR. Well?

SOLDIER. The citizens rose against us when the army entered the gates. I was with two others in the market place when the news came. They set upon us. I cut my way out; and here I am.

CAESAR. Good. I am glad to see you alive. *(Rufio enters the loggia hastily, passing behind the soldier to look out through one of the arches at the quay beneath.)* Rufio, we are besieged.

RUFIO. What! Already?

CAESAR. Now or to-morrow: what does it matter? We shall be besieged.

Britannus runs in.

BRITANNUS. Caesar—

CAESAR *(anticipating him)*. Yes: I know. *(Rufio and Britannus come down the hall from the loggia at opposite sides, past Caesar, who waits for a moment near the step to say to the soldier)* Comrade: give the word to turn out on the beach and stand by the boats. Get your wound attended to. Go. *(The soldier hurries out. Caesar comes down the hall between Rufio and Britannus)* Rufio: we have some ships in the west harbor. Burn them.

RUFIO *(staring)*. Burn them!!

CAESAR. Take every boat we have in the east harbor, and seize the Pharos—that island with the lighthouse. Leave half our men behind to hold the beach and the quay outside this palace: that is the way home.

RUFIO (disapproving strongly). Are we to give up the city?

CAESAR. We have not got it, Rufio. This palace we have and—what is that building next door?

RUFIO. The theatre.

CAESAR. We will have that too: it commands the strand. For the rest, Egypt for the Egyptians!

RUFIO. Well, you know best, I suppose. Is that all?

CAESAR. That is all. Are those ships burnt yet?

RUFIO. Be easy: I shall waste no more time. (He runs out.)

BRITANNUS. Caesar: Pothinus demands speech of you. In my opinion he needs a lesson. His manner is most insolent.

CAESAR. Where is he?

BRITANNUS. He waits without.

CAESAR. Ho there! admit Pothinus.

Pothinus appears in the loggia, and comes down the hall very haughtily to Caesars left hand.

CAESAR. Well, Pothinus?

POTHINUS. I have brought you our ultimatum, Caesar.

CAESAR. Ultimatum! The door was open: you should have gone out through it before you declared war. You are my Prisoner now. (He goes to the chair and loosens his toga.)

POTHINUS (scornfully). I your prisoner! Do you know that you are in Alexandria, and that King Ptolemy, with an army outnumbering your little troop a hundred to one, is in possession of Alexandria?

CAESAR (unconcernedly taking off his toga and throwing it on the chair). Well, my friend, get out if you can. And tell your friends not to kill any more Romans in the market place. Otherwise my soldiers, who do not share my celebrated clemency, will probably kill you. Britannus, pass the word to the guard; and fetch my armor. (Britannus runs out. Rufio returns.) Well?

Rufio (*pointing from the loggia to a cloud of smoke drifting over the harbor*). See there! (*Pothinus runs eagerly up the steps to look out.*)

Caesar. What, ablaze already! Impossible!

Rufio. Yes, five good ships, and a barge laden with oil grappled to each. But it is not my doing: the Egyptians have saved me the trouble. They have captured the west harbor.

Caesar (*anxiously*). And the east harbor? The lighthouse, Rufio?

Rufio (*with a sudden splutter of raging ill usage, coming down to Caesar and scolding him*). Can I embark a legion in five minutes? The first cohort is already on the beach. We can do no more. If you want faster work, come and do it yourself?

Caesar (*soothing him*). Good, good. Patience, Rufio, patience.

Rufio (*Patience! Who is impatient here, you or I? Would I be here, if I could not oversee them from that balcony?

Caesar. Forgive me, Rufio; and (*anxiously*) hurry them as much as—

He is interrupted by an outcry as of an old man in the extremity of misfortune. It draws near rapidly; and Theodotus rushes in, tearing his hair, and squeaking the most lamentable exclamations. Rufio steps back to stare at him, amazed at his frantic condition. Pothinus turns to listen.

Theodotus (*on the steps, with uplifted arms*). Horror unspeakable! Woe, alas! Help!

Rufio. What now?

Caesar (*frowning*). Who is slain?

Theodotus. Slain! Oh, worse than the death of ten thousand men! Loss irreparable to mankind!

Rufio. What has happened, man?

Theodotus (*rushing down the hall between them*). The fire has spread from your ships. The first of the seven wonders of the world perishes. The library of Alexandria is in flames.

Rufio. Psha! (*Quite relieved, he goes up to the loggia and watches the preparations of the troops on the beach.*)

Caesar. Is that all?

Theodotus (*unable to believe his senses*). All! Caesar: will you go down to posterity as a barbarous soldier too ignorant to know the value of books?

CAESAR. Theodotus: I am an author myself; and I tell you it is better that the Egyptians should live their lives than dream them away with the help of books.

THEODOTUS *(kneeling, with genuine literary emotion: the passion of the pedant).* Caesar: once in ten generations of men, the world gains an immortal book.

CAESAR *(inflexible).* If it did not flatter mankind, the common executioner would burn it.

THEODOTUS. Without history, death would lay you beside your meanest soldier.

CAESAR. Death will do that in any case. I ask no better grave.

THEODOTUS. What is burning there is the memory of mankind.

CAESAR. A shameful memory. Let it burn.

THEODOTUS. *(wildly).* Will you destroy the past?

CAESAR. Ay, and build the future with its ruins. *(Theodotus, in despair, strikes himself on the temples with his fists.)* But harken, Theodotus, teacher of kings: you who valued Pompey's head no more than a shepherd values an onion, and who now kneel to me, with tears in your old eyes, to plead for a few sheepskins scrawled with errors. I cannot spare you a man or a bucket of water just now; but you shall pass freely out of the palace. Now, away with you to Achillas; and borrow his legions to put out the fire. *(He hurries him to the steps.)*

POTHINUS *(significantly).* You understand, Theodotus: I remain a prisoner.

THEODOTUS. A prisoner!

CAESAR. Will you stay to talk whilst the memory of mankind is burning? *(Calling through the loggia)* Ho there! Pass Theodotus out. *(To Theodotus)* Away with you.

THEODOTUS *(to Pothinus).* I must go to save the library. *(He hurries out.)*

CAESAR. Follow him to the gate, Pothinus. Bid him urge your people to kill no more of my soldiers, for your sake.

POTHINUS. My life will cost you dear if you take it, Caesar. *(He goes out after Theodotus.)*

Rufio, absorbed in watching the embarkation, does not notice the departure of the two Egyptians.

RUFIO *(shouting front the loggia to the beach)*. All ready, there?

A CENTURION *(from below)*. All ready. We wait for Caesar.

CAESAR. Tell them Caesar is coming—the rogues! *(Calling)* Britannicus. (*This magniloquent version of his secretary's name is one of Caesar's jokes. In later years it would have meant, quite seriously and officially, Conqueror of Britain.)*

RUFIO. *(calling down)*. Push off, all except the longboat. Stand by it to embark, Caesar's guard there. *(He leaves the balcony and comes down into the hall.)* Where are those Egyptians? Is this more clemency? Have you let them go?

CAESAR *(chuckling)*. I have let Theodotus go to save the library. We must respect literature, Rufio.

RUFIO. *(raging)*. Folly on folly's head! I believe if you could bring back all the dead of Spain, Gaul and Thessaly to life, you would do it that we might have the trouble of fighting them over again.

CAESAR. Might not the gods destroy the world if their only thought, were to be at peace next year? *(Rufio, out of all patience, turns away in anger. Caesar suddenly grips his sleeve, and adds slyly in his ear)* Besides, my friend: every Egyptian we imprison means imprisoning two Roman soldiers to guard him. Eh?

RUFIO. Agh! I might have known there was some fox's trick behind your fine talking. *(He gets away from Caesar with an ill-humored shrug, and goes to the balcony for another look at the preparations; finally goes out.)*

CAESAR. Is Britannus asleep? I sent him for my armor an hour ago. *(Calling)* Britannicus, thou British islander. Britannicus!

Cleopatra runs in through the loggia with Caesar's helmet and sword, snatched from Britannus, who follows her with a cuirass and greaves. They come down to Caesar, she, to his left hand, Britannus to his right.

CLEOPATRA. I am going to dress you, Caesar. Sit down. *(He*

obeys.) These Roman helmets are so becoming! *(She takes* off *his wreath.)* Oh! *(She bursts out laughing at him.)*

CAESAR. What are you laughing at?

CLEOPATRA. You're bald *(beginning with a big B, and ending with a splutter).*

CAESAR *(almost annoyed).* Cleopatra! *(He rises, for the convenience of Britannus, who puts the cuirass on him.)*

CLEOPATRA. So that is why you wear the wreath—to hide it.

BRITANNUS. Peace, Egyptian: they are the bays of the conqueror. *(He buckles the cuirass.)*

CLEOPATRA. Peace, thou: islander! *(To Caesar)* You should rub your head with strong spirits of sugar, Caesar. That will make it grow.

CAESAR *(with a wry face).* Cleopatra: do you like to be reminded that you are very young?

CLEOPATRA *(pouting).* No.

CAESAR *(sitting down again, and setting out his leg for Britannus, who kneels to put on his greaves).* Neither do I like to be reminded that I am—middle aged. Let me give you ten of my superfluous years. That will make you 26, and leave me only—no matter. Is it a bargain?

CLEOPATRA. Agreed. 26, mind. *(She puts the helmet on him.)* Oh! How nice! You look only about 50 in it!

BRITANNUS *(looking up severely at Cleopatra).* You must not speak in this manner to Caesar.

CLEOPATRA. Is it true that when Caesar caught you on that island, you were painted all over blue?

BRITANNUS. Blue is the color worn by all Britons of good standing. In war we stain our bodies blue; so that though our enemies may strip us of our clothes and our lives, they cannot strip us of our respectability. *(He rises.)*

CLEOPATRA *(with Caesar's sword).* Let me hang this on. Now you look splendid. Have they made any statues of you in Rome?

CAESAR. Yes, many statues.

CLEOPATRA. You must send for one and give it to me.

RUFIO *(coming back into the loggia, more impatient than ever).* Now Caesar: have you done talking? The moment your foot is aboard there will be no holding our men back: the boats will race one another for the lighthouse

CAESAR (*drawing his sword and trying the edge*). Is this well set to-day, Britannicus? At Pharsalia it was as blunt as a barrel-hoop.

BRITANNUS. It will split one of the Egyptian's hairs to-day, Caesar. I have set, it myself.

CLEOPATRA (*suddenly throwing her arms in terror round Caesar*). Oh, you are not really going into battle to be killed ?

CAESAR. No, Cleopatra. No man goes to battle to be killed.

CLEOPATRA. But they do get killed. My sister's husband was killed in battle. You must not go. Let him go (*pointing to Rufio. They all laugh at her*). Oh please, please don't go. What will happen to me if you never come back?

CAESAR (*gravely*). Are you afraid?

CLEOPATRA. No.

CAESAR (*with quiet authority*). Go to the balcony; and you shall see us take the Pharos. You must learn to look on battles. Go. (*She goes, downcast, and looks out from the balcony.*) That is well. Now, Rufio. March.

CLEOPATRA (*suddenly clapping her hands*). Oh, you will not be, able to go!

CAESAR. Why? What now?

CLEOPATRA. They are drying up the harbor with buckets—a multitude of soldiers—over there (*pointing out across the sea to her left*)—they are dipping up the water.

RUFIO. (*hastening to look*). It is true. The Egyptian army! Crawling over the edge of the west harbor like locusts. (*With sudden anger he strides down to Caesar.*) This is your accursed clemency, Caesar. Theodotus has brought them.

CAESAR (*delighted with his own cleverness*). I meant him to, Rufio. They have come to put out the fire. The library will keep them busy whilst we seize the lighthouse. Eh? (*He rushes out buoyantly through, the loggia, followed by Britannus.*)

RUFIO (*disgustedly*). More foxing! Agh! (*He rushes off. A shout from the soldiers announces the appearance of Caesar below.*)

CENTURION *(below)*. All aboard. Give way there. *(Another shout.)*

CLEOPATRA *(waving her scarf through the loggia arch)*. Goodbye, goodbye, dear Caesar. Come back safe. Goodbye!

END OF ACT II

PART IV

SHAPES: VERSE

POETRY: INFINITY OF REFLECTIONS

Stand before a mirror. Look into it, first at yourself, then around you. Notice the slight alterations of light and form, created by the glass and the silver backing. In a reflection, or even a representation, such as a digital image, you do not look quite the same as you do in person. Now place the mirror opposite another mirror. Look into either one. Notice the infinite hall of reflections, ever smaller, extending out infinitely? Poetry is like a mirror before a mirror. Like the mirror, poetry creates representations of ideas, forms, and nature. Like two mirrors reflecting each other, it evokes an infinite array of interpretations in readers. It compresses and transforms ideas into symbolic or visual form, through words, that open out in varied understanding.

Poetry is one of the oldest forms of human expression, whether in the form of ritual chants to gods; stories of the great deeds of heroes such as the epic *Beowulf*, or their weaknesses, as in the romance *Sir Gawain and the Green Knight*; expressions of spiritual and physical love, as in John Donne's "The Good Morrow"; or private reflections on a landscape, as in Wordsworth's "Lines Composed a Few Miles Above Tintern Abbey," and many of the works from Japanese poetry in this volume.

Poetry has a long history of oral recitation. For example, the oldest surviving poem in English, "Caedmon's Hymn," in Bede's *Ecclesiastical History of the English People*, tells the story of how the poet invented the poem in a dream, through divine inspiration, and later sang it to Hilda, abbess of Whitby, the religious

community where the poet worked sometime between 650 and
680 C.E. The poem, about creation, embodies the act of creating.
The history of poetry long precedes Caedmon's experience,
with elements in common. Poets in many cultures attribute creative
power to a divine source; poetry is often set to or accompanied by
music, or recited, and recorded in some form. Poetry also has much
in common with music: rhythmic patterns of sounds and words;
stress and/or quantity of syllables. The poet shapes the flow of
language as the composer does the notes in a musical composition,
aware of the harmonies of words and counterpoint of meaning.
Poetry also shares parallels with art, through the visual imagery
evoked by language.

Some of the oldest forms of poetry in western cultures are
those classified in Aristotle's *Poetics*: epic, lyric, comedy, and tragedy.
The latter two terms are now associated with drama, once a form
of poetry recited by actors, such as Aristophanes's *Lysistrata*, or
centuries later, William Shakespeare's *Othello*. The former terms
still refer to genres of poetry. The epic, such as Homer's *Iliad* or
the Old English *Beowulf*, is a long narrative involving a hero who
overcomes many challenges to accomplish a goal that few others
could achieve, often with travel across grand expanses of land and
sea. The lyric poem, once sung to the accompaniment of a lyre in
ancient Greece, now refers to a shorter, usually non-narrative poem.
Thus we get the term "lyrics" for the words of a song. Examples of
lyric poetry in this volume include the works of Sappho and the
Kagura, "God-music." However, poetry transcends and defies
classification. Poets are continually experimenting and challenging
the conventions of their times, altering and combining old forms
in new ways.

Transference of meaning, or figurative language, makes such
creative invention possible. At the heart of poetry is metaphor,
which allows a writer to use language symbolically. Metaphors, or
words whose meaning have been transferred to a new context, create
the hall of mirrors. One metaphor evokes many associations and
interpretations, yet they all "reflect" the poem, which in turn
reflects, interprets the world it describes. The reader can look into

a poem through its metaphors, which often evoke visual images, and enter a new landscape that envelops and reshapes one's understanding, being, to the point of oneness. Like all great art, a poem invites the imagination of the reader to become that other mirror, to lose the self, to find the self, reflected infinitely in a transcendent time, place, reborn.

Elza C. Tiner, Ph.D.
Professor of English

Sappho

ca. 630 B.C.E.

Selected poems

Sappho was born on the island of Lesbos, which produced exceptional lyric poets. What we know of her life is derived largely from her poetry, which indicates that she had a daughter, Cleïs, whom she loved greatly. She was of the Æolian race of Asia Minor, a people devoted to art and poetry, with a passion for beauty, joy, and love. In antiquity, she was known simply as the Poetess. Greek philosophers and historians including Plato and Herodotus considered her the greatest genius among women.

Sappho is known primarily for her poetry about love, which often expresses strong feelings for other women. Some fragments of exceedingly beautiful poetry about nature also survive. Her lyricism and clear, direct style express a strong sense of emotion. Beauty and love, as revealed through her poetry, are not abstract concepts, nor frivolous and cheerful; rather they are intense and all-consuming, often described in great personal detail. Much of her poetry was burned in 1073 at Rome and Constantinople, judged to be too immoral for the times.

Source

Sappho. *ca.* 630 B.C.E. *Sappho: A New Translation.* Mary Barnard, Trans. Berkeley: University of California Press, 1958. Poems 1, 24, 37, 64, 82, 86.*

1.

Tell everyone

Now, today, I shall
sing beautifully
for my friends' pleasure

2.

We shall enjoy it

As for him who finds
fault, may silliness
and sorrow take him!

24.

Awed by her splendor

Stars near the lovely
Moon cover their own
bright faces
          when she
is roundest and lights
earth with her silver.

37.

You know the place: then

Leave Crete and come to us
waiting where the grove is
pleasantest, by precincts

sacred to you; incense
smokes on the altar, cold
streams murmur through the

apple branches, a young
rose thicket shades the ground
and quivering leaves pour

down deep sleep; in meadows
where horses have grown sleek
among spring flowers, dill

scents the air. Queen! Cyprian!
Fill our gold cups with love
stirred into clear nectar.

64.
Tonight I've watched

The moon and then
the Pleiades
go down

The night is now
half-gone; youth
goes; I am

in bed alone.

82.
Rich as you are

Death will finish
you: afterwards no
one will remember

or want you: you
had no share in
the Pierian roses

You will flitter
invisible among
the indistinct dead
in Hell's palace
darting fitfully.

86.
Experience shows us

Wealth unchaperoned
by Virtue is never
an innocuous neighbor

CAEDMON

ca. 648-680 C.E.

"CAEDMON'S HYMN"

No Date

"Caedmon's Hymn" is the first known English poem and Caedmon the first English poet. The Anglo-Saxon version of the poem was recorded by the Venerable Bede (673-735), a Northumbrian monk, in his *Ecclesiastical History of the English People*, *Historia Ecclesiastica Gentis Anglorum*. Although he was an illiterate herdsman, he was admitted as a brother to the Streoneshalh monastery (now Whitby, on the coast of Yorkshire). Church history tells the story:

> One night, when the servants of the monastery were gathered about the table for good-fellowship, and the harp was passed from hand to hand, Caedmon, knowing nothing of poetry, left the company for shame, as he had often done, and retired to the stable, as he was assigned that night to the care of the draught cattle. As he slept, there stood by him in vision [*sic*] one who called him by name, and bade him sing. "I cannot sing, and therefore I left the feast." "Sing to me, however, sing of Creation." Thereupon Caedmon began to

sing in praise of God verses which he had never heard before. Of these verses, called Caedmon's hymn, Bede gives the Latin equivalent, the Alfredian translation of Bede gives a West-Saxon poetic version, and one manuscript of Bede appends a Northumbrian poetic version, perhaps the very words of Caedmon. In the morning Caedmon recited his story and his verses to Hilda and the learned men of the monastery, and all agreed that he had received a Divine gift. Caedmon, having further shown his gift by turning into excellent verse some sacred stories recited to him, yielded to the exhortation of Hilda that he take the monsastic habit. (*C.E.*)

In this translation, the concept of God as "shaper" in the creative process, which is central to this poem, has been emphasized, with the West Saxon phrases "he aerest sceop" and "halig scyppend," or "he first shaped" and "Sacred Shaper," respectively.

SOURCE

Caedmon. No date. "Caedmon's Hymn." Translation of the West Saxon version by Elza C. Tiner. Reproduced by permission. Original Old English version available at: http://georgetown.edu/labyrinth/library/oe/texts/a32.2.html.
Catholic Encyclopedia. 2005. Online at www.newadvent.org/cathen/03131c.htm

CAEDMON'S HYMN

Now we must praise Heaven's Protector,
The Lord's might and his mind-heart,
The Glory-Father's work, just as his wonders,
The Eternal Lord, their origins began.
He first shaped for earth's children,

Heaven as a roof, he, the Sacred Shaper;
Then the Guardian of Mankind,
The Eternal Lord, made middle earth
For men, for earth, our Leader Almighty.

BEOWULF

ca. 750-1000

Anonymous

Beowulf is a story of enormous cultural and historical importance, recounting life in the mead halls (the sites of warriors' celebrations) and describing other features of Anglo-Saxon social life. The oldest surviving epic in English literature, *Beowulf* was originally composed to be sung or spoken in a public performance by a "scop"—a singer with a stringed instrument. It is the earliest English epic to be adapted into a literary form and remains the only long heroic poem to survive in its entirety in Old English, though the only surviving manuscript has been burned and mutilated in some places. While the Old English version dates from around 1000, the story itself was composed nearly 250 years earlier in the vernacular West Saxon dialect.

The story tells of the achievements of the hero, Beowulf, who brings his superhuman strength and courage to save King Hrothgar and his palace, Heorot, from the terror wrought by the monster Grendel and Grendel's mother. The story of Beowulf's battles parallels the human struggle between good and evil—created over a period of time when Christianity was beginning to become popular and replace earlier beliefs. The poem shows how the scop deliberately interpolates the language of Christian salvation into the hero's ancient, pagan story. The source of the truths of human lives is clearly under revision.

The story begins when Hrothgar, prosperous king of the Geats (Danes), builds a great mead hall—Heorot. Here, his warriors gather to drink, receive rewards, and listen to stories of their bravery as created by the scop. The noise of the mead hall angers Grendel, a demon who lives in the swamplands. Grendel terrorizes Hrothgar's kingdom for over 12 years until Beowulf, a warrior from another kingdom, hears of the trouble and comes to help.

The selections here presented tell the story of Grendel's attack after Beowulf has joined Hrothgar's troops—Beowulf wounds the monster gravely and it flees to its subterranean world to recover. In XXI, Grendel's mother attacks in revenge, but Beowulf tracks her to her "mere" (lake) and plunges into its magical world after her. In the final excerpts, Beowulf has become old but must fight a new terror: a dragon. Although his loyal retainer, Wiglaf, battles valiantly, the Dragon kills Beowulf, who is then given a hero's funeral.

Readers will enjoy the vivid action and detail of Anglo-Saxon life, as well as the battles with the monsters.* The text also provides an example of the conventions of this very early form of English. Each poetic line is traditionally broken by a space midway to reflect the design of the original manuscript. Excerpts from the translated text and from the narrative summaries provided by the translator have been selected also to give readers a good sense of the language and design of the poem, its narrative line, and its thematic concerns. Notes in brackets indicate additions or summaries provided by the editors of this volume.

SOURCE

Anonymous. *ca.* 750-1000. *Beowulf.* In *Beowulf: A New Verse Translation for Fireside and Classroom.* William Ellery Leonard, Ed. and Trans. New York: Century, 1923. 32-38 (XI-XII), 62-65 (XXI), 118 (XXXVII), 121 (XLIII), 130 (XLII), 134 (XLIII).

---

*   In imagining the "mere" where Grendel and his mother live, it helps to associate it with the very deep, enchanted "loch" of Scottish legend, Loch Ness, and its monster.

Beowulf [Excerpts]

XI

The Scop strikes louder notes upon his harp and he chants with so much fire that we in our banquet hall keep our hands fixed in the handles of our tankards and forget to drink. For he tells how Grendel burst the door of Heorot, greedy for man-flesh and unwitting the welcome he would get, and how Grendel ate up a sleeping Geat, and how, to his eternal sorrow, he then laid paws upon Beowulf. Fierce indeed was that wrestling, and it was a wonder that Heorot, so battered and shaken, did not tumble down on the heads of all. And the Danes, who were waiting yonder on the wall of the Burg, heard the night-shrieks of Grendel in the grip of the Strong One.

And now from out the moorland,   under the misty slopes,
Came astalking Grendel—   God's anger on his hopes.
That Scather foul was minded   to snare of human kin
Some one, or sundry,   that high hail within.
Under the welkin[1] strode he,   until full well he spied
The wine-house, the gold-hall, with fret-work glittering wide.
Nor was that the first time   Hrothgar's home he sought.
Yet never in his life-days,   late or early, aught
Like this harsh welcome found he   from thanemen[2] in the hall.
He came afooting onward   to the house withal,
This warring One that ever   had been from bliss out-cast;
Forthwith the door sprang open,   with forgéd-bolts though fast,
When with his paws he pressed it;   yea, then, on bale-work bent,
Swoln as he was with fury,   that house's mouth he rent.
Anon the Fiend was treading   the shining floor in there;
On he moved in anger;   from eyes of him did glare,
Unto fire likest,   a light unfair.
He saw within the chamber   many a man asleep,—
Kinsman band together,   of clanfolk a heap;

---

[1]   Sky, heavens

[2]   warriors commited to be loyal to the king.

Laughed his mood, was minded that Hobgoblin grim,
Ere the dawn to sunder each his life from limb,
Now that fill-of-feeding he weened awaited him!
But Wyrd³ it was that would not longer grant him might
To seize on more of mankind after that same night.
    Was watching he, the stalwart Kin of Hygelac,⁴
How with grip the Grisly would go at his attack.
He had no thought, this Goblin, that business to put off;
But pounced upon a sleeping man, starting quick enough!
Unthwartedly he slit him, bit his bone-box, drunk
From his veins the blood of him, gulped him chunk by chunk,
Till soon, then, he had there this un-living Geat
Altogether eaten down, even to hands and feet.
Then stepped he forth and nearer, and pawed by bed to him
The hardy-headed Hero, reaching toward him
With his claws he be-deviled: with thoughts that boded harm,
Beowulf received him, propped upon an arm.
But soon he found, did Grendel,— this herdsman-over crimes,—
That never in this Middle-World,⁵ this earth of many climes,
He'd met a mightier hand-grip in any man than here.
Afeared in mood and spirit, small help he gat from fear!
Was bent on making-off, ho!— out to the dark would flee,
Would seek the din of devils! Not now in Heorot he
Fared as in the old-days!— And then the Bold-in-pride,
Hyglac's Thane, remembered his speech of eventide.
Up he stood and grasped him so tight the fingers cracked
The Ettin started outward— the Jarl upon him packed.
The monstrous One was minded, whereso'er he may,
To fling himself but farther, and from thence away
To flee to boggy dingles; his fingers' power he wist
Was in the grip of the Grim One. That was a sorry quest
Whereon the Scather Grendel to Heorot Hall had pressed.

---

³   Fate (the pagan concept)

⁴   i.e., Beowulf

⁵   Between heaven and hell, i.e., earth

The lordly room resounded;   and all the Danes did quail,
Those warrior jarls of walled-town,   lest reft for aye of ale.
Wroth were the ramping twain there,   those warders of the house;
The chamber rang with uproar;   mickle wonder 'twas
How the wine-hall held out   'gainst shock of fighters there,
How adown did fall not   that earthly dwelling fair.
But inside and outside   it was too firmly wrought,
With the bands of iron,   forged by cunning thought.
I've heard that many a mead-bench,   with gold gilded o'er,
There where tugged the foemen,   started from the floor.
So had weened the wise ones   of the Scyldings erst
That never any man by force   might asunder burst
That brave house and bone-bright,   nor by craft might split—
Save that bosoming fire   in flame should swallow it.
Up there rose a shriek then,   strange enough o'night;
On each and every North-Dane   seized a grisly fright,
On each who from the wall there   heard that 'well-a way'—
Heard this God-Forsaker   chant his gruesome lay,
His song of loss-in-battle,   heard bewail his wound
This Grendel, Hell's Bondsman.   For held him tightly bound
That man into was of all men   between the seas confessed,
In the days of this our life here,   in strength the mightiest.

XII

*The Scop chants how Beowulf's men hacked in vain at Grendel
with their ancestral swords, apparently forgetting in their fury and
terror what Beowulf had said, that Grendel bore a charmed life against
all weapons of mankind. But Beowulf at last tore out Grendel's arm,
and the wounded Monster fled forth into the night to die in his dark,
murky fens; and Beowulf hung the bloody trophy under the roof of
Heorot—as it would seem, on the outside just over the door.*

The jarls' [thanes'] Defender would not,   forsooth with a will,
Let him loose aliving—him who came to kill,
Deeming not his life-days   of use to any folk.
More than once did jarlman   of Beowulf try a stroke

With his father's falchion,[6] fain the life to ward
Of the faméd Chieftain, their great Lord,
They wist not, these warsmen, these hardy-headed few,
The while they fell asmiting and thought the while to hew
On this side, on that side, seeking soul to kill,
That best of earthly iron blades, nor never battle-bill,
This acccurséd Scather could hurt or harm:
For over victor-weapons he had cast a charm,
Over every sword-edge. Yet his passing-o'er,
In the days of his life here, was to be full sore;
And this alien Elf-Thing was to fare afar
To the under-places where the devils are.
For he had found, had Grendel,— this Striver against God,—
Who in such merry mood of old so oft on man had trod,
That his bulk-of-body would not help him moe,
Now Hygelac's stout Kinsman held his fore-paw so!
Was each unto the other alive a loathly thing.
A body-sore he gat there, this wretched Ogreling:
There showed upon his shoulder a cureless wound anon;
His sinews sprang asunder; from socket burst the bone.
To Beowulf was given the glory of the fray;
And Grendel was to flee hence, sick-to-death, away,—
Off under fen-slopes, off to dens of gloom.
He wist, O well he wist it, his end-of-life had come,
His full tale of days now.— The wish of Danemen all,
After that gory set-to, had come to pass withal.
He had now y-cleanséd, he who came from far,
The Wise-Head and Stout-Heart, the House of high Hrothgár
Had freed it now from fury. His night-work made him glad,
His deed of might and glory. The Geatmen's Leader had
Now before the East-Danes fulfilled his vaunting[7] there,—
Aye, all ills amended and the carking care,
Which they had dreed aforetime, and by stress and strain

---

[6] sword

[7] i.e., boasting, which was a conventional, competitive occupation among
such heroes

Long been doomed to suffer—   more than little pain.
Of this there was a token,   clear enough in proof,
When the Victor-Fighter   under the gabled roof
Hung on high the fore-paw   the arm and shoulder grim—
And there ye had together   all Grendel's clutching-limb!

[In the following sections, Grendel's enraged mother raids Hrothgar's palace in revenge and takes one of the men (a "retainer") when she leaves. Beowulf and a posse take off after her, tracking her through the fens and the bogs.]

XXI

The scop chants Beowulf's confident reply and the journey of Hrothgar, Beowulf, and the band along the trail of the Witch-Wife [Grendel's mother] on to the bleak regions, till of a sudden along the cliff they came upon the head of the retainer the Witch-Wife had slaughtered and eaten. And he chants how the waters below were alive with Nicors [monsters] and Sea-Serpents, and how Beowulf shot one of them dead with an arrow, and how Beowulf then donned his armor and received from Unferth, who was now a staunch believer in Beowulf, the loan of Unferth's famous sword called Hrunting. (For a sword in those days was so near and dear to a man that it often bore a personal name, like a trusted servant.)

Beowulf made a speech then,   son of Ecgtheow, he:
"Sorrow not, thou Sage One,—   for each it better be
That his friend he wreaketh   than bemourn him late.
Our end of life in world here   we must all await;
Let who is able win him   glory ere his death;
In after-years for warrior dead   that chiefly profiteth.
Arise thou Kingdom's Warden!   Speedily let us hie
Of this Kin of Grendel   the trail for to spy.
Thus to thee I promise: She'll refuge in nor rest.—
Neither in earth's bosom   nor in hill-forést,
Nor in sea-bottom,   wheresoe'er she go!
For this day have patience   in thine every woe,
As I ween thou wilt have."

Upleapt the Graybeard [Hrothgar] now;
Thanked the Lord Almighty   for what this man did vow.
Then Hrothgar's horse was bridled,   his steed with braided mane;
Stately rode the royal Sage;   and afoot his train
Of shield-bearers was stepping.   Wide was there to see
Her tracks across the wood-ways,   her trail along the lea,
Whither fared she forward   over the murky moor,
And with her bare the dead man,   the best of kin-thanes sure
Of all who once with Hrothgar   warded well the home.
Then the Son of Aethelings [Beowulf]   now did over-roam
The narrow-passes,   the steep cliff-stone,
The close defiles   and the paths unknown,
The beetling cragheads,   the Nicors' [water monsters] den.
All ahead he hastened   with a few wise men
For to view the region, till a sudden he
Found the joyless forest,   found the mountain tree,
Leaning o'er the hoar cliff.   Under the wood,
Blood-stained and troubled,   there the waters stood.
Unto the friends of Scvldings,   unto every Dane,
It was a thing of sorrow,   a burden of heart's pain,
Aye, to many a clansman   a grief it was and dread,
When, upon the sea-cliff they   met with Aescher [the stolen retainer]'s head!
The flood with blood was boiling,   yes, with the hot gore;
The folk saw down upon it;   the horn was singing o'er
Its battle-blast of onset.   The band all sate;
They watched along the water   the sea-worms great,
Monsters of the dragon-breed,   trying there the sea,
And on the foreland ledges   Nicors lying free
(Who're wont at early morning   their grievous quest to take
Out upon the sail-road)—   and wild-beast and snake.
Bitter and puffed with anger,   they [the Nicors] hastened away—
They had heard that clangor,   the war-horn's lay.
One did the Geatish Leader   with arrow-bow from shore
Berob of life forever   and of the waves' uproar.
The warrior-shaft, the hardy,   unto his heart went home—
He whom death had taken swam   more sluggish on the foam![8]

Speedily on the billows   with barbed boar-spear
They pressed him so sorely,   they harried him so fierce,
And dragged him up the ledges,   this wave-tossing Ranger.
The marvelling warriors looked upon   the grim and grisly Stranger.
Girded himself, did Beowulf,   with his jarlman's weeds;
Naught for his life he mourned. His coat of mail must needs,
Bright with deft devices,   be trying the sea-quest—
This hand-woven byrnie big,   that girt his bony-chest,
So never a grip-in-battle   might do his bosom scath,
Nor life by hurt by vengeful grasp   of this Thing-of-Wrath.
The head of him was guarded   by the helmet white
That soon must seek the sounding surge   and stir the deeps below:
With lordly bands 'twas bounden,   with treasure-work 'twas dight,
As the weapon-smith had wroght it   in days of long ago,
And wondrously had decked it   and set with shapes of boar,
That brand nor blade of battle   might bite it nevermore.
Nor was that the smallest   of helps to mighty deed
Which Spokesman of Hrothgar   had loaned him in his need:
A good sword hafted,   and Hrunting its name
Of all old heirlooms   the first it was in fame.
The edge of it was iron,   etched with twig and spray,[9]
Hardened by the battle-blood;   ne'er did it betray
Any man that clasped it   with hand amid the fray,—
Any man that dared to go   on war-paths away,
To folk-stead of foemen.   Nor this the first time now
That Hrunting-sword of Unferth   in mighty works should dow.
In sooth the bairn of Eeglaf [Unferth],   great though his prowess be,
Remembered not his speech of late   when drunk with wine was he,—
Now as he lent his weapon   to a stouter swordsman [Beowulf] here.
Himself he durst not hazard   his own life in the mere,
Nor dree a warrior's duty.   And thus he lost the fame,
The glory of a doughty deed.   For the Other 'twas not so,
When he himself had girded   for battle with the Foe.

---

[8]   Characteristic understatement—being dead, he couldn't swim at all [WEL]

[9]   That is, the blade was adorned on all its length with cunning and beautiful
       scrollwork. [WEL]

[...]

XXXVII

The Scop chants how Wiglaf succeeded in piercing the Dragon in the belly (where the hide was softer and where probably there were no protecting scales); and how the dying Beowulf then cut him down the middle with his war-knife. And so an end to the Dragon. But Beowulf sat down a little before the cavern's entrance, while Wiglaf ministered to him. Then he spoke, reconciled to death, because he felt he had lived the good life, as defender of his homeland, as a man of his word, and as one who had not murdered his kinsmen (as so many chiefs and kings used to do). And he bade Wiglaf go and fetch forth some of the treasure.)

XXXVIII

The Scop chants how Wiglaf, at the dying Beowulf's bidding, went and fetched all the treasure he could carry and laid it before Beowulf; and how Beowulf, generously thinking of his people to the last, thanked God that he had won them such golden gifts; and how, thinking too of his fame in aftertimes, he gave instructions for a memorial mound on the promontory; and how, in gratitude to his loyal young Kinsman, he gave Wiglaf his collar and war-gear, and passed to his reward among those who had lived righteously on earth. (Here are two questions for us: was Beowulf a Christian? and did Wiglaf become King of the Geats?)

XXXIX

The Scop chants how the Dragon was surely dead too; and how the cowardly deserters emerged shame-faced from the woods, and how Wiglaf upbraided them as ingrates and poltroons. (The simple men of those days thought there was no crime more shameful than disloyalty; and some wise philosophers of today have told me those simple men were right.)

[...]

XLII

The Scop chants how in truth Beowulf had been doomed to die because the treasure was under a fatal spell. (Yet he tells us that Beowulf was under God's protecting care and it would seem that here, as in several places in his poem, he has mingled heathen and Christian ideas—as many people do still.) He chants next the speech of the faithful kinsman, Wiglaf, who now bethought him of the funeral pyre. And then Wiglaf went with seven chosen men and pillaged the Hoard of all that remained. And the warriors pushed the Monster's bulk over the cliff into the sea. And they laded a wagon with the treasure, and marched with the body of Beowulf to Whale's Ness.

XLIII

The Scop chants the funeral rites, how they built a pyre and hung it with war-gear and set on it the body of Beowulf, and how they all mourned about the flames. And with them his Wife. (The Scop has not mentioned his wife before—[. . .]. The Geats raised, as Beowulf had bidden, a memorial mound on the headland, and they surrounded the place of the burning with a wall, and they laid away in the mound all the treasure that Beowulf thought he had won for his people's joy. And then,—last scene of all that ends this strange, eventful history—twelve of the Geats rode around the mound singing their sorrow and their praise. It must have been a beautiful and majestic ceremony. But is it not strange that Beowulf should have been honored with such purely pagan rites, and that no cross was set over the mound? Not really strange. For, in spite of all the Scop says about the Christian's God, Beowulf and Hrothgar and Hygelac and all of those bygone worthies were still little touched in their real feelings and customs by the new doctrines and customs of the Christian missionaries and monks; and the Scop, for all his wistful piety, was at heart something of a pagan too. But Beowulf was a good man and great, for all that.

Sir Gawain and the Green Knight

14th Century

Anonymous

Claiming he offers not war but a Yuletide / New Year's game to the "beardless boys at this banqueting board," the Green Knight appears on the 15th day of the annual Christmas celebration at Camelot, where King Arthur and his Knights of the Roundtable are gathered at holiday festivities. He invites any of the Round Table knights to come forward and strike his head off with his axe; in a year, he will return to offer the same blow to the one who takes up the challenge. None of the Knights comes forward, so to save face, King Arthur himself accepts. Just as King Arthur is about to swing his axe, Sir Gawain steps forward to take his place and restore the eminence of the Knights of the Round Table. In one blow, he chops off the head of the Green Knight, but to the amazement of everyone, the Green Knight picks up his severed head by the hair and remounts his green horse. The bloody body aims the severed head at the queen, its eyes flashing, and it speaks, reminding Gawain that he is honor-bound to seek out the Green Knight by the next New Year's Day. So, the next year, Gawain rides out in search of the Green Knight. The balance of the action concerns what he finds and how he distinguishes himself as a worthy knight, the personification of chivalry—courtly, courteous, courageous, honorable, and loyal. Throughout, he remains a believable individual, defined by his brave actions—and his flaws.

Sir Gawain and the Green Knight was a product of the 14th-century Alliterative Revival, written by an unknown author who is believed to be a contemporary of Chaucer. The poetry is distinguished by its alliterations (multiple words beginning with the same sound), and by its form in which each verse or stanza is followed "bob and wheel": a line of 2-3 syllables is followed by a quatrain of lines that use 3 or 4 poetic feet. The character of Sir Gawain figures prominently in Arthurian romances. The nephew of King Arthur, he takes center stage in *Sir Gawain and the Green Knight*, where he is subjected to tests of his character rather than the tests of his courage that he expects.

SOURCE

Anonymous. *ca.* 1350. [*Sir Gawain and the Green Knight.* One: v.III-XI].[1] Brian Stone, Trans. Baltimore:Penguin, 1958. 24-33.

SIR GAWAIN AND THE GREEN KNIGHT* [EXCERPT]

Part One, Verses III-XI

[Verses I and II: The poet opens the poem with two stanzas that situate Britain as a cultural descendant of Troy, validating Britain's importance in Western culture as other civilizations of classical antiquity.]

III

THIS king lay at Camelot one Christmastide
With loyal lords, liegemen peerless,
Members rightly reckoned of the Round Table,
In splendid celebration, seemly and carefree.

---

[1]　The manuscript bears no title, nor are the Parts or stanzas numbered.

*　"Sir Gawain and the Green Knight." Brain Stone, Translator. © 1958. Used by Permission of Penguin Book Company, United Kingdom.

There tussling in tournament time and again
Jousted in jollity these gentle knights,
Then in court carnival sang catches and danced;
For there the feasting flowed for fully fifteen days
With all the meat and merry-making men could devise,
Gladly ringing glee, glorious to hear
Debonair rejoicing by day, dancing at night!
All was happiness in the height in halls and chambers
For lords and their ladies, delectable joy.
With all delights on earth they housed there together,
The most renowned knights acknowledging Christ,
The loveliest ladies to live in all time,
And the comeliest[2] king ever to keep court.
For this goodly gathering was in its golden age
                    Far famed,
         Well graced by God's good will,
         With its mettlesome[3] king acclaimed:
         So hardy a host on hill
         Could not with ease be named.

IV

THE year being so young that yester-even saw its birth,
That day double on the dais[4] were the diners served.
When the singing and psalms had ceased in the chapel,
The King and his company came into hall
Called on with cries from clergy and laity,
Noël was newly announced, named time and again.
Then lords and ladies leaped forth, largesse distributing,
Granted New Year gifts graciously, gave them by hand,
Bustling and bantering about these offerings.
Ladies laughed full loudly, though losing their wealth,
And the winners were not woeful, you may well believe.

---

[2]   handsomest

[3]   Strong, sturdy, and brave

[4]   Raised platform at the front of the room for dignitaries

All this merriment they made until meal time.
Then in progress to their places they passed after washing,
In authorized order, the high-ranking first;
With glorious Guinevere,[5] gay in the midst,
On the princely platform with its precious hangings
Of splendid silk at the sides, silk of Toulouse;
Turkestan tapestry toweringly canopied her,
Brilliantly embroidered with the best gems
Of warranted worth that wealth at any time
        Could buy.
      Fairest of form was this queen,
      Glinting and grey of eye;
      No man could say he had seen
      A lovelier, but with a lie.

V

BUT Arthur would not eat until all were served.
He was charming and cheerful, child-like and gay,
And taking life lightly, little he loved
Lying down for long or lolling on a seat,
So robust his young brain and his beating blood.
However, something else now had his attention:
His noble announcement that he never would eat
On such a fair feast-day till informed in full
Of some unusual adventure, as yet untold,[6]
Of some momentous marvel that he might believe,
About ancestors, or arms, or other high theme;
Or till a stranger should seek out a strong knight of his,
To join with him in jousting, in jeopardy to lay
Life against life, each allowing the other

---

[5]   Wife of King Arthur

[6]   This custom is often referred to in medieval romances. Sometimes the
adventure had to befall the court or some member of it; sometimes, as here,
it was enough to have a report of it. [BS]

The favour of Fortune, the fairer lot.
Such was the King's custom when he kept court,
At all famous feasts among his free retinue
              In hall.
          So he throve amid the throng,
          A ruler royal and tall,
          Still standing staunch and strong—
          The year being young withal.

VI

ERECT stood the strong king, stately of mien,[7]
Trifling time with talk before the topmost table.
Good Gawain was placed at Guinevere's side,
And Agravain of the Hard Hand[8] sat on the other side,
Both the King's sister's sons, staunchest of knights.
Above, Bishop Baldwin[9] began the board,
And Ywain,[10] Urien's son, ate next to him.
These were disposed on the dais and with dignity served,
And many mighty men next, marshalled at side tables.
Then the first course came in with such cracking of trumpets,
(Whence bright bedecked blazons in banners hung)
Such din of drumming and a deal of fine piping,
Such wild warbles whelming in whirlpools of sound,
That hearts were uplifted high at the strains.
Then delicacies and dainties were delivered to the guests,
Fresh food in foison,[11] such freight of full dishes

---

7   Facial expression

8   Agravain, Gawain's brother. Both were sons of King Lot of Orkney and
    Arthur's half-sister Anna (or Belisent).[BS]

9   Bishop Baldwin, the King's bishop and counsellor, sits in the place of
    honour nearest to the King.

10 Ywain, son of King Urien and Brimesent, another half-sister of Arthur's. [BS]

11 Of plentiful harvest

That space was scarce at the social tables
When the broth was brought in in bowls of silver
       To the cloth.
     Each feaster made free with the fare,
     Took lightly and nothing loth;
     Twelve plates were for every pair,
     Good beer and bright wine both.

VII

Of their meal I shall mention no more just now,
For it is evident to all that ample was served;
Near at hand the noise of a new fanfare
Gave the lords leave to lift food to their lips.
But barely had the blast of trump abated one minute
And the first course in the court been courteously served,
When there pressed in from the porch an appalling figure,
Who in height outstripped all earthly men.
From throat to thigh he was thickset and square;
His loins and limbs were so long and great
That he was half a giant on earth, I believe,
Yet mainly and most of all a man he seemed,
And the handsomest of horsemen, though huge, at that;
For though at back and at breast his body was broad,
His hips and haunches were elegant and small,
And perfectly proportioned were all parts of the man,
       As seen.
     Amazed at the hue of him,
     A foe with furious mien,
     Men gaped, for the giant grim
     Was coloured a gorgeous green.

VIII

AND garments of green girt the fellow about—
A two-third length tunic, tight at the waist,

A comely cloak on top, accomplished with lining
Of the finest fur to be found, manifest to all,
Marvellous fur-trimmed material, with matching hood
Lying back from his locks and laid on his shoulders;
Fitly held-up hose, in hue the same green,
That was caught at the calf, with clinking spurs beneath
Of bright gold on bases of embroidered silk,
With shields for the shanks and shins when riding.
And verily his vesture was all vivid green,
So were the bars on his belt and the brilliants set
In ravishing array on his rich accoutrements.
It would be tedious to tell a tithe[12] of the trifles
Embossed and embroidered, such as birds and flies,[13]
In green gay and gaudy, with gold in the middle,
About himself and his saddle on silken work.
The breast-hangings of the horse, its haughty crupper,
The enamelled knobs and nails on its bridle,
And the stirrups that he stood on, were all stained with the same;
So were the saddle-bows and splendid tail-straps,
That ever glimmered and glinted with their green stones.
The steed that he spurred on was similar in hue
                To the sight,
          Green and huge of grain,
          Mettlesome in might
          And brusque with bit and rein—
          A steed to serve that knight!

IX

YES, garbed all in green was the gallant rider.
His hair, like his horse in hue, hung light,
Clustering in curls like a cloak round his shoulders,
And a great bushy beard on his breast flowing down,

---

12   A tenth part or small portion
13   Probably dragonflies

With the lovely locks hanging loose from his head,
Was shorn below the shoulder, sheared right round,
So that half his arms were under the encircling hair,
Covered as by a king's cape, that closes at the neck.
The mane of that mighty horse, much like the beard,
Well crisped and combed, was copiously plaited
With twists of twining gold, twinkling in the green,
First a green gossamer, a golden one next.
His flowing tail and forelock followed suit,
And both were bound with bands of bright green,
Ornamented to the end with exquisite stones,
While a thong running thwart threaded on high
Many bright golden bells, burnished and ringing.
Such a horse, such a horseman, in the whole wide world
Was never seen or observed by those assembled before,
     Not one.
     Lightning-like he seemed
     And swift to strike and stun.
     His dreadful blows, men deemed,
     Once dealt, meant death was done.

X

YET hauberk[14] and helmet had he none,
Nor plastron[15] nor plate-armour proper to combat,
Nor shield for shoving, nor sharp spear for lunging;
But he held a holly cluster in one hand, holly[16]
That is greenest when groves are gaunt and bare,

---

[14]   Long, chain-mail tunic

[15]   Breastplate

[16]   The holly cluster, or wassail bob, was a symbol of Christmas good luck
though its origin as such is wholly pagan. The early Christians in Rome
probably took it over from the Saturnalia, in which it figured prominently.
Saturn's club was made of holly wood. [BS]

And an axe in his other hand, huge and monstrous,
An axe fell[17] and fearsome, fit for a fable;
For fully forty inches frowned the head.
Its handle-base was hued in green, in hammered gold and steel.
The blade was burnished bright, with a broad edge,
Acutely honed for cutting, as keenest razors are.
The grim man gripped it by its great strong handle,
Which was wound with iron all the way to the end,
And graven in green with graceful designs.
A cord curved round it, was caught at the head,
Then hitched to the haft at intervals in loops,
With costly tassels attached thereto in plenty
On bosses[18] of bright green embroidered richly.
In he rode, and up the hall, this man,
Pressing forward to the platform, no peril fearing.
He gave no one a greeting, but glared over all.
His opening utterance was, "Who and where
Is the governor of this gathering? Gladly would I
Behold him with my eyes and have speech with him."
        He frowned;
     He studied the standers-by
     And rolled his eye around,
     Essaying to espy
     The noble most renowned.[19]

XI

THE assembled folk stared, long scanning the man,
For all men marvelled what it might mean
That a chevalier and charger should achieve such a hue

---

[17]   Fierce, lethal; sharp and biting

[18]   Raised ornaments

[19]   The Green Knight evidently sees the place of honour empty, King Arthur
     having not yet taken his place.[BS]

As to grow green as grass, and greener yet, it seemed,
More gaudily glowing than green enamel on gold.
The people pondered him, in perplexity neared him,
With all the world's wonder as to what he would do.
For astonishing sights they had seen, but such a one never;
Therefore a phantom from Fairyland the folk there deemed him
So even the doughty[20] were daunted and dared not reply,
All standing stock-still, astounded by his voice.
Throughout the high hall was a hush like death;
Quiet suddenly descended, as if deep had stolen them
> To rest;
>> For some were still for fear,
>> And others at honour's behest;
>> But let him who all revere
>> Greet that gruesome guest.

---

[20]   brave

THOMAS DE CELANO

ca. 1200-1255

"*DIES IRAE*"

The author of "*Dies Irae*" is uncertain but the poem is frequently attributed to Thomas of Celano, a well-known Franciscan, a disciple of St. Francis of Assisi and his biographer. "*Dies Irae*" (Day of Wrath) probably comes from the "*Libera me*" sung at the Absolution following the Mass. The oldest known inscription of the poem survives in a Dominican missal of the late 14th century. Originally a hymn sung with the Gospel on the first Sunday of Advent, the "*Dies Irae*" became accepted for general liturgical use by the Roman Catholic Church at the end of the 15th century.

The poem begins with a description of the Judgment, followed by a prayer to Christ and repentance, with the hope to be with God when the Judgment is over. It was adapted for use in Masses for the Dead by the addition of the final six lines, and it provides part of the text for Mozart's *Requiem*.

SOURCE

Celano, Thomas de. *ca.*1250. *Dies Irae*. Elza C. Tiner, Trans. The original Latin text may be found in *The Oxford Book of Medieval Latin Verse*. F.J. E. Raby, Ed. Oxford: Clarendon, 1959. 392-394.

DIES IRAE

Day of wrath, that fiery day,
When the world will melt away,
So David, Sybil truly say.

What a trembling there will be,
When the Judge will come to see
All divided righteously!

The horn will sound its wondrous tone,
Through the graveyards loudly blown,
Calling all before the throne.

Death will marvel, as will nature,
At the rise of every creature
Summoned to the Judge's answer.

Then the book will be unchained;
There the sum of deeds retained:
So mankind will be arraigned.

Lastly when the judgement's near,
Our hidden sins will then appear:
Unpunished crimes no longer here!

What words remain to wretched me,
What patron shall I ask to see,
When the just are scarcely free?

King of awesome majesty,
Whose saving grace flows openly,
Save me, font of piety!

Blessed Jesus, think of me,
I am why you came to be;
Do not destroy me finally.

Seeking me you, overcome,
On the cross my ransom won:
This labor's not a wasted one.

Justly judge of punishment,
A gift of pardon implement
Before the day of settlement.

Like a sinner I do shudder,
Guilty blushes red in color:
God, pardon your petitioner!

You set Mary free of sin,
And the souls of thieves did win,
You also gave me hope therein.

Prayers of mine are hardly worthy;
Greatest good, but grant me mercy:
Not the fire burning fiercely.

With the sheep my place assure,
From the goats keep me secure,
Setting law both right and sure.

When the cursed receive their blame,
Awarding them the sharpest flame,
With the blessed call my name.

At your feet I've fallen, lying,
Contrite heart in ashes sighing:
Look after me as I am dying.

LI-PO

ca. 701-762

"NOCTURNE"
"ON A PICTURE SCREEN"
"BY THE GREAT WALL"
"ON HEARING THE FLUTE"

ca. 750

Li Po was a major poet of China's T'ang Dynasty. His name stems from the planet Chang-keng (Venus), known in China as Tai-po Hsing, the great white star, that appeared in his mother's dream on the night of his birth. Around 742, he was placed under imperial patronage with the duties to write poems, but like Wordsworth, he preferred the solitude of hills and lakes, and soon began to wander the countryside. Li Po sometimes went by the name "Old Wine Genius," and according to legend, drowned, while drunk, when he tried to embrace the reflection of the moon on the water.

China's classical poetry reached its pinnacle in the T'ang Dynasty (beginning in the 7th century), a time of border wars and palace intrigues, and also an era of ecomomic prosperity, cultural refinement, and artistic brilliance. The known anthology of T'ang

Dynasty poetry consists of more than forty-eight thousand poems by more than two thousand poets, evidence of the importance and popularity of poetry. The poetry of Li Po was included in French and German anthologies of Chinese poems in the late 18th century; it became widely known in the West in the 19th century.

SOURCE:

Li Po. *ca.*750. "Nocturne," "On a Picture Screen," "By the Great Wall," "On Hearing the Flute at Lo-Cheng One Spring Night." In *The Works of Li Po, the Chinese Poet.* Shigeyoshi Obata, Trans. New York: E. P. Dutton & Co., 1922. 28, 40-41, 77, 169.

NOCTURNE

Blue water . . . a clear moon . . .
In the moonlight the white herons are flying.
Listen! Do you hear the girls who gather water-chestnuts?
They are going home in the night, singing.

ON A PICTURE SCREEN

Whence these twelve peaks of Wu-shan!
Have they flown into the gorgeous screen
From heaven's one corner?

Ah, those lonely pines murmuring in the wind!
Those palaces of Yang-tai, hovering yonder—
Oh, the melancholy of it!—
Where the jeweled couch of the king
With brocade covers is desolate,—
His elfin maid voluptuously fair
Still haunting them in vain!

Here a few feet
Seem a thousand miles.
The craggy walls glisten blue and red,
A piece of dazzling embroidery.
How green those distant trees are
Round the river strait of Ching-men!
And those ships—they go on,
Floating on the waters of Pa.
The water sings over the rocks
Between countless hills
Of shining mist and lustrous grass.

How many years since these valley flowers bloomed
To smile in the sun?
And that man traveling on the river,
Hears he not for ages the monkeys screaming?
Whoever looks on this
Loses himself in eternity;
And entering the sacred mountains of Sung,
He will dream among the resplendent clouds.

By the Great Wall

Came the barbarian horde with the autumn;
Out went the imperial army from the House of Han.
The general has divided the tiger tallies,
And the dunes of White Dragon are now
The camping ground of the brave.
The moon in the wilderness
Follows the movement of his bow,
And upon his sword the desert frost blossoms.
He has not even entered this side of the Jewel Gate Pass.
But do not heave a long sigh, O little wife!

On Hearing the Flute at Lo Cheng
One Spring Night

Whence comes this voice of the sweet bamboo,
Flying in the dark?
It flies with the spring wind,
Hovering over the city of Lo.
How memories of home come back to-night!
Hark! The plaintive tune of "Willow-breaking." . . .

SELECTED POETRY IN JAPANESE

660-1943

Poetry is engrained in Japanese culture and has, in turn, influenced the literature of many cultures. It became especially important in the West in the 19th century with the advent of trade with Japan. It is notable for its conciseness, vividness, and its connection of emotions to ideas or objects. No written Japanese literature exists before the 8th century, although numerous ballads, ritual prayers, myths, and legends were preserved through oral traditions. Selected below are examples of various forms: lyric, Kagura, Tanka, and haiku.

From the 12th to 17th centuries, Japan was in a state of warfare and turmoil. The poetry of this period reflects a mood of gloom and solitude, with Buddhist overtones. With the establishment of peace in 1603 under the Edo (Tokyo) government, commerce and its new merchant class flourished. The literature of the Edo period is more worldly, and often amorous, vulgar, and comic. The haiku form was refined during this time. Throughout the modern period, beginning in 1867, Japanese writers sought to maintain traditional aesthetic values while assimilating Western techniques.

Lyric poetry developed from early ballads, including those in the early anthology of Japanese poetry *Man'yôshû* (alternatively translated as *Ten Thousand Leaves* or *Myriad Leaves*), compiled after 759 with its emphasis on truth and the personal participation. "Hitomaro" (Kakinomoto no Asomi Hitomaro, ca. 660-708) was a foremost poet of the Yamato period and one of four principal poets of *Man'yôshû*. His lyric poems show a reverence for nature's beauty and the intensity of emotions for the loss of a loved one.

Kagura is an ancient dance set in austere and natural settings, and made as offerings to entertain the Shinto gods. Often no one other than the performers were allowed to witness Kagura.

The Tanka form emphasizes emotions in poems about nature, a loved one, or daily life. A Tanka was also written after a special event.

Kawahigashi Hekigoto is considered a pioneer of modern haiku, a poem in seventeen syllables (in Japanese), reflecting the influence of Zen.

SOURCE

Brownas, Geoffrey and Anthony Thwaite. 1964. *The Penguin Book of Japanese Verse.* Brownas and Thwaite, Trans. Baltimore: Penguin. 14-15, 88,142-143, 166, 177-179.*

WORKMAN (HITOMARO)

ca. 759

THE CONSTRUCTION OF THE PALACE OF FUJIWARA

(Lyric)

Our Great Empress
Who rules the eight quarters,
August child
Of the sun on high,
Governs her domain
And controls her palace
On the Fujiwara Plain.

---

*   From the PENGUIN BOOK OF JAPANESE VERSE, Brownas and Thaite, Trans. Thwaite, Norfolk, England.

At her divine desire
Gods of heaven and earth
Came and offered service.
The stout cypress logs
Of Tanakami Mount in Ömi,
Ömi, where waves dash the rocks,
Trailing like jewel duckweed,
We floated down the Uji waters.
Our homes forgotten,
Not thinking of ourselves,
Like a flight of wild duck
We, her servants, bobbed in the water,
Thronging to gather the beams
And carry them to the streams of Izumi.
'To the shining Palace of the Sun we build
May unknown kingdoms come in homage.'

On the Kuse Highway there appeared
That magic tortoise with the letters on his shell—
'Our land shall never fail'—
Marking a new era.
We lashed the logs as rafts
And vied to take them
Up Izumi's stream.
I look on our scurryings—
The fruit of a divinity.

Anonymous
No date

God-music
(Kagura)

On the leaves of the bamboo-grass
Snow falls, piles up.
On a winter night,
To make fine music
To the gods is pleasing.

From the first age
Of the timeless gods
We have held
The leaf of the bamboo-grass.

Silver Clasp
On his sword
Slung proudly at his thigh,
As he swaggers down
The broad walks of Nara:
Who might he be?

O for a mighty sword,
Mighty as Furu's
Shrine above the Stone!
I'd plait thread to thong
And so I would lord it
Down the Royal Palace Way.

TACHIBANA AKEMI
1812-1868

POEMS OF SOLITARY DELIGHTS
(Tanka)

WHAT a delight it is
When on the bamboo matting
In my grass-thatched hut,
All on my own,
I make myself at ease.

WHAT a delight it is
When, borrowing
Rare writings from a friend,
I open out
The first sheet.

WHAT a delight it is
When, spreading paper,
I take my brush
And find my hand
Better than I thought.

WHAT a delight it is
When, after a hundred days
Of racking my brains,
That verse that wouldn't come
Suddenly turns out well.

WHAT a delight it is
When, of a morning,
I get up and go out
To find in full bloom a flower
That yesterday was not there.

WHAT a delight it is
When, skimming through the pages
Of a book, I discover
A man written of there
Who is just like me.

WHAT a delight it is
When everyone admits
It's a very difficult book,
And I understand it
With no trouble at all.

WHAT a delight it is
When I blow away the ash,
To watch the crimson
Of the glowing fire
And hear the water boil.

WHAT a delight it is
When a guest you cannot stand
Arrives and says to you
'I'm afraid I can't stay long,'
And soon goes home.

WHAT a delight it is
When I find a good brush,
Steep it hard in water,
Lick it on my tongue
And give it its first try.

KAWAHIGASHI HEKIGOTŌ
(1873-1937)

Hekigotō is considered a pioneer of modern haiku.

COLD SPRING DAY
(Haiku)

COLD spring day:
Above the fields
Rootless clouds.

THE *Nō* by torchlight:
On the woman's mask
One shaft of light.

TSUCHIĬ BANSUI
1871-1952

Bansui is the pen name for Tsuchiĭ Rinkichi, also known as Doĭ Bansui. Bansui studied English at the Imperial University of Tokyo, where he was on the editorial staff of the college magazine, *Teïkoko Bungaku* (Imperial Literature). He went on to study in London, Paris, and Leipzig, Germany, from 1901 to 1904. He later taught English and translated many great literary works into Japanese, including Homer's *Iliad* and *Odyssey*. "Moon over the ruined castle" (Kôjô-no-Tsuki) is the lyric for a musical composition by Taki Rentarô (1879-1903). It was first published in "Songs for High School Students" by the Tokyo Music School in 1901. It became one of the most popular songs in Japan.

MOON OVER THE RUINED CASTLE
(Lyric)

SPRING in its tall towers, flower-viewing banquets,
The wine-cup passed and glinting in the light
Streaming through pine branches a thousand ages:
That moonlight of the past—where is it now?

Autumn: the white hoarfrost across the camp,
Counting the wild geese, crying as they flew:
Light of the past flashing on row on row
Of planted swords: that light—where is it now?

Now, over the ruined castle the midnight moon,
Its light unchanged; for whom does it shine?
In the hedge, only the laurel is left behind:
In the pines, only the wind of the storm still sings.

High in the heavens the light remains unchanged.
Glory and decay are the mark of this shifting earth.
Is it to copy them now, brighter yet,
Over the ruined castle the midnight moon?

SHIMAZAKI TŌSON
1872-1943

Shimazaka Tōson was a poet and novelist known for his semi-autobiographical prose fiction. *Hakai* (The Broken Commandment), the story of an outcast youth, is considered the first Japanese naturalist novel and shows the influence of French naturalism and subjectivity. Tōson, along with Tokuda Shusei, Masamune Hakucho, and Tayama Katai, became established as the four pillars of naturalism.

BY THE OLD CASTLE AT KOMORO
(Lyric)

By the old castle at Komoro
The clouds are white and the wanderer grieves.
The green chickweed does not sprout
And the young grass is too thin for carpet.

The silver quilt covering the hills
Melts in the sun to make a stream of shallow snow.

The light of the sun is warm
But the scent does not fill the fields;
Spring is only shallow, hazed.
The colour of the corn is a wan green.
Some bands of travellers
Hurry along the path through the fields.

It grows dark, Asama disappears:
Sounds of a reed flute, its note plaintive.
The waves of Chikuma River falter.
I put up in an inn near its bank
And drink, fuddled by *sake* dregs,
And, grass for pillow, rest on my journeying.

MICHELANGELO

1475-1564

"IN THIS MERE LIVING STONE"
"THE COURSE OF MY LONG LIFE"

No date

Michelangelo Buonarroti Simoni, known simply as Michelangelo, was a Renaissance sculptor, painter, architect, and poet who has had incalculable influence on the development of Western art. Born in Florence to a family of minor aristocracy, Michelangelo began to work in the Medici sculpture garden under the patronage of Lorenzo de Medici (Lorenzo the Magnificent) in 1489. One of his most renowned sculptures, a *Pieta* (1499), now stands in the Vatican. Pope Julius II called him to Rome to work on his tomb where he later completed the ceiling of the Sistene Chapel (1508-1512). The ceiling shows scenes of creation from the Book of Genesis, most famously the Creation of Adam. Exposed to the classical writings of Plato, Aristotle, and Virgil, as well as to Dante and Petrarch, Michelangelo understood beauty as a divine communication from God to humanity.

Poems by Michelangelo were found scribbled on paper in his workshop; some of them did circulate during his lifetime. Personal reflections of his moods, contemplations of his sculpture or painting, and his religious beliefs, many of his poems were published 60 years after his death. In the first poem below, he expresses his theory of art; the second reveals his concern for his own salvation.

SOURCE

Buonarroti, Michelangelo. *ca.* 1550. "In this mere living stone" and "The course of my long life" In *The Poetry of Michelangelo.* Robert J. Clements, Ed. New York: New York University Press, 1965. g240 (p. 68), g285 (p.85).*

IN THIS MERE LIVING STONE

In this mere living stone
Art would have milady's face
Go on living here throughout the years:
How should heaven feel about her,
She being its handiwork, but this being mine,
Not mortal now, but divine,
And not merely so in my eyes?
Yet she must depart, sojourning here a short time.
Her fortune is crippled on its stronger side,
If a stone remains while death hustles her away.

(G 240)

THE COURSE OF MY LONG LIFE

The course of my long life hath reached at last,
In fragile bark o'er a tempestuous sea,
The common harbor where must rendered be
Account of all the actions of the past.
The impassioned fantasy, that, vague and vast,
Made art an idol and a king to me,

---

*   Used by permission of New York University Press

Was an illusion, and but vanity
Were the dreams that lured me and harassed.
The dreams of love, that were so sweet of yore—
What are they now, when two deaths may be mine,
One sure, and one forecasting its alarms?
Painting and sculpture satisfy no more
The soul now turning to the Love Divine,
That oped, to embrace us, on the cross its arms.

                    (G 285) (H.W. Longfellow)

SHAKESPEARE

1564-1609

SONNETS: 21, 23, 24

1590s

The 14-line sonnet form, established as early as the 14th century in Italy by Petrarch, was perfected in English by Shakespeare. Most English sonnets of the period were produced during the 1590s when there was a particular vogue for sonnet writing, which disappeared toward the end of the decade. The "English" or "Shakespearean" sonnet seeks greater spontaneity than the Italian, using iambic pentameter with a set rhyme scheme, which divides the lines into 3 groups of 4 lines and a concluding couplet (abab—cdcd—efef—gg). Sonneteers wrote their poems and circulated them among their friends at court, often anonymously, needling each other or giving advice and/or criticism across a range of subjects. Gentlemen sought to write good sonnets as a mark of their status—if they could not, patrons paid good sonneteers for their work, especially to court a lady. Some sonnet collections are "sequences" that narrate events over time, but Shakespeare's collection defies an easy ordering. Shakespeare's 154 sonnets address love, aging, art, nature, passion, and often, the ironies of life.

SOURCE

Shakespeare, William. 1598-1609. Sonnets 21, 23, 24. In *Shakespeare's Sonnets: Reconsidered, and in part Rearranged with Introductory Chapters, Notes, and a Reprint of the Original 1609 Edition.* Samuel Butler, Ed. London: A.C.Fifield, 1899. 142, 143, 145.

21.

1585 Summer]

To Mr. W.H. extolling his beauty.

So is it not with me as with that Muse
Stirr'd by a painted beauty to his verse,
Who heaven itself for ornament doth use
And every fair with his fair doth rehearse,
Making a couplement of proud compare
With sun and Moon, with earth and sea's rich gems,
With April's first-born flowers, and all things rare
That heaven's air in this huge rondure hems.
O, let me, true in love, but truly write,
And then believe me, my love is as fair
As any mother's child, though not so bright
As those gold candles fix'd i' the heavens are.
    Let them say more that like of hearsay well;
    I will not praise that purpose not to sell.

1585 Summer]

23.

To W.H. Shakespeare's looks must say what he cannot bring his tongue to speak

As an unperfect actor on the stage
Who with his fear is put beside his part,

Or some fierce thing replete with too much rage
Whose strength's abundance weakens his own heart;
So I, for fear of trust, forget to say
The perfect ceremony of love's rite,
And in mine own love's strength seem to decay,
O'ercharg'd with burthen of mine own love's might.
O, let my looks be then the eloquence
And dumb presagers of my speaking breast;
Who plead for love and look for recompense,
More than that tongue that less hath more express'd;
　　　O, learn to read what silent love hath writ:
　　　To hear with eyes belongs to love's fine wit.

1585 Summer]

24.

To Mr. W.H. A Sonnet full of conceits after the manner of the time.

Mine eye hath play'd the painter and hath steel'd
Thy beauty's form in the table of my heart;
My body is the frame wherein 'tis held,
And perspective it is best Painter's art.
For through the Painter must you see his skill,
To find where your true Image pictur'd lies;
Which in my bosom's shop is hanging still,
That hath his windows glazed with thine eyes.
Now see what good turns eyes for eyes have done:
Mine eyes have drawn thy shape, and thine for me
Are windows to my breast where-through the Sun
Delights to peep, to gaze therein on thee:
　　　Yet eyes this cunning want to grace their art,
　　　They draw but what they see, know not the heart.

WILLIAM BLAKE

1757-1827

"TO THE MUSES"

1783

One of the earliest English Romantic poets, William Blake was also a painter and engraver who rebelled against the constraints of the artistic establishment. Blake developed the innovative method of engraving text and illustration on the same plate. The results were the volumes *Songs of Innocence* (1789), *Songs of Experience* (1794), *Milton* (1804-08), and *Jerusalem* (1804-1820). As an artist, he is best known for the 21 etchings that illustrate the Book of Job from the Old Testament; these works are both realistic in their representation of anatomy and imaginative in their use of fantastic creatures. Catherine Boucher, his wife, printed the copper plates of his engravings, hand-colored the images, and bound the books. Blake's thought was influenced by Emanuel Swedenborg (1688-1772), a Swedish scientist, philosopher and theologian, who advocated a new spiritual era of increased human freedom and sincere, rational approaches to religion. Neither Blake's artwork nor his poetry enjoyed commercial or critical success in his lifetime.

SOURCE

Blake, William. 1783. "To the Muses." In *The Poetical Works of William Blake Lyrical and Miscellaneous*. William Rossetti, Editor. London: George Bell and Sons, 1900. 50.

TO THE MUSES.*

Whether on Ida's[1] shady brow,
    Or in the chambers of the East,
The chambers of the Sun, that now
    From ancient melody have ceased;

Whether in heaven ye wander fair,
    Or the green corners of the earth,
Or the blue regions of the air
    Where the melodious winds have birth;

Whether on crystal rocks ye rove,
    Beneath the bosom of the sea,
Wandering in many a coral grove;
    Fair Nine, forsaking Poetry;

How have you left the ancient love
    That bards of old enjoyed in you!
The languid strings do scarcely move,
    The sound is forced, the notes are few!

---

* The Greek Muses, nine goddesses of creative inspiration, preside over human production of various arts. They are Clio (history), Euterpe (music and lyric poetry), Thalia (comedy and pastoral poetry), Melpomene (tragedy), Terpsichore (dancing and song), Erato (lyric and love poetry), Urania (astronomy), Calliope (epic poetry), and Polyhymnia (heroic hymns). [Ed.]

[1] Mount Ida is the highest mountain on the Greek island of Crete. [Ed.]

JOHN KEATS

1795-1821

"ODE ON A GRECIAN URN"

1819

John Keats is often considered the quintessential poet of the Romantic Period of English poetry. Keats's youth was marked by a lively social life punctuated by depression, amorous despair, poverty, and illness. Educated at Clarke's School in Enfield, Keats cultivated his passion for poetry by translating the *Aeneid*. His first volume of poetry was published in 1817, though not a critical success. However, his second volume (1820) was praised, but at 25, ill and too poor to marry the woman he loved, he traveled to Italy to recuperate from tuberculosis. In Rome, the English physician who attended him believed that emotional excitement was a danger to the life of a consumptive patient; he did not allow Keats to write. Keats attempted suicide by overdosing on laudanum but was stopped by his friend, the portrait painter Joseph Severn. He died shortly thereafter, the example of his youth, his despair, and his profound passion becoming part of the legacy of his poetic work.

Keats believed the meaning of life could be found in the contemplation of material beauty. His poetry expresses profound sensory perception while acknowledging a debt to Classical antiquity. These characteristics are clearly exemplified in Keats's odes, meditations in lyric form on emotions or on observed objects, both natural and created—such as a Grecian urn.

SOURCE

Keats, John. 1819. "Ode on a Grecian Urn." In *The English Poets.* Thos. H. Ward, Ed. Vol. IV. Second Edition, Revised. New York: Macmillan, 1888. 454-455.

ODE ON A GRECIAN URN

1.

Thou still unravished bride of quietness!
   Thou foster-child of Silence and slow Time,
Sylvan historian, who canst thus express
   A flowery tale more sweetly than our rhyme:
What leaf-fringed legend haunts about thy shape
   Of deities or mortals, or of both,
In Tempe or the dales of Arcady?
   What men or gods are these? What maidens loath?
What mad pursuit? What struggle to escape?
   What pipes and timbrels? What wild ecstasy?

2.

Heard melodies are sweet, but those unheard
   Are sweeter; therefore, ye soft pipes, play on;
Not to the sensual ear, but, more endeared,
   Pipe to the spirit ditties of no tone:
Fair youth, beneath the trees, thou canst not leave
   Thy song, nor ever can those trees be bare;
     Bold Lover, never, never canst thou kiss,
Though winning near the goal—yet, do not grieve;
     She cannot fade, though thou hast not thy bliss,
For ever wilt thou love, and she be fair!

3.

Ah, happy, happy boughs! that cannot shed
  Your leaves, nor ever bid the Spring adieu;
And, happy melodist, unwearied,
  For ever piping songs for ever new;
More happy love! more happy, happy love!
  For ever warm and still to be enjoyed,
    For ever panting and for ever young;
All breathing human passion far above,
  That leaves a heart high sorrowful and cloyed,
    A burning forehead, and a parching tongue.

4.

Who are these coming to the sacrifice?
  To what green alter, O mysterious priest,
Lead'st thou that heifer lowing at the skies,
  And all her silken flanks with garlands drest?
What little town by river or sea-shore,
  Or mountain-built with peaceful citadel,
    Is emptied of its folk, this pious morn?
And, little town, thy streets for evermore
  Will silent be; and not a soul, to tell
    Why thou art desolate, can e'er return.

5.

O Attic shape! Fair attitude! with brede
  Of marble men and maidens overwrought,
With forest branches and the trodden weed;
  Thou, silent form! dost tease us out of thought
As doth eternity. Cold Pastoral!
  When old age shall this generation waste,
    Thou shalt remain, in midst of other woe
Than ours, a friend to man, to whom thou say'st:
  'Beauty is truth, truth beauty,—that is all
    Ye know on earth, and all ye need to know.'

PERCY BYSSHE SHELLEY

1792-1827

"OZYMANDIAS"

1818

Born to an aristocratic family, Percy Bysshe Shelley was educated at Eton and Oxford where, in 1811, his pamphlet, "The Necessity Of Atheism," resulted in his expulsion. His father disinherited him after his marriage to Harriet Westbrook, a 16-year-old daughter of a tavern keeper. When his marriage to Harriet began to fail, Shelley fell in love with Mary Wollstonecraft Godwin.[1] Rejected by Shelley, Harriet drowned in the Thames in 1816. Shelley then married Mary Wollstonecraft. In 1818, Shelley and his family moved to Italy and settled in the Bay of Lerici. On July 8, 1822, he and a friend set out in a small boat to visit another friend. Their boat sank in a squall and Shelley drowned; his body was found three days later. His cremated remains are interred in Rome.

SOURCE

Shelley, Percy Bysshe. 1818. "Ozymandias." In *The Poetical Works of Percy Bysshe Shelley*. Edward Dowden, Ed. New York: A.L. Burt, 1880. 378.

---

[1] This is the Mary Shelley who wrote *Frankenstein.* She was the daughter of

OZYMANDIAS[2]

I MET a traveller from an antique land
Who said: "Two vast and trunkless legs of stone
Stand in the desert. Near them, on the sand,
Half sunk, a shattered visage lies, whose frown,
And wrinkled lip and sneer of cold command,
Tell that its sculptor well those passions read
Which yet survive, stampt on these lifeless things,
The hand that mockt them and the heart that fed.
And on the pedestal these words appear:
'My name is Ozymandias, king of kings:
Look on my works, ye Mighty, and despair!'
Nothing beside remains. Round the decay
Of that colossal wreck, boundless and bare,
The lone and level sands stretch far away."

---

the philosopher and anarchist William Godwin (1756-1836) and feminist
Mary Wollstonecraft, author of *A Vindication of the Rights of Woman* (1792).
Mary Shelley helped edit the 1880 volume from which "Ozymandias" is
here reprinted.

[2]   Egyptian pharaoh Rameses II (Dynasty 19, ca. 1279-1213 B.C.E.), son of
Sety I. *Ozymandias* is derived from the Greek translation of one of his many
names, User-maat-re. An obelisk carved at his direction, now in Paris, reads
in Egyptian hieroglyphic, "As long as the skies exist, your monuments shall
exist, your name shall exist, firm as the skies." The poem "Ozymandias"
describes the ruins of these monuments, built to memorialize the pharoah's
immortal self.

ROBERT BROWNING

1812-1889

"MY LAST DUCHESS"

1842

Robert Browning had a prolific career, with the last of his poems published on the day of his death. His fame as a poet is often overshadowed by the story of his courtship of and marriage to the poet Elizabeth Barrett, whom he met first through correspondence. The Brownings spent happy years together in Italy; many of their poems reflect their fascination with Italian culture and history.

Browning is known for his invention of the dramatic monologue, a form in which a single, imaginary or historical character speaks, revealing surprising and questionable character features to an unnamed auditor. Part of the delight of the poetry is the reader's discovery of the relationship between speaker and auditor. The drama is often ironic. "My Last Duchess" is just such a piece. The Renaissance setting in the ducal palace of Ferrara (northern Italy), presents the Duke of Ferrara entertaining an offer of a dowry to accompany the woman who will be his next wife. While considering the offer brought to him by the envoy of the Count of Tyrol, the Duke reveals his true nature in front of the portrait of his "last Duchess"; the artist "Fra Pandolf" is invented by Browning.

SOURCE

Browning, Robert. 1842. "My Last Duchess." *Selections from the Poems of Robert Browning.* Selected by Robert Browning. [Publication Information missing] London, 1872. 2-4.

MY LAST DUCHESS

Ferrara

That's my last Duchess painted on the wall,
Looking as if she were alive. I call
That piece a wonder, now: Frà Pandolf's hands
Worked busily a day, and there she stands.
Will 't please you sit and look at her? I said
"Frà Pandolf" by design, for never read
Strangers like you that pictured countenance,
The depth and passion of its earnest glance,
But to myself they turned (since none puts by
The curtain I have drawn for you, but I)
And seemed as they would ask me, if they durst,
How such a glance came there; so, not the first
Are you to turn and ask thus. Sir, 't was not
Her husband's presence only, called that spot
Of joy into the Duchess' cheek: perhaps
Frà Pandolf chanced to say "Her mantle laps
"Over my lady's wrist too much," or "Paint
"Must never hope to reproduce the faint
"Half-flush that dies along her throat:" such stuff
Was courtesy, she thought, and cause enough
For calling up that spot of joy. She had
A heart—how shall I say?—too soon made glad,
Too easily impressed; she liked whate'er
She looked on, and her looks went everywhere.
Sir, 't was all one! My favour at her breast,
The dropping of the daylight in the West,

The bough of cherries some officious fool
Broke in the orchard for her, the white mule
She rode with round the terrace—all and each
Would draw from her alike the approving speech,
Or blush, at least. She thanked men,—good! but thanked
Somehow—I know not how—as if she ranked
My gift of a nine-hundred-years-old name
With anybody's gift. Who'd stoop to blame
This sort of trifling? Even had you skill
In speech—(which I have not)—to make your will
Quite clear to such an one, and say, "Just this
"Or that in you disgusts me; here you miss,
"Or there exceed the mark"—and if she let
Herself be lessoned so, nor plainly set
Her wits to yours, forsooth, and made excuse,
—E'en then would be some stooping; and I choose
Never to stoop. Oh sir, she smiled, no doubt,
Whene'er I passed her; but who passed without
Much the same smile? This grew; I gave commands;
Then all smiles stopped together. There she stands
As if alive. Will 't please you rise? We'll meet
The company below, then. I repeat,
The Count your master's known munificence
Is ample warrant that no just pretence
Of mine for dowry will be disallowed;
Though his fair daughter's self, as I avowed
At starting, is my object. Nay, we'll go
Together down, sir. Notice Neptune, though,
Taming a sea-horse, thought a rarity,
Which Claus of Innsbruck cast in bronze for me?

ALFRED, LORD TENNYSON

1809-1892

"ULYSSES"

1842

Alfred, Lord Tennyson was the fourth of twelve children of a minister, whose epilepsy and alcoholism instilled in Tennyson a fear of mental illness. At Trinity College, Cambridge, Tennyson joined The Apostles, an undergraduate club whose members, including Arthur Henry Hallam, were to become his lifelong friends. Hallam's death at the age of 22 caused Tennyson heartfelt grief and led to some of his greatest poetry, including "Ulysses." Written soon after Arthur Hallam's death, the poem was inspired by a passage in Dante's *Inferno*, Canto XXVI, which he and Hallam had studied together. As a dramatic monologue* the poem can be read as the declaration of the old hero whose life no longer holds adventure and danger, but who resolves to move on. Contemporary interpretations, however, see it as a dramatic poem of greater complexity.

Much of Tennyson's poetry was composed in his head over a period of years and transcribed by others, as his poor vision made reading and writing difficult. In 1850, he was named Great Britain's Poet Laureate. Queen Victoria bestowed on him the title, Lord Tennyson, First Baron of Aldworth and Freshwater.

---

*   See introduction to Robert Browning, 385

SOURCE

Tennyson, Alfred, Lord. 1842. "Ulysses." In *The Poetic* and *Dramatic Works of Alfred, Lord Tennyson*. Student's Cambridge Edition. New York: Houghton Mifflin, 1898. 88-89.

ULYSSES

First Printed in 1842, and unaltered

It little profits that an idle king,
By this still hearth, among these barren crags,
Match'd with an aged wife, I mete and dole
Unequal laws unto a savage race,
That hoard, and sleep, and feed, and know not me.
I cannot rest from travel; I will drink
Life to the lees. All times I have enjoy'd
Greatly, have suffer'd greatly, both with those
That loved me, and alone; on shore, and when
Thro' scudding drifts the rainy Hyades
Vext the dim sea. I am become a name;
For always roaming with a hungry heart
Much have I seen and known,—cities of men
And manners, climates, councils, governments,
Myself not least, but honour'd of them all,—
And drunk delight of battle with my peers,
Far on the ringing plains of windy Troy.
I am a part of all that I have met;
Yet all experience is an arch wherethro'
Gleams that untravell'd world, whose margin fades
For ever and for ever when I move.
How dull it is to pause, to make an end,
To rust unburnish'd, not to shine in use!
As tho' to breathe were life! Life piled on life
Were all too little, and of one to me
Little remains; but every hour is saved

From that eternal silence, something more,
A bringer of new things; and vile it were
For some three suns to store and hoard myself,
And this gray spirit yearning in desire
To follow knowledge like a sinking star,
Beyond the utmost bound of human thought.
This is my son, mine own Telemachus,
To whom I leave the sceptre and the isle,—
Well-loved of me, discerning to fulfil
This labor, by slow prudence to make mild
A rugged people, and thro' soft degrees
Subdue them to the useful and the good.
Most blameless is he, centred in the sphere
Of common duties, decent not to fail
In offices of tenderness, and pay
Meet adoration to my household gods,
When I am gone. He works his work, I mine.
There lies the port; the vessel puffs her sail;
There gloom the dark, broad seas. My mariners,
Souls that have toil'd, and wrought, and thought with me,—
That ever with a frolic welcome took
The thunder and the sunshine, and opposed
Free hearts, free foreheads,—you and I are old;
Old age hath yet his honor and his toil.
Death closes all; but something ere the end,
Some work of noble note, may yet be done,
Not unbecoming men that strove with Gods.
The lights begin to twinkle from the rocks;
The long day wanes; the slow moon climbs; the deep
Moans round with many voices. Come, my friends,
'Tis not too late to seek a newer world.
Push off, and sitting well in order smite
The sounding furrows; for my purpose holds
To sail beyond the sunset, and the baths
Of all the western stars, until I die.
It may be that the gulfs will wash us down;

It may be we shall touch the Happy Isles,
And see the great Achilles, whom we knew.
Tho' much is taken, much abides; and tho'
We are not now that strength which in old days
Moved earth and heaven; that which we are, we are,—
One equal temper of heroic hearts,
Made weak by time and fate, but strong in will
To strive, to seek, to find, and not to yield.

WILLIAM WORDSWORTH

1770-1850

"LINES COMPOSED A FEW MILES ABOVE TINTERN ABBEY ON REVISITING THE BANKS OF THE WYE DURING A TOUR. JULY 13, 1798."

William Wordsworth is one of the great poets of English Romanticism. His emphasis on the senses and on nature underscores the Romantic concept of the human condition. Wordsworth's most treasured contribution to English poetry is the volume that heralded the Romantic era, *Lyrical Ballads* (1798), a collaboration with the poet Samuel Taylor Coleridge ("The Rime of the Ancient Mariner"). The *Lyrical Ballads* were written as a reaction against the highly wrought artificiality of 18th-century verse and sought to reclaim natural, rustic simplicity for English poetry. Although his poems were frequently panned by critics, including Lord Byron, they remained widely popular. In 1843, he was named England's Poet Laureate, a position he held until his death.

In 1802, he married a childhood friend, Mary Hutchinson, and with his sister Dorothy, the three lived in the Lake District of England, where Wordsworth's position as Distributor of Stamps for Westmorland gave him enough money to support the family while still writing. Clearly, Wordsworth's poetry is deeply infused with his love of nature, especially by the sights and scenes of the Lake District. He even published a guide for explorers of the area.

While arranging for the printing of *Lyrical Ballads,* Wordsworth and Coleridge traveled to Wales, where Wordsworth wrote "Tintern Abbey," one of his most famous poems. His inspiration was the ruins of the old abbey, the second Cistercian monastery in Britain and the first in Wales, founded in 1131. Its great church was built between 1269 and 1301; as other monasteries, it was dissolved as an institution by Henry VIII in 1536.

Source

Wordsworth, William. 1798. "Lines Composed a Few Miles Above Tintern Abbey." In *The English Poets.* Thomas Ward, Ed. Vol. IV. Second Ed. New York: Macmillan, 1888. 18-22.

Lines Composed a Few Miles Above Tintern Abbey on Revisiting the Banks of the Wye During a Tour. July 13, 1798.

Five years have past; five summers, with the length
Of five long winters! and again I hear
These waters, rolling from their mountain-springs
With a soft inland murmur.—Once again
Do I behold these steep and lofty cliffs,
That on a wild secluded scene impress
Thoughts of more deep seclusion; and connect
The landscape with the quiet of the sky.
The day is come when I again repose
Here, under this dark sycamore, and view
These plots of cottage-ground, these orchard-tufts,
Which at this season, with their unripe fruits,
Are clad in one green hue, and lose themselves
'Mid groves and copses. Once again I see
These hedge-rows, hardly hedge-rows, little lines
Of sportive wood run wild; these pastoral farms,
Green to the very door; and wreaths of smoke
Sent up, in silence, from among the trees!

With some uncertain notice, as might seem
Of vagrant dwellers in the houseless woods,
Or of some Hermit's cave, where by his fire
The hermit sits alone.
                   These beauteous forms
Through a long absence, have not been to me
As is a landscape to a blind man's eye:
But oft, in lonely rooms, and 'mid the din
Of towns and cities, I have owed to them
In hours of weariness, sensations sweet
Felt in the blood, and felt along the heart;
And passing even into my purer mind,
With tranquil restoration:—feelings too
Of unremembered pleasure: such, perhaps,
As have no slight or trivial influence
On that best portion of a good man's life,
His little, nameless, unremembered acts
Of kindness and of love. Nor less, I trust,
To them I may have owed another gift,
Of aspect more sublime; that blessed mood,
In which the burthen of the mystery,
In which the heavy and the weary weight
Of all this unintelligible world,
Is lightened:—that serene and blessed mood
In which the affections gently lead us on,—
Until, the breath of this corporeal frame
And even the motion of our human blood
Almost suspended, we are laid asleep
In body, and become a living soul:
While with an eye made quiet by the power
Of harmony, and the deep power of joy,
We see into the life of things.
                       If this
Be but a vain belief, yet, oh! how oft—
In darkness and amid the many shapes
Of joyless daylight; when the fretful stir

Unprofitable, and the fever of the world,
Have hung upon the beatings of my heart—
How oft, in spirit, have I turned to thee,
O sylvan Wye! thou wanderer thro' the woods,
How often has my spirit turned to thee!
And now, with gleams of half-extinguished thought,
With many recognitions dim and faint,
And somewhat of a sad perplexity,
The picture of the mind revives again:
While here I stand, not only with the sense
Of present pleasure, but with pleasing thoughts
That in this moment there is life and food
For future years. And so I dare to hope,
Though changed, no doubt, from what I was when first
I came among these hills; when like a roe
I bounded o'er the mountains, by the sides
Of the deep rivers, and the lonely streams
Wherever nature led: more like a man
Flying from something that he dreads, than one
Who sought the thing he loved. For nature then
(The coarser pleasures of my boyish days,
And their glad animal movements all gone by)
To me was all in all.—I cannot paint
What then I was. The sounding cataract
Haunted me like a passion; the tall rock,
The mountain, and the deep and gloomy wood,
Their colours and their forms, were then to me
An appetite; a feeling and a love,
That had no need of a remoter charm,
By thought supplied, nor any interest
Unborrowed from the eye.—That time is past
And all its aching joys are now no more,
And all its dizzy raptures. Not for this
Faint I, nor mourn, nor murmur; other gifts
Have followed; for such loss, I would believe,
Abundant recompense. For I have learned

To look on nature, not as in the hour
Of thoughtless youth; but hearing oftentimes
The still, sad music of humanity,
Nor harsh nor grating, though of ample power
To chasten and subdue. And I have felt
A presence that disturbs me with the joy
Of elevated thoughts; a sense sublime,
Of something far more deeply interfused,
Whose dwelling is the light of setting suns,
And the round ocean and the living air,
And the blue sky, and in the mind of man:
A motion and a spirit, that impels
All thinking things, all objects of all thought,
And rolls through all things. Therefore am I still
A lover of the meadows and the woods,
And mountains; and of all that we behold
From this green earth; of all the mighty world
Of eye, and ear,—both what they half create,
And what perceive; well pleased to recognize
In nature and the language of the sense
The anchor of my purest thoughts, the nurse,
The guide, the guardian of my heart, and soul
Of all my moral being.
　　　　　　　　　Nor perchance,
If I were not thus taught, should I the more
Suffer my genial spirits to decay:
For thou art with me here upon the banks
Of this fair river; thou my dearest Friend,
My dear, dear Friend; and in thy voice I catch
The language of my former heart, and read
My former pleasure in the shooting lights
Of thy wild eyes. Oh! yet a little while
May I behold in thee what I was once,
My dear, dear Sister! and this prayer I make,
Knowing that Nature never did betray
The heart that loved her; 'tis her privilege

Through all the years of this our life, to lead
From joy to joy: for she can so inform
The mind that is within us, so impress
With quietness and beauty, and so feed
With lofty thoughts, that neither evil tongues,
Rash judgements, nor the sneers of selfish men,
Nor greetings where no kindness is, nor all
The dreary intercourse of daily life,
Shall e'er prevail against us, or disturb
Our cheerful faith, that all which we behold
Is full of blessings. Therefore let the moon
Shine on thee in thy solitary walk;
And let the misty mountain-winds be free
To blow against thee: and, in after years,
When these wild ecstasies shall be matured
Into a sober pleasure; when thy mind
Shall be a mansion for all lovely forms,
Thy memory be as a dwelling-place
For all sweet sounds and harmonies; oh! then,
If solitude, or fear, or pain, or grief,
Should be thy portion, with what healing thoughts
Of tender joy wilt thou remember me,
And these my exhortations! Nor, perchance—
If I should be where I no more can hear
Thy voice, nor catch from thy wild eyes these gleams
Of past existence.—wilt thou then forget
That on the banks of this delightful stream
We stood together; and that I, so long
A worshipper of Nature, hither came
Unwearied in that service: rather say
With warmer love—oh! with far deeper zeal
Of holier love. Nor wilt thou then forget
That after many wanderings, many years
Of absence, these steep woods and lofty cliffs,
And this green pastoral landscape, were to me
More dear, both for themselves and for thy sake!

EMMA LAZARUS

1849-1887

"THE NEW COLOSSUS"

1883

Raised in New York and Rhode Island, Emma Lazarus wrote many poems that reflect her Jewish heritage and consciousness. In 1866, her father, Moses Lazarus, had published for private circulation her *Poems and Translations: Written Between the Ages of Fourteen and Sixteen*. In the 1880s, Lazarus worked with the Hebrew Emigrant Aid Society, the Hebrew Technical Institute, and agricultural communities of Eastern European Jews in the United States. A regular contributor to the periodical *American Hebrew*, she published an essay in 1883, "The Jewish Problem," calling for the founding of a state by Jews for Jews in Palestine.

The sonnet "The New Colossus" was written in 1883 for an auction to raise money for the pedestal of the Statue of Liberty and printed in the *Catalogue of the Pedestal Fund Art Loan Exhibition at the National Academy of Design*. Engraved on the pedestal of the Statue of Liberty, it greets immigrants as they arrive in New York Harbor.

SOURCE

Emma Lazarus. 1883. "The New Colossus." Available on the National Park Service website: http://www.nps.gov/stli/newcolossus/

THE NEW COLOSSUS

Not like the brazen giant of Greek fame
With conquering limbs astride from land to land;
Here at our sea-washed, sunset gates shall stand
A mighty woman with a torch, whose flame
Is the imprisoned lightning, and her name
Mother of Exiles. From her beacon-hand
Glows world-wide welcome; her mild eyes command
The air-bridged harbor that twin cities frame,
"Keep, ancient lands, your storied pomp!" cries she
With silent lips. "Give me your tired, your poor,
Your huddled masses yearning to breathe free,
The wretched refuse of your teeming shore,
Send these, the homeless, tempest-tossed to me,
I lift my lamp beside the golden door!"

W.H. Auden

1907-1973

"Musée des Beaux Arts"

1938

W. H. Auden became involved with a group of literary intellectuals—Stephen Spender and Christopher Isherwood among them—while at Oxford, and later in the 1930s, he joined other young leftist poets in London. His importance as a 20th-century poet was established by his volume of verse, *Poems* (1930), in which he examined the failure of English capitalist society. In 1937, he was awarded the King's Gold Medal for Poetry; that same year, he drove an ambulance for the Loyalist forces in the Spanish Civil War. Leaving a war-wearied Europe in 1939, Auden moved to the United States, where he worked as a poet, lecturer, and editor, and where, in 1948, he was awarded the Pulitzer Prize for poetry. In 1956, he returned to England as a professor of poetry and later writer in residence at Oxford. He was a Chancellor of The Academy of American Poets from 1954 to 1973.

The first book published after his move to America, *Another Time* (1940), included the free verse "Musée des Beaux Arts." Written after a visit to the Museum of Fine Arts in Brussels, the poem challenges humanity's seemingly benign, indifferent response to tragedy. Auden considers human suffering by referring to the painting *Landscape with the Fall of Icarus*[1] (*ca.*1558) by Pieter Bruegel, in which Icarus falls from the sky while others plow their fields, tend their flocks, and go about their daily lives, unaware. Readers should consider W.C. Williams's poem "Landscape with the Fall of Icarus" as well. (418)

SOURCE

Auden, W. H. 1938. "Musée des Beaux Arts." In *Collected Shorter Poems, 1927-1957*. Vintage Edition. New York: Random, 1975 [Reprint of 1952 edition]. 123-124.*

MUSÉE DES BEAUX ARTS

About suffering they were never wrong,
The Old Masters: how well they understood
Its human position; how it takes place
While someone else is eating or opening a window or just walking
    dully along;
How, when the aged are reverently, passionately waiting
For the miraculous birth, there always must be
Children who did not specially want it to happen, skating
On a pond at the edge of the wood:

---

[1] The painting is derived from the classical myth of Icarus, son the Athenian craftsman Daedalus, who constructed wings by which they hoped to fly from their imprisonment on Crete. Daedalus attached the wings to their shoulders with wax, and warned Icarus not to fly too high or too low. But Icarus flew too near the sun, the wax melted, the wings fell off, and Icarus plunged to his death in the sea.

* "Musée des Beaux Arts," copyright 1940 and renewed 1968 by W. H. Auden, from COLLECTED POEMS, by W. H. Auden. Used by Permission of Random House, Inc

They never forgot
That even the dreadful martyrdom must run its course
Anyhow in a corner, some untidy spot
Where the dogs go on with their doggy life and the torturer's horse
Scratches its innocent behind on a tree.
In Brueghel's Icarus, for instance: how everything turns away
Quite leisurely from the disaster; the ploughman may
Have heard the splash, the forsaken cry,
But for him it was not an important failure; the sun shone
As it had to on the white legs disappearing into the green
Water; and the expensive delicate ship that must have seen
Something amazing, a boy falling out of the sky,
Had somewhere to get to and sailed calmly on.

ANNE SPENCER

1882-1975

"LIFE-LONG, POOR BROWNING"
"DUNBAR"

ca. 1920

At the age of 11, Annie Bethel Scales came from Henry County, Virginia, to the Virginia Seminary and College (now Virginia University of Lynchburg) where she stayed for six years. She met her husband, Edward Spencer, and settled in Lynchburg, where the Spencers became homeowners and hosts to many black artists, political activists, and intellectuals traveling between points south or west and the east coast or New York. Their home became a center of intellectual life during the otherwise grim Jim Crow era. Their friends and visitors included James Weldon Johnson, W.E.B.DuBois, Thurgood Marshall, Paul Robeson, Langston Hughes, Gwendolyn Brooks, and other luminaries of the period.

With a steady job as the librarian at Dunbar High School, an exemplary secondary school which, before integration, turned out many successful professionals and famous artists, Anne Spencer helped put her three children through college. The Spencers founded the Lynchburg chapter of the NAACP, Virginia's first chapter, in 1918. James Weldon Johnson is credited with discovering Spencer's talent and introducing her to H. L. Mencken, who helped her publish her first poem, "Before the Feast at Shushan." Most of her poems were published in the 1920s in compilations such as Johnson's *The Book of American Negro Poetry* (1922).

Much of Spencer's poetry concerns the human search for beauty, a quest that was likewise evident in her garden, preserved and maintained as part of her legacy at her home. Also famous is her garden cottage, Edankraal, where she did much of her writing. Spencer frequently gave her poetry as gifts, wrote poems on scraps of paper around the house, and even on the wallpaper in her bedroom. What has been published so far is just a portion of her work. She also wrote of love and friendship, as well as of racism and oppression.

"Life-Long, Poor Browning" is her lament for the poet Robert Browning, for he never visited the state of Virginia she found so beautiful and inspiring; had he seen it he would not have longed for English gardens from his home in Italy(see introduction to Browning, p. 385). In "Dunbar," (referring to poet Paul Laurence Dunbar), she exclaims over the transitory lives of poets.

SOURCE

Spencer, Anne. *ca.* 1920. "Life-long, Poor Browning" and "Dunbar." In *Anne Spencer: "Ah, how poets sing and die!"* Nina V. Salmon, Ed. Lynchburg, VA: The Anne Spencer Memorial Foundation, 2001. 66, 29.*

LIFE-LONG, POOR BROWNING

Life-long, poor Browning never knew Virginia,
Or he'd not grieved in Florence for April sallies
Back to English gardens after Euclid's linear:
Clipt yews, Pomander Walks, and pleachéd alleys;

---

*   Reprinted with permission from The Anne Spencer Memorial Foundation

Primroses, prim indeed, in quiet ordered hedges,
Waterways, soberly, sedately enchanneled,
No thin riotous blade even among the sedges,
All the wild country-side tamely impaneled . . .

Dead, now, dear Browning lives on in heaven,—
(Heaven's Virginia when the year's at its Spring)
He's haunting the byways of wine-aired leaven
And throating the notes of the wildings on wing:

Here canopied reaches of dogwood and hazel,
Beech tree and redbud fine-laced in vines,
Fleet clapping rills by lush fern and basil,
Drain blue hills to lowlands scented with pines . . .

Think you he meets in this tender green sweetness
Shade that was Elizabeth . . . immortal completeness!

DUNBAR

Ah, how poets sing and die!
Make one song and Heaven takes it;
Have one heart and Beauty breaks it;
Chatterton, Shelley, Keats and I—
Ah, how poets sing and die!

RAINER MARIA RILKE

1876-1926

"ARCHAIC TORSO OF APOLLO"

1908

Rainer Maria Rilke, one of the great poets of modern German literature, was born in Prague. After publishing *Leben und Lieder* (Life and Songs), his first collection of poems, in 1894, he attended Prague's Charles University. He then studied philosophy and art history at the University of Munich and the University of Berlin. In 1899, he traveled to Russia, where he met Tolstoy and spent the summer at the artists' colony at Worpswede, where he met and married Clara Westhoff, a former pupil of the French sculptor Auguste Rodin. But Rilke's marriage soon ended, and he journeyed to Paris, where he met the sculptor Rodin, serving for a brief time as his private secretary.

Rodin's influence on Rilke was profound—the poet moved away from his early sentimental style and began writing more lyrical poems, noted for their intensity and their striking imagery influenced by the visual arts. When World War I broke out, Rilke wrote *War Songs*, which reveal his emotional transformation from zeal to desolation. At the age of forty, Rilke was drafted into the Austrian army and assigned to the War Archive in Vienna. He took up residence in Switzerland after the war and lived there until his death from leukemia in 1926.

Although he was widely admired in his international circle of artistic friends, Rilke was almost unknown to the public in his lifetime. In "Archaic Torso of Apollo," he explores the moment when the object of aesthetic contemplation speaks to the viewer, penetrating the complacency of mere viewing. Apollo, the embodiment of the classical Greek spirit, represents the rational and civilized side of human nature, the god of poetry and music, of the arts that heal the soul.

SOURCE

Rilke, Rainer Maria. 1908. "Archaic Torso of Apollo." Howard Landman, Trans. 2001. http://www.polyamory.org/~howard/ Poetry/rilke_archaic_apollo.html*

ARCHAIC TORSO OF APOLLO

We never knew his fantastic head,
where eyes like apples ripened. Yet
his torso, like a lamp, still glows
with his gaze which, although turned down low,

lingers and shines. Else the prow of his breast
couldn't dazzle you, nor in the slight twist
of his loins could a smile run free
through that center which held fertility.

Else this stone would stand defaced and squat
under the shoulders' diaphanous dive
and not glisten like a predator's coat;

and not from every edge explode
like starlight: for there's not one spot
that doesn't see you. You must change your life.

---

*   Used by permission of Howard A. Landman, translator

FEDERICO GARCÍA LORCA

1898-1936

"LAMENT FOR IGNACIO SÁNCHEZ MEJÍAS"

1935

Born near Granada, Spain, Federico García Lorca studied law at Granada University, and philosophy and letters at Madrid University. His first book of poetry was published in 1921, although his poems were already known through recitation. Lorca's work encompasses features of the folklore of his native Andalusia, such as *Romancero Gitano* (1928), *Lament for the Death of a Bullfighter, and Other Poems* (1937) and the folk tragedy *Bodas de sangre* (Blood Wedding), 1935), dark in mood and imagery, and as surrealistic as the paintings of his friend Salvador Dalí. Lorca is perhaps the most famous victim of the Spanish Civil War. In August 1936, he was dragged into a field and executed by the Escuadra Negra, one of Franco's death squads, ostensibly for his left-wing sympathies and homosexuality. As many as 30,000 people were killed by Franco's death squads and executioners, with many, as Lorca, thrown into unmarked graves. Lorca became a martyr, a symbol of the victims of fascist tyranny, so his books were officially banned until the early 1970s, although some plays were produced in Spain beginning in the 1950s.

Lorca is respected as one of the greatest Spanish writers of the 20th century and an author whose work extends the achievements of Spain's "Golden Age." His work, focused as it is on the Andalusian landscape and culture, has often been labeled as "regional" or "provincial." Yet his voice is considered universal, ringing true both inside and outside of Spain. His musical and descriptive verse pulsates in its imagery. The "Llanto por Ignacio Sánchez Mejías" (Lament for Ignacio Sánchez Mejías) is perhaps Lorca's greatest poetic achievement. He expresses his grief for his friend, one of the greatest of all matadors, killed attempting a comeback in the bullring. Many of Lorca's contemporaries talked of abolishing the bullfight, but Lorca was committed to its importance as a cultural festival in which death is surrounded by beauty. "Lament for Ignacio Sánchez Mejías" is divided into four parts. In this selection (the first part only), Lorca recounts the moment the matador was wounded by the bull, poetically intensified by the lyrical repetition of the refrain "at five in the afternoon." (Part two tells of blood and death; the third describes his wake, and the fourth provides an epitaph.)

SOURCE

Lorca, Federico García. 1935. "Lament for Ignacio Sánchez Mejías." Stephen Spender and J.I.Gili, Trans. In *The Selected Poems of Federico García Lorca.* Francisco García Lorca and Donald M. Allen, Eds. New York: New Directions, 1955. 135,137,139.*

LAMENT FOR IGNACIO SÁNCHEZ MEJÍAS

1. *Cogida and Death*

At five in the afternoon.
It was exactly five in the afternoon.

A boy brought the white sheet
at five in the afternoon.
A frail of lime ready prepared
at five in the afternoon.
The rest was death, and death alone
at five in the afternoon.

The wind carried away the cottonwool
at five in the afternoon.
And the oxide scattered crystal and nickel
at five in the afternoon.
Now the dove and the leopard wrestle
at five in the afternoon.
And a thigh with a desolate horn
at five in the afternoon.
The bass-string struck up
at five in the afternoon.
Arsenic bells and smoke
at five in the afternoon.
Groups of silence in the corners
at five in the afternoon.
And the bull alone with a high heart!
At five in the afternoon.
When the sweat of snow was coming
at *five in the afternoon,*
when the bull ring was covered in iodine
at five in the afternoon.
death laid eggs in the wound
at five in the afternoon.
At five in the afternoon.
Exactly at five o'clock in the afternoon.

A coffin on wheels is his bed
at five in the afternoon.
Bones and flutes resound in his ears
at five in the afternoon.
Now the bull was bellowing through his forehead
at five in the afternoon.
The room was iridescent with agony
at five in the afternoon.
In the distance the gangrene now comes
at five in the afternoon.
Horn of the lily through green groins
at five in the afternoon.
The wounds were burning like suns
at five in the afternoon,
and the crowd was breaking the windows
at five in the afternoon.
At five in the afternoon.
Ah, that fatal five in the afternoon!
It was five by all the clocks!
It was five in the shade of the afternoon!
                    Stephen Spender and J.L.Gili, Trans.

Pablo Neruda

1904-1973

"Arise to Birth with Me My Brother"
1966

Pablo Neruda, born Neftalí Ricardo Reyes Basoalto in Chile, adopted the pseudonym Pablo Neruda in 1946 in memory of the Czech poet, Jan Neruda. At 12, Neruda became acquainted with the poet Gabriela Mistral, who encouraged his writing of poetry. He published his first poem at the age of 13, and by 16 he was a contributor to the literary journal *Selva Austral*. After his studies at the University of Chile, he worked in Chilean consulates in Asia, South America, and Spain. During this time, his poetry became increasingly focused on political and social issues, especially after the murder of García Lorca, whom he knew, and his involvement with Spain's Republican movement during the Spanish Civil War.

In 1939, he moved to Paris as the consul for Spanish emigration and later was named Consul General in Mexico. After returning to Chile in 1945, he took a Senate position and joined the Communist party. His protests against the government's repressive policies sent him underground until he could flee the country in1949. Returning in 1952, he continued writing. He received the Nobel Prize for Literature in 1971.

"Arise to birth with me, my brother" is Canto XII from *The Heights of Macchu Picchu*.[1] A long poem written after the poet had visited the site of the ancient Incan ruins in the Andes, *The Heights of Macchu Picchu* draws parallels between the universal life journey and the life of the poet, himself. The poem speaks through the voices of the dead who had lived in the city long ago. *The Heights of Macchu Picchu* celebrates life, questions the human condition, mourns the loss of idealistic innocence, and accepts the inevitability of death. "Arise to birth with me, my brother" celebrates the Inca and their achievements, symbolized by the site of Macchu Picchu.

SOURCE

Neruda, Pablo. 1966. "Arise to birth with me, my brother." In *The Heights of Macchu Picchu*. Nathaniel Tarn, Trans. New York: Farrar, Straus & Giroux, 1974. 67-71.*

ARISE TO BIRTH WITH ME, MY BROTHER

Arise to birth with me, my brother.

Give me your hand out of the depths
sown by your sorrows.
You will not return from these stone fastnesses.
You will not emerge from subterranean time.
Your rasping voice will not come back,
nor your pierced eyes rise from their sockets.

---

[1] The ruins at Macchu Picchu are the remains of an Inca royal estate deep in the jungle and high in the mountains. It was never conquered by the Spaniards. Indeed, it had probably been abandoned before they arrived. It was rediscovered by Hiram Bingham about 1912 and reported in the *National Geographic*. (www.rexmwess.com/wonders/macchu.htm)

* Reprinted by permission of Farrar, Strauss and Giroux, LLC.

Look at me from the depths of the earth,
tiller of fields, weaver, reticent shepherd,
groom of totemic guanacos,[2]
mason high on your treacherous scaffolding,
iceman of Andean tears,
jeweler with crushed fingers,
farmer anxious among his seedlings,
potter wasted among his clays—
bring to the cup of this new life
your ancient buried sorrows.
Show me your blood and your furrow;
say to me: here I was scourged
because a gem was dull or because the earth
failed to give up in time its tithe of corn or stone.
Point out to me the rock on which you stumbled,
the wood they used to crucify your body.
Strike the old flints
to kindle ancient lamps, light up the whips
glued to your wounds throughout the centuries
and light the axes gleaming with your blood.

I come to speak for your dead mouths.

Throughout the earth
let dead lips congregate,
out of the depths spin this long night to me
as if I rode at anchor here with you.

---

[2]   a large mammal related to the llama that lives in the mountains of South
       America. A member of the camelid family, the guanaco has loose lips,
       pointed ears, and long wooly fur, dark chestnut in color.

And tell me everything, tell chain by chain,
and link by link, and step by step;
sharpen the knives you kept hidden away,
thrust them into my breast, into my hands,
like a torrent of sunbursts,
an Amazon of buried jaguars,
and leave me cry: hours, days and years,
blind ages, stellar centuries.

And give me silence, give me water, hope.

Give me the struggle, the iron, the volcanoes.

Let bodies cling like magnets to my body.

Come quickly to my veins and to my mouth.

Speak through my speech, and through my blood.

WILLIAM CARLOS WILLIAMS

1883-1963

"LANDSCAPE WITH THE FALL OF ICARUS"
"THE HUNTERS IN THE SNOW"

1949

In addition to his poetry, novels, and plays, William Carlos
Williams maintained a medical practice throughout his life. The
most profound influence on his poetry was Ezra Pound, whom he
met at the University of Pennsylvania. Both were members of the
Imagist movement, begun in 1912 by a group of American and
English poets seeking to produce an innovative and inherently
American form of poetry. Characterized by a clarity of expression
achieved through visual images, an imagist poem used a new
"variable foot" meter, a measured line, and the thematic engagement
of everyday lives of common people. Williams's poetry clearly
influenced the work of other well-known American poets, including
those of the Beat Generation like Allen Ginsburg, and others such
as H.D., Ezra Pound, Amy Lowell, and Denise Levertov. Imagist
works were promoted by *Poetry* magazine, a journal begun in 1912
devoted to publishing "the best poetry written today, in whatever
style, genre, or approach."

For the Roman poet Horace in *Ars Poetica* (*ca.* 13 B.C.E.), *ut
pictura poesis* (as is painting, so is poetry). Such a symbiosis of the
arts emerges in poems that Williams published in his collection,

Pictures from Brueghel and other poems (Collected Poems 1950-1962). In "Landscape with the Fall of Icarus," the poet reflects on the painting *Landscape with the Fall of Icarus* (*ca*.1558) by Pieter Bruegel (or Brueghel). In both the painted image and the written word, we observe the young Icarus falling to the sea, unnoticed by the farmer who goes about the tilling of his field. The painting, and thus the poem, are darkly ironic: flying too close to the heavens ends in young Icarus's fatal fall, and even in spring, the time of re-birth, there is death. In both works, the fall of Icarus is subordinate to the landscape itself. Yet in the poem's last line, "Icarus drowning," the poet matter-of-factly forces us to take notice (compare this poem with Auden's "Musée des Beaux Arts"). In "The Hunters in the Snow," Williams again engages Bruegel's art by simply and directly describing the 1565 painting, showing the reader the image through characteristically austere diction, unpunctuated.

SOURCE

Williams, William Carlos. 1949. "Landscape with the Fall of Icarus" and "The Hunters in the Snow." In *Pictures from Brueghel and other poems (Collected Poems 1950-1962)*. New York: New Directions. 1962, 4, 5.*

II LANDSCAPE WITH THE FALL OF ICARUS

According to Brueghel
when Icarus fell
it was spring

a farmer was ploughing
his field
the whole pageantry

of the year was
awake tingling
near

the edge of the sea
concerned
with itself

sweating in the sun
that melted
the wings' wax

unsignificantly
off the coast
there was

a splash quite unnoticed
this was
Icarus drowning

III THE HUNTERS IN THE SNOW

The over-all picture is winter
icy mountains
in the background the return

from the hunt it is toward evening
from the left
sturdy hunters lead in

their pack the inn-sign
hanging from a
broken hinge is a stag a crucifix

between his antlers the cold
inn yard is
deserted but for a huge bonfire

that flares wind-driven tended by
women who cluster
about it to the right beyond

the hill is a pattern of skaters
Brueghel the painter
concerned with it all has chosen

a winter-struck bush for his
foreground to
complete the picture . . .

PART V

SHAPES: MUSIC

WHAT IS MUSIC?

What is music? The answer to this question is an elusive one, continuously changing over time. The most objective definition is that music is sound organized by human beings in a certain time frame. We do not call sounds in nature such as the singing of birds or murmuring of streams "music," despite how pleasing they are. They can be called music once organized and manipulated with musical elements by a composer, such as in Vivaldi's *Four Seasons*.

Music is an art, reflecting human thoughts and emotions. It is often considered the most powerful among all of the arts; it seems to bypass the intellect and touch the soul and senses directly. As Beethoven said, ". . . music is higher revelation than all wisdom and philosophy." Yet music is also a science, involving principles of mathematics and physics among many other disciplines. Notes and rests are the musical parallel of fractions, all divided evenly into the confines of a measure. The tuning of a guitar by tightening or loosening of the strings is a phenomenon explained by physical science. Music is largely interdisciplinary, requiring knowledge across the arts and the sciences for a complete understanding of what it is and how it works.

Musical activity incorporates three participants: the composer, the performer, and the listener; the function of these three parties often overlaps. A musical piece is the expression of the composer's sincere intentions. Beethoven wrote, "Stimulated by those moods that poets turn into words, I turn my ideas into tones, which resound, roar, and rage until at last they stand before me in form of notes." The performer then recreates the composer's intentions as closely as possible through musical notation, his own musical intuition, and a process called interpretation. The listener is the final piece of the puzzle. To become a true listener, one would need considerable training and discipline, as with any other language. Yet music communicates in a more oblique fashion unlike conventional spoken languages, which have fixed meanings for each word. There are two thoughts on how music communicates. Some insist that musical meaning lies exclusively within the context of the work itself; others believe that it exists as extramusical ideas.

Historically, musical elements were often linked to certain emotions and moral qualities. Plato thought the "proper" sort of music encouraged the young men of Athens to be diligent and avoid the temptations of wine, women, and wanton song. Music is able to change a person's feelings and attitude. It has a persuasive power. Music is a force for change in society as well as a reflection of the values of society. Goethe stated, "It is perhaps in music that the dignity of art is most eminently apparent, for it elevates and ennobles everything that it expresses."

So what is music? It is an art, and a science. It is a language, a way of conveying thoughts as well as emotions. It is a mirror of the society in which we live. It is all-encompassing and universal. It has as many exceptions as rules, as many boundaries as unlimited freedom. It is a form of expression. We innately know it and understand it, but cannot completely define it.

Jong Kim, Ph.D.
Assistant Professor of Music

Ludwig van Beethoven

1770-1827

Heiligenstadt Testament

1806

Ludwig von Beethoven, one of the world's greatest composers, was the son of a German court musician who made young Ludwig's childhood difficult by the exploitation of the son's prodigious musical talents. Although his formal education did not continue past the elementary level, he studied with Haydn in Vienna where he was first recognized as a piano virtuoso. His explosive musical power was an anomaly amid the restrained, refined elegant style of the music popular at the time.

Beethoven's work is generally divided into three periods: early (prior to 1802), middle (characterized by highly dramatic and monumental compositions), and late (beginning around 1815), showing deep, introspective elements. Although Beethoven remained committed to the classical principles of composition throughout his career, the drama, passion, and intensity of his work broke new ground for the self-expression of later composers. Beethoven was the first great composer to declare himself an "artist," and in the process, he became a symbol of the artist-hero for the emerging modern world, no longer the artist-craftsman confined to the restrictions dictated by the court or the aristocracy of earlier times.

Beethoven gradually lost his hearing in his early 30s. Eventually he revealed his secret "miserable life" in letters to friends. His correspondence reveals that the impact of his disheartening condition was more social than musical, in part because he could no longer perform in public. The letter here translated reveals his anger, defiance, depression, and despair, giving full expression to his emotional turbulence—the same quality that makes his music so distinctive. In the letter he tells his brothers "goodbye" and wills them his belongings. He then lives 25 years longer. Even after he was totally deaf (at 48), he continued to compose for many more years in his unceasing search for musical truth. When he could no longer hear all of the sounds of the world around him, his music passionately and eloquently still resonated in his mind.

The translator of this document, Dr. Piero Weiss, has chosen to retain the letter's punctuation—it provides its own dimension of eloquence.

SOURCE

van Beethoven, Ludwig. 1802. *Heiligenstadt Testament*. In *Letters of Composers Through Six Centuries*. Piero Weiss, Ed. and Tr. Philadelphia: Chilton, 1967. 167-69.*

HEILIGENSTADT TESTAMENT

This famous document, drafted in the form of a testament addressed to his two brothers, was found among Beethoven's effects when he died. It had been written twenty-five years earlier in the village of Heiligenstadt, on the outskirts of Vienna, at the most critical moment in the composer's life, when he had had to face the fact that his deafness was progressive and, probably, incurable.[PW]

For my brothers Carl and [Johann] Beethoven.

O ye men who think or declare that I am hostile stubborn or Misanthropic, how you wrong me you do not know the secret

---

*   Reprinted by permission of Dr. Piero Weiss.

motive of what seems thus to you, from Childhood my Heart and Mind were inclined to the Gentle Feeling of goodwill, indeed I was ever disposed To accomplish great Feats, but only reflect that for the last 6 years an incurable condition has seized me, worsened by senseless physicians, cheated from year to year in the Hope of improvement, finally compelled to the prospect of a *lasting Ailment* (whose Curing may perhaps last for years or indeed be impossible) born with a fiery Lively Temperament susceptible even to the Diversions of Society, I soon had to keep to myself, pass my life in solitude, if I attempted from time to time to place myself beyond all this, o how harshly then was I repulsed by the doubly sad Experience of my bad Hearing, and yet I could not say to People: speak louder, shout, for I am deaf, alas how could I possibly then admit the Weakness of *a Faculty* which should exist in me to a more perfect degree than in others, a Faculty I once possessed to the highest Perfection, to such Perfection as few of my Calling surely have or have had—o I cannot do it, therefore forgive me, if you see me shrinking back when I should gladly join you my misfortune afflicts me doubly, since it causes me to be misunderstood, Diversion in Human Society, civilized Conversation, mutual Effusions cannot take place for me, all but alone I may enter into society no more than the greatest Necessity requires, I must live like a Banished man, if I approach a company, a hot anxiety invades me, as I am afraid of being put in Danger of letting my Condition be noticed—and thus has it been this half-year too, which I have spent in the country, my wise Physician having ordered me to spare my Hearing as much as possible, he nearly met my present Disposition, even though I have sometimes let myself be led astray by an Urge for Society, but what a Mortification if someone stood next to me and heard a flute from afar and I heard *nothing;* or someone *heard a Shepherd Singing,* and I heard nothing, such Happenings brought me close to Despair, I was not far from ending my own life—only Art, only art held me back, ah, it seemed impossible to me that I should leave the world before I had produced all that I felt I might, and so I spared this wretched life—truly wretched; a body so susceptible that a somewhat rapid

change can remove me from the Best Condition to the worst—
Patience—so now I must choose Her for my guide, I have done
so—I hope that my decision to persevere may be permanent, until
it please the inexorable Parcae [Fates] to break the Thread, perhaps
I will improve, perhaps not, I am resigned—to be forced already
in my 28th year already to become a Philosopher, that is not easy,
for an Artist harder than for anyone else—deity thou lookest down
into my innermost being; thou knowest it, thou seest that charity
and benevolence dwell within,—o Men, when some day you read
this, think then that you have wronged me, and the unhappy one,
let him console himself by finding another like himself who, despite
Nature's Impediments, yet did what was in his Power to be admitted
to the Ranks of worthy Artists and Men—you my Brothers Carl
and [Johann], as soon as I am dead, and professor schmid still
lives, ask him in my Name to describe my Illness, and append this
Sheet of writing to this History of my illness, so that at least after
my Death the world may make its peace with me as much as
possible—At the same time I here declare you two as the Heirs of
the small Riches (if one may call them such) belonging to me,
share them fairly, and tolerate and help one another, you know
what you have done against me, it has long been forgiven, you
Brother Carl I thank again especially for the Attachment you have
shown me in these more recent later days, My wish is that you
may have a better more untroubled Life than I, commend *Virtue* to
your children, it alone can bring happiness, not Money, I speak
from Experience, it was Virtue raised me in my Distress, I have it
to thank besides my Art if I did not put an end to my Life through
suicide—farewell and love each other,—I thank all Friends,
particularly *Prince Lichnowski* and *Professor Schmidt*.—I wish that
Prince L.'s Instruments may be preserved by one of you, yet let
there arise no Strife between you on that account, but as soon as
they can serve you for a more useful purpose, you may sell them if
you like, how happy am I, if I can still be of use to you even in my
Grave—And so it's done—I hasten with joy towards my Death—
should it come before I have had an Opportunity to disclose all
my Artistic Capacities, then it shall have come still too soon in

spite of my Hard Destiny, and I should indeed wish it later—yet even then am I content, does it not free me from an endless Suffering State?—Come *when* you will, I'll meet you bravely—farewell and do not wholly forget me in Death, I have deserved it of you, since in Life I have often thought of you, to make you happy, so may you be—

Heiglnstadt   Ludwig van Beethoven
   6th october
     1 8 0 2   [SEAL]

IGOR STRAVINSKY

1882-1971

POETICS OF MUSIC IN THE FORM OF SIX LESSONS

1939-1940

Born in Russia, where he studied under 19th-century Russian musical giant Rimsky-Korsakov, Igor Stravinsky is recognized as an enormously important composer of the 20th century. He won early acclaim for controversial works such as *The Firebird* (1910) and *Petrushka* (1911), working in Paris with Diaghilev's Ballets Russes. His *Le Sacre du Printemps* (*The Rite of Spring*, 1913) inspired riots at its premier performance. In the 1930s, Stravinsky, who had gained French citizenship, toured Europe and the United States as a pianist and conductor of his own works. When World War II broke out, he stayed in the United States, settling in Hollywood, becoming a U.S. citizen in 1945. He continued to compose and conduct into his 80s.

Stravinsky is a major theoretician of modernist musical aesthetics. *The Poetics of Music in the Form of Six Lessons* provides a view into Stravinsky's idea of where his music fits in western tradition as well as insights into his compositional aesthetic. The "Lessons" were originally delivered in French as six lectures in the highly esteemed Charles Eliot Norton series at Harvard in 1939-1940. The excerpts here are taken from two of his six his topics:

"Getting Acquainted," "The Phenomenon of Music," The Composition of Music," "Musical Typology," "The Avatars of Music," and "The Performance of Music."

SOURCE

Stravinsky, Igor. 1939-1940. *The Poetics of Music in the Form of Six Lessons.* "1: Getting Acquainted" and "3: The Composition of Music." Arthur Knodel and Ingolf Dahl, Trans. Cambridge, MA: Harvard, 1942, 1947. 11-12, 47-52, 56-57, 63-65.*

THE POETICS OF MUSIC IN THE FORM OF SIX LESSONS

1: Getting Acquainted

[. . .]

In truth, I should be hard pressed to cite for you a single fact in the history of art that might be qualified as revolutionary. Art is by essence constructive. Revolution implies a disruption of equilibrium. To speak of revolution is to speak of a temporary chaos. Now art is the contrary of chaos. It never gives itself up to chaos without immediately finding its living works, its very existence, threatened.

The quality of being revolutionary is generally attributed to artists in our day with a laudatory intent, undoubtedly because we are living in a period when revolution enjoys a kind of prestige among yesterday's elite. Let us understand each other: I am the first to recognize that daring is the motive force of the finest and greatest acts, which is all the more reason for not putting it unthinkingly at the service of disorder and base cravings in a desire to cause sensation at any price. I approve of daring; I set no limits to it. But likewise there are no limits to the mischief wrought by arbitrary acts.

To enjoy to the full the conquests of daring, we must demand that it operate in a pitiless light. We are working in its favor when we denounce the false wares that would usurp its place. Gratuitous excess spoils every substance, every form that it touches. In its blundering it impairs the effectiveness of the most valuable discoveries and at the same time corrupts the taste of its devotees— which explains why their taste often plunges without transition from the wildest complications to the flattest banalities.

A musical complex, however harsh it may be, is legitimate to the extent to which it is genuine. But to recognize genuine values in the midst of the excesses of sham one must be gifted with a sure instinct that our snobs hate all the more intensely for being themselves completely deprived thereof.

Our vanguard elite, sworn perpetually to outdo itself, expects and requires that music should satisfy the taste for absurd cacophony.

[...]

3: The Composition of Music

We are living at a time when the status of man is undergoing profound upheavals. Modern man is progressively losing his understanding of values and his sense of proportions. This failure to understand essential realities is extremely serious. It leads us infallibly to the violation of the fundamental laws of human equilibrium. In the domain of music, the consequences of this misunderstanding are these: on one hand there is a tendency to turn the mind away from what I shall call the higher mathematics of music in order to degrade music to servile employment, and to vulgarize it by adapting it to the requirements of an elementary utilitarianism—as we shall soon see on examining Soviet music. On the other hand, since the mind itself is ailing, the music of our time and particularly the music that calls itself and believes itself *pure*, carries within it the symptoms of a pathologic blemish and spreads the germs of a new original sin. The old original sin was chiefly a sin of knowledge; the new original sin, if I may speak in these terms, is first and foremost a sin of non-acknowledgment—a refusal to acknowledge the truth and the laws that proceed therefrom, laws that we have called fundamental. What then is this truth in the domain of music? And what are its repercussions on creative activity?

Let us not forget that it is written: "Spiritus ubi vult spirat" (St. John, 3:8). What we must retain in this proposition is above all the word WILL. The Spirit is thus endowed with the capacity of willing. The principle of speculative volition is a fact.

Now it is just this fact that is too often disputed. People question the direction that the wind of the Spirit is taking, not the rightness of the artisan's work. In so doing, whatever may be your feelings about ontology or whatever your own philosophy and beliefs may be, you must admit that you are making an attack on the very freedom of the spirit—whether you begin this large word with a capital or not. If a believer in Christian philosophy, you would then also have to refuse to accept the idea of the Holy Spirit. If an agnostic or atheist, you would have to do nothing less than refuse to be a freethinker . . .

It should be noted that there is never any dispute when the listener takes pleasure in the work he hears. The least informed of music-lovers readily clings to the periphery of a work; it pleases him for reasons that are most often entirely foreign to the essence of music. This pleasure is enough for him and calls for no justification. But if it happens that the music displeases him, our music-lover will ask you for an explanation of his discomfiture. He will demand that we explain something that is in its essence ineffable.

By its fruit we judge the tree. Judge the tree by its fruit then, and do not meddle with the roots. Function justifies an organ, no matter how strange the organ may appear in the eyes of those who are not accustomed to see it functioning. Snobbish circles are cluttered with persons who, like one of Montesquieu's characters, wonder how one can possibly be a Persian. They make me think unfailingly of the story of the peasant who, on seeing a dromedary in the zoo for the first time, examines it at length, shakes his head and, turning to leave, says, to the great delight of those present: "It isn't true."

It is through the unhampered play of its functions, then, that a work is revealed and justified. We are free to accept or reject this play, but no one has the right to question the fact of its existence. To judge, dispute, and criticize the principle of speculative volition which is at the origin of all creation is thus manifestly useless. In the pure state, music is free speculation. Artists of all epochs have unceasingly testified to this concept. For myself, I see no reason for not trying to do as they did. Since I myself was created, I cannot help having the desire to create. What sets this desire in motion, and what can I do to make it productive?

The study of the creative process is an extremely delicate one. In truth, it is impossible to observe the inner workings of this process from the outside. It is futile to try and follow its successive phases in someone else's work. It is likewise very difficult to observe one's self. Yet it is only by enlisting the aid of introspection that I may have any chance at all of guiding you in this essentially fluctuating matter.

Most music-lovers believe that what sets the composer's creative imagination in motion is a certain emotive disturbance generally designated by the name of inspiration.

I have no thought of denying to inspiration the outstanding role that has devolved upon it in the generative process we are studying; I simply maintain that inspiration is in no way a prescribed condition of the creative act, but rather a manifestation that is chronologically secondary.

Inspiration, art, artist—so many words, hazy at least, that keep us from seeing clearly in a field where everything is balance and calculation through which the breath of the speculative spirit blows. It is afterwards, and only afterwards, that the emotive disturbance which is at the root of inspiration may arise—an emotive disturbance about which people talk so indelicately by conferring upon it a meaning that is shocking to us and that compromises the term itself. Is it not clear that this emotion is merely a reaction on the part of the creator grappling with that unknown entity which is still only the object of his creating and which is to become a work of art? Step by step, link by link, it will be granted him to discover the work. It is this chain of discoveries, as well as each individual discovery, that give rise to the emotion—an almost physiological reflex, like that of the appetite causing a flow of saliva—this emotion which invariably follows closely the phases of the creative process.

All creation presupposes at its origin a sort of appetite that is brought on by the foretaste of discovery. This foretaste of the creative act accompanies the intuitive grasp of an unknown entity already possessed but not yet intelligible, an entity that will not take definite shape except by the action of a constantly vigilant technique.

This appetite that is aroused in me at the mere thought of putting in order musical elements that have attracted my attention is not at all a fortuitous thing like inspiration, but as habitual and periodic, if not as constant, as a natural need.

This premonition of an obligation, this foretaste of a pleasure, this conditioned reflex, as a modern physiologist would say, shows clearly that it is the idea of discovery and hard work that attracts me.

The very act of putting my work on paper, of, as we say, kneading the dough, is for me inseparable from the pleasure of creation. So far as I am concerned, I cannot separate the spiritual effort from the psychological and physical effort; they confront me on the same level and do not present a hierarchy.

The word *artist* which, as it is most generally understood today, bestows on its bearer the highest intellectual prestige, the privilege of being accepted as a pure mind—this pretentious term is in my view entirely incompatible with the role of the *homo faber.*[7] At this point it should be remembered that, whatever field of endeavor has fallen to our lot, if it is true that we are *intellectuals,* we are called upon not to cogitate, but to perform.

---

[7]   the man who makes, the craftsman

The philosopher Jacques Maritain reminds us that in the mighty structure of medieval civilization, the artist held only the rank of an artisan. "And his individualism was forbidden any sort of anarchic development, because a natural social discipline imposed certain limitative conditions upon him from without." It was the Renaissance that invented the artist, distinguished him from the artisan and began to exalt the former at the expense of the latter.

At the outset the name artist was given only to the Masters of Arts: philosophers, alchemists, magicians; but painters, sculptors, musicians, and poets had the right to be qualified only as artisans.

> Plying divers implements,
> The subtile artizan implants
> Life in marble, copper, bronze,

says the poet Du Bellay. And Montaigne enumerates in his *Essays* the "painters, poets and other artizans." And even in the seventeenth century, La Fontaine hails a painter with the name of *artisan* and draws a sharp rebuke from an ill-tempered critic who might have been the ancestor of most of our present-day critics.

The idea of work to be done is for me so closely bound up with the idea of the arranging of materials and of the pleasure that the actual doing of the work affords us that, should the impossible happen and my work suddenly be given to me in a perfectly completed form, I should be embarrassed and nonplussed by it, as by a hoax.

We have a duty towards music, namely, to invent it. [. . .]

Invention presupposes imagination but should not be confused with it. For the act of invention implies the necessity of a lucky find and of achieving full realization of this find. What we imagine does not necessarily take on a concrete form and may remain in a state of virtuality, whereas invention is not conceivable apart from its actual being worked out.

Thus, what concerns us here is not imagination itself, but rather creative imagination: the faculty that helps us to pass from the level of conception to the level of realization. [. . .]

The faculty of observation and of making something out of what is observed belongs only to the person who at least possesses, in his particular field of endeavor, an acquired culture and an innate taste. A dealer, an art-lover who is the first to buy the canvases of an unknown painter who will be famous twenty-five years later under the name of Cézanne—doesn't such a person give us a clear example of this innate taste? What else guides him in his choices? A flair, an instinct from which this taste proceeds, a completely spontaneous faculty anterior to reflection.

As for culture, it is a sort of upbringing which, in the social sphere, confers polish upon education, sustains and rounds out academic instruction. This upbringing is just as important in the sphere of taste and is essential to the creator who must ceaselessly refine his taste or run the risk of losing his perspicacity. Our mind, as well as our body, requires continual exercise. It atrophies if we do not cultivate it.

It is culture that brings out the full value of taste and gives it a chance to prove its worth simply by its application. The artist imposes a culture upon himself and ends by imposing it upon others. That is how tradition becomes established.

Tradition is entirely different from habit, even from an excellent habit, since habit is by definition an unconscious acquisition and tends to become mechanical, whereas tradition results from a conscious and deliberate acceptance. A real tradition is not the relic of a past that is irretrievably gone; it is a living force that animates and informs the present. In this sense the paradox which banteringly maintains that everything which is not tradition is plagiarism, is true. . . .

Far from implying the repetition of what has been, tradition presupposes the reality of what endures. It appears as an heirloom, a heritage that one receives on condition of making it bear fruit before passing it on to one's descendants.

Brahms was born sixty years after Beethoven. From the one to the other, and from every aspect, the distance is great; they do not dress the same way, but Brahms follows the tradition of Beethoven without borrowing one of his habiliments. For the borrowing of a method has nothing to do with observing a tradition. "A method is replaced: a tradition is carried forward in order to produce something new." Tradition thus assures the continuity of creation. The example that I have just cited does not constitute an exception but is one proof out of a hundred of a constant law. This sense of tradition which is a natural need must not be confused with the desire which the composer feels to affirm the kinship he finds across the centuries with some master of the past. [. . .]

A mode of composition that does not assign itself limits becomes pure fantasy. The effects it produces may accidentally amuse but are not capable of being repeated. I cannot conceive of a fantasy that is repeated, for it can be repeated only to its detriment.

Let us understand each other in regard to this word fantasy. We are not using the word in the sense in which it is connected with a definite musical form, but in the acceptation which presupposes an abandonment of one's self to the caprices of imagination. And this presupposes that the composer's will is voluntarily paralyzed. For imagination is not only the mother of caprice but the servant and handmaiden of the creative will as well.

The creator's function is to sift the elements he receives from her, for human activity must impose limits upon itself. The more art is controlled, limited, worked over, the more it is free.

As for myself, I experience a sort of terror when, at the moment of setting to work and finding myself before the infinitude of possibilities that present themselves, I have the feeling that everything is permissible to me. If everything is permissible to me, the best and the worst; if nothing offers me any resistance, then any effort is inconceivable, and I cannot use anything as a basis, and consequently every undertaking becomes futile.

Will I then have to lose myself in this abyss of freedom? To what shall I cling in order to escape the dizziness that seizes me before the virtuality of this infinitude? However, I shall not succumb. I shall overcome my terror and shall be reassured by the thought that I have the seven notes of the scale and its chromatic intervals at my disposal, that strong and weak accents are within my reach, and that in all of these I possess solid and concrete elements which offer me a field of experience just as vast as the upsetting and dizzy infinitude that had just frightened me. It is into this field that I shall sink my roots, fully convinced that combinations which have at their disposal twelve sounds in each octave and all possible rhythmic varieties promise me riches that all the activity of human genius will never exhaust.

What delivers me from the anguish into which an unrestricted freedom plunges me is the fact that I am always able to turn immediately to the concrete things that are here in question. I have no use for a theoretic freedom. Let me have something finite, definite—matter that can lend itself to my operation only insofar as it is commensurate with my possibilities. And such matter presents itself to me together with its limitations. I must in turn impose mine upon it. So here we are, whether we like it or not, in the realm of necessity. And yet which of us has ever heard talk of art as other than a realm of freedom? This sort of heresy is uniformly widespread because it is imagined that art is outside the bounds of ordinary activity. Well, in art as in everything else, one can build only upon a resisting foundation: whatever constantly gives way to pressure, constantly renders movement impossible.

My freedom thus consists in my moving about within the narrow frame that I have assigned myself for each one of my undertakings.

I shall go even further: my freedom will be so much the greater and more meaningful the more narrowly I limit my field of action and the more I surround myself with obstacles. Whatever diminishes constraint, diminishes strength. The more constraints one imposes, the more one frees one's self of the chains that shackle the spirit. [. . .]

AARON COPLAND

1900-1990

THE GIFTED LISTENER

1952

Aaron Copland was a pioneer of American music. Born in Brooklyn, New York, to Jewish immigrants from Poland and Lithuania, he studied at the music school for Americans at Fontainebleau under the tutelage of Nadia Boulanger in the 1920s. Among his most famous compositions are the ballets *Rodeo* (1942) and *Billy the Kid* (1938), and *Appalachian Spring* (1944), a work commissioned by the modern dance choreographer Martha Graham. Many are familiar with the Shaker hymn "Simple Gifts," which Copland incorporated into this ballet. His symphonies include *Lincoln Portrait* and *Fanfare for the Common Man*.

Copland was also an impresario of modern music concerts, founding the Copland-Sessions Concerts with Roger Sessions in 1928-31 and organizing the American Festivals of Contemporary Music at Saratoga Springs, New York, beginning in 1932. Copland scored many successful films, including *Of Mice and Men* (1938), *Our Town* (1940) and *The Heiress* (1948), for which he won an Academy Award.

His music is distinguished by its quintessentially American themes, its energy, and its elegance of expression. It has mirrored the times: in the 1920s, jazz; in the Great Depression of the 1930s,

American folk music, old hymns, and cowboy songs, all created for the large radio audiences; and in the 1950s, abandoning the American pastoral ideal, his work reflected the new tonalities and techniques of techniques of Arnold Schoenberg.

In "The Gifter Listener," Copland extends the concept of musical giftedness beyond the composer and the performer to listeners— non-musicians who can be absorbed into the experience and import of music by informed listening. Of equal importance is his insistence that live performance refuse to function as the "musical museum" and offer listeners new, surprising, and challenging pieces.

SOURCE

Copland, Aaron. 1952. "The Gifted Listener." In *Music and Imagination.* "Chapter One." Cambridge, MA: Harvard, 1972. 7-20.*

THE GIFTED LISTENER

The more I live the life of music the more I am convinced that it is the freely imaginative mind that is at the core of all vital music making and music listening. When Coleridge put down his famous phrase, "the sense of musical delight, with the power of producing it, is a gift of the imagination," he was referring, of course, to the musical delights of poetry. But it seems to me even more true when applied to the musical delights of music. An imaginative mind is essential to the creation of art in any medium, but it is even more essential in music precisely because music provides the broadest possible vista for the imagination since it is the freest, the most abstract, the least fettered of all the arts: no story content, no pictorial representation, no regularity of meter, no strict limitation of frame need hamper the intuitive functioning of the imaginative mind. In saying this I am not forgetting that music has its disciplines: its strict forms and regular rhythms, and even in some cases its programmatic content. Music as mathematics, music as architecture or as image, music in any static, seizable form has always held fascination for the lay mind. But as a musician, what fascinates me is the thought that by its very nature music invites imaginative treatment, and that the facts of music, so called, are only meaningful insofar as the imagination is given free play. It is for this reason that I wish to consider especially those facets of music that are open to the creative influences of the imagination.

Imagination in the listener—in the gifted listener—is what concerns us here. It is so often assumed that music's principal stumbling block is the backward listener that it might be instructive to contemplate for a change the qualities of the sensitive listener.

Listening is a talent, and like any other talent or gift, we possess it in varying degrees. I have found among music-lovers a marked tendency to underestimate and mistrust this talent, rather than to overestimate it. The reason for these feelings of inferiority are difficult to determine. Since there is no reliable way of measuring the gift for listening, there is no reliable way of reassuring those who misjudge themselves. I should say that there are two principal requisites for talented listening: first, the ability to open oneself up to musical experience; and secondly, the ability to evaluate critically that experience. Neither of these is possible without a certain native gift. Listening implies an inborn talent of some degree, which, again like any other talent, can be trained and developed. This talent has a certain "purity" about it. We exercise it, so to speak, for ourselves alone; there is nothing to be gained from it in a material sense. Listening is its own reward; there are no prizes to be won, no contests of creative listening. But I hold that person fortunate who has the gift, for there are few pleasures in art greater than the secure sense that one can recognize beauty when one comes upon it.

When I speak of the gifted listener I am thinking of the nonmusician primarily, of the listener who intends to retain his amateur status. It is the thought of just such a listener that excites the composer in me. I know, or I think I know, how the professional musician will react to music. But with the amateur it is different; one never can be sure how he will react. Nothing really tells him what he should be hearing, no treatise or chart or guide can ever sufficiently pull together the various strands of a complex piece of music—only the inrushing floodlight of one's own imagination can do that. Recognizing the beautiful in an abstract art like music partakes somewhat of a minor miracle; each time it happens I remain slightly incredulous.

The situation of the professional musician as listener, especially of the composer, is rather different. He is an initiate. Like the minister before the altar his contact with the Source gives him an inner understanding of music's mysteries, and a greater familiarity in their presence. He possesses a dual awareness: on the one hand of the inscrutable mystery that gives certain common tones meaning; on the other of the human travail that enters into every creation. It is an awareness that no layman can hope to share. There is a nicety of balance in the musician's awareness that escapes the musical amateur. The amateur may be either too reverent or too carried away; too much in love with the separate section or too limited in his enthusiasm for a single school or composer. Mere professionalism, however, is not at all a guarantee of intelligent listening. Executant ability, even of the highest order, is no guarantee of instinct in judgment. The sensitive amateur, just because he lacks the prejudices and preconceptions of the professional musician, is sometimes a surer guide to the true quality of a piece of music. The ideal listener, it seems to me, would combine the preparation of the trained professional with the innocence of the intuitive amateur.

All musicians, creators and performers alike, think of the gifted listener as a key figure in the musical universe. I should like, if I can, to track down the source of this gift, and to consider the type of musical experience which is most characteristically his.

The ideal listener, above all else, possesses the ability to lend himself to the power of music. The power of music to move us is some thing quite special as an artistic phenomenon. My intention is not to delve into its basis in physics—my scientific equipment is much too rudimentary—but rather to concentrate on its emotional overtones. Contrary to what you might expect, I do not hold that music has the power to move us beyond any of the other arts. To me the theater has this power in a more naked form, a power that is almost too great. The sense of being overwhelmed by the events that occur on a stage sometimes brings with it a kind of resentment at the ease with which the dramatist plays upon my emotions. I feel like a keyboard on which he can improvise any tune he pleases. There is no resisting, my emotions have the upper hand, but my mind keeps protesting: by what right does the playwright do this to me? Not infrequently I have been moved to tears in the theater; never at music. Why never at music? Because there is something about music that keeps its distance even at the moment that it engulfs us. It is at the same time outside and away from us and inside and part of us. In one sense it dwarfs us, and in another we master it. We are led on and on, and yet in some strange way we never lose control. It is the very nature of music to give us the distillation of sentiments, the essence of experience transfused and heightened and expressed in such fashion that we may contemplate it at the same instant that we are swayed by it. When the gifted listener lends himself to the power of music, he gets both the event and the idealization of the "event"; he is inside the "event," so to speak, even though the music keeps what Edward Bullough rightly terms its "psychical distance."

What another layman, Paul Claudel, wrote about the listener seems to me to have been well observed. "We absorb him into the concert," Claudel says. "He is no longer anything but expectation and attention . . . ." I like that, because expectancy denotes the ability to lend oneself, to lend oneself eagerly to the thing heard, while attention bespeaks an interest in the thing said, a preoccupation with an understanding of what is being heard. I've watched the absorbed listener in the concert hall numerous times, half absorbed myself in trying to fathom the exact nature of his response. This is an especially fascinating pastime when the listener happens to be listening to one's own music. At such times I am concerned not so much with whatever pleasure the music may be giving, but rather with the question whether I am being understood.

Parenthetically, I should like to call attention to a curious bit of artist psychology: the thought that my music might, or might not give pleasure to a considerable number of music-lovers has never particularly stirred me. At times I have been vigorously hissed, at other times as vigorously applauded; in both circumstances I remain comparatively unmoved. Why should that be? Probably because I feel in some way detached from the end result. The writing of it gives me pleasure, especially when it seems to come off; but once out of my hands the work takes on a life of its own. In a similar way I can imagine a father who takes no personal credit for the beauty of a much admired daughter. This must mean that the artist (or father) considers himself an unwitting instrument whose satisfaction is not to produce beauty, but simply to produce.

But to return to my absorbed listener. The interesting question, then, is not whether he is deriving pleasure, but rather, whether he is understanding the import of the music. And if he has understood, then I must ask: *what* has he understood?

As you see, I am warily approaching one of the thorniest problems in aesthetics, namely, the meaning of music. The semanticist who investigates the meaning of words, or even the meaning of meaning, has an easy time of it by comparison with the hardy soul who ventures forth in quest of music's meaning. A composer might easily side-step the issue; aesthetics is not his province. His gift is one of expression, not of theoretic speculation. Still the problem persists, and the musical practitioner ought to have something to say that could be of interest to the mind that philosophizes about art.

I have seldom read a statement about the meaning of music, if seriously expressed, that did not seem to me to have some basis in truth. From this I conclude that music is many-sided and can be approached from many different angles. Basically, however, two opposing theories have been advanced by the aestheticians as to music's significance. One is that the meaning of music, if there is any meaning, must be sought in the music itself, for music has no extramusical connotation; and the other is that music is a language without a dictionary whose symbols are interpreted by the listener according to some unwritten esperanto of the emotions. The more I consider these two theories the more it seems to me that they are bound together more closely than is generally supposed, and for this reason: music as a symbolic language of psychological and expressive value can only be made evident through "music itself," while music which is said to mean only itself sets up patterns of sound which inevitably suggest some kind of connotation in the mind of the listener, even if only to connote the joy of music making for its own sake. Whichever it may be, pure or impure, an object or a language, I cannot get it out of my head that all composers derive their impulse from a similar drive. I cannot be persuaded that Bach, when he penned the *Orgelbüchlein,* thought he was creating an object of "just notes," or that Tchaikovsky in composing *Swan Lake* was wallowing in nothing but uncontrolled emotion. Notes can be manipulated as if they were objects, certainly—they can be made to do exercises, like a dancer. But it is only when these exerciselike patterns of sound take on meaning that they become music. There is historical justification for the weighted emphasis sometimes on one side, sometimes on the other, of this controversy. During periods when music became too cool and detached, too scholastically conventionalized, composers were enjoined to remember its origin as a language of the emotions, and when, during the last century, it became overly symptomatic of the inner *Sturm und Drang* of personalized emotion, composers were cautioned not to forget that music is a pure art of a self-contained beauty. This perennial dichotomy was neatly summarized by Eduard Hanslick, standard bearer for the "pure music" defenders of the nineteenth century, when he wrote that "an inward singing, and not an inward feeling, prompts a gifted person to compose a musical piece." But my point is that this dichotomous situation has no reality to a functioning composer.

Singing *is* feeling to a composer, and the more intensely felt the singing, the purer the expression.

The precise meaning of music is a question that should never have been asked, and in any event will never elicit a precise answer. It is the literary mind that is disturbed by this imprecision. No true music-lover is troubled by the symbolic character of musical speech; on the contrary, it is this very imprecision that intrigues and activates the imagination. Whatever the semanticists of music may uncover, composers will blithely continue to articulate "subtle complexes of feeling that language cannot even name, let alone set forth." This last phrase I came upon in Susanne Langer's cogent chapter, "On Significance in Music." Reviewing the various theories of musical significance from Plato to Schopenhauer and from Roger Fry to recent psychoanalytical speculation, Mrs. Langer concludes: "Music is our myth of the inner life—a young, vital, and meaningful myth, of recent inspiration and still in its 'vegetative' growth." Musical myths—even more than folk myths—are subject to highly personalized interpretations, and there is no known method of guaranteeing that my interpretation will be a truer one than yours. I can only recommend reliance on one's own instinctive comprehension of the unverbalized symbolism of musical sounds.

All this is of minor concern to the gifted listener—primarily intent, as he should be, on the enjoyment of music. Without theories and without preconceived notions of what music ought to be, he lends himself as a sentient human being to the power of music. What often surprises me is the basically primitive nature of this relationship. From self-observation and from observing audience reaction I would be inclined to say that we all listen on an elementary plane of musical consciousness. I was startled to find this curious phrase in Santayana concerning music: "the most abstract of arts," he remarks, "serves the dumbest emotions." Yes, I like this idea that we respond to music from a primal and almost brutish level—dumbly, as it were, for on that level we are firmly grounded. On that level, whatever the music may be, we experience basic reactions such as tension and release, density and transparency, a smooth or angry surface, the music's swellings and subsidings, its pushing forward or hanging back, its length, its speed, its thunders and whisperings—and a thousand other psychologically based reflections of our physical life of movement and gesture, and our inner, subconscious mental life. That is fundamentally the way we all hear music—gifted and ungifted alike—and all the analytical, historical, textual material on or about the music heard, interesting though it may be, cannot—and I venture to say should not—alter that fundamental relationship.

I stress this point, not so much because the layman is likely to forget it, but because the professional musician tends to lose sight of it. This does not signify, by any means, that I do not believe in the possibility of the refinement of musical taste. Quite the contrary. I am convinced that the higher forms of music imply a listener whose musical taste has been cultivated either through listening or through training or both. On a more modest level refinement in musical taste begins with the ability to distinguish subtle nuances of feeling. Anyone can tell the difference between a sad piece and a joyous one. The talented listener recognizes not merely the joyous quality of the piece, but also the specific shade of joyousness— whether it be troubled joy, delicate joy, carefree joy, hysterical joy, and so forth. I add "and so forth" advisedly, for it covers an infinitude of shadings that cannot be named, as I have named these few, because of music's incommensurability with language.

An important requirement for subtle listening is a mature understanding of the natural differences of musical expression to be anticipated in music of different epochs. An awareness of musical history should prepare the talented listener to distinguish stylistic differences, for example, in the expression of joyousness. Ecstatic joy as you find it in the music of Scriabin ought not to be sought for in the operas of Gluck, or even of Mozart. A sense of being "at home" in the world of the late fifteen hundreds makes one aware of what not to seek in the music of that period; and in like fashion, being "at home" in the musical idioms of the late baroque period will immediately suggest parallelisms with certain aspects of contemporary music. To approach all music in the vain hope that it will soothe one in the lush harmonies of the late nineteenth century is a common error of many present-day music-lovers.

One other gift is needed, this one perhaps the most difficult and at the same time the most essential: the gift of being able to see all around the structural framework of an extended piece of music. Next to fathoming the meanings of music, I find this point the most obscure in our understanding of the auditory faculty. Exactly in what manner we sort out and add up and realize in our own minds the impressions that can only be gained singly in the separate moments of the music's flowing past us is surely one of the rarer manifestations of consciousness. Here if anywhere the imagination must take fire. Sometimes it seems to me that I do not at all comprehend how other people put together a piece in their mind's ear. It is a difficult feat in any of the arts, especially those that exist in point of time, such as the drama or fiction. But there the chronology of events usually guides the spectator or reader. The structural organization of the dance is somewhat analogous to that of music, but here too, despite the fluidity of movement each separate moment presents a picture, not unlike that of the painter's canvas. But in music where there is no chronology of events, no momentary picture, nothing to "hang on to," as it were, it is the imagination and the imagination alone that has the power of balancing the combined impressions made by themes, rhythms, tone colors, harmonies, textures, dynamics, developments, contrasts.

I don't mean to make this more mysterious than it is. To draw a graph of a particular musical structure is generally possible, and may be of some help to the cultivated listener; but we do not usually wish to listen to music with diagrams in our laps. And if we did, I question the wisdom of such an idea, for too great concentration on the purely formal outlines of a piece of music might distract from free association with other elements in the piece.

No, however one turns the problem, we come back always to the curious gift that permits us to sum up the complex impressions of a piece of absolute music so that the incidents of the harmonic and melodic and textural flow of the work as it streams past us result finally in a unified and total image of the work's essence. Our success in this venture depends first on the clarity of the composer's conception, and second, on a delicate balance of heart and brain that makes it possible for us to be moved at the same instant that we retain the sensation of our emotional responses, using it for balanced judgment later in other and different moments of response. Here, most of all, the listener must fall back upon his own gift; here, especially, analysis and experience and imagination must combine to give us the assurance that we have made our own the composer's complex of ideas.

Now, perhaps, is the moment to return to one of my principal queries: *what* has the listener understood? If anything was understood, then it must have been whatever it was the composer tried to communicate. Were you absorbed? Was your attention held? That, then, was it; for what you heard were patterns of sounds that represent the central core of the composer's being—or that aspect of it reflected in the particular work in question. One part of everything he is and knows is implicit in each composer's single work, and it is that central fact of his being that he hopes he has communicated.

It occurs to me to wonder: are you a better person for having heard a great work of art? Are you morally a better person, I mean? In the largest sense, I suppose you are, but in the more immediate sense, I doubt it. I doubt it because I have never seen it demonstrated. What happens is that a masterwork awakens in us reactions of a spiritual order that are already in us, only waiting to be aroused. When Beethoven's music exhorts us to "be noble," "be compassionate," "be strong," he awakens moral ideas that are already within us. His music cannot persuade: it makes evident. It does not shape conduct: it is itself the exemplification of a particular way of looking at life. A concert is not a sermon. It is a performance— a reincarnation of a series of ideas implicit in the work of art.

As a composer and a musical citizen I am concerned with one more problem of the gifted listener: one that is special to our own period. Despite the attractions of phonograph and radio, which are considerable, true music-lovers insist on hearing live performances of music. An unusual and disturbing situation has gradually become all-pervasive at public performances of music: the universal preponderance of old music on concert programs.

This unhealthy state of affairs, this obsession with old music, tends to make all music listening safe and unadventurous since it deals so largely in the works of the accepted masters. Filling our halls with familiar sounds induces a sense of security in our audiences; they are gradually losing all need to exercise freely their own musical judgement. Over and over again the same limited number of bona fide, guaranteed masterpieces are on display; by inference, therefore, it is mainly these works that are worth our notice. This narrows considerably in the minds of a broad public the very conception of how varied musical experience may be, and puts all lesser works in a false light. It conventionalizes programs, obviously, and overemphasizes the interpreter's role, for only through seeking out new "readings" is it possible to repeat the same works year after year. Most pernicious of all, it leaves a bare minimum of wall space for the showing of the works of new composers, without which the supply of future writers of masterworks is certain to dry up.

This state of affairs is not merely a local or national one—it pervades the musical life of every country that professes love for western music. Nine-tenths of the time a program performed in a concert hall in Buenos Aires provides an exact replica of what goes on in a concert hall of London or of Tel-Aviv. Music is no longer merely an international language, it is an international commodity.

This concentration on masterworks is having a pronounced influence on present-day musical life. A solemn wall of respectability surrounds the haloed masterpieces of music and deadens their impact. They are written about too often out of a sticky sentiment steeped in conventionality. It is both exhilarating and depressing to think of them: exhilarating to think that great masses of people are put in daily contact with them, have the possibility of truly taking sustenance from them; and depressing to watch these same classics used to snuff out all liveliness, all immediacy from the contemporary musical scene.

Reverence for the classics in our time has been turned into a form of discrimination against all other music. Professor Edward Dent spoke his mind on this same subject when he came to the United States in 1936 to accept an honorary doctorate from Harvard University. Reverence for the classics, in his opinion, was traceable to the setting up of a "religion of music" intrinsic to the ideas of Beethoven and promulgated by Richard Wagner. "In the days of Handel and Mozart," he said, "nobody wanted old music; all audiences demanded the newest opera or the newest concerto, as we now naturally demand the newest play and the newest novel. If in those two branches of imaginative production we habitually demand the newest and the latest, why is it that in music we almost invariably demand what is old-fashioned and out of date, while the music of the present day is often received with positive hostility. All music, even church music," he added, "was 'utility music,' music for the particular moment."

This situation, remarked upon fifteen years ago by Professor Dent, is now intensified through the role played by commercial interests in the purveying of music. Professor Dent was himself aware of that fact, for he pointed out then that "the religious outlook on music is an affair of business as well as of devotion." The big public is now frightened of investing in any music that doesn't have the label "Masterwork" stamped on it. Thus along with the classics themselves we are given the "light classics," the "jazz classics," and even "modern classics." Radio programs, record advertisements, adult appreciation courses—all focus attention on a restricted list of the musical great in such a way that there appears to be no other raison *d'etre* for music. In the same way musical references in books harp upon the names of a few musical giants. The final irony is that the people who are persuaded to concern themselves only with the best in music are the very ones who would have most difficulty in recognizing a real masterpiece when they heard one.

The simple truth is that our concert halls have been turned into musical museums—auditory museums of a most limited kind. Our musical era is sick in that respect—our composers invalids who exist on the fringe of musical society, and our listeners impoverished through a relentless repetition of the same works signed by a handful of sanctified names.

Our immediate concern is the effect all this has on the listener of unusual gifts. A narrow and limited repertoire in the concert hall results in a narrow and limited musical experience. No true musical enthusiast wants to be confined to a few hundred years of musical history. He naturally seeks out every type of musical experience; his intuitive understanding gives him a sense of assurance whether he is confronted with the recently deciphered treasures of Gothic art, or the quick wit of a Chabrier or a Bizet, or the latest importation of Italian dodecaphonism.[1] A healthy musical curiosity and a broad musical experience sharpens the critical faculty of even the most talented amateur.

All this has bearing on our relation to the classic masters also. To listen to music in a familiar style and to listen freshly, ignoring what others have said or written and testing its values for oneself, is a mark of the intelligent listener. The classics themselves must be reinterpreted in terms of our own period if we are to hear them anew and "keep their perennial humanity living and capable of assimilation." But in order to do that, we must have a balanced musical diet that permits us to set off our appraisals of the old masters against the varied and different musical manifestations of more recent times. For it is only in the light of the whole musical experience that the classics become most meaningful.

The dream of every musician who loves his art is to involve gifted listeners everywhere as an active force in the musical community. The attitude of each individual listener, especially the gifted listener, is the principal resource we have in bringing to fruition the immense musical potentialities of our own time.

---

[1] Music using the 12-tone scale

LEONARD BERNSTEIN

1918-1990

THE JOY OF MUSIC

1959

Leonard Bernstein is perhaps best known for composing the musical *West Side Story* (the re-telling of the Romeo and Juliet story set in a New York slum, 1957). The film version of the musical won five Academy Awards (1961). One of America's foremost music conductors, composers, and authors on the philosophy of music and composition, Leonard Bernstein studied piano at the New England Conservatory of Music and graduated from Harvard University in 1939. He continued to study piano, conducting, and orchestration at the Curtis Institute of Music in Philadelphia; his first permanent conducting post was as an assistant conductor for the New York Philharmonic in 1943.

A cultural force, Bernstein was a gifted teacher, a passionate arts advocate, and a politically committed American. In 1957, as musical director of the New York Philharmonic (the first American named to that post), Bernstein began his annual, televised Young Peoples' Concerts. Throughout the 1960s and 1970s he served as a guest conductor for orchestras world-wide, as a composer, as an advocate for American composers, including his friend Aaron Copland, and as a humanitarian, especially for Jewish causes. He premiered his *Fanfare* at the Inaugural Gala for President John F.

Kennedy (1961), and in 1963, led the Kennedy memorial concert with a performance of Mahler's *Symphony No. 2* (Resurrection). He refused to accept the National Medal of the Arts from President George H.W. Bush in protest of the revocation of an NEA grant for a New York exhibition on AIDS (1990). Following his death, the corner of Broadway and 65th Street in New York City was renamed "Leonard Bernstein Place."

Leonard Bernstein, in the "Introduction" of the volume excerpted here, speaks of having talked about music with friends, colleagues, teachers, students, and others, and of the "doomed" efforts to "explain the unique phenomenon of human reaction to organized sound" (11). *The Joy of Music* presents a compilation of conversations with imaginary characters on American society's philosophy of music and how a composer/conductor thinks about music. The dialogue that follows fancifully explores the persistent tension Bernstein must have felt between putting his talent into composing symphonies or Broadway musicals. In the long run, Bernstein created new forms to serve American cultural enthusiasms.

SOURCE

Bernstein, Leonard. 1959. "Whatever Happened to That Great American Symphony?" In *The Joy of Music*. New York: Anchor, 1994. 40-51.*

WHATEVER HAPPENED TO THAT GREAT AMERICAN SYMPHONY?

(The following, not properly a conversation, is an exchange of documents between L.B. and Broadway Producer, henceforth known as B.P., a man who interests himself, curiously enough, in some facets of art generally unknown to his calling. A born gentleman of average producer height; chin framed by a luxurious Persian-lamb collar which

---

*   Reprinted by permission of the Joy Harris Literary Agency, Inc. New York, on behalf of the author, Leonard Bernstein *adorns his fifty-per-cent-cashmere evening coat; a man with an emerald tie pin and a wise, sweaty look—a man, in short, who carries his five feet two with pride and power. LB)*

I. Via Western Union

B.P.
HOTEL GORBEDUC
NEW YORK
    VERY SORRY CANNOT ACCEPT KIND OFFER SHOW BASED BURTON'S ANATOMY MELANCHOLY SPLENDID IDEA WISH YOU ALL LUCK WITH IT REGRET UNABLE BUT DEEPLY INVOLVED WRITING NEW SYMPHONY GREETINGS

L.B.

II. Via Post

L.B.
Steinway Hall
New York City
DEAR L.B.:
    My associates and I were very much disappointed to receive your refusal by wire yesterday of our offer to collaborate with us, and with many other artists of outstanding merit and importance, on our new project for this season. I have long felt (and now feel corroborated by my associates in that opinion) that Burton's *Anatomy of Melancholy* would one day serve as the basis of a great work in the musical theater. We think that you are just the man to write the music for it, thereby enriching our stage which this season cries for such a work. Instead you tell us that you are writing a new symphony, a commendable enough enterprise. But if you will allow me to take a few minutes of your time, I should like to point out a few facts which you may not have taken into account in making your decision.

I begin with a question: why? Why continue to write symphonies in America for a public which does not care one way or the other about them? Can you honestly name me two or three people in all America who actually *care* whether you or anybody else ever writes another symphony or not? Do not answer this too hastily, or too defensively. The more you consider the question, the clearer will come the answer: that nobody, with the possible exception of some other composers and some critics who live by denouncing or flattering new works, will be any the sorrier if you or any of your symphonic colleagues never writes a symphony again. There seems to me to be no historical necessity for symphonies in our time: perhaps our age does not express itself truly through the symphonic form; I really am not in a position to know. I am a simple man, and know mainly through intuition whatever it is I know. I think I have my fingers on the pulse of the people, and believe me, L.B., it is not a symphonic pulse that I feel.

So there you are, writing music for which there is no historical necessity, probably; for which there is no public demand, certainly; and from which, if you will pardon me, there is no economic gain. Perhaps now you can see more clearly why I asked: why? Now let me ask: why not? Why not give of your talents to that sector of musical art in America where there is hot, live, young blood—the theater? Here you will find the public waiting for you, and you will be complying with the demands of history. All art, in all times, I believe, has been created to meet a public or private demand, whether it be the art of building Gothic cathedrals, or of painting the portrait of a wealthy patron, or of writing a play for the Elizabethan public, or of composing a Mass. Or, if you will again pardon me, the art of writing a symphony. Hadyn and Mozart and Brahms surely didn't write their symphonies in a vacuum; their symphonies were expected of them. Nobody today really *expects* a symphony of anybody. Our American composers have an obligation to the theater, which is alive and which needs them. Won't you think seriously about it again?

Faithfully,
B.P.

P.S. How had you planned for this new symphony to feed, clothe and house your charming wife and baby (to whom warmest personal regards)?

III. Via Post

B.P.
Hotel Gorbeduc
New York City
DEAR B.P.:

I have read and reread your most interesting letter of yesterday, and I am impressed. I say *impressed* rather than *convinced,* since I cannot honestly report a change of heart as a result. But I have rarely met a producer operating in the Broadway area who has given so much sincere and deeply felt thought to a situation which basically does not concern his immediate livelihood. I am further impressed with your legal style, which is persuasive to a point where, if I were not more closely acquainted than you with the facts of the case (which is only natural), I might yield to your arguments. But the facts stand, and I feel obliged to report them to you.

There has never in history, by statistical record, been so great an interest in the symphony and in the symphony orchestra as is at this moment manifested in the United States. There are orchestras everywhere, in every small city, in every university and high school, in even some of our most provincial areas. How can you speak of "no public demand" when the latest figures of the League of Symphony Orchestras shows xx orchestras of major proportions now operating in the United States, as against xx orchestras of similar size in 19xx? The League further reports xx orchestras of smaller proportions now professionally active. Everywhere there have arisen festivals to which the public flocks in unprecedented numbers—and they are festivals which emphasize contemporary music almost as much as the standard repertory. Summer concerts have became as great an attraction as canoeing once was; and the winter seasons of our major orchestras are enjoying a lively increase in both attendance and interest. Community concert services send out great numbers of artists to cities large and small from coast to coast, where they are heard by audiences that a decade ago would not have dreamed of attending a concert.

I am sorry to bore you with statistics this way, but these facts are a matter of record. And think of all the new works being commissioned by such agencies as the Louisville Orchestra. xx works this year alone! And then think of the prizes, fellowships, awards of various kinds, all of which encourage the writing of concert music. Think of the enormous increase in the sale of records: why, it amounts almost to a craze. No, you cannot say that the public is indifferent to concert music. As to your reference to historical necessity, I simply do not understand you. And when you speak of economic gain, you are right; but economic considerations cannot enter into this area. One is an artist by necessity, and there are other ways of making money.

As you know, I love to write for the theater: I have done it before, and hope to do it often again. But this is a moment when other things come first. Thank you again for having asked me and for having taken the trouble to write.

Sincerely,
L.B.

IV. VIA POST

L.B.
Yaddo*
Saratoga Springs, New York
Dear L.B.:

Forgive me for breaking into your privacy again, but in the week that has elapsed since I received your letter I have given a lot of thought to the subject we have been discussing, and have even done some reading to back me up. Besides, your letter was so

---

*   An artist's retreat

incredibly solemn, and, were it not for its obvious sincerity, so
dull, if you will pardon me, that I am intrigued. I cannot believe
that a young fellow like you, grown up in America, with the sense
of fun that you have exhibited in some of your works, can possibly
be such a fuddy-duddy. This letter is written partly to find out,
and partly to acquaint you with my more recent thoughts about
the symphonic form. I have given up the idea of trying to persuade
you to do our show with us, and we are now negotiating with
another composer. But you have awakened in me, by your refusal
and your reasons for refusing, a real interest in this whole subject.
I now have what might almost be called a theory. I explained it
yesterday to our mutual friend P., who was in town for a day, and
he found it silly. But what can you expect of a poet? As you know,
he is also up at Yaddo for a month, working on his new volume,
Greaves of Brass, and that's how I knew where to write you. Please
avoid discussing my theory with him when you see him; his sense
of historical necessity is appalling, if I can judge by the two poems
from *Greaves of Brass* that he showed me yesterday.

Well, then, the theory. All music must begin in the theater,
historically speaking. Does that amaze you? Just think about it.
The origins of music are mostly folklore, comprising songs and
dances of prayer, of work, of celebration, of love. This means that
music first arises attached to words and ideas. There is no folk
music, to my knowledge, that is abstract. It is music for working
to, or for dancing to, or for singing words to. It is always about
something. Then, as it develops, music becomes more sophisticated,
more complicated; but it is still attached to concepts, as it is in the
theater. Where music really grew up was in the church, wasn't it?
The greatest theater of them all! (If ever there was theater music in
the truest and best sense it was simple plain-chant.) Now we find
little operas beginning to emerge, in Italy and in Germany and in
Austria. The little operas (or masques, or singspiels, or whatever
they were) become bigger operas—and we have Mozart. While in
the church, little motets have grown into large requiems and
cantatas. Now is the moment when the big switch can happen,
and not until this moment. Now musical idioms have become

familiar; and the procedures of Western music are enough alike so that the music can be *separated* from the words or the ideas or the concepts—that is, from the theater—and can exist for the audience in its own right. Now that there is a Mozart opera, there can also be a Mozart symphony. (But never forget that the symphony, as my books tell me, came from the opera overture!) And now that there are Bach Passions, there can also be Bach preludes and fugues. (But remember that the preludes and fugues were first of all reverie-pieces used in the church service!) In short, the audience had grown up *with* the music in the theater, and had reached the point where they could relate to the music *without* the theater. Their ears were ready for abstract sound: F-sharps and E-flats had become in themselves interesting and moving, without benefit of words to tell why they ought to be. But it had taken the audience a long time to reach this point.

Does all this sound like nonsense to you? I hope not; I'm banking on that solemnity of yours. But now to the meat of the theory.

The point I want to make with all my might is that America right now seems to me to be, musically, just about where Germany was around the seventeenth century. Deep in the singspiel. (We mustn't talk about present-day church music: that must be traditional, and has all been inherited.) But our secular music is just about where German music was fifty years before Mozart. Only our singspiels are called *Oklahoma!* and *Can-Can.* This is a period we must pass through before we can arrive at a real American symphonic form, or a real American style of whatever kind of concert music. It may not be the symphony as we have known it: we may produce something very different. But the musical language it will speak must first be created in our theater; then one day it can be divorced from "meaning" and stand alone, abstract. Do you see what I mean? For all our technical mastery and sophistication we are not really ready yet to produce our own concert music. As a result, all the stuff that is being turned out by the mile every day for concert performance in American halls is really European, and *old* European at that, with perhaps some American spice added by way of cowboy tunes or blues harmonies or jazz rhythms. But the music remains essentially European, because the whole notion of the symphonic form is a German notion, and don't let anybody tell you anything else. All the Russian symphonies are really German ones with vodka substituted for beer; and Franck's is German with some cornets making the difference; and Liszt's are German with nothing making the difference, and so are Elgar's and Grieg's and Dvořák's. Whatever national touches have been added, it's all German deep down, because the line of the symphony is a straight one smack from Mozart to Mahler.

Now here we are, remember, a brand-new country, comparatively speaking, a baby only a hundred and seventy-five years old. Which is nothing at all when you think of the old empires that produced that straight line I just mentioned. And actually we have been writing music in this country for only fifty years, and half of that fifty years the music has been borrowed clean out of the pockets of Brahms and Company. Of course we have the disadvantage here of having been born already grown up, so we don't start with folk dances and prayers for rain. We started with the leavings of the European development, handed to us on an old cracked dish. But then, we have an advantage after all: we have jazz. Which is the beginning of some other straight line which will grow here as certainly as the symphonic line grew out of another folk-strain for about a hundred years in Germany. Whatever jazz is, it's our own folk music, naïve, sophisticated, and exciting. And out of it has been born something we call the musical comedy. Well, 175 years isn't very long for that to have happened (and it really took only the last fifty years) compared to the centuries it took for the singspiel to arrive. And here we are at the point of building that singspiel into real opera—or, in our terms, developing *Pal Joey* into whatever American music is going to become. We are all ready and waiting for the Mozart to come along and just simply do it. That's why I'm in the producing business: I want to be there when it happens, if I live that long. I'm taking bids on the new Mozart. Any comers?

Well, there you have it. Very rough, not really thought out, but as plain as day to me. What I would love to make plain as day to you is the difference that arises out of all this between Europe and America as they relate to concert music. A new Brahms symphony to a Viennese of that period was of consuming interest to him: it caused endless speculation about what it would turn out to be, how it would differ from the last one, and all the rest, just as we speculate now about a forthcoming Rodgers-Hammerstein show. It made table-talk the next morning; it was everybody's concern; it was part of daily living, the air breathed, food taken. As a result, the Viennese or German of today has inherited some of that possessiveness about the Brahms music: it is almost as though he had written it himself. The same is true of the relation between Italians and Italian opera. But in America the listener cannot share these feelings, no matter how wildly he loves the music of Brahms or Verdi, and no matter how much talk he makes about music being a universal language. There will always be the element of the museum about this repertory for him—the revered classic, always slightly remote. It can never be his private property, so to speak. And since he doesn't give a damn about whether anyone is writing new symphonies or not, there is no real vitality for him in our concert life, except the vitality of a visit to the museum. Q.E.D.

This has been a really long one, and I hope you will forgive my going on and on. But I was excited about this when it occurred to me and I wanted you to hear it all right away, even if you are trying to write that long, useless piece up there in your retreat. My best to P., and whatever you do don't let him talk you into setting *Greaves of Brass* to music. You're being abstract now, remember; you're committed.

Faithfully,
B.P.

V. Via Air Mail

B.P.
Hotel Gorbeduc
New York City
DEAR B.P.:

It is a month since I had your last long, astonishing letter, and I apologize for my lateness in answering; but I have been to Yaddo and back to New York and then here to Milan all rather quickly. I had to suspend work on my symphony temporarily to fill this engagement conducting at La Scala, and now that the rehearsals and first performance are over I finally have a chance to answer you.

I must admit that I see to some extent what you mean about the sense of possessiveness toward music. Here in Milan people are still spending their time and energy at parties and luncheons arguing loudly about which is the greater opera, *Rigoletto* or *Trovatore*. As though it had all been written yesterday, hot off the presses. These Italians (or at least these Milanese) really own that music; and as you say, they seem to think they have written it all themselves. And you are right when you say that the wildest music-lover in the States can never relate that closely and familiarly to the same music. I am reminded of people at similar parties and luncheons in New York who will talk for hours about the relative merits of two hit musical shows, and even get excited or angry or hurt as they attack or defend them. All that part of your letter is perfectly true.

But I must take issue with your historical survey. It all sounds so easy and slick as you put it; and I admire you enormously for going into books and digging out all those facts and making them into ideas. Perhaps your main idea has some validity, but there are remarkable holes in your reasoning. What of the Frescobaldi *ricercare*, and the whole seventeenth-century school of organ music? What of Froberger and Pachelbel, who preceded Bach? Oh, all right, I'm being solemn and dull again, and I won't go into a lot of boring musicology. But you don't say the most obvious fact: that even if America is now in a period analogous to the singspiel period in Germany, she is at the same time equipped with the fore-knowledge of the next 250 years. What a difference that makes, after all! Don't you see that the great development of German music was dependent on its very naïveté in its early stages? American composers can never be that naïve now, writing as they are after the world has already known Mozart and Strauss and Debussy and Schönberg. Perhaps they are condemned after all to be epigonous, and to follow in the line handed them by an already overdeveloped Europe. It may not be so exciting to compose now as it must have been in 1850; perhaps this is all very sad, but perhaps it is true. And anyway, what would you have all these serious American composers do? Go *en masse* into the shoe business? They are writing out of some sort of inner necessity, so there most be a real validity to it, whether or not it is explainable by your new theory.

I have a matinee today and so I must leave this and run to the theater. How is your show coming? Have you found a composer yet? I wish you luck and hope that whoever finally writes it will turn out to be your Mozart, in spades.

Sincerely,
L.B.

VI. VIA TRANSATLANTIC CABLE

LB
SCALA
MILANO
    SHOE BUSINESS GOOD IDEA LETTER FOLLOWS GREETINGS

BP

VII. VIA AIR MAIL

L.B.
Teatro alla Scala
Milano, Italy

Dear L.B.:
    Hooray! You are a dead duck! You have obviously been convinced of my theory, and that makes me very happy. Your letter clearly shows that you have no real, sensible rebuttal. Of course what I said was full of holes; what do you expect from a brand-new musicologist? What do I know about Pachbelbel and Frescobaldi and that other guy? But what I know I know on all twelves, and at

this point I am more certain than ever that I am right. Why, I went to the Philharmonic concert the other night, just to see what is happening in your thrilling concert world. There were empty seats everywhere. People were sleeping on all sides, some noisily, and I do not exclude one or two critics. It was all as dull as it could be, and the applause was polite and seemed intended more as something to start people's circulation going again after their nap than approval of the music. Dull, dull, dull! After the concert the audience shuffled out in a stupor, not talking much about it or about anything; and I shuffled to Sardi's for a double stinger. It was like waking up. The theater, the theater, on all sides: people arguing, recalling scenes and jokes with gales of laughter, people singing snatches of tunes to each other to prove some point, everyone alive. Alive, I tell you!

Sure, there are some American composers who will have to go on writing their symphonies which may get heard twice with indifference. They may even be geniuses. I wish them all the luck in the world, and I hope they make it. But I have a sneaky feeling that they will continue to do symphonies because they *can't* do music for the theater. Don't think it is so easy to be a theater composer! In some ways it's harder: there is a discipline of the stage. You're not your own boss; it is the whole work that counts. A composer of symphonies has all the notes in the rainbow before him: he can choose as he wishes; not the theater composer. He really has to *work*! A great theater composer is a rare thing: he must have the sense of timing of a Duse, a sense of when to go easy and when to lay it on, a preknowledge of what the audience will feel every second of the work. He must have lightness and weight, wit and sentiment, pathos and brilliance. He must know his craft and everyone else's as well. Don't disparage him. I listened to *Tosca* the other day, and what a wallop it gave me! That man knew theater. And that man does not exactly languish in dishonor.

I tell you again: what is alive and young and throbbing, with historic current in America is musical theater. And I tell you another thing: you know it as well as I do! You know in your heart that the real pieces of importance and interest to America now are not X's

Fourteenth Symphony and Y's Flute Soliloquy, but *Finian's Rainbow* and *Carousel* and maybe even *Wonderful Town,* though I doubt it, and *South Pacific.* And all your long lists of dead statistics and all your Pachelbels put together cannot make you feel otherwise.

I want to thank you for giving me the push to go out and investigate all this stuff. I have never been so glad or so proud to be a producer of musical theater on Broadway. We are going ahead with our show at full speed, as soon as we find the right composer, and I can't wait to begin. I want to be part of this big new line that is forming to the right in the musical history of America, and I want to watch it take its place in the musical history of the world.

Faithfully,

B.P.

VIII. VIA TRANSATLANTIC CABLE

B.P.
HOTEL GORBEDUC
NEW YORK
PLANS CHANGED HAVE DECIDED ACCEPT YOUR SHOW STILL DISAGREE HEARTILY YOUR THEORY HOME NEXT WEEK WARMEST REGARDS

LB

(NOVEMBER 1954)

ROGER SESSIONS

1896-1985

THE MUSICAL EXPERIENCE OF COMPOSER, PERFORMER, AND LISTENER

1950

Roger Sessions, a distinguished teacher and composer, entered Harvard University at 14 years old. There, he wrote for and edited the *Harvard Musical Review*, submitting articles that dealt with the important music of the day. After finishing graduate studies at Yale at the age of 20, he began a long and renowned teaching career with a position at Smith College. In 1925, he moved to Europe, living in Florence, Rome, and Berlin before returning to the US to teach at Princeton in the early 1930s. By that time, he had already collaborated with Aaron Copland in launching a series of concerts designed to promote younger American composers. Subsequently, he took teaching positions at Princeton and the University of California, Berkeley, before retiring in 1983 to accept a position with the Juilliard School in New York. He was awarded the Pulitzer Prize for his final composition, *Concerto for Orchestra*.

Roger Sessions is recognized primarily as a preeminent teacher of musical composition. While Stravinsky is among his early influences, his own compositions are noted for their melodic, vibrant, intense, and cohesive qualities, although they are considered technically challenging for both performer and listener. To Sessions, music is an experience of communication that demands a conscious effort on the part of both performer and listener. And Sessions, like Franz Boas, recognizes the fundamental aspect of the musical impulse in the human experience.

SOURCE

Sessions, Roger. 1950. "The Musical Impulse." In *The Musical Experience of Composer, Performer, and Listener.* Princeton, NJ: Princeton University Press, 1971. 3-20.*

THE MUSICAL EXPERIENCE OF COMPOSER, PERFORMER, AND LISTENER

The Musical Impulse

How shall we explain the power that men and women of all times have recognized in music, or account for the enormous importance they have ascribed to it? Why did primitive peoples endow it with supernatural force and create legends, persisting into times and places far from primitive, in which musicians of surpassing ability were able to tame wild beasts, to move stones, and to soften the hard hearts of gods, demons, and even human tyrants? Why have serious and gifted men—in imaginative force and intellectual mastery the equals of any that ever lived—why have such men at all periods devoted their lives to music and found in it a supremely satisfying medium of expression?

Music, of all the arts, seems to be the most remote from the ordinary concerns and preoccupations of people; of all things created by man, its utility, as that word is generally understood, is least easy to demonstrate. Yet it is considered among the really important manifestations of our western culture, and possibly the one

---

manifestation in which our western contribution has been unique. Those who have created its lasting values are honored as among the truly great. We defend our convictions concerning it with the utmost intensity; and at least in some parts of the world we bitterly excoriate those whose convictions differ, or seem to differ, from our own. We regard music as important, as vitally connected with ourselves and our fate as human beings. But what is the nature of our vital connection with it? What has impelled men to create music? What, in other words, are the sources of the musical impulse? I would like to explore here some approaches to an answer to this question.

Our way will be easier, I think, if we ask ourselves first: is music a matter of tones sung or played, or should we consider it rather from the standpoint of the listener? A close examination of this question leads to some rather surprising conclusions. We find that listening to music, as we understand it, is a relatively late, a relatively sophisticated, and even a rather artificial means of access to it, and that even until fairly recent times composers presumably did not think of their music primarily as being listened to, but rather as being played and sung, or at most as being heard incidentally as a part of an occasion, of which the center of attention for those who heard it lay elsewhere than in the qualities of the music as such.

In fact, composer, performer, and listener can, without undue exaggeration, be regarded not only as three types or degrees of relationship to music, but also as three successive stages of specialization. In the beginning, no doubt, the three were one. Music was vocal or instrumental improvisation; and while there were those who did not perform, and who therefore heard music, they were not listeners in our modern sense of the word. They heard the sounds as part of a ritual, a drama, or an epic narrative, and accepted it in its purely incidental or symbolic function, subordinate to the occasion of which it was a part. Music, in and for itself can hardly be said to have existed, and whatever individual character it may have had was essentially irrelevant.

Later, however, as certain patterns became fixed or traditional, the functions of composer and performer began to be differentiated. The composer existed precisely because he had introduced into the raw material of sound and rhythm patterns that became recognizable and therefore capable of repetition—which is only another way of saying that composers began to exist when music began to take shape. The composer began to emerge as a differentiated type exactly at the moment that a bit of musical material took on a form that its producer felt impelled to repeat.

The same event produced the performer in his separate function; the first performer was, in the strictest sense, the first musician who played or sang something that had been played or sung before. His type became more pronounced in the individual who first played or sang music composed by someone other than himself. At both of these points the performer's problems began to emerge, and whether or not he was aware of the fact, his problems and his characteristic solutions and points of view began to appear at the same time. These will be discussed in detail later on. Here it is important only to envisage clearly that the differentiation of composer and performer represents already a second stage in the development of musical sophistication. The high degree of differentiation reached in the course of the development of music should not obscure the fact that in the last analysis composer and performer are not only collaborators in a common enterprise but participants in an essentially single experience.

I am not, of course, talking in terms of musical history. The developments I have cited are not in any precise sense historical, and I have not presented them even as hypothetically so. It would certainly be in accordance with historical fact, however, to think of them as a long, somewhat involved, gradual development, of which I have given a condensed and symbolical account. And this very qualification underlines better the point I am making: namely, that the performer, as distinct from the composer, is the product of already advanced musical refinement. While the relationship of the composer to music is a simple, direct, and primary one, that of the performer is already complex and even problematical. To be sure, the composer as an individual may be the most complex of creatures and the performer the simplest—I have personally known examples of both such types! But while the act of composition, of production, is a primary act, that of performance—that is, re-production—is already removed by one step. The music passes through the medium of a second personality, and necessarily undergoes something of what we call interpretation. I am not raising here the much discussed question of what interpretation is, or what it may or should be; whether it should be "personal" or "objective," whether it can be or should be historically accurate, and so forth. I am simply pointing to it as an inevitable aspect of the performer's activity, of which the other aspect is, of course, projection. The performer, in other words, not only interprets or reconceives the work, but, so to speak, processes it in terms of a specific occasion: he projects it as part of a recitation or a concert, as the embodiment of a dramatic moment or situation, a part of a ritual, or finally and perhaps most simply as a piece performed solely for his own delectation. Whether or not he is aware of the fact, the nature of his performance is conditioned by the circumstances under which it takes place.   *freewill!*

It hardly need be pointed out that the relation to music of the listener is even more complex than that of the performer. As I have pointed out, the listener, as we think of him today, came fairly recently on the musical scene. Listening to music, as distinct from reproducing it, is the product of a very late stage in musical sophistication, and it might with reason be maintained that the listener has existed as such only for about three hundred and fifty years. The composers of the Middle Ages and the Renaissance composed their music for church services and for secular occasions, where it was accepted as part of the general background, in much the same manner as were the frescoes decorating the church walls or the sculptures adorning the public buildings. Or else they composed it for amateurs, who had received musical training as a part of general education, and whose relationship with it was that of the performer responding to it through active participation in its production. Even well into the nineteenth century the musical public consisted largely of people whose primary contact with music was through playing or singing in the privacy of their own homes. For them concerts were in a certain sense occasional rituals which they attended as adepts, and they were the better equipped as listeners because of their experience in participating, however humbly and however inadequately, in the actual process of musical production. By the "listener," I do not mean the person who simply hears music—who is present when it is performed and who, in a general way, may either enjoy or dislike it, but who is in no sense a real participant in it. To listen implies rather a real participation, a real response, a real sharing in the work of the composer and of the performer, and a greater or less degree of awareness of the individual and specific sense of the music performed. For the listener, in this sense, music is no longer an incident or an adjunct but an independent and self-sufficient medium of expression. His ideal aim is to apprehend to the fullest and most complete possible extent the musical utterance of the composer as the performer delivers it to him.

And how, through what means, does he do this? Let us think for a moment of a similar instance of artistic experience, which is however not quite so complex in structure. The reader of a poem does not generally receive the poem through the medium of an interpreter, nor does he, generally, actually "perform," i.e. read aloud, the poem himself. Yet the rhymes and the meters, as well as the sense of the words, are as vivid to him as they would be if the poem were actually read to or by him. What he does in fact is to "perform" it in imagination, imaginatively to re-create and re-experience it. The "listener" to music does fundamentally the same thing. In "following" a performance, he recreates it and makes it his own. He really listens precisely to the degree that he does this, and really hears to precisely the extent that he does it successfully.

I have discussed this question in some detail here not in order either to belittle the listener or to minimize the validity or the intensity of his relationship to music. What I do wish to point out is that if we are to get at the sources of the musical impulse, we *transition*

must start with the impulse to make music; it is not a question of why music appeals to us, but why men and women in every generation have been impelled to create it. I have tried to show as clearly as possible that composer, performer, and listener each fulfill one of three separate functions in a total creative process, which was originally undifferentiated and which still is essentially indivisible. It is true that there are listeners—as, alas, there are composers and performers!—of every degree of talent and achievement. But the essential is that music is an activity: it is something done, an experience lived through, with varying intensity, by composer, performer, and listener alike.

An understanding of these matters will help us to seek and perhaps to understand the basic facts regarding the musical impulse. We will know better, for instance, than to seek them in the science of acoustics or even primarily with reference to sounds heard.

Let me make this a little clearer. A great deal of musical theory has been formulated by attempting to codify laws governing musical sound and musical rhythm, and from these to deduce musical principles. Sometimes these principles are even deduced from what we know of the physical nature of sound, and as a result are given what seems to me an essentially specious validity. I say "essentially specious" because while the physical facts are clear enough, there are always gaps, incomplete or unconvincing transitions, left between the realm of physics and the realm of musical experience, even if we leave "art" out of account. Many ingenious and even brilliant attempts, it is true, have been made to bridge these gaps. One of the difficulties of trying to do so, however, is apparent, in the way in which the physical fact of the overtone series has been used by various harmonic theorists to support very different and even diametrically contradictory ideas. Because the first six partial tones obviously correspond exactly with the tones composing the major triad, theorists are fond of calling the latter the "chord of nature." On that premise, Heinrich Schenker, for example, a brilliant and at times profound writer, has reconstructed the theory of tonality as basically an elaboration of that chord or its "artificial"

And ... I'm lost

counterpart, the minor triad. He bases what he considers the immutable laws of music on these deductions, even though in doing so he virtually excludes the music written before Bach, after Brahms, and outside of a rather narrowly Germanic orbit. Furthermore, what is perhaps even more problematical, he is forced to disregard the evolutionary factors within even those limits, and to regard the musical language of Bach and Mozart and Beethoven and Brahms in exactly the same light; and he remonstrates with even those composers whenever he catches them punching holes in the system he has thus established. Or again, Paul Hindemith, also a brilliant and certainly a more creative writer, has carefully examined the overtone series and made very interesting deductions regarding it, but he gives it an even more outspoken status than has Schenker, as a kind of musical court of last appeal, with the triad as final arbiter, on the basis not of musical experience, but of physical science. Other writers, however, noting that the overtone series extends well beyond the first six partials, have found in this fact justification for harmonic daring of a much more far-reaching type, and have in some cases sought to discover new harmonic principles based on the systematic use of these upper partials.

Such speculations have been in many cases the product of brilliant minds, of indisputable musical authority, and I do not wish in any way to minimize this fact. Yet it would be easy to point out that each author, in a manner quite consistent with his musical stature, found in the overtone series a tool he could adapt to his individual and peculiar purpose. Above all it seems to me clear that physics and music are different spheres, and that, though they certainly touch at moments, the connection between them is an occasional and circumstantial, not an essential, one. For the musician at any level of sophistication, it is his experience, his relationship with sound, not the physical properties of sound as such, which constitute his materials. Experience, and only experience, has always been his point of departure, and while it has often led him to results which find apparent confirmation in the non-human world, this is by no means always the case. Even when it is the case, it can be regarded as no more than an interesting coincidence until a clear connection with musical experience can be demonstrated.

What I wish to stress is the fact that since music is created by human beings, we must regard the sources, or raw materials, first of all as human facts. For it is not rhythm and sound as such but their nature as human facts which concerns us. And if we look at them closely we perceive that they are actually human facts of the most intimate kind. We see that these basic facts—the raw materials, the primitive sources, of music—are facts of musical experience and not the physical facts of sound and rhythm.

Let us look at rhythm first, since it is perhaps the primary fact. It is quite customary to refer our feeling for rhythm to the many rhythmical impressions constantly received from experience—the non-human as well as the human, the subconscious as well as those of which we are aware, and the sophisticated and complex as well as the naive and simple. Reference is made not only to the act of breathing and walking, but to the alternation of day and night, the precession of the equinoxes, and the movement of the tides; to the beating of the heart, to the dance, and to many another instances of rhythmic recurrence in nature and man, even the mechanical rhythms which everywhere impose themselves on our consciousness, Such illustrations certainly have their place and their relevance; anything so fundamental as our rhythmic sense certainly is nourished and no doubt refined by impressions of every kind, and I believe we may truly say that it remains impervious actually to none. It seems to me also, however, that such generalizations miss a fundamental point. For our rhythmic sense is based ultimately on something far more potent than mere observation.

It seems to me clear indeed that the basic rhythmic fact is not the fact simply of alternation, but of a specific type of alternation with which we are familiar from the first movement of our existence as separate beings. We celebrate that event by drawing a breath, which is required of us if existence is to be realized. The drawing of the breath is an act of cumulation, of tension which is then released by the alternative act of exhalation.

Passion = Rhythm

⇨ what is your "musical phrase?"

Is it, then, in any way far-fetched to say that our first effective experience of rhythm, and the one that remains most deeply and constantly with us, is characterized not only by alternation as such, but by the alternation of cumulative tension with its release in a complementary movement? This is, actually, the primary fact of musical rhythm too. We recognize it in the technical terms "up-beat" and "down-beat," arsis and thesis; and we apply it, consciously as well as instinctively, to our conception of larger musical structure, as well as to the more familiar matters of detail to which these terms are generally applied.

What, for instance, is a so-called "musical phrase" if not the portion of music that must be performed, so to speak without letting go, or, figuratively, in a single breath? The phrase is a constant movement toward a goal—the cadence—and the rhythmic nature of the latter is admirably characterized in the term itself, derived from the Italian verb *cadere,* to fall: that is, the "falling" or down-beat, the movement of release.

I am tempted to call this the most important musical fact and am sure I have done so on occasion. More than any other fact, it seems to me, it bears on the nature of what I shall call "musical movement"; on it depends the appropriateness to their context of harmonies, of melodic intervals, and details of rhythmic elaboration. From it are derived the principles on which satisfactory musical articulation is based; and many an otherwise excellent performance is ruined through inadequate attention to what it implies. How often, unfortunately, in the performance of music, do we hear so much emphasis put on the first part of the phrase that its conclusion is left dangling in the air! The phrase does not, if I may put it that way, sit: the effect is one of breathlessness because the tension is not quite released, or to put it a little differently, the goal of the phrase is not clearly felt. It is not a question of what is generally called accent, but rather of solidity and firmness. [. . .]

I am not implying that our rhythmic sense is derived from the act of breathing alone, or even from the alternation between tension and release which contributes such a tremendous part of our

Meaning of Musical Impulse

physiological and therefore of our psychological existence. Actually our sense of rhythm is a fundamental organic fact, the product of many forces within us working together toward a common end. Nor have I forgotten that the term "rhythm" is often used in an inclusive sense, embracing not only the facts I have described, but what we define more strictly as tempo and meter as well.

Once more I should like to emphasize that it is through our perception of these elements, our awareness of them, that they have meaning for us, and that we gain this perception through the experiences of our psycho-physical organism. Here it is not a question of the alternation of tension and relaxation but of our experience of time itself. We gain our experience, our sensation of time, through movement, and it is movement, primarily, which gives it content for us. It is unnecessary to seek scientific proof of this. We need only a clear analysis of ordinary experience, and it is the latter, in any case, which is relevant to the nature of music. We judge tempo first of all by the relation of basic metrical pulsations to the speed with which we accomplish the ordinary actions of our existence, such as walking and speaking; but, in a more extended sense, we judge it by the amount of effort required to reproduce or respond to it. Heavy accents call forth more energy because we subconsciously assume more energy in producing them, they suggest, and therefore actually call forth in our imagination, greater effort, of which the physiology can be demonstrated many times and in many contexts. Similarly, music rich in detail or elaboration, whether melodic, rhythmic, harmonic, or polyphonic, requires greater effort on the part of the hearer than when the changes are less constant or the detail less elaborate. Consequently music of the former type performed at a fast tempo will seem energetic and strained, while music of simple texture may move along, however rapidly, with the utmost ease and grace.

Nietzsche, always a profound writer on music though not himself a musician, laments in his *Jenseits von Gut und Böse* ("Beyond Good and Evil") the passing of what he calls the "good old time" of Mozart and Haydn, when, to paraphrase his words, a true Presto movement was possible in music. He cites Mendelssohn as the last composer who could write a real Presto. To be sure, he did not know Verdi's "Falstaff"; and needless to say, he was speaking of the music of genuine composers and not of imitators of past styles. Everything, he said, had become ponderous, heavy in spirit, and weighted down with preoccupation, a vital ease had disappeared from the life and hence the culture of Europe. Leaving aside his psychological judgment, which does not concern us at this point, and translating his statements into analytic terms, is he not drawing true conclusions from the indisputable fact that the music of the nineteenth century was, actually, far richer in texture and in coloring than that which had preceded it, and that this fact in itself precluded the type of movement which Haydn embodied so often in his Finales, or Mozart in such a work as the Overture to *The Marriage of Figaro*, in which detail is reduced to a minimum of elaboration, and contrasts are of the subtlest kind?

These few observations lay no claim to exhaustiveness. The subject of rhythm is a vast one, and indeed an adequate definition of rhythm comes close to defining music itself. It is a subject, too, that lends itself all too easily to oversimplification, a clear case of this being the abstraction of the rhythmic element in music from that of musical sound.

Now, if we consider musical sound from the standpoint of the impulse to produce it, we find that in a very real sense and to a very real degree this impulse, too, is rooted in our earliest, most constantly present and most intimate experiences. From almost the first moments of our existence the impulse to produce vocal sound is a familiar one, almost as familiar as the impulse to breathe, though not so indispensable. The sound, to be sure, is at first presumably a by-product. But is it not clear that much of our melodic feeling derives from this source; that is, from a vocal impulse which first of all is connected with the vital act of breathing and is subject to its nuances? In the second place melodic feeling undergoes vast refinement during the growth of even the most unmusical individuals. From the vocal impulse we acquire, for instance, our sensitive response to differences in pitch. I mean here powers not of discrimination, but of response, the kind of response that is instinctive and that precedes discrimination and possibly even precedes consciousness. In simple terms, when we raise our voices we increase the intensity of our vocal effort, a rise in pitch implies an increase in tension, and therefore in intensity of energy, or, in other terms, of expressiveness in one direction. When we lower our voices we make a different kind of effort, and gain an intensity of a different and more complex kind. Similarly, an increase in volume denotes, not only in terms of the physical effort of production, but in the sympathetic effort of response, also an increase in tension and hence of intensity. I have spoken of intensity of expression, which of course is synonymous or commensurable with the degree of contrast involved. If we like, we may speculate on the combinations possible between two directions of movement of pitch, and two directions of movement in volume. We may try to formulate, for instance, the effect of high or rising notes sung or played very softly or of a descending passage sung or played crescendo. What I believe will be indisputable is the fact that with only slight qualifications we carry over these primitive responses from music produced vocally to our more complex response to that heard instrumentally, independently of the particular character of the instrument involved. Though subject to definition, qualification, and refinement, it is a very basic music response of which I am speaking, and possibly more than any single factor it governs our response to melody in its largest features. I shall discuss actual discrimination, the refined sense of pitch, later; here I am referring to the purely instinctive bases of musical expression, as nearly as I can define them, quite apart from the coordinative function of the musical ear. It is true that the line of demarcation is an arbitrary one. But the discrimination of delicate shades of difference in pitch, such as all civilized musical systems demand, only refines the basis responses. It makes possible, through the fact of notes of fixed and definite pitch, greater precision in rhythmic and melodic contour.

Nevertheless, a melodic motif or phrase is in essence and origin a vocal gesture; it is a vocal movement with a clearly defined and therefore clearly expressed profile. And, one final point, it too is *reflection of human press in music*

sensitive to infinitely delicate nuances of tension and relaxation, as these are embodied in the breathing which animates the vocal gesture and shapes its contours. Thus, agitated breathing will be reflected in agitated melodic and rhythmic movement; or conversely, sharp, irregular accents, or successive violent contrasts in pitch will call forth subconscious associations suggesting the kind of agitation which produces violent or irregular breathing, just as quieter melodic movement will evoke a more serene response.

I am oversimplifying, of course. These are not the only elements in musical expression, but I am deliberately restricting the discussion here to primitive, direct, and simple responses to music. Even at this level, may we not say that the basic ingredient of music is not so much sound as movement, conceived in the terms I have indicated? I would even go a step farther, and say that music is significant for us as human beings principally because it embodies movement of a specifically human type that goes to the roots of our being and takes shape in the inner gestures which embody our deepest and most intimate responses. This is of itself not yet art; it is not yet even language. But it is the material of which musical art is made, and to which musical art gives significance.   *Music is in orientation*

If we appreciate these facts, we can understand the more readily why music is the art of sound. For of all the five senses, the sense of hearing is the only one inexorably associated with our sense of time. The gestures which music embodies are, after all, invisible gestures; one may almost define them as consisting of movement in the abstract, movement which exists in time but not in space, movement, in fact, which gives time its meaning and its significance for us. If this is true, then sound is its predestined vehicle. For what apprehend through the eye is for us static, monumental. Even movement seen is bounded by our range of vision; we never can closely follow it off into space unless we ourselves move. Sound, at least in our experience, is never static, but invariably impermanent; it either ceases or changes. By its very nature it embodies for us movement in time, and as such imposes no inherent limits.

To sum up: the experience of music is essentially indivisible, whether it is embodied in the impulse to produce, or in the response, through reproduction, actual as by the performer or imaginary as by the listener, of the musical experience embodied in music already produced. Secondly, what we may call the raw, formal materials of music are also the expressive elements, and these, again, have their basis in certain of the most elementary, intimate, and vital experiences through which we live as human beings. Let us consider now the means through which these raw materials are coordinated, become coherent, and are rendered significant; through which, in other words, they begin to be music.

PART VI

SHAPES: PAINTING AND SCULPTURE

POETRY, SCULPTURE, AND ARCHITECTURE

PAINTING, SCULPTURE, AND ARCHITECTURE

In the visual arts are found the earliest evidence of the innate human urge to create representations of the individual and the common struggle with natural and spiritual forces that are experienced by the senses, ordered within the mind, and given symbolic expression within the imagination. These arts, of painting, sculpture, and architecture, are therefore the concrete expression of the search for an understanding of the highest definition of the meaning of human existence, namely, the good, the true, and the beautiful. The creative expression of this quest predates not only the appearance of written texts, but also human attempts to organize socially. The history of art documents this quest through the centuries, identifying and tracing its variations among cultures and its response to changed historical circumstances.

It was during the Paleolithic Period, dating roughly from 30,000 to 8,000 B.C.E., that sculpture—the art of shaping material in three-dimensional form through carving, modeling, or the assemblage of natural materials—became the first of the arts to appear. Not surprisingly, the earliest sculpted forms are of human beings and animals. Painting, which is the representation of three-dimensional forms on a two-dimensional surface or plane, and achieved through the skilled application of paints concocted for the purpose, soon followed. Architecture grew out of the complementary needs for simple shelter from the forces of nature and for creation of a sacred space in which to worship and commune with God. Consisting of the design and construction of buildings, architecture is, therefore, the most concrete and absolute expression of a culture's spiritual resolve. Because buildings exist *in situ*, that is, within a permanently communal situation or space, they inscribe the very landscape in which a people, culturally speaking, live and move and have their being. Architecture is, thus, unique as a vehicle for conserving shared memories and for the symbolic expression of the spiritual achievements and aspirations of a particular people in their cultural existence across time.

It was during the Classical Period, dating from 480 to 323 B.C.E., that the first texts in the visual arts appeared. These were treatises on sculpture and architecture. Written references to painting are to be found only in the form of allusions and references to lost works. By the time of the Renaissance in the early fifteenth century, artists and architects had already demonstrated that an unwritten tradition, dating to the Classical Period, had been formed and directed the imaginative quest of visual representations of the good, the true, and the beautiful. This tradition was codified into what we now recognize as the Western Canon.

During the Renaissance, leading humanists demonstrated that the past could be adapted for use in the present by appropriating, for painting, sculpture, and architecture, the classical forms of the past. In these treatises are to be found the origins of aesthetic *modernity*, a term signifying a conscious philosophical and spiritual abandonment of the past and the concomitant determination to establish *modern* (that is, *new*) principles for understanding—and representing artistically—human nature and destiny.

Prior to the Renaissance, all three of the principal arts strove to represent the created order and to establish in human culture a mirror image of the forms ascribed to the Divine—the forms of the good, the true, and the beautiful. In effect, artists in every medium gradually abandoned the attempt to represent human destiny as a pilgrimage between Heaven and Earth and through

Time unto Eternity, and turned from the perceived objects of creation to the interior mysteries of the human subject, or consciousness, itself. The effects of these modern theories of human existence and destiny naturally called into question the very premises upon which the arts—especially in Western culture—had arisen. This "project of modernity," which can be defined as the attempt to conceive and to construct human existence without regard to what Plato termed the Divine forms (here again we refer to the good, the true, and the beautiful) gradually displaced virtually every symbolic and thematic reference in the Western artistic tradition.

For example, during the nineteenth century, Baudelaire successfully summoned many artists to abandon any hopes of representing spiritual qualities and to concentrate instead on depicting the everyday objects of contemporary life. Appropriating the Enlightenment's thrust that human reason wholly apart from Divine revelation is the source of truth about human nature and destiny, the modern project in intellectual and therefore in artistic terms abandoned interest in the spiritual cosmos and concentrated on the mastery of nature through science and the exploration of human nature or consciousness through the methods of science, principally psychology. Accordingly, human consciousness, which previously had been seen as a subject in response to the objective realities of nature and the Divine, became itself the sole subject of inquiry—hence of artistic representation.

By the midpoint of the twentieth century, this project of modernity, or modernism, had been completed. Consequently, many historians of art dismissed methodologies based on traditional iconographic analysis and textual exegesis. However, as worldwide wars and scientific discoveries undermined the Enlightenment confidence in unaided human reason, modernism collapsed as a philosophical system and artistic program. Whereas modernism had supplanted religious faith in spiritual realities, postmodernism supplanted modernism's faith in autonomous human reason. Accordingly, postmodernism, which is the condition and concept within which the arts at present are to be understood, rejects any thesis purporting to represent the truth about either religious faith or intellectual reason. All distinctions, for example, between cosmos and culture, or between high culture and common culture, or between various cultures, are dismissed as mere fabrications, or constructs, deriving only from political power and having nothing to do with any possible timeless definition of the true, the good, or the beautiful. The history of the visual arts explores the aesthetic response in painting, sculpture, and architecture to these and other fundamental beliefs about the origin, nature, and destiny of human existence.

Delane Bovenizer, Ph.D.

LEONARDO DA VINCI

1452-1519

NOTEBOOKS

No date

Leonardo da Vinci is often referred to as the quintessential Renaissance Man. He was a painter, architect, engineer, mathematician, philosopher, inventor, scientist, and writer. He was a genius ahead of his time. Sigmund Freud observed that "Leonardo da Vinci was like a man who awoke too early in the darkness, while the others were all still asleep" (Kausal 2004). Leonardo was born in Anchiano, near Vinci, the illegitimate son of a notary. In 1468, he was sent to Florence as an apprentice to painter and sculptor Andrea del Verrocchio. According to legend, after Leonardo painted the head of an angel in Verrocchio's *Baptism of Christ*, the master was so moved by the image that he laid down his brush and devoted himself entirely to sculpture. Leonardo's interest in the science of painting flourished, including the use of linear perspective, and he soon developed his personal style of diffused shadows and subtle hues.

In Verrocchio's studio, Leonardo also encountered, among others, the artists Uccello, Pollaiuolo, Botticelli, Ghirlandaio, and Perugino. In 1481, many of these painters were invited by Pope Sixtus IV to Rome to work in the Sistene Chapel. Leonardo was slighted, and instead, in 1482, entered the service of Lodovico Sforza, Duke of Milan, where he stayed until 1499. Among his greatest works of this time was *The Last Supper* in the refectory of S. Maria delle Grazie, a consummate example of the assimilation of art and science. He went on to work in Florence as architect and general engineer Cesare Borgia, for the French governor Charles II d'Amboise in Milan, and in Rome for Giuliano de Medici, brother of Pope Leo X. In 1516-17, he left Rome for France at the request of Francis I, to work as first painter, engineer, and architect to the king. One of the possessions he took with him was the *Mona Lisa*.

Throughout his life, Leonardo produced thousands of pages of text and illustrations on all manner of things scientific and artistic. He was highly regarded by his contemporaries as a thinker, although none of his treatises was published in his lifetime, left unfinished like other creative endeavors that no longer held his interest. At his death in 1519, he bequeathed all of his writings and the paintings in his possession to his young friend and companion Francesco Melzi. After Melzi's death in 1570, Leonardo's writings became scattered among collections in Spain, Milan, and England.

Passages from 18 of Leonardo's notebooks, inscribed in reverse writing from right to left, expressing his ideas on painting, were compiled and published in the 16th century. Leonardo's notebooks reveal the mind of a complex genius and demonstrated the intellectual power of art as a mode of inquiry into nature.

SOURCES

Da Vinci, Leonardo. *ca.* 1465-1519. "How Painting Surpasses All Human Works by Reason of the Subtle Possibilities which It Contains." In *Leonardo da Vinci's Notebooks*: Book III, "Art 1: Painting, Poetry, and Sculpture." Edward McCurdy, Ed. and Trans.1923. New York: Empire State Book Company, 1935. 156-162.

Kausal, Martin. 2004. Website: http://www.kausal.com/leonardo/index.html

How Painting Surpasses All Human Works by Reason of the Subtle Possibilities which It Contains

The eye, which is called the window of the soul, is the chief means whereby the understanding may most fully and abundantly appreciate the infinite works of nature; and the ear is the second inasmuch as it acquires its importance from the fact that it hears the things which the eye has seen. If you historians, or poets, or mathematicians had never seen things with your eyes you would be ill able to describe them in your writings. And if you, O poet, represent a story by depicting it with your pen, the painter with his brush will so render it as to be more easily satisfying and less tedious to understand. If you call painting 'dumb poetry,' then the painter may say of the poet that his art is 'blind painting.' Consider then which is the more grievous affliction, to be blind or be dumb! Although the poet has as wide a choice of subjects as the painter, his creations fail to afford as much satisfaction to mankind as do paintings, for while poetry attempts with words to represent forms, actions and scenes, the painter employs the exact images of the forms in order to reproduce these forms. Consider, then, which is more fundamental to man; the name of man or his image? The name changes with change of country; the form is unchanged except by death.

And if the poet serves the understanding by way of the ear, the painter does so by the eye which is the nobler sense. I will only cite as an instance of this how if a good painter represents the fury of a battle and a poet also describes one, and the two descriptions are shown together to the public, you will soon see which will draw most of the spectators, and where there will be most discussion, to which most praise will be given and which will satisfy the more. There is no doubt that the painting which is by far the more useful and beautiful will give the greater pleasure. Inscribe in any place the name of God and set opposite to it his image, you will see which will be held in greater reverence!

Since painting embraces within itself all the forms of nature you have nothing omitted except the names, and these are not universal like the forms. If you have the results of her processes we have the processes of her results.

Take the case of a poet describing the beauties of a lady to her lover and that of a painter who makes a portrait of her; you will see whither nature will the more incline the enamoured judge. Surely the proof of the matter ought to rest upon the verdict of experience!

You have set painting among the mechanical arts! Truly were painters as ready equipped as you are to praise their own works in writing I doubt whether it would endure the reproach of so vile a name. If you call it mechanical because it is by manual work that the hands represent what the imagination creates, your writers are setting down with the pen by manual work what originates in the mind. If you call it mechanical because it is done for money, who fall into this error—if indeed it can be called an error—more than you yourselves? If you lecture for the Schools do you not go to whoever pays you the most? Do you do any work without some reward? And yet I do not say this in order to censure such opinions, for every labour looks for its reward. And if the poet should say, "I will create a fiction which shall express great things," so likewise will the painter also, for even so Apelles made the Calumny. If you should say that poetry is the more enduring,—to this I would reply that the works of a coppersmith are more enduring still, since time preserves them longer than either your works or ours; nevertheless they show but little imagination; and painting if it be done upon copper in enamel colours can be made far more enduring.

In Art we may be said to be grandsons unto God. If poetry treats of moral philosophy, painting has to do with natural philosophy; if the one describes the workings of the mind, the other considers what the mind effects by movements of the body; if the one dismays folk by hellish fictions, the other does the like by showing the same things in action. Suppose the poet sets himself to represent some image of beauty or terror, something vile and foul, or some monstrous thing, in contest with the painter, and suppose in his own way he makes a change of forms at his pleasure, will not the painter still satisfy the more? Have we not seen pictures which bear so close a resemblance to the actual thing that they have deceived both men and beasts?

If you know how to describe and write down the appearance of the forms, the painter can make them so that they appear enlivened with lights and shadows which create the very expression of the faces; herein you cannot attain with the pen where he attains with the brush.

(Bib. Nat. MS. 2038, 19 r and v, 20 r).

So soon as the poet ceases to represent in words what exists in nature, then the poet ceases to be like the painter; for if the poet were to leave such representation and describe the polished and persuasive words of him whom he wishes to represent speaking, then he becomes an orator and is no longer a poet or a painter; and if he speaks of the heavens he becomes an astrologer; and a philosopher and theologian when discoursing of the works of nature or of God. But if he confines himself to the representation of specific objects he will vie with the painter only if by his words he can satisfy the eye to the same extent as he does.

(Windsor MSS. Notes et dessins sur la Génération [Rouveyre], 1 r.).

How He Who Despises Painting Has No Love for the Philosophy in Nature

If you despise painting, which is the sole imitator of all the visible works of nature, it is certain that you will be despising a subtle invention which with philosophical and ingenious speculation takes as its theme all the various kinds of forms, airs, and scenes, plants, animals, grasses and flowers, which are surrounded by light and shade. And this truly is a science and the true-born daughter of nature, since painting is the offspring of nature. But in order to speak more correctly we may call it the grandchild of nature; for all visible things derive their existence from nature, and from these same things is born painting. So therefore we may justly speak of it as the grandchild of nature and as related to God himself.

(MS. 2038 Bib. Nat. 20 r.)

THAT SCULPTURE IS LESS INTELLECTUAL THAN PAINTING, AND LACKS MANY OF ITS NATURAL PARTS

As practising myself the art of sculpture no less than that of painting, and doing both the one and the other in the same degree, it seems to me that without suspicion of unfairness I may venture to give an opinion as to which of the two is the more intellectual, and of the greater difficulty and perfection. In the first place sculpture is dependent on certain lights, namely those from above, while a picture carries everywhere with it its own light and shade; light and shade therefore are essential to sculpture. In this respect, the sculptor is aided by the nature of the relief, which produces these of its own accord, but the painter artificially creates them by his art in places where nature would normally do the like. The sculptor cannot render the difference in the varying natures of the colours of objects; painting does not fail to do so in any particular. The lines of perspective of sculptors do not seem in any way true; those of painters may appear to extend a hundred miles beyond the work itself. The effects of aerial perspective are outside the scope of their work; they can neither represent transparent bodies nor luminous bodies nor angles of reflection nor shining bodies such as mirrors and like things of glittering surface, nor mists, nor dull weather, nor an infinite number of things which I forbear to mention lest they should prove wearisome.

The one advantage which it has is that of offering greater resistance to time; yet painting offers a like resistance if it is done upon thick copper covered with white enamel and then painted upon with enamel colours and placed in a fire and fused. In degree of permanence it then surpasses even sculpture.

It may be urged that if a mistake is made it is not easy to set it right, but it is a poor line of argument to attempt to prove that the fact of a mistake being irremediable makes the work more noble. I should say indeed that it is more difficult to correct the mind of the master who makes such mistakes than the work which he has spoiled. We know very well that a good experienced painter will not make such mistakes; on the contrary following sound rules he will proceed by removing so little at a time that his work will progress well. The sculptor also if he is working in clay or wax can either take away from it or add to it, and when the model is completed it is easy to cast it in bronze; and this is the last process and it is the most enduring form of sculpture, since that which is only in marble is liable to be destroyed, but not when done in bronze.

But painting done upon copper, which by the methods in use in painting may be either taken from or altered, is like the bronze, for when you have first made the model for this in wax it can still be either reduced or altered. While the sculpture in bronze is imperishable, this painting upon copper and enamel is absolutely eternal; and while bronze remains dark and rough, this is full of an infinite variety of varied and lovely colours, of which I have already made mention. But if you would have me speak only of panel painting I am content to give an opinion between it and sculpture by saying that painting is more beautiful, more imaginative, and richer in resource, while sculpture is more enduring, but excels in nothing else. Sculpture reveals what it is with little effort; painting seems a thing miraculous, making things intangible appear tangible, presenting in relief things which are flat, in distance things near at hand. In fact, painting is adorned with infinite possibilities of which sculpture can make no use.

(MS. 2038, Bib Nat. 25 r. and 24 v.)

The sculptor cannot represent transparent or luminous things.
(C. A. 215 v. d.)

WASHINGTON IRVING

1783-1859

TALES OF THE ALHAMBRA

1832

The first American author to achieve international fame, Washington Irving is best known as the author "The Legend of Sleepy Hollow" and "Rip Van Winkle," published in *Sketch Book* (1819-1820). A New Yorker by birth, Irving studied law and was admitted to the bar in 1806, but his interest was in writing, so he began publishing satirical essays to New York newspapers as early as 1802. His first literary success came with *A History of New York* (1809), a satire of Jeffersonian democracy written as the witty—and fictional—Dutch-American scholar, Diedrich Knickerbocker. From 1826 to 1829, Irving was on the staff of the U.S. delegation to Madrid. For three months, he lived in the Alhambra, the ancient Moorish palace in Granada. The literary result was *Tales of the Alhambra*, first published in 1832. Part short story and part travelogue, *Tales of the Alhambra* concerns the history and legends of the Moors in Spain, complete with hidden treasure and romantic princesses, reminiscent of *The Arabian Nights*. "The Court of Lions" is a tour steeped in visual imagery focused on the fountain at the center of the fortified place that was the seat of the Nasrids (1232-1492), the last Muslim dynasty in Spain.

SOURCE

Irving, Washington. 1832. "The Court of Lions." In *Tales of the Alhambra*. Philadelphia: David McKay, 1894. 113-119.

THE COURT OF LIONS

The peculiar charm of this old dreamy palace is its power of calling up vague reveries and picturings of the past, and thus clothing naked realities with the illusions of the memory and the imagination. As I delight to walk in these "vain shadows," I am prone to seek those parts of the Alhambra which are most favorable to this phantasmagoria of the mind; and none are more so than the Court of Lions and its surrounding halls. Here the hand of time has fallen the lightest, and the traces of Moorish elegance and splendor exist in almost their original brilliancy. Earthquakes have shaken the foundations of this pile and rent its rudest towers, yet see! not one of those slender columns has been displaced, not an arch of that light and fragile colonnade given way, and all the fairy fretwork of these domes, apparently as unsubstantial as the crystal fabrics of a morning's frost, exist after the lapse of centuries, almost as fresh as if from the hand of the Moslem artist. I write in the midst of these mementos of the past, in the fresh hour of early morning, in the fated Hall of the Abencerrages. The blood-stained fountain, the legendary monument of their massacre, is before me; the lofty jet almost casts its dew upon my paper. How difficult to reconcile the ancient tale of violence and blood with the gentle and peaceful scene around! Everything here appears calculated to inspire kind and happy feelings, for everything is delicate and beautiful. The very light falls tenderly from above through the lantern of a dome tinted and wrought as if by fairy hands. Through the ample and fretted arch of the portal I behold the Court of Lions with brilliant sunshine gleaming along its colonnades and sparkling in its fountains. The lively swallow dives into the court, and, rising with a surge, darts away twittering over the roofs; the busy bee toils humming among the flower-beds, and painted butterflies hover from plant to plant and flutter up and sport with each other in the sunny air. It needs but a slight exertion of the fancy to picture some pensive beauty of the harem loitering in these secluded haunts of Oriental luxury.

He, however, who would behold this scene under an aspect more in unison with its fortunes, let him come when the shadows of evening temper the brightness of the court and throw a gloom into the surrounding halls. Then nothing can be more serenely melancholy or more in harmony with the tale of departed grandeur.

At such times I am apt to seek the Hall of Justice, whose deep shadowy arcades extend across the upper end of the court. Here was performed, in presence of Ferdinand and Isabella and their triumphant court, the pompous ceremonial of high mass on taking possession of the Alhambra. The very cross is still to be seen upon the wall where the altar was erected, and where officiated the grand cardinal of Spain and others of the highest religious dignitaries of the land. I picture to myself the scene when this place was filled with the conquering host, that mixture of mitred prelate and shaven monk and steel-clad knight and silken courtier—when crosses and crosiers and religious standards were mingled with proud armorial ensigns and the banners of the haughty chiefs of Spain, and flaunted in triumph through these Moslem halls. I picture to myself Columbus, the future discoverer of a world, taking his modest stand in a remote corner, the humble and neglected spectator of the pageant. I see in imagination the Catholic sovereigns prostrating themselves before the altar and pouring forth thanks for their victory, while the vaults resound with sacred minstrelsy and the deep-toned Te Deum.

The transient illusion is over, the pageant melts from the fancy; monarch, priest, and warrior return into oblivion with the poor Moslems over whom they exulted. The hall of their triumph is waste and desolate. The bat flits about its twilight vault, and the owl hoots from the neighboring Tower of Comares.

Entering the Court of the Lions a few evenings since, I was almost startled at beholding a turbaned Moor quietly seated near

the fountain. For a moment one of the fictions of the
realized: an enchanted Moor had broken the spell of c
become visible. He proved, however, to be a mere ordir.
a native of Tetuan in Barbary, who had a shop in the ∠acatin of
Granada, where he sold rhubarb, trinkets, and perfumes. As he
spoke Spanish fluently, I was enabled to hold conversation with
him, and found him shrewd and intelligent. He told me that he
came up the hill occasionally in the summer to pass a part of the
day in the Alhambra, which reminded him of the old palaces in
Barbary, being built and adorned in similar style, though with
more magnificence.

As we walked about the palace he pointed out several of the
Arabic inscriptions as possessing much poetic beauty.

"Ah, señor," said he, "when the Moors held Granada they were
a gayer people than they are now-a-days. They thought only of
love, music and poetry. They made stanzas upon every occasion,
and set them all to music. He who could make the best verses and
she who had the most tuneful voice might be sure of favor and
preferment. In those days, if anyone asked for bread, the reply
was, Make me a couplet; and the poorest beggar, if he begged in
rhyme, would often be rewarded with a piece of gold."

"And is the popular feeling for poetry," said I, "entirely lost
among you?"

"By no means, señor: the people of Barbary, even those of the
lower classes, still make couplets, and good ones too, as in the old
times; but talent is not rewarded as it was then; the rich prefer the
jingle of their gold to the sound of poetry or music."

As he was talking his eye caught one of the inscriptions which
foretold perpetuity to the power and glory of the Moslem
monarchs, the masters of this pile. He shook his head and shrugged
his shoulders as he interpreted it. "Such might have been the case,"
said he, "the Moslems might still have been reigning in the
Alhambra, had not Boabdil been a traitor and given up his capital
to the Christians. The Spanish monarchs would never have been
able to conquer it by open force."

I endeavored to vindicate the memory of the unlucky Boabdil from this aspersion, and to show that the dissensions which led to the downfall of the Moorish throne originated in the cruelty of his tiger-hearted father, but the Moor would admit of no palliation.

"Muley Hassan," said he, "might have been cruel, but he was brave, vigilant, and patriotic. Had he been properly seconded, Granada would still have been ours; but his son Boabdil thwarted his plans, crippled his power, sowed treason in his palace and dissension in his camp. May the curse of God light upon him for his treachery!" With these words the Moor left the Alhambra.

The indignation of my turbaned companion agrees with an anecdote related by a friend who, in the course of a tour in Barbary, had an interview with the Pacha of Tetuan. The Moorish governor was particular in his inquiries about Spain, and especially concerning the favored region of Andalusia, the delights of Granada, and the remains of its royal palace. The replies awakened all those fond recollections, so deeply cherished by the Moors, of the power and splendor of their ancient empire in Spain. Turning to his Moslem attendants, the Pacha stroked his beard, and broke forth in passionate lamentations that such a sceptre should have fallen from the sway of true believers. He consoled himself, however, with the persuasion that the power and prosperity of the Spanish nation were on the decline; that a time would come when the Moors would reconquer their rightful domains; and that the day was perhaps not far distant when Mahommedan worship would again be offered up in the mosque of Cordova and a Mahommedan prince sit on his throne in the Alhambra.

Such is the general aspiration and belief among the Moors of Barbary, who consider Spain and especially Andalusia their rightful heritage, of which they have been despoiled by treachery and violence. These ideas are fostered and perpetuated by the descendants of the exiled Moors of Granada scattered among the cities of Barbary. Several of these reside in Tetuan, preserving their ancient names, such as Páez and Medina, and refraining from intermarriage with any families who cannot claim the same high origin. Their vaunted lineage is regarded with a degree of popular deference rarely shown in Mahommedan communities to any hereditary distinction excepting in the royal line.

These families, it is said, continue to sigh after the terrestrial paradise of their ancestors, and to put up prayers in their mosques on Fridays imploring Allah to hasten the time when Granada shall be restored to the faithful—an event to which they look forward as fondly and confidently as did the Christian crusaders to the recovery of the Holy Sepulchre. Nay, it is added that some of them retain the ancient maps and deeds of the estates and gardens of their ancestors at Granada, and even the keys of the houses, holding them as evidences of their hereditary claims, to be produced at the anticipated day of restoration.

The Court of the Lions has also its share of super-natural legends. I have already mentioned the belief in the murmuring of voices and clanking of chains, made at night by the spirits of the murdered Abencerrages. Mateo Jiménez, a few evenings since, at one of the gatherings in Dame Antonia's apartment related a fact which happened within the knowledge of his grandfather, the legendary tailor.

There was an invalid soldier, who had charge of the Alhambra to show it to strangers. As he was one evening about twilight passing through the Court of Lions, he heard footsteps in the Hall of the Abencerrages. Supposing some visitors to be lingering there, he advanced to attend upon them, when to his astonishment he beheld four Moors richly dressed with gilded cuirasses and scimitars and poniards glittering with precious stones. They were walking to and fro with solemn pace, but paused and beckoned to him. The old soldier, however, took to flight an could never afterwards be prevailed upon to enter the Alhambra. Thus it is that men sometimes turn their back upon fortune, for it is the firm opinion of Mateo that the Moors intended to reveal the place where their treasures lay buried. A successor to the invalid soldier was more knowing; he came to the Alhambra poor, but at the end of a year went off to Malaga, bought houses, set up a carriage and still lives there one of the richest as well as oldest men of the place, all which, Mateo sagely surmises, was in consequence of his finding out the golden secret of the phantom Moors.

CHARLES BAUDELAIRE

1821-1867

THE SALON OF 1846

Charles Baudelaire was a poet, translator, and critic of literature and art. He was educated at the Collège Royal in Lyons, the Lycée Louis-le-Grand in Paris, and briefly studied law at the École de Droit, but Baudelaire preferred living a bohemian life immersed in the literary community of the Paris Latin Quarter—where he contracted the venereal disease that ultimately claimed his life. His teachers considered his earliest poems to be obscenely depraved affectations. Afflicted with depression and a sense of isolation, he was sent to India in 1841 by his stepfather, who tried to remove him from his disreputable way of life. Baudelaire jumped ship in Mauritius, however, and made his way back to France, soon to squander his inheritance on clothes, books and art, as well as wine, hashish, and opium.

Baudelaire's poetry was innovative and introspective, characterized by a search for truth in every aspect of life. His most influential work was *Les Fleurs du mal* (The Flowers of Evil, 1857). He also wrote essays on art, literature, and music. As a powerful art critic, he could advance the reputation of an artist with a review. Imbued with his belief that the critic should write exactly what he feels, his reviews reveal his ideas on aesthetics, imagination, and the art movements that dominated the 19th century.

Baudelaire was concerned with modernity in art and befriended many artists whose work heralded modernism. In *Le Salon de 1846*, he expounds on his belief that beauty, being allied with horror and melancholy, is the goal of art. For Baudelaire, beauty was both eternal and absolute, and determined individually by the artist; romanticism was a contemporary expression of beauty, as it was most concerned not with subject matter or exact truth, but with feelings and introspection. In *Le Salon de 1846*, he focused on the Romantic artist Eugène Delacroix (1798-1863), whose work often depicted victims and anti-heroes. Ironically, Delacroix was inspired by ancient Greece and Rome, and by Renaissance painters. For Baudelaire, however, Delacroix's modernism lay in his poetic use of color, emotion, spirituality, and epic character.

SOURCE

Charles Baudelaire. 1846. Excerpt from *Le Salon de 1846*. Luc Guglielmi, Trans. Reproduced by Permission. The original French version of the text is available online at: *http://www.ac-rouen.fr/lycees/jeanne-d-arc/romantik/louvre-1/ reseau/salon-46.html*

SALON OF 1846

The romanticism and the color lead me right to Eugène Delacroix. I don't know if he is proud of his romantic quality: but his place is here, because the majority of the public for a long time, and even since his first work, has seen him as the most influential artist in the *modern* school.

By entering into this part, my heart is full of joy and I chose my finest and newest pens, because I want to be clear and lucid, since I want to start talking about my most favorite and sensitive subject. To be sure to be as clear as possible and to understand the conclusion of this chapter, I must put some historical pieces of evidence for the public from the court cited by historians and critics. And it isn't with some joy that the pure enthusiasts of Eugène

Delacroix will reread an article from the *Constitutionnel* of 1822, coming from the Salon of Thiers, journalist.

> No art work reveals better the future of a great painter than the one from Mr. Delacroix, representing *Dante and Virgil in Hell.* It is in that art work that we can see his talent, that superior outburst which revives the hopes a little discouraged by the ability too moderate from the rest of the work.
>
> Dante and Virgil, driven by Charon, cross the River of Hell and with difficulty cut through the people who are trying to get into their barge. Dante, supposedly alive, reflects the horrible atmosphere of that place; Virgil, crowned with a dark laurel, has the colors of death. The poor people, condemned for ever to the desire to go on the opposite side of the river, tie themselves to the barge: one is trying to catch it but cannot, and, turned upside down by too rapid a current, dives into the water; another one is kissing it[the barge] and pushes with his feet the others who are trying to come aboard like him; two others are biting the wood with their teeth but in vain. There is the selfishness of distress, the despair of Hell. In this subject, so close to exaggeration, one can find it to be too harsh for good taste; in other words, which come from the drawing, for which some hard judges would critique it for the lack of nobility. The brush is wide and firm, the color simple and vigorous.
>
> The artist has, on top of that poetic imagination common to the writer and the painter, that imagination of art, that we could call in other words the imagination of drawing, and which is different from all the others. He is throwing his

figures, grouping them and bend them with the will and Michelangelo's boldness and the richness of Rubens. I don't know which artist's memory touches me when I view that painting; I find in it that wild, natural power which breaks without effort to its own impulse, to its own heat, its own impetus.

I don't think that I am wrong, Mr. Delacroix is a genius; that he goes forward with assurance, that he is doing all those huge works, is the necessary condition for talent; and what should have given him more confidence, it is the opinion that I express here of his person, that he is one of the most talented of the school masters.

Pierre-Auguste Renoir

1841-1919

[On Irregularity]

No date

The French painter Pierre-Auguste Renoir was a leading member of the Impressionists, a group that included Claude Monet, Alfred Sisley, and Jean-Frédéric Bazille. Renoir was born in Limoges and as a young child moved to Paris, where his father found work as a tailor. In 1854, Renoir was apprenticed as a painter in the porcelain factory of Lévy frères, but the firm went bankrupt several years later. Renoir began the common practice of honing his craft as a painter by copying paintings in the Louvre. In 1861, he enrolled at the École des Beaux Arts, where studio techniques and the influence of the Old Masters and historical subjects dominated. Soon, he and the others who would come to be called Impressionists began the revolutionary practice of painting outdoors in the forest at Fontainebleau, using newly available paint in tubes and recent scientific studies of light and color. The artists sought to catch a fleeting moment of time through the use of bright colors and quick brush strokes.

Their work was rejected by the Salon, an annual exhibition that could establish—or destroy—an artist's reputation. In response, they staged the Salon des Réfusés, and critics coined the then-derogatory term "Impressionists," derived from Monet's painting *Impression, Sunrise*. Throughout his career, Renoir was considered a master of light, although he never relinquished his admiration for the Old Masters, returning to a more classical style in his later years. As an elderly man, Renoir was stricken by crippling arthritis especially in his hands. Unable to hold his paintbrushes, he strapped them to his wrists, thus painting in thick, heavy brush strokes. Renoir died at his home in the south of France at the age of 79.

Renoir's *Notebook* is included in *Renoir, My Father,* a biography by his son, the filmmaker Jean Renoir. In *Notebook*, Renoir expresses his philosophy of art and the concept of irregularity as found in nature—its laws and its splendor—which he saw as the true master of art.

SOURCE

Renoir, Pierre-Auguste. No date. [On Irregularity]. Excerpt from Auguste Renoir's Notebook. In Jean Renoir. *Renoir, My Father.* New York: Little Brown, 1958. 240-245.*

[ON IRREGULARITY]

FROM AUGUSTE RENOIR'S NOTEBOOK

Everything that I call grammar on primary notions of Art can be summed up in one word: Irregularity.

The earth is not round. An orange is not round. Not one section of it has the same form or weight as another. If you divide it into quarters, you will not find in a single quarter the same number of pips as in any of the other three; nor will any of the pips be exactly alike.

Take the leaf of a tree—take a hundred thousand other leaves of the same kind of tree—not one will exactly resemble the other.

Take a column. If I make it symmetrical with a compass, it loses its vital principle.

Explain the irregularity in regularity. The value of regularity is in the eye only . . . the non-value of the regularity of the compass.

It is customary to prostrate oneself in front of the (obvious) beauty of Greek art. The rest has no value. What a farce! It is as if you told me that a blonde is more beautiful than a brunette; and vice versa.

Do not restore; only remake the damaged parts.

Do not think it is possible to repeat another period.

The artist who uses the least of what is called imagination will be the greatest.

To be an artist you must learn to know the laws of nature.

The only reward one should offer an artist is to buy his work.

An artist must eat sparingly and give up a normal way of life.

Delacroix never won a prize.

How is it that in the so-called barbarian ages art was understood, whereas in our age of progress exactly the opposite is true.

When art becomes a useless thing, it is the beginning of the end . . . . A people never loses half, or even just a part, of its value. Everything comes to end at the same time.

If art is superfluous, why caricature or make a pretense of it? . . . I only wish to be comfortable? Therefore I have furniture made of rough wood for myself, and a house without ornament or decoration . . . I only want what is strictly necessary . . . . If I could obtain that result, I should be a man of taste. But the ideal of simplicity is almost impossible to achieve.

The reason for this decadence is that the eye has lost the habit of seeing.

Artists do exist. But one doesn't know where to find them. An artist can do nothing if the person who asks him to produce work is blind. It is the eye of the sensualist that I wish to open.

Not everyone is a sensualist just because he wishes to be.

There are some who never become sensualists no matter how hard they try.

Someone gave a picture by one of the great masters to one of my friends, who was delighted to have an object of undisputed value in his drawing room. He showed it off to everyone. One day he came rushing in to see me. He was overcome with joy. He told me naively that he had never understood until that morning why the picture was beautiful. Until then, he had always followed the crowd in being impressed only by the signature. My friend had just become a sensualist.

It is impossible to repeat in one period what was done in another. The point of view is not the same, any more than are the tools, the ideas, the needs or the painters' techniques.

A gentleman who has become newly rich decides that he wants a chateau. He makes inquiries as to the style most in fashion at the time. It turns out to be Louis XIII; and off he goes. And of course, he finds an architect who builds him an imitation Louis XIII. Who is to blame?

To own a beautiful palace, you should be worthy of it.

The art lover is the one who should be taught. He is the one to whom the medals should be given and not to the artist, who doesn't care a hang about them.

Painters on porcelain only copy the work of others. Not one of them would think of looking at the canary he has in a cage to see how its feet are made.

They ought to have cheaply priced inns in luxuriant surroundings for those in the decorative arts. I say inns; but, if you wish, schools minus teachers. I don't want my pupils to be polished up any more than I want my garden to be tidied up.

Young people should learn to see things for themselves, and not ask for advice.

Look at the way the Japanese painted birds and fish. Their system is quite simple. They sat down in the countryside and watched birds flying. By watching them carefully, they finally came to understand movement; and they did the same as regards fish.

Don't be afraid to look at the great masters of the best periods. They created irregularity within regularity. Saint Mark's Cathedral in Venice: symmetrical, as a whole, but not one detail is like another!

An artist, under pain of oblivion, must have confidence in himself, and listen only to his real master: Nature.

The more you rely on good tools, the more boring your sculpture will be.

The Japanese still have a simplicity of life, which gives them time to go about and to contemplate. They still look, fascinated, at a blade of grass, or the flight of birds, or the wonderful movements of fish, and they go home, their minds filled with beautiful ideas, which they have no trouble in putting on the objects they decorate.

To get a good idea of what decadence is, you only have to go and sip a beer in some café on one of the boulevards, and watch the passing crowd. Nothing could be more comical. And magistrates with side whiskers! Could anybody look at a gentleman "tattooed" that way, and not die laughing?

Catholics who, like all the others, have fallen for the tinseled rubbish and for the plaster statuettes sold in the rue Bonaparte, will tell you there is no salvation outside the Catholic religion. Don't believe a word of it. Religion is everywhere. It is in the mind, in the heart, in the love you put into what you do.

Don't try to make a fortune, whatever you do. Because, as soon as you've made your fortune, you'll die of boredom.

I believe that I am nearer to God by being humble before this splendor (nature); by accepting the role I have been given to play in life; by honoring this majesty without self-interest, and, about all, without asking for anything, being confident that He who has created everything has forgotten nothing.

I believe, therefore, without seeking to understand. I don't wish to give any name, and especially I do not wish to give the name of God, to statues or to paintings. For He is above everything that is known. Everything that is made for this purpose, is, in my humble opinion, *a fraud.*

The sick and the infirm ought to be fed, without having to beg, in a country like France.

Go and see what others have produced, but never copy anything except nature. You would be trying to enter into a temperament that is not yours and nothing that you would do would have any character.

The greatest enemy of the worker and the industrial artist is certainly the machine.

The modern architect is, generally speaking, art's greatest enemy.

We are proud of the renown of our old masters, and the countless works of art this marvelous country has produced. But we must not behave like those nobles, who owe their titles to their ancestors, and spend their last sou to hear themselves addressed as "Monsieur le Baron" by the waiters in cafés—which costs them twenty francs each time.

Since you love the Republic so much, why are there no statues of the Republic as beautiful as the Athenas of the Greeks? Do you love the Republic less than the Greeks did their gods?

There are people who imagine that one can re-do the Middle Ages and the Renaissance with impunity. One can only copy: that is the watchword. And after such folly has continued long enough, go back to the sources. You will see how far away we have got from them.

God, the King of artists, was clumsy.

Not only do I not wish to see one capital of a column exactly resemble another, I do not wish it to resemble itself; or to be uniform any more than are the heads, feet and hands which God created. I do not wish a column to be perfectly round, any more than a tree is.

I say to young people, therefore: throw away your compasses, otherwise there is no art.

Consider the great masters of the past. They were aware that there are two regularities: that of the eye and that of the compass. The great masters rejected the latter.

I propose to found a society. It is to be called "The Society of Irregulars." The members would have to know that a circle should never be round.

PAUL CÉZANNE

1839-1906

LETTERS

1904-1905

Paul Cézanne is regarded as one of the clearest harbingers of modern art. He was born in Aix-en-Provence in the south of France, where he studied law, attended drawing classes, and became friends with the novelist Émile Zola. Against the wishes of his father, he moved to Paris in 1861, where he joined Zola and began to work as a painter. His father later relented and provided an inheritance that allowed Cézanne to live comfortably. From 1864 to 1869, Cézanne submitted his work to the Salon, but was consistently rejected. During this time, he also met the artist Camille Pissarro and other members of the Impressionist group. Although he assimilated the principles of light and color and the loose brushwork of the group and exhibited with them in 1874 and 1877, Cézanne did not consider himself an Impressionist. In later life, Cézanne settled again in Aix, where he concentrated on still lifes, scenes of bathers, and views of Mont Sainte-Victoire, a landmark visible from his studio. At the time of his death, Cézanne was already considered a fundamental influence on the Fauve and Cubist movements, an influence that advanced modernism in the 20th century.

By 1889, Cézanne had returned to his home in Aix-en-Provence, where he would spend the remainder of his life. In 1895,

Ambroise Vollard organized the first major exhibition of Cézanne's work. The resulting debate about Cézanne's art brought him many devotees among the younger generation of artists, many of whom sought his advice. The subsequent correspondence addressed to his followers includes his theories and ideas about art. Most notable was his counsel to treat nature in the forms of a cone, sphere, and cylinder, a theory that is the foundation of early modernism.

SOURCE

Cézanne, Paul.1904-1905. "[Selections from]Letters to Young Friends: Letters on Painting, 1889-1906." In *Letters.* John Rewald, Ed. Marguerite Kay, Trans. Oxford: Bruno Cassier, 1941 and 1944. Letters Numbered CLXVII, CLXVIII, CLXIX, CLXXI, CLXXIV, CLXXV, CLXXX, CLXXXIII, CLXXXIV.

LETTERS
LETTERS TO YOUNG FRIENDS:
LETTERS ON PAINTING [SELECETIONS]

Not having exhibited in Paris for more than ten years, Cézanne was entirely unknown there. Only a small group of initiated used to go to the little shop of père Tanguy to admire the pictures of the recluse of Aix. Gradually this circle grew, critics such as Roger Marx and Gustave Geffroy began to take an interest in Cézanne's work and Octave Maus, secretary of the Art-Association of the "Vingts," invited him to exhibit with them at Brussels. In 1895 Ambroise Vollard followed the urgent advice of Camille Pissarro and his friends and organized the first great exhibition of Cézanne's pictures in his gallery in the rue Laffite. This was soon followed by other exhibitions all of which gave rise to the most heated discussions. As well as fanatical opponents they also brought Cézanne sincere and ardent admirers among the young generation of artists who soon sought the friendship and advice of the master at Aix. It is to them, young painters and writers, that Cézanne addressed those of his letters which contain his ideas and artistic theories.[JR]

CLXVII To Émile Bernard

Aix en Provence, 15th April, 1904

Dear Monsieur Bernard,

When you get this letter you will very probably already have received a letter coming from Belgium I think, and addressed to you to the rue Boulegon. I am well content with the expression of fine sympathy in art which you sent me in your letter.

May I repeat what I told you here: treat nature by the cylinder, the sphere, the cone, everything in proper perspective so that each side of an object or a plane is directed towards a central point. Lines parallel to the horizon give breadth, that is a section of nature or, if you prefer, of the spectacle that the Pater Omnipotens Eterne Deus [Father Omnipotent Eternal God] spreads out before our eyes. Lines perpendicular to this horizon give depth. But nature for us men is more depth than surface whence the need of introducing into our light vibrations, represented by reds and yellows, a sufficient amount of blue to give the impression of air.

I must tell you that I had another look at the study you made in the lower floor of the studio, it is good. You should, I think, only continue in this way. You have the understanding of what must be done and you will soon turn your back on the Gauguins and the Van Goghs!

Please thank Madame Bernard for the kind thoughts that she has reserved for the undersigned, a kiss from *père Goriot* for the children, all my best regards for your dear family.

CLXVIII To Émile Bernard

Aix, 12th May, 1904

My dear Bernard,

My absorption in my work and my advanced age will explain sufficiently my delay in answering your letter.

Moreover, in your last letter you discourse on such widely divergent topics, though all are connected with art, that I cannot follow you in all your phases.

I have already told you that I like Redon's talent enormously, and from my heart I agree with his feeling for and admiration of Delacroix. I do not know if my indifferent health will allow ever to realize my dream of painting his apotheosis.

I am progressing very slowly, for nature reveals herself to me in very complex forms; and the progress needed is incessant. One must see one's model correctly and experience it in the right way; and furthermore express oneself forcibly and with distinction.

Taste is the best judge. It is rare. Art only addresses itself to an excessively small number of individuals.

The artist must scorn all judgement that is not based on an intelligent observation of character. He must beware of the literary spirit which so often causes painting to deviate from its true path— the concrete study of nature—to lose itself all too long in intangible speculations.

The Louvre is a good book to consult but it must only be an intermediary. The real and immense study that must be taken up is the manifold picture of nature.

Thank you for sending me the book; I am waiting so as to be able to read it with a clear head.

You can if you think it right, send Vollard what he asked you for.

Please give my kind regards to Madame Bernard, and a kiss from *père Goriot* for Antoine and Irene.

CLXIX To Émile Bernard

Aix, 26th May, 1904

My dear Bernard,

On the whole I approve of the ideas you are going to expound in your next article for the *Occident*. But I must always come back to this: painters must devote themselves entirely to the study of nature and try to produce pictures which are an instruction. Talks on art are almost useless. The work which goes to bring progress in one's own subject is sufficient compensation for the incomprehension of imbeciles.

Literature expresses itself by abstractions whereas painting by means of drawing and colour, gives concrete shape to sensations and perceptions. One is neither too scrupulous nor too sincere nor too submissive to nature; but one is more or less master of one's model, and above all, of the means of expression. Get to the heart of what is before you and continue to express yourself as logically as possible.

Please give my kindest regards to Madame Bernard, a warm handclasp for you, love to the children.

Pictor P. Cézanne.

CLXXI To Émile Bernard

Aix, 25th July, 1904

My dear Bernard,

I received the "Revue Occidentale" and can only thank you for what you wrote about me. [Bernard's article on Paul Cézanne had just been published in the July number of the revue *Occident*—JR.]

I am sorry that we cannot be together now, for I do not want to be right in theory but in nature. Ingres, in spite of his "estyle" (Aixian pronunciation) and his admirers, is only a very little painter. You know the greatest painters better than I do; the Venetians and the Spaniards.

To achieve progress nature alone counts, and the eye is trained through contact with her. It becomes concentric by looking and working. I mean to say that in an orange, an apple, a bowl, a head, there is a culminating point; and this point is always—in spite of the tremendous effect of light and shade and colourful sensations—the closest to our eye; the edges of the objects recede to a centre on our horizon. With a small temperament one can be very much of a painter. One can do good things without being very much of a harmonist or a colourist. It is sufficient to have a sense of art—and this sense is doubtless the horror of the bourgeois. Therefore institutions, pensions, honours can only be made for cretins, rogues and rascals. Do not be an art critic, but paint, therein lies salvation.

A warm handclasp from your old comrade

P. Cézanne

My kind regards to Madame Bernard and love to the children.

CLXXIV To Charles Camoin

Aix, 9th December, 1904

My dear Camoin,

I received your kind letter dated from Martigues. Come whenever you like, you will always find me at work; you can accompany me to the motif if you like. Tell me the date of your arrival for if you come to the studio on the Lauves I can have lunch brought up for us both.

I have lunch at 11 o'clock, and from there I set off for the motif unless it rains. I have a baggage depot 20 minutes away from my house.

Studying the model and realizing it is sometimes very slow in coming for the artist.

Whoever the master is whom you prefer this must only be a directive for you. Otherwise you will never be anything but an imitator. With any feeling for nature whatever, and some fortunate gifts—and you have some—you should be able to dissociate yourself; advice, the methods of another must not make you change your own manner of feeling. Should you at the moment be under the influence of one who is older than you, believe me as soon as you begin to feel yourself, your own emotions will finally emerge and conquer their place in the sun,—*get the upper hand)* confidence,—what you must strive to attain is a good method of *construction*. Drawing is merely the outline of what you see.

Michelangelo is a constructor, and Rafael an *artist* who, great as he is, is always limited by the model.—When he tries to be thoughtful he falls below the *niveau* [standard] of his great rival.

Very sincerely yours,

P. Cézanne.

CLXXV To Émile Bernard

Aix, 23rd December, 1904

My dear Bernard,

I received your kind letter dated from Naples. I shall not dwell here on aesthetic problems. Yes I approve of your admiration for the strongest of all the Venetians; we are celebrating Tintoretto. Your desire to find a moral, an intellectual point of support in the works, which assuredly we shall never surpass, makes you continually on the *qui vive* [alert], searching incessantly for the way that you dimly apprehend, which will lead you surely to the recognition in front of nature, of what your means of expression are; and the day you will have found them, be convinced that you will find also without effort and in front of nature, the means employed by the four or five great ones of Venice.

This is true without possible doubt—I am very positive:—an optical impression is produced on our organs of sight which makes us classify as *light*, half-tone or quarter-tone the surfaces represented by colour sensations. (So that light does not exist for the painter). As long as we are forced to proceed from black to white, the first of these abstractions being like a point of support for the eye as much as for the mind, we are confused, we do not succeed in mastering ourselves in *possessing ourselves*. During this period (I am necessarily repeating myself a little) we turn towards the admirable works that have been handed down to us throughout the ages, where we find comfort, a support such as a plank is for the bather.—Everything you tell me in your letter is very true.

I am happy to hear that Madame Bernard and the children are well. My wife and my son are in Paris at the moment. We shall be together again soon I hope.

I wish to reply as far as possible to the principal points in your kind letter, and please give my warmest regards to Madame Bernard and a good kiss for Antoine and Irene, and for you my friend, after wishing you a happy New Year I send you a warm handclasp.

P. Cézanne.

CLXXX To Roger Marx

Aix, 23rd January, 1905

Monsieur le Rédacteur [Editor],

I read with interest the lines that you were kind enough to write about me in the two articles in the *Gazette des Beaux-Arts*. Thank you for the favourable opinion that you express on my behalf [in the December 1904 issue—JR].

My age and my health will never allow me to realize the dream of art that I have been pursuing all my life. But I shall always be grateful to the public of intelligent amateurs who had—despite my own hesitations—the intuition of what I wanted to attempt for the renewal of my art. To my mind one should not substitute oneself for the past, one has merely to add a new link. With the temperament of a painter and an ideal of art, that is to say a conception of nature, sufficient powers of expression would have been necessary to be intelligible for man and to occupy a suitable position in the history of art.

Please accept, Monsieur le Rédacteur, the expression of my warmest sympathy as an artist.

P. Cézanne.

CLXXXIII To Émile Bernard

Aix, 1905, Friday

My dear Bernard,

I am replying briefly to some of the paragraphs of your last letter. As you write, I think I really have made some slight progress in the last studies that you saw at my house. It is, however, very painful to have to register that the improvement produced in the comprehension of nature from the point of view of the form of the picture and the development of the means of expression should be accompanied by old age and a weakening of the body.

If the official Salons remain so inferior it is because they only employ more or less widely known methods of production. It would be better to bring more personal feeling, observation and character.

The Louvre is the book in which we learn to read. We must not, however, be satisfied with retaining the beautiful formulas of our illustrious predecessors. Let us go forth to study beautiful nature, let us try to free our minds from them, let us strive to express ourselves according to our personal temperaments. Time and reflection, moreover, modify little by little our vision, and at last comprehension comes to us.

It is impossible in this rainy weather to practise out of doors these theories which are yet so right. But perseverance leads us to understand interiors like everything else. It is only the old duffers who clog our intelligence, which needs spurring on.

Very sincerely yours and my regards to Madame Bernard and love to the children.

P. Cézanne.

You will understand me better when we see each other again; study modifies our vision to such a degree that the humble and colossal Pissarro finds himself justified in his anarchist theories.

Draw; but it is the reflection which *envelops;* light, through the general reflection, is the envelope.

Sincerely yours,
P.C.

CLXXXIV To Émile Bernard

Aix, 23rd October, 1905

My dear Bernard,

Your letters are precious to me for a double reason, because their arrival lifts me out of the monotony which is caused by the incessant and constant search for the sole and unique aim and this produces, in moments of physical fatigue, a kind of intellectual exhaustion; secondly I am able to describe to you again, rather too much I am afraid, the obstinacy with which I pursue the realization of that part of nature, which, coming into our line of vision, gives the picture. Now the theme to develop is that—whatever our temperament or power in the presence of nature may be—we must tender the image of what we see, forgetting everything that existed before us. Which, I believe, must permit the artist to give his entire personality whether great or small.

Now, being old, nearly 70 years, the sensations of colour, which give light, are the reason for the abstractions which prevent me from either covering my canvas or continuing the delimitation of the objects when their points of contact are fine and delicate; from which it results that my image or picture is incomplete. On the other hand the planes are placed one on top of the other from whence neo-impressionism emerged, which outlines the contours with a black stroke, a failing that must be fought at all costs. Well, nature when consulted, gives us the means of attaining this end.

I remembered quite well that you were at Tonnerre but the difficulties of settling down in my house make me place myself entirely at the disposal of my family, which makes use of this to seek their own comforts and neglect me a little. That is life; at my age I should have more experience and use it for the general good. I owe you the truth and shall tell it to you in painting.

Please give my kind regards to Madame Bernard; I must love the children seeing that St. Vincent de Paul is the one to whom I must recommend myself most.

Your old
Paul Cézanne.

A warm handclasp and good courage.
Optics, which are developed in us by study teach us to see.

LEO TOLSTOY

1828-1910

WHAT IS ART?

1896

Leo Tolstoy was born in Czarist Russia as a Count entitled to a life of privilege. Although he attended Kazou University, he did not receive a degree. He served as an officer in the artillery in the Caucasus from 1851-55, after which he traveled to Romania, France, Switzerland, and Germany. He is best known for his three major novels, *War and Peace* (1863-69), *Anna Karenina* (1873-77), and *Resurrection* (1899), which reflect the lifelong search for morals and values, that led him to both Christian philosophy and simple living.

What is Art? is a treatise on the nature and purpose of art. The essay reflects his personal interpretation of Christianity, which called for non-resistance to evil and for the need to look inward and to God, rather than outward to the State, when seeking answers to questions of morality. He explored the concept of art as communication, requiring interaction between the work of art and the observer, in which the observer must rely on senses and feelings to take part in the conversation. He further examined how moral values define aesthetic values. To be good art, according to Tolstoy, it must express original thoughts and feelings, and be comprehensible to the most people. Writing in a cultural environment that valued elitist works and devalued domestic or folk works, Tolstoy's position offers truly revolutionary claims.

SOURCE

Tolstoï, Lyof N. [Leo Tolstoy] 1898. *What is Art?* In *The Complete Works of Lyof N. Tolstoï.* Aline Delano, Tr. New York: Thomas Y. Crowell Co., 1899.

WHAT IS ART?
Chapter Five

What is art, if we put aside the conception of beauty, which confuses the whole matter? The latest and most comprehensible definitions of art, apart from the conception of beauty, are the following: (1 *a*) Art is an activity arising even in the animal kingdom, and springing from sexual desire and the propensity to play (Schiller, Darwin, Spencer), and, (I 1*b*) accompanied by a pleasurable excitement of the nervous system (Grant Allen). This is the physiological-evolutionary definition. (2) Art is the external manifestation, by means of lines, colors, movements, sounds, or words, of emotions felt by man (Véron). This is the experimental definition. According to the very latest definition (Sully), (3) Art is "the production of some permanent object or passing action, which is fitted, not only to supply an active enjoyment to the producer, but to convey a pleasurable impression to a number of spectators or listeners, quite apart from any personal advantage to be derived from it."

Notwithstanding the superiority of these definitions to the metaphysical definitions which depended on the conception of beauty, they are yet far from exact. (1 *a*) The first, the physiological-evolutionary definition, is inexact, because, instead of speaking about the artistic activity itself, which is the real matter in hand, it treats of the derivation of art. The modification of it, (1 *b*) based on the physiological effects on the human organism, is inexact, because within the limits of such definition many other human activities can be included, as has occurred in the neo-aesthetic theories, which reckon as art the preparation of handsome clothes, pleasant scents, and even victuals.

The experimental definition (2), which makes art consist in the expression of emotions, is inexact, because a man may express his emotions by means of lines, colors, sounds, or words, and yet may not act on others by such expression; and then the manifestation of his emotions is not art.

The third definition (that of Sully) is inexact, because in the production of objects or actions affording pleasure to the producer and a pleasant emotion to the spectators or hearers apart from personal advantage may be included the showing of conjuring tricks or gymnastic exercises, and other activities which are not art. And, further, many things, the production of which does not afford pleasure to the producer, and the sensation received from which is unpleasant, such as gloomy, heart-rending scenes in a poetic description or a play, may nevertheless be undoubted works of art.

The inaccuracy of all these definitions arises from the fact that in them all (as also in the metaphysical definitions) the object considered is the pleasure art may give, and not the purpose it may serve in the life of man and of humanity.

In order correctly to define art, it is necessary, first of all, to cease to consider it as a means to pleasure, and to consider it as one of the conditions of human life. Viewing it in this way, we cannot fail to observe that art is one of the means of intercourse between man and man.

Every work of art causes the receiver to enter into a certain kind of relationship both with him who produced, or is producing, the art, and with all those who, simultaneously, previously, or subsequently, receive the same artistic impression.

Speech, transmitting the thoughts and experiences of men, serves as a means of union among them, and art acts in a similar manner. The peculiarity of this latter means of intercourse, distinguishing it from intercourse by means of words, consists in this, that whereas by words a man transmits his thoughts to another, by means of art he transmits his feelings.

The activity of art is based on the fact that a man, receiving through his sense of hearing or sight another man's expression of feeling, is capable of experiencing the emotion which moved the man who expressed it. To take the simplest example: one man laughs, and another, who hears, becomes merry; or a man weeps, and another, who hears, feels sorrow. A man is excited or irritated, and another man, seeing him, comes to a similar state of mind. By his movements, or by the sounds of his voice, a man expresses courage and determination, or sadness and calmness, and this state of mind passes on to others. A man suffers, expressing his sufferings by groans and spasms, and this suffering transmits itself to other people; a man expresses his feeling of admiration, devotion, fear, respect, or love to certain objects, persons, or phenomena, and others are infected by the same feelings of admiration, devotion, fear, respect, or love to the same objects, persons, and phenomena.

And it is on this capacity of man to receive another man's expression of feeling, and experience those feelings himself, that the activity of art is based.

If a man infects another or others, directly, immediately, by his appearance, or by the sounds he gives vent to at the very time he experiences the feeling; if he causes another man to yawn when he himself cannot help yawning, or to laugh or cry when he himself is obliged to laugh or cry, or to suffer when he himself is suffering—that does not amount to art.

Art begins when one person, with the object of joining another or others to himself in one and the same feeling, expresses that feeling by certain external indications. To take the simplest example: a boy, having experienced, let us say, fear on encountering a wolf, relates that encounter; and, in order to evoke in others the feeling he has experienced, describes himself, his condition before the encounter, the surroundings, the wood, his own light-heartedness, and then the wolf's appearance, its movements, the distance between himself and the wolf, etc. All this, if only the boy, when telling the story, again experiences the feelings he had lived through and infects the hearers and compels them to feel what the narrator had experienced, is art. If even the boy had not seen a wolf but had frequently been afraid of one, and if, wishing to evoke in others the fear he had felt, he invented an encounter with a wolf, and recounted it so as to make his hearers share the feelings he experienced when he feared the wolf, that also would be art. And just in the same way it is art if a man, having experienced either the fear of suffering or the attraction of enjoyment (whether in reality or in imagination), expresses these feelings on canvas or in marble so that others are infected by them. And it is also art if a man feels or imagines to himself feelings of delight, gladness, sorrow, despair, courage, or despondency, and the transition from one to another of these feelings, and expresses these feelings by sounds, so that the hearers are infected by them, and experience them as they were experienced by the composer.

The feelings with which the artist infects others may be most various,—very strong or very weak, very important or very insignificant, very bad or very good: feelings of love for native land, self-devotion and submission to fate or to God expressed in a drama, raptures of lovers described in a novel, feelings of voluptuousness expressed in a picture, courage expressed in a triumphal march, merriment evoked by a dance, humor evoked by a funny story, the feeling of quietness transmitted by an evening landscape or by a lullaby, or the feeling of admiration evoked by a beautiful arabesque—it is all art.

If only the spectators or auditors are infected by the feelings which the author has felt, it is art.

To evoke in oneself a feeling one has once experienced, and having evoked it in oneself, then, by means of movements, lines, colors, sounds, or forms expressed in words, so to transmit that feeling that others may experience the same feeling—this is the activity of art.

Art is a human activity, consisting in this, that one man consciously, by means of certain external signs, hands on to others feelings he has lived through, and that other people are infected by these feelings, and also experience them.

Art is not, as the metaphysicians say, the manifestation of some mysterious Idea of beauty, or God; it is not, as the aesthetical physiologists say, a game in which man lets off his excess of stored-up energy [i.e., in Greek tragedy, catharsis]; it is not the expression of man's emotions by external signs; it is not the production of pleasing objects; and, above all, it is not pleasure; but it is a means of union among men, joining them together in the same feelings, and indispensable for the life and progress toward well-being of individuals and of humanity.

As, thanks to man's capacity to express thoughts by words, every man may know all that has been done for him in the realms of thought by all humanity before his day, and can, in the present, thanks to this capacity to understand the thoughts of others, become a sharer in their activity, and can himself hand on to his contemporaries and descendants the thoughts he has assimilated from others, as well as those which have arisen within himself; so, thanks to man's capacity to be infected with the feelings of others by means of art, all that is being lived through by his contemporaries is accessible to him, as well as the feelings experienced by men thousands of years ago, and he has also the possibility of transmitting his own feelings to others.

If people lacked this capacity to receive the thoughts conceived by the men who preceded them, and to pass on to others their own thoughts, men would be like wild beasts, or like Kaspar Hauser [a 16-year-old boy who appeared in 1828 in Germany who had supposedly been kept confined for his entire life and lacked socialization].

And if men lacked this other capacity of being infected by art, people might be almost more savage still, and, above all, more separated from, and more hostile to, one another.

And therefore the activity of art is a most important one, as important as the activity of speech itself and as generally diffused.

We are accustomed to understand art to be only what we hear and see in theaters, concerts, and exhibitions; together with buildings, statues, poems, novels . . . . But all this is but the smallest part of the art by which we communicate with each other in life. All human life is filled with works of art of every kind,—from cradlesong, jest, mimicry, the ornamentation of houses, dress, and utensils, up to church services, buildings, monuments, and triumphal processions. It is all artistic activity. So that by art, in the limited sense of the word, we do not mean all human activity transmitting feelings, but only that part which we for some reason select from it and to which we attach special importance.

This special importance has always been given by all men to that part of this activity which transmits feelings flowing from their religious perception, and this small part of art they have specifically called art, attaching to it the full meaning of the word.

That was how men of old—Socrates, Plato, and Aristotle— looked on art. Thus did the Hebrew prophets and the ancient Christians regard art; thus it was, and still is, understood by the Mahommedans, and thus is it still understood by religious folk among our own peasantry.

Some teachers of mankind—as Plato in his *Republic* and people such as the primitive Christians, the strict Mahommedans, and the Buddhists—have gone so far as to repudiate all art.

People viewing art in this way (in contradiction to the prevalent view of to-day, which regards any art as good if only it affords pleasure) considered, and consider, that art (as contrasted with speech, which need not be listened to) is so highly dangerous in its power to infect people against their wills, that mankind will lose far less by banishing all art than by tolerating each and every art.

Evidently such people were wrong in repudiating all art, for they denied that which cannot be denied,—one of the indispensable means of communication, without which mankind could not exist. But not less wrong are the people of civilized European society of our class and day, in favoring any art if it but serves beauty, *i.e.*, gives people pleasure.

Formerly people feared lest among the works of art there might chance to be some causing corruption, and they prohibited art altogether. Now, they only fear lest they should be deprived of any enjoyment art can afford, and patronize any art. And I think the last error is much grosser than the first, and that its consequences are far more harmful.

BERNHARD BERENSON

1865-1959

FLORENTINE PAINTERS OF THE RENAISSANCE

1896

Bernhard Berenson is considered a foremost critic and connoisseur of Italian art. Born in Lithuania, he moved to the United States and graduated from Harvard University in 1887. He was an art advisor for many important collectors, including Isabella Stewart Gardner, whose home is now a museum in Boston. In 1900, he settled in Settignano, near Florence, Italy, where he built his personal collection. Berenson was a brilliant raconteur as well as an art collector and authority on Italian Renaissance art, and his home, I Tatti (later willed to Harvard University) became a destination for European and American intellectuals. Although scholars now question some of his judgments, Berenson's many publications continue to be an invaluable reference on the painters of the Italian Renaissance.

Berenson begins his exploration of the Italian Renaissance in Florence with the painter Giotto di Bondone (active 1300-1337). Vasari credited Giotto with setting art on a true path, one that drew accurately from life. Berenson likewise differentiates Giotto's work. He does so by examining the use of perspective to create a three-dimensional form and the stimulation of tactile values. In the latter, he acclaims Giotto as the supreme master. It is this that, to Berenson, gives a figure artistic existence.

SOURCE

Berenson, Bernhard. 1896. "II [On Giotto and Values of Touch]." In *The Florentine Painters of the Renaissance*. 3rd Edition. New York: G.P. Putnam's Sons, 1909. 3-19.

FLORENTINE PAINTERS OF THE RENAISSANCE
II. [On Giotto and Values of Touch]

The first of the great personalities in Florentine painting was Giotto. Although he affords no exception to the rule that the great Florentines exploited all the arts in the endeavour to express themselves, he, Giotto, renowned as architect and sculptor, reputed as wit and versifier, differed from most of his Tuscan successors in having peculiar aptitude for the essential in painting *as an art.*

But before we can appreciate his real value, we must come to an agreement as to what in the art of figure-painting—the craft has its own altogether diverse laws—*is* the essential; for figure-painting, we may say at once, was not only the one preoccupation of Giotto, but the dominant interest of the entire Florentine school.

Psychology has ascertained that sight alone gives us no accurate sense of the third dimension. In our infancy, long before we are conscious of the process, the sense of touch, helped on by muscular sensations of movement, teaches us to appreciate depth, the third dimension, both in objects and in space.

In the same unconscious years we learn to make of touch, of the third dimension, the test of reality. The child is still dimly aware of the intimate connection between touch and the third dimension. He cannot persuade himself of the unreality of Looking-Glass Land until he has touched the back of the mirror. Later, we entirely forget the connection, although it remains true, that every time our eyes recognise reality, we are, as a matter of fact, giving tactile values to retinal impressions.

Now, painting is an art which aims at giving an abiding impression of artistic reality with only two dimensions. The painter must, therefore, do consciously what we all do unconsciously,— construct his third dimension. And he can accomplish his task only as we accomplish ours, by giving tactile values to retinal impressions. His first business, therefore, is to rouse the tactile sense, for I must have the illusion of being able to touch a figure, I must have the illusion of varying muscular sensations inside my palm and fingers corresponding to the various projections of this figure, before I shall take it for granted as real, and let it affect me lastingly.

It follows that the essential in the art of painting—as distinguished from the art of colouring, I beg the reader to observe— is somehow to stimulate our consciousness of tactile values, so that the picture shall have at least as much power as the object represented, to appeal to our tactile imagination.

Well, it was of the power to stimulate the tactile consciousness— of the essential, as I have ventured to call it, in the art of painting— that Giotto was supreme master. This is his everlasting claim to greatness, and it is this which will make him a source of highest aesthetic delight for a period at least as long as decipherable traces of his handiwork remain on mouldering panel or crumbling wall. For great though he was as a poet, enthralling as a story-teller, splendid and majestic as a composer, he was in these qualities superior in degree only, to many of the masters who painted in various parts of Europe during the thousand years that intervened between the decline of antique, and the birth, in his own person, of modern painting. But none of these masters had the power to stimulate the tactile imagination, and, consequently, they never painted a figure which has artistic existence. Their works have value, if at all, as highly elaborate, very intelligible symbols, capable, indeed, of communicating something, but losing all higher value the moment the message is delivered.

Giotto's paintings, on the contrary, have not only as much power of appealing to the tactile imagination as is possessed by the objects represented—human figures in particular—but actually more, with the necessary result that to his contemporaries they conveyed a *keener* sense of reality, of life-likeness than the objects themselves! We whose current knowledge of anatomy is greater, who expect more articulation and suppleness in the human figure, who, in short, see much less naively now than Giotto's contemporaries, no longer find his paintings more than life-like; but we still feel them to be intensely real in the sense that they still powerfully appeal to our tactile imagination, thereby compelling us, as do all things that stimulate our sense of touch while they present themselves to our eyes, to take their existence for granted. And it is only when we can take for granted the existence of the object painted that it can begin to give us pleasure that is genuinely artistic, as separated from the interest we feel in symbols.

At the risk of seeming to wander off into the boundless domain of aesthetics, we must stop at this point for a moment to make sure that we are of one mind regarding the meaning of the phrase "artistic pleasure," in so far at least as it is used in connection with painting.

What is the point at which ordinary pleasures pass over into the specific pleasures derived from each one of the arts? Our judgment about the merits of any given work of art depends to a large extent upon our answer to this question. Those who have not yet differentiated the specific pleasures of the art of painting from the pleasures they derive from the art of literature, will be likely to fall into the error of judging the picture by its dramatic presentation of a situation or its rendering of character; will, in short, demand of the painting that it shall be in the first place a good *illustration*. Those others who seek in painting what is usually sought in music, the communication of a pleasurable state of emotion, will prefer pictures which suggest pleasant associations, nice people, refined amusements, agreeable landscapes. In many cases this lack of clearness is of comparatively slight importance, the given picture containing all these pleasure-giving elements in addition to the qualities peculiar to the art of painting. But in the case of the Florentines, the distinction is of vital consequence, for they have been the artists in Europe who have most resolutely set themselves to work upon the specific problems of the art of figure-painting, and have neglected, more than any other school, to call to their aid the secondary pleasures of association. With them the issue is clear. If we wish to appreciate their merit, we are forced to disregard the desire for pretty or agreeable types, dramatically interpreted situations, and, in fact, "suggestiveness" of any kind. Worse still, we must even forego our pleasure in colour, often a genuinely artistic pleasure, for they never systematically exploited this element, and in some of their best works the colour is actually harsh and unpleasant. It was in fact upon form, and form alone, that the great Florentine masters concentrated their efforts, and we are consequently forced to the belief that, in their pictures at least, form is the principal source of our aesthetic enjoyment.

Now in what way, we ask, can form in painting give me a sensation of pleasure which differs from the ordinary sensations I receive from form? How is it that an object whose recognition in nature may have given me no pleasure, becomes, when recognised in a picture, a source of aesthetic enjoyment, or that recognition pleasurable in nature becomes an enhanced pleasure the moment it is transferred to art? The answer, I believe, depends upon the fact that art stimulates to an unwonted activity psychical processes which are in themselves the source of most (if not all) of our pleasures, and which here, free from disturbing physical sensations, never tend to pass over into pain. For instance: I am in the habit of realising a given object with an intensity that we shall value as 2. If I suddenly realise this familiar object with an intensity of 4, I receive the immediate pleasure which accompanies a doubling of my mental activity. But the pleasure rarely stops here. Those who are capable of receiving direct pleasure from a work of art, are generally led on to the further pleasures of self-consciousness. The fact that the psychical process of recognition goes forward with the unusual intensity of 4 to 2, overwhelms them with the sense of having twice the capacity they had credited themselves with: their whole personality is enhanced, and, being aware that this enhancement is connected with the object in question, they for some time after take not only an increased interest in it, but continue to realise it with the new intensity. Precisely this is what form does in painting: it lends a higher coefficient of reality to the object represented, with the consequent enjoyment of accelerated psychical processes, and the exhilarating sense of increased capacity in the observer. (Hence, by the way, the greater pleasure we take in the object painted than in itself.)

And it happens thus. We remember that to realise form we must give tactile values to retinal sensations. Ordinarily we have considerable difficulty in skimming off these tactile values, and by the time they have reached our consciousness, they have lost much of their strength. Obviously, the artist who gives us these values more rapidly than the object itself gives them, gives us the pleasures consequent upon a more vivid realisation of the object, and the further pleasures that come from the sense of greater psychical capacity.

Furthermore, the stimulation of our tactile imagination awakens our consciousness of the importance of the tactile sense in our physical and mental functioning, and thus, again, by making us feel better provided for life than we were aware of being, gives us a heightened sense of capacity. And this brings us back once more to the statement that the chief business of the figure painter, as an artist, is to stimulate the tactile imagination.

The proportions of this small book forbid me to develop further a theme, the adequate treatment of which would require more than the entire space at my command. I must be satisfied with the crude and unillumined exposition given already, allowing myself this further word only, that I do not mean to imply that we get no pleasure from a picture except the tactile satisfaction. On the contrary, we get much pleasure from composition, more from colour, and perhaps more still from movement, to say nothing of all the possible associative pleasures for which every work of art is the occasion. What I do wish to say is that *unless* it satisfies our tactile imagination, a picture will not exert the fascination of an ever-heightened reality; first we shall exhaust its ideas, and then its power of appealing to our emotions, and its "beauty" will not seem more significant at the thousandth look than at the first.

My need of dwelling upon this subject at all, I must repeat, arises from the fact that although this principle is important indeed in other schools, it is all-important in the Florentine school. Without its due appreciation it would be impossible to do justice to Florentine painting. We should lose ourselves in admiration of its "teaching," or perchance of its historical importance—as if historical importance were synonymous with artistic significance!—but we should never realise what artistic idea haunted the minds of its great men, and never understand why at a date so early it became academic.

Let us now turn back to Giotto and see in what way he fulfils the first condition of painting as an art, which condition, as we agreed, is somehow to stimulate our tactile imagination. We shall understand this without difficulty if we cover with the same glance two pictures of nearly the same subject that hang side by side in the Florence Academy, one by "Cimabue," and the other by Giotto. The difference is striking, but it does not consist so much in a difference of pattern and types, as of realisation. In the "Cimabue" we patiently decipher the lines and colours, and we conclude at last that they were intended to represent a woman seated, men and angels standing by or kneeling. To recognise these representations we have had to make many times the effort that the actual objects would have required, and in consequence our feeling of capacity has not only not been confirmed, but actually put in question. With what sense of relief, of rapidly rising vitality, we turn to the Giotto! Our eyes scarcely have had time to light on it before we realise it completely—the throne occupying a real space, the Virgin satisfactorily seated upon it, the angels grouped in rows about it. Our tactile imagination is put to play immediately.

Our palms and fingers accompany our eyes much more quickly than in presence of real objects, the sensations varying constantly with the various projections represented, as of face, torso, knees; confirming in every way our feeling of capacity for coping with things,—for life, in short. I care little that the picture endowed with the gift of evoking such feelings has faults, that the types represented do not correspond to my ideal of beauty, that the figures are too massive, and almost unarticulated; I forgive them all, because I have much better to do than to dwell upon faults.

But how does Giotto accomplish this miracle? With the simplest means, with almost rudimentary light and shade, and functional line, he contrives to render, out of all the possible outlines, out of all the possible variations of light and shade that a given figure may have, only those that we must isolate for special attention when we are actually realising it. This determines his types, his schemes of colour, even his compositions. He aims at types which both in face and figure are simple, large-boned, and massive,—types, that is to say, which in actual life would furnish the most powerful stimulus to the tactile imagination. Obliged to get the utmost out of his rudimentary light and shade, he makes his scheme of colour of the lightest that his contrasts may be of the strongest. In his compositions, he aims at clearness of grouping, so that each important figure may have its desired tactile value. Note in the *Madonna* we have been looking at, how the shadows compel us to realise every concavity, and the lights every convexity, and how, with the play of the two, under the guidance of line, we realise the significant parts of each figure, whether draped or undraped. Nothing here but has its architectonic reason. Above all, every line is functional; that is to say, charged with purpose. Its existence, its direction, is absolutely determined by the need of rendering the tactile values. Follow any line here, say in the figure of the angel kneeling to the left, and see how it outlines and models, how it enables you to realise the head, the torso, the hips, the legs, the feet, and how its direction, its tension, is always determined by the action. There is not a genuine fragment of Giotto in existence but has these qualities, and to such a degree that the worst treatment has not been able to spoil them. Witness the resurrected frescoes in Santa Croce at Florence!

The rendering of tactile values once recognised as the most important specifically artistic quality of Giotto's work, and as his personal contribution to the art of painting, we are all the better fitted to appreciate his more obvious though less peculiar merits— merits, I must add, which would seem far less extraordinary if it were not for the high plane of reality on which Giotto keeps us. Now what is back of this power of raising us to a higher plane of reality but a genius for grasping and communicating real significance? What is it to render the tactile values of an object but to communicate its material significance? A painter who, after generations of mere manufacturers of symbols, illustrations, and allegories had the power to render the material significance of the objects he painted, must, as a man, have had a profound sense of the significant. No matter, then, what his theme, Giotto feels its real significance and communicates as much of it as the general limitations of his art, and of his own skill permit. When the theme is sacred story, it is scarcely necessary to point out with what processional gravity, with what hieratic dignity, with what sacramental intentness he endows it; the eloquence of the greatest critics has here found a darling subject. But let us look a moment at certain of his symbols in the Arena at Padua, at the *Inconstancy*, the *Injustice* the *Avarice*, for instance. "What are the significant traits," he seems to have asked himself, "in the appearance and action of a person under the exclusive domination of one of these vices? Let me paint the person with these traits, and I shall have a figure that perforce must call up the vice in question." So he paints *Inconstancy* as a woman with a blank face, her arms held out aimlessly, her torso falling backwards, her feet on the side of a wheel. It makes one giddy to look at her. *Injustice*, is a powerfully built man in the vigour of his years dressed in the costume of a judge, with his left hand clenching the hilt of his sword, and his clawed right hand grasping a double hooked lance. His cruel eye is sternly on the watch, and his attitude is one of alert readiness to spring in all his giant force upon his prey. He sits enthroned on a rock, overtowering the tall waving trees, and below him his underlings are stripping and murdering a wayfarer. *Avarice* is a horned hag with ears like trumpets. A snake issuing from her mouth curls back and bites her forehead. Her left hand clutches her money-bag, as she moves forward stealthily, her right hand ready to shut down on whatever it can grasp. No need to label them: as long as these vices exist, for so long has Giotto extracted and presented their visible significance.

Still another exemplification of his sense for the significant is furnished by his treatment of action and movement. The grouping, the gestures never fail to be just such as will most rapidly convey the meaning. So with the significant line, the significant light and shade, the significant look up or down, and the significant gesture, with means technically of the simplest, and, be it remembered, with no knowledge of anatomy, Giotto conveys a complete sense of motion such as we get in his Paduan frescoes of the *Resurrection of the Blessed*, of the *Ascension of our Lord*, of the God the Father in the *Baptism*, or the angel in *Zacharias' Dream*.

This, then, is Giotto's claim to everlasting appreciation as an artist: that his thorough-going sense for the significant in the visible world enabled him so to represent things that we realise his representations more quickly and more completely than we should realise the things themselves, thus giving us that confirmation of our sense of capacity which is so great a source of pleasure.

JOHN BERGER

1926-

WAYS OF SEEING

1972

Award-winning novelist, painter, and art historian, John Berger's many distinctions include screenplays and stage plays, as well as a series for BBC based on one of his many books on art criticism, *Ways of Seeing,* excerpted here. This influential volume on art criticism aims to start a process of questioning: art is all around us, everywhere we go, every day of our lives. The eye is receptive to the visual world, and therefore to art, at all times. Yet we frequently see art in the form of reproduction, which changes the way in which we see it. Berger questions how we look at paintings, how images and artistic conventions develop social implications and psychological impact; he is also interested in how women are depicted in art from the Renaissance onward.

The artist often plays an important role as the articulator of shared beliefs and values, which are expressed through an ongoing tradition to the intended audience. For Berger, "[t]he way we see things is affected by what we know or what we believe." A work of art as a representation of an idea is, therefore, best understood within an historical, cultural, and religious framework. As is clear in this excerpt, Berger's point of view aligns itself with a Marxist criticism of culture and social relations.

SOURCE

Berger, John. 1972. *Ways of Seeing.* "[Chapter] 1." New York: Penguin, 1983. 8-11, 16-20, 26-33.*

Note: the Penguin edition includes images of art works referenced. They are noted here in < > to aid the interested reader's further study.

WAYS OF SEEING

1

Seeing comes before words. The child looks and recognizes before it can speak.

But there is also another sense in which seeing comes before words. It is seeing which establishes our place in the surrounding world; we explain that world with words, but words can never undo the fact that we are surrounded by it. The relation between what we see and what we know is never settled. Each evening we *see* the sun set. We *know* that the earth is turning away from it. Yet the knowledge, the explanation, never quite fits the sight. The Surrealist pointer Magritte commented on this always-present gap between words and seeing in a painting called *The Key of Dreams*.

< Image of *The Key of Dreams* by Magritte >

The way we see things is affected by what we know or what we believe. In the Middle Ages when men believed in the physical existence of Hell the sight of fire must have meant something different from what it means today. Nevertheless their idea of Hell owed a lot to the sight of fire consuming and the ashes remaining—as well as to their experience of the pain of burns.

When in love, the sight of the beloved has a completeness which no words and no embrace can match: a completeness which only the act of making love can temporarily accommodate.

Yet this seeing which comes before words, and can never be quite covered by them, is not a question of mechanically reacting to stimuli. (It can only be thought of in this way if one isolates the small part of the process which concerns the eye's retina.) We only see what we look at. To look is an act of choice. As a result of this act, what we see is brought within our reach—though not necessarily within arm's reach. To touch something is to situate oneself in relation to it. (Close your eyes, move round the room and notice how the faculty of touch is like a static, limited form of sight.) We never look at just one thing; we are always looking at the relation between things and ourselves. Our vision is continually active, continually moving, continually holding things in a circle around itself, constituting what is present to us as we are.

Soon after we can see, we are aware that we can also be seen. The eye of the other combines with our own eye to make it fully credible that we are part of the visible world.

If we accept that we can see that hill over there, we propose that from that hill we can be seen. The reciprocal nature of vision is more fundamental than that of spoken dialogue. And often dialogue is an attempt to verbalize this—an attempt to explain how, either metaphorically or literally, "you see things," and an attempt to discover how "he sees things."

In the sense in which we use the word in this book, all images are man-made.

< Assemblage of 12 images in various media >

An image is a sight which has been recreated or reproduced. It is an appearance, or a set of appearances, which has been detached from the place and time in which it first made its appearance and preserved—for a few moments or a few centuries. Every image embodies a way of seeing. Even a photograph. For photographs are not, as is often assumed, a mechanical record. Every time we look at a photograph, we are aware, however slightly, of the photographer selecting that sight from an infinity of other possible sights. This is true even in the most casual family snapshot. The photographer's way of seeing is reflected in his choice of subject. The painter's way of seeing is reconstituted by the marks he makes on the canvas or paper. Yet, although every image embodies a way of seeing, our perception or appreciation of an image depends also upon our own way of seeing. (It may be, for example, that Sheila is one figure among twenty; but for our own reasons she is the one we have eyes for.)

Images were first made to conjure up the appearances of something that was absent. Gradually it became evident that an image could outlast what it represented; it then showed how something or somebody had once looked—and thus by implication how the subject had once been seen by other people. Later still the specific vision of the image-maker was also recognized as part of the record. An image became a record of how X had seen Y. This was the result of an increasing consciousness of individuality, accompanying an increasing awareness of history. It would be rash to try to date this last development precisely. But certainly in Europe such consciousness has existed since the beginning of the Renaissance.

No other kind of relic or text from the past can offer such a direct testimony about the world which surrounded other people at other times. In this respect images are more precise and richer than literature. To say this is not to deny the expressive or imaginative quality of art, treating it as mere documentary evidence; the more imaginative the work, the more profoundly it allows us to share the artist's experience of the visible.

Yet when an image is presented as a work of art, the way people look at it is affected by a whole series of learnt assumptions about art. Assumptions concerning:

   Beauty
   Truth

Genius
Civilization
Form
Status
Taste, etc.

Many of these assumptions no longer accord with the world as
it is. (The world-as-it-is is more than pure objective fact, it includes
consciousness.) Out of true with the present, these assumptions
obscure the past. They mystify rather than clarify. The past is never
there waiting to be discovered, to be recognized for exactly what it
is. History always constitutes the relation between a present and
its past. Consequently fear of the present leads to mystification of
the past. The past is not for living in; it is a well of conclusions
from which we draw in order to act. Cultural mystification of
the past entails a double loss. Works of art are made unnecessarily
remote. And the past offers us fewer conclusions to complete in
action.

When we 'see' a landscape, we situate ourselves in it. If we
'saw' the art of the past, we would situate ourselves in history.
When we are prevented from seeing it, we are being deprived of
the history which belongs to us. Who benefits from this
deprivation? In the end, the art of the past is being mystified
because a privileged minority is striving to invent a history which
can retrospectively justify the role of the ruling classes, and such
a justification can no longer make sense in modern terms. And
so, inevitably, it mystifies.

Let us consider a typical example of such mystification. A two-
volume study was recently published on Frans Hals [Seymour Silve,
Frans Hals (Phaidon, London)-JB]. It is the authoritative work to
date on this painter. As a book of specialized art history it is no
better and no worse than the average.

<Images of 2 paintings: *Regents of the Old Men's Alms House* and
Regentesses of the Old Men's Alms House, both by Hals 1580-1666>

The last two great paintings by Frans Hals portray the Governors and the Governesses of an Alms House for old paupers in the Dutch seventeenth-century city of Haarlem. They were officially commissioned portraits. Hals, an old man of over eighty, was destitute. Most of his life he had been in debt. During the winter of 1664, the year he began painting these pictures, he obtained three loads of peat on public charity; otherwise he would have frozen to death. Those who now sat for him were administrators of such public charity.

The author records these facts and then explicitly says that it would be incorrect to read into the paintings any criticism of the sitters. There is no evidence, he says, that Hals painted them in a spirit of bitterness. The author considers them, however, remarkable works of art and explains why. Here he writes of the Regentesses:

> Each woman speaks to us of the human condition with equal importance. Each woman stands out with equal clarity against the *enormous* dark surface, yet they are linked by a firm rhythmical arrangement and the subdued diagonal pattern formed by their heads and hands. Subtle modulations of the *deep*, glowing blacks contribute to the harmonious fusion of the whole and form an *unforgettable contrast* with the *powerful* whites and vivid flesh tones where the detached strokes reach *a peak of breadth and strength*. (our italics[-JB])

The compositional unity of a painting contributes fundamentally to the power of its image. It is reasonable to consider a painting's composition. But here the composition is written about as though it were in itself the emotional charge of the painting. Terms like *harmonious fusion, unforgettable contrast*, reaching *a peak of breadth and strength* transfer the emotion provoked by the image from the plane of lived experience, to that of disinterested "art appreciation." All conflict disappears. One is left with the unchanging "human condition," and the painting considered as a marvellously made object.

Focus on the composition instead of what it mean

Very little is known about Hals or the Regents who commissioned him. It is not possible to produce circumstantial evidence to establish what their relations were. But there is the evidence of the paintings themselves: the evidence of a group of men and a group of women as seen by another man, the painter. Study this evidence and judge for yourself.

< Details of 3 heads in Hals's paintings above >

The art historian fears such direct judgement:

> As in so many other pictures by Hals, the penetrating
> characterizations almost seduce us into believing that
> we know the personality traits and even the habits
> of the men and women portrayed.

What is this "seduction" he writes of? It is nothing less than the paintings working upon us. They work upon us because we accept the way Hals saw his sitters. We do not accept this innocently. We accept it in so far as it corresponds to our own observation of people, gestures, faces, institutions. This is possible because we still live in a society of comparable social relations and moral values. And it is precisely this which gives the paintings their psychological and social urgency. It is this—not the painter's skill as a "seducer"— which convinces us that we *can* know the people portrayed.

The author continues:

> In the case of some critics the seduction has been a
> total success. It has, for example, been asserted that
> the Regent in the tipped slouch hat, which hardly
> covers any of his long, lank hair, and whose curiously
> set eyes do not focus, was shown in a drunken state.

This, he suggests, is a libel. He argues that it was a fashion at that time to wear hats on the side of the head. He cites medical opinion to

I saw this painting at Rill museum
in Amstad 2006

(handwritten marginalia at top: "Hal has to suppress how he sees the way he sees" ... "before he can be ... objective")

prove that the Regent's expression could well be the result of a facial paralysis. He insists that the painting would have been unacceptable to the Regents if one of them had been portrayed drunk. One might go on discussing each of these points for pages. (Men in seventeenth-century Holland wore their hats on the side of their heads in order to be thought of as adventurous and pleasure-loving. Heavy drinking was an approved practice. Etcetera.) But such a discussion would take us even farther away from the only confrontation which matters and which the author is determined to evade.

In this confrontation the Regents and Regentesses stare at Hals, a destitute old painter who has lost his reputation and lives off public charity; he examines them through the eyes of a pauper who must nevertheless try to be objective, i.e., must try to surmount the way he sees as a pauper. This is the drama of these paintings. A drama of an "unforgettable contrast."

Mystification has little to do with the vocabulary used. Mystification is the process of explaining away what might otherwise be evident. Hals was the first portraitist to paint the new characters and expressions created by capitalism. He did in pictorial terms what Balzac did two centuries later in literature. Yet the author of the authoritative work on these paintings sums up the artist's achievement by referring to

> Hals's unwavering commitment to his personal vision, which enriches our consciousness of our fellow men and heightens our awe for the ever-increasing power of the mighty impulses that enabled him to give us a close view of life's vital forces.

That is mystification.

In order to avoid mystifying the past (which can equally well suffer pseudo-Marxist mystification) let us now examine the particular relation which now exists, so far as pictorial images are concerned, between the present and the past. If we can see the present clearly enough, we shall ask the right questions of the past.

Today we see the art of the past as nobody saw it before. We actually perceive it in a different way.

This difference can be illustrated in terms of what was thought of as perspective. The convention of perspective, which is unique to European art and which was first established in the early Renaissance, centres everything on the eye of the beholder. It is like a beam from a lighthouse—only instead of light travelling outwards, appearances travel in. The conventions called those appearances *reality*. Perspective makes the single eye the centre of the visible world. Everything converges on to the eye as to the vanishing point of infinity. The visible world is arranged for the spectator as the universe was once thought to be arranged for God.

According to the convention of perspective there is no visual reciprocity. There is no need for God to situate himself in relation to others: he is himself the situation. The inherent contradiction in perspective was that it structured all images of reality to address a single spectator who, unlike God, could only be in one place at a time.

<Figural sketches showing concepts of perspective/perceivers>

After the invention of the camera this contradiction gradually became apparent.

< Still from *Man with Movie Camera* by Vertov >

I'm an eye. A mechanical eye. I, the machine, show you a world the way only I can see it. I free myself for today and forever from human immobility. I'm in constant movement. I approach and pull away from objects. I creep under them. I move alongside a running horse's mouth. I fall and rise with the falling and rising bodies. This is I, the machine, manoeuvring in the chaotic movements, recording one movement after another in the most complex combinations.

Freed from the boundaries of time and space, I
co-ordinate any and all points of the universe,
wherever I want them to be. My way leads towards
the creation of a fresh perception of the world. Thus
I explain in a new way the world unknown to you.
*(This quotation is from an article
written in 1923 by Dziga Vertov,
the revolutionary Soviet film director.)*

The camera isolated momentary appearances and in so doing
destroyed the idea that images were timeless. Or, to put it another
way, the camera showed that the notion of time passing was
inseparable from the experience of the visual (except in paintings).
What you saw depended upon where you were when. What you
saw was relative to your position in time and space. It was no
longer possible to imagine everything converging on the human
eye as on the vanishing point of infinity.

This is not to say that before the invention of the camera men
believed that everyone could see everything. But perspective organized
the visual field as though that were indeed the ideal. Every drawing or
painting that used perspective proposed to the spectator that he was
the unique centre of the world. The camera—and more particularly
the movie camera—demonstrated that there was no centre.

The invention of the camera changed the way men saw. The
visible came to mean something different to them. This was
immediately reflected in painting.

For the Impressionists the visible no longer presented itself to
man in order to be seen. On the contrary, the visible, in continual
flux, became fugitive. For the Cubists the visible was no longer
what confronted the single eye, but the totality of possible views
taken from points all round the object (or person) being depicted.

<*Still Life with Wicker Chairs* by Picasso 1881->

The invention of the camera also changed the way in which men
saw paintings painted long before the camera was invented. Originally

paintings were an integral part of the building for which they were designed. Sometimes in an early Renaissance church or chapel one has the feeling that the images on the wall are records of the building's interior life, that together they make up the building's memory—so much are they part of the particularity of the building.

< Exterior and interior photos of Church of St. Francis at Assisi >

The uniqueness of every painting was once part of the uniqueness of the place where it resided. Sometimes the painting was transportable. But it could never be seen in two places at the same time. When the camera reproduces a painting, it destroys the uniqueness of its image. As a result its meaning changes. Or, more exactly, its meaning multiplies and fragments into many meanings.

This is vividly illustrated by what happens when a painting is shown on a television screen. The painting enters each viewer's house. There it is surrounded by his wallpaper, his furniture, his mementoes. It enters the atmosphere of his family. It becomes their talking point. It lends its meaning to their meaning. At the same time it enters a million other houses and, in each of them, is seen in a different context. Because of the camera, the painting now travels to the spectator rather than the spectator to the painting. In its travels, its meaning is diversified.

< Photo of young person laughing, wearing t-shirt bearing a large image of the *Mona Lisa* >

One might argue that all reproductions more or less distort, and that therefore the original painting is still in a sense unique. Here is a reproduction of the *Virgin of the Rocks* by Leonardo da Vinci.

< Image of *Virgin of the Rocks* by Leonardo da Vinci 1452-1519, National Gallery >

Having seen this reproduction, one can go to the National Gallery to look at the original and there discover what the reproduction lacks. Alternatively one can forget about the quality of the reproduction and simply be reminded, when one sees the original, that it is a famous painting of which somewhere one has already seen a reproduction. But in either case the uniqueness of the original now lies in it being *the original of a reproduction*. It is no longer what its image shows that strikes one as unique; its first meaning is no longer to be found in what it says, but in what it is.

This new status of the original work is the perfectly rational consequence of the new means of reproduction. But it is at this point that a process of mystification again enters. The meaning of the original work no longer lies in what it uniquely says but in what it uniquely is. How is its unique existence evaluated and defined in our present culture? It is defined as an object whose value depends upon its rarity. This value is affirmed and gauged by the price it fetches on the market. But because it is nevertheless "a work of art"—and art is thought to be greater than commerce—its market price is said to be a reflection of its spiritual value. Yet the spiritual value of an object, as distinct from a message or an example, can only be explained in terms of magic or religion. And since in modern society neither of these is a living force, the art object, the "work of art," is enveloped in an atmosphere of entirely bogus religiosity. Works of art are discussed and presented as though they were holy relics: relics which are first and foremost evidence of their own survival. The past in which they originated is studied in order to prove their survival genuine. They are declared art when their line of descent can be certified.

Before the *Virgin of the Rocks* the visitor to the National Gallery would be encouraged by nearly everything he might have heard and read about the painting to feel something like this: "I am in front of it. I can see it. This painting by Leonardo is unlike any other in the world. The National Gallery has the real one. If I look at this painting hard enough, I should somehow be able to feel its authenticity. The *Virgin of the Rocks* by Leonardo da Vinci: it is authentic and therefore it is beautiful."

To dismiss such feelings as naïve would be quite wrong. They accord perfectly with the sophisticated culture of art experts for whom the National Gallery catalogue is written. The entry on the *Virgin of the Rocks* is one of the longest entries. It consists of fourteen closely printed pages. They do not deal with the meaning of the image. They deal with who commissioned the painting, legal squabbles, who owned it, its likely date, the families of its owners. Behind this information lie years of research. The aim of the research is to prove beyond any shadow of doubt that the painting is a genuine Leonardo. The secondary aim is to prove that an almost identical painting in the Louvre is a replica of the National Gallery version.

< Images of both paintings labeled accordingly >

French art historians try to prove the opposite.

< Image of 15 postage stamps (5 over 3)
bearing reproduction of *The Virgin and Child with St. Anne and St. John the Baptist* by Leonardo da Vinci 1542-1519 >

The National Gallery sells more reproductions of Leonardo's cartoon of The Virgin and Child with St Anne and St John the Baptist than any other picture in their collection. A fear years ago it was known only to scholars. It became famous because an American wanted to buy it for two-and-a-half million pounds.

Now it hangs in a room by itself. The room is like a chapel. The drawing is behind bullet-proof perspex. It has acquired a new kind of impressiveness. Not because of what it shows—not because of the meaning of its image. It has become impressive, mysterious, because of its market value.

The bogus religiosity which now surrounds original works of art, and which is ultimately dependent upon their market value, has become the substitute for what paintings lost when the camera made them reproducible. Its function is nostalgic. It is the final empty claim for the continuing values of an oligarchic, undemocratic culture. If the image is no longer unique and exclusive, the art object, the thing, must be made mysteriously so.

The majority of the population do not visit art museums. The following table shows how closely an interest in art is related to privileged education.

National proportion of art museum visitors according to level of education: Percentage of each educational category who visit art museums

	Greece	Poland	France	Holland		Greece	Poland	France	Holland
With no educational qualification	0.02	0.12	0.15	—	Only Secondary education	10.5	10.4	10	20
Only primary education	0.3	1.5	0.45	0.5	Further and higher education	11.5	11.7	12.5	17.3

Source: Pierre Bourdieu and Alain Darbel. *L'Amour de l'Art*, Editions de Minuit, Paris 1969. Appendix 5, table 4

The majority take it as axiomatic that the museums are full of holy relics which refer to a mystery which excludes them: the mystery of unaccountable wealth. Or, to put this another way, they believe that original masterpieces belong to the preserve (both materially and spiritually) of the rich. Another table indicates what the idea of an art gallery suggests to each social class.

Of the places listed below which does a museum remind you of most?

	Manual workers	Skilled and white collar workers	Professional and upper management
	%	%	%
Church	66	45	30.5
Library	9	34	28
Lecture hall	--	4	4.5
Department store or entrance hall in public building	--	7	2
Church and library	9	2	4.5
Church and lecture hall	4	2	--
Library and lecture hall	--	--	2
None of these	4	2	19.5
No reply	8	4	9
	100 (n=53)	100 (n=98)	100 (n=99)

Source: as above, appendix 4, table 8

In the age of pictorial reproduction the meaning of paintings is no longer attached to them; their meaning becomes transmittable: that is to say it becomes information of a sort, and, like all information, it is either put to use or ignored; information carries no special authority within itself. When a painting is put to use, its meaning is either modified or totally changed. One should be quite clear about what this involves. It is not a question of reproduction failing to reproduce certain aspects of an image faithfully; it is a question of reproduction making it possible, even inevitable, that an image will be used for many different purposes and that the reproduced image, unlike an original work, can lend itself to them all. Let us examine some of the ways in which the reproduced image lends itself to such usage.

<Image of *Venus and Mars* by Botticelli 1445-1510>

Reproduction isolates a detail of a painting from the whole. The detail is transformed. An allegorical figure becomes a portrait of a girl.

< Detail of girl's head from work pictured above >

When a painting is reproduced by a film camera it inevitably becomes material for the film-maker's argument.

A film which reproduces images of a painting leads the spectator, through the painting, to the film-maker's own conclusions. The painting lends authority to the film-maker. This is because a film unfolds in time and a painting does not.

< 6 details from *Procession to Calvary* by Breughel 1525-1569 >

In a film the way one image follows another, their succession, constructs an argument which becomes irreversible. In a painting all its elements are there to be seen simultaneously. The spectator may need time to examine each element of the painting but whenever he reaches a conclusion, the simultaneity of the whole painting is there to reverse or qualify his conclusion. The painting maintains its own authority.

<*Procession to Calvary* by Breughel 1525-1569>

Paintings are often reproduced with words around them.

< Demonstration of how words create meaning in painting using *Wheatfield with Crows* by Van Gogh 1853-1890 >

Reproduced paintings, like all information, have to hold their own against all the other information being continually transmitted.

Consequently a reproduction, as well as making its own references to the image of its original, becomes itself the reference point for other images. The meaning of an image is changed according to what one sees immediately beside it or what comes immediately after it. Such authority as it retains, is distributed over the whole context in which it appears.

< images from advertising >

Because works of art are reproducible, they can, theoretically, be used by anybody. Yet mostly—in art books, magazines, films or within gilt frames in living-rooms—reproductions are still used to bolster the illusion that nothing has changed, that art, with its unique undiminished authority, justifies most other forms of authority, that art makes inequality seem noble and hierarchies seem thrilling. For example, the whole concept of the National Cultural Heritage exploits the authority of art to glorify the present social system and its priorities.

The means of reproduction are used politically and commercially to disguise or deny what their existence makes possible. But sometimes individuals use them differently.

< Photo of bulletin board with pictures >

Adults and children sometimes have boards in their bedrooms or living-rooms on which they pin pieces of paper: letters, snapshots, reproductions of paintings, newspaper cuttings, original drawings, postcards. On each board all the images belong to the same language and all are more or less equal within it, because they have been chosen in a highly personal way to match and express the experience of the room's inhabitant. Logically, these boards should replace museums.

What are we saying by that? Let us first be sure about what we are not saying.

We are not saying that there is nothing left to experience before original works of art except a sense of awe because they have survived. The way original works of art are usually approached—through museum catalogues, guides, hired cassettes, etc.—is not the only way they might be approached. When the art of the past ceases to be viewed nostalgically, the works will cease to be holy relics—although they will never re-become what they were before the age of reproduction. We are not saying original works of art are now useless.

< *Woman Pouring Milk* by Vermeer 1632-1675 >

Original paintings are silent and still in a sense that information never is. Even a reproduction hung on a wall is not comparable in this respect for in the original the silence and stillness permeate the actual material, the paint, in which one follows the traces of the painter's immediate gestures. This has the effect of closing the distance in time between the painting of the picture and one's own act of looking at it. In this special sense all paintings are contemporary. Hence the immediacy of their testimony. Their historical moment is literally there before our eyes. Cézanne made a similar observation from the painter's point of view. "A minute in the world's life passes! To paint it in its reality, and forget everything for that! To become that minute, to be the sensitive plate . . . give the image of what we see, forgetting everything that has appeared before our time . . . ." What we make of that painted moment when it is before our eyes depends upon what we expect of art, and that in turn depends today upon how we have already experienced the meaning of paintings through reproductions.

Nor are we saying that all art can be understood spontaneously. We are not claiming that to cut out a magazine reproduction of an archaic Greek head, because it is reminiscent of some personal experience, and to pin it on to a board beside other disparate images, is to come to terms with the full meaning of that head.

The idea of innocence faces two ways. By refusing to enter a conspiracy, one remains innocent of that conspiracy. But to remain innocent may also be to remain ignorant. The issue is not between innocence and knowledge (or between the natural and the cultural) but between a total approach to art which attempts to relate it to every aspect of experience and the esoteric approach of a few specialized experts who are the clerks of the nostalgia of a ruling class in decline. (In decline, not before the proletariat, but before the new power of the corporation and the state.) The real question is: to whom does the meaning of the art of the past properly belong? To those who can apply it to their own lives, or to a cultural hierarchy of relic specialists?

The visual arts have always existed within a certain preserve; originally this preserve was magical or sacred. But it was also physical: it was the place, the cave, the building, in which, or for which, the work was made. The experience of art, which at first was the experience of ritual, was set apart from the rest of life— precisely in order to be able to exercise power over it. Later the preserve of art became a social one. It entered the culture of the ruling class, whilst physically it was set apart and isolated in their palaces and houses. During all this history the authority of art was inseparable from the particular authority of the preserve.

What the modern means of reproduction have done is to destroy the authority of art and to remove it—or, rather, to remove its images which they reproduce—from any preserve. For the first time ever, images of art have become ephemeral, ubiquitous, insubstantial, available, valueless, free. They surround us in the same way as a language surrounds us. They have entered the mainstream of life over which they no longer, in themselves, have power.

Yet very few people are aware of what has happened because the means of reproduction are used nearly all the time to promote the illusion that nothing has changed except that the masses, thanks to reproductions, can now begin to appreciate art as the cultured minority once did. Understandably, the masses remain uninterested and sceptical.

If the new language of images were used differently, it would, through its use, confer a new kind of power. Within it we could begin to define our experiences more precisely in areas where words are inadequate. (Seeing comes before words.) Not only personal experience, but also the essential historical experience of our relation to the past: that is to say the experience of seeking to give meaning to our lives, of trying to understand the history of which we can become the active agents.

The art of the past no longer exists as it once did. Its authority is lost. In its place there is a language of images. What matters now is who uses that language for what purpose. This touches upon questions of copyright for reproduction, the ownership of art presses and publishers, the total policy of public art galleries and museums. As usually presented, these are narrow professional matters. One of the aims of this essay has been to show that what is really at stake is much larger. A people or a class which is cut off from its own past is far less free to choose and to act as a people or class than one that has been able to situate itself in history. This is why—and this is the only reason why—the entire art of the past has now become a political issue.

INDEX

F

M

Edwards Brothers Malloy
Thorofare, NJ USA
August 2, 2012